PAULA DEEN'S
Southern
Cooking
BIBLE

ALSO BY PAULA DEEN

Paula Deen's The Deen Family Cookbook

Paula Deen's Kitchen Wisdom and Recipe Journal

Christmas with Paula Deen

Paula Deen: It Ain't All About the Cookin'

Paula Deen Celebrates!

Paula Deen & Friends: Living It Up, Southern Style

The Lady & Sons Just Desserts

The Lady & Sons Savannah Country Cookbook

The Lady & Sons, Too!: A Whole New Batch of Recipes from Savannah

Paula Deen's Cookbook for the Lunch-Box Set

Paula Deen's My First Cookbook

Paula Deen's Savannah Style

PAULA DEEN'S
Southern Cooking
BIBLE

The New Classic Guide to Delicious Dishes
with More Than 300 Recipes

PAULA DEEN
WITH MELISSA CLARK

RODALE

© 2011 by Paula Deen
Illustrations © 2011 by Jason Snyder
Color photographs © 2013 by Rodale Inc. —Banana Cream Pie, BBQ Pork Loin, Blackberry Cobbler, Brunswick Stew, Catfish Po' Boy, Cinnamon Glazed Sour Cream Apple Bundt, Country Captain, Cream Cheese Choc Chip Bread Pudding, Easy Chicken and Dumplings, Fried Chicken Salad, Lady and Sons Chicken Pot Pie, Mississippi Mud Cake, My Favorite Lasagna, Pecan Spice Layer Cake, Praline French Toast, Red Velvet Cake, Red Wine Beef Stew, Southern Chili in a Biscuit Bowl, Ultimate Easy Fudge, Nutty Brittle and Popcorn Balls, Yam Casserole

The original *Paula Deen's Southern Cooking Bible* was published in 2011 and is reprinted with permission by Simon & Schuster, Inc. Exclusive direct mail edition published in March 2013 by Rodale Inc.

Printed in the United States of America
Rodale Inc. makes every effort to use acid-free ♾, recycled paper ♻.

Recipes appearing on back cover *(clockwise from top left)*: Praline French Toast Casserole (page 100); Brunswick Stew (page 73) with Sweet Potato Biscuits (page 279); Southern Chili in a Biscuit Bowl (page 134); Banana Cream Pie (page 317)

Book designed by Nancy Singer

Library of Congress Cataloging-in-Publication Data is on file with the printer.

ISBN 978–1–62336–084–9 hardcover

6   8   10   9   7   hardcover

We inspire and enable people to improve their lives and the world around them.
For more of our products, visit rodalestore.com or call 800–848–4735.

This book is dedicated to my
three precious grandsons,
Jack, Matthew, and Henry.
I look forward to seeing them blossom
into fine grown men who I hope
will always be extremely proud
of their Southern roots.

Contents

- - - - - -

Chapter 7
POULTRY

Chapter 8
FISH AND SHELLFISH

xi

Introduction

Y'all know I was born and raised on Southern food and made my name sharing my version of down-home cooking with the world. But the funny thing is that until I began to travel outside of my own little town of Albany, Georgia, I couldn't have told you what Southern cooking is all about. Sure, my mama, grandmama, and Aunt Peggy taught me just about everything there was to know about the traditional dishes I grew up eating: the pork chops and gravy, the chicken and dumplin's, the fried peach pies. And when I moved to Savannah as an adult, I learned mighty fast how differently folks eat there, with all the fruits of the sea—beautiful blue crab and sweet shrimp—just swimming right outside their back doors. When I married Michael, I married into Savannah red rice, shrimp and grits, and a big old Low-Country boil full of seafood.

Southern food is simply not one thing or another. In fact, it's about as regional as you can get: drive around the South and you'll soon discover that the gravy, the barbecue sauce, and the corn bread change with the countryside. You haven't eaten Southern food until you've had a taste of the Tennessee mountains' stack cakes and chowchow, North Carolina's hill-country barbecue, South Carolina's Low-Country dirty rice, and a she-crab soup from the beautiful port cities of Charleston and Savannah, not to mention Cajun blackened fish, Creole gumbo, and soul food like hoppin' John and collards from southern Louisiana.

All of this good food comes out of a rich history. In Louisiana, for instance, exiled French refugees known as the Acadians arrived in South Louisiana from Nova Scotia, Canada, in the mid-1700s. They were known for their use of wild game, seafood, wild vegetation, and herbs. But when those Acadians, who later became known as Cajuns, started mixing with the Native Americans, they learned techniques for using what was available from the swamps, bayous, lakes, rivers, and woods. Nowadays, Cajun food is a cuisine all its own, famous for its one-pot meals, such as gumbo, and its sausages, like andouille and tasso.

Creole food, on the other hand, is also Louisiana-based but traces its roots back to the early 1700s. Originating with Spanish immigrants and later blending with Native American, French, Spanish, English, African, German, and Italian cuisines, Creole cuisine gave us such traditional favorites as jambalaya, which probably descended from a Spanish paella. Creole food also tends to be fancier and closer to European cuisine than Cajun, since many of the Creoles were rich planters, and their chefs came from France or Spain.

Each time I learn something new about what all the great cooks of the South have simmering, I hold my head a little higher. I am just so proud to count myself among them.

Good, down-home Southern cooking isn't fancy, but when y'all sit down to a simple plate of crisp fried chicken; a fluffy, warm, just-buttered biscuit; a mess of greens cooked down with a bit of ham; and a tall, handsome banana cream pie topped with ice-cold whipped cream afterward, well, you'll have to agree: there is just nothing better.

This book is my way of celebrating the wonderful food I grew up on, and many of those classic dishes are included in these pages. I didn't stop there, though. I was eager to share the recipes I've learned and loved over the years as I've met other cooks all across the South, and all the amazing people and stories behind all that great food. There's so much good eating from Louisiana to Kentucky, from Virginia to Florida. So what I wanted to put together was my Southern cooking bible.

I could spend the rest of my days crisscrossing the states south of the Mason-Dixon with my cast-iron skillet, and I still wouldn't be able to round up even a fraction of the wonderful, traditional recipes out there. Heck, you can get in a war down here over barbecue sauce: Do you like a mustard base like the folks do in South Carolina, a vinegar base from eastern North Carolina, or a red tomato base from eastern Alabama? Or maybe you like a sweet and spicy base made with ketchup, like they do in western North Carolina? Sometimes, you just got to pick sides. I love it all, but my daddy's tangy barbecue sauce is the one true sauce I could never do without. Still, you got to keep trying 'em, because when it comes to Southern food, it's especially true that variety is the spice of life.

Most anytime you put two Southern cooks in the same kitchen, you will sense a little cordial disagreement. For example, I would never put sugar in my vegetables. But some folks in the South do like their vegetables sweet. And even though you won't find two Southerners with identical recipes, I do believe that the recipes in the *Southern Cooking Bible* contain the essential ingredients that bring together all great Southern cooking, from the deep, dark beefy flavor of Louisiana's Cajun Gril- lades and Grits (page 149) to the cheese and turkey melt known as a Kentucky Hot Brown (page 99). I'll tell you, even if a comforting meal of South Carolina Chicken Bog (page 169), simmered with rice and sausage, might not seem to have much in common with a big ol' smoking platter of Memphis Dry-Rub Ribs (page 225), you can be sure they are served up with the single most important, most commonplace ingredient used throughout the entire South: hospitality.

The first thing a Southerner will ask when somebody walks into the house is, "Are y'all thirsty? Y'all hungry?" Now, probably it has something to do with how dirt poor many parts of the South were at one point or another in history. Offering their guests a meal was a Southerner's way of sharing as much as they could even if they didn't have much in the bank. Putting out a big, ample spread is a point of pride for every Southern hostess: that's her way of letting her guests know they'll be taken care of, and they don't need to hold back. That's why our meals tend to be served family style, with big old bowls on the table heaped full of corn, slaw, fried okra, sweet potatoes, beans, sliced tomatoes, cucumbers, and onions. It doesn't matter how much meat you serve once you got your fresh vegetables, your pickles, relishes, biscuits, butter, and syrup set out: there will be fine food for all. And of course, as sure as day follows night, you can be sure there will be plenty of dessert to come.

In fact, even when times were hard, Southerners typically used their resourcefulness and the bounty of berry bushes, streams and brooks, and a kitchen garden to get them through. So many of the beloved recipes in these pages were born through the combination of a talented cook and a scant pantry: flour, shortening, cornmeal, maybe a bit of smoked ham, and the occasional old laying hen, plus a bushel of homegrown fruits and vegetables. These are the main ingredients in the majority of recipes in this book.

It is so interesting to think about how many different foods come from the simplest items in the Southern pantry. We got our cornmeal, introduced to European settlers by the Native Americans, along with beans, peppers, and squash. And right there you can make a meal out of hoecakes, those little skillet corn breads that Southerners just adore with a plate of vegetables.

Of course corn doesn't go just into corn bread: we also turn it into hominy and, maybe the most uniquely Southern ingredient of all, grits. Oh my, it's no wonder that folks call the area from Louisiana to the Carolinas the Grits Belt. Down here, we could eat grits from sunup to sundown. And we do. There's grits and eggs and bacon for breakfast, maybe with some steaming buttered biscuits on the side. Grits with gravy makes a side dish for anything at lunch or dinner or can even be its own meal in harder times. And if you haven't had a dinner of shrimp and grits, you've got to get yourself down to Charleston and try some out: simple, hearty, and filling, that is a meal that fishermen invented and you will not find a better way to end the day. Once you have grits in your cabinet, you're ready to do like any good Southern cook and just keep on cooking them: I make grits cakes with leftover grits just like my mama used to, all buttery and crisp around the edges. And I have even invented a Down-Home Grits Pie (page 327)!

African-American traditions are another great big piece of Southern cooking. Cooking with produce like black-eyed peas, okra, yams, benne seeds, watermelon, and peanuts—all grew roots in African soil. Techniques like smoking meat, preparing pot greens with their liquor, and deep-frying existed in Africa before crossing the Atlantic. And now, Southern fried chicken, fish, and fruit fritters are just about the pinnacle of our cooking, y'all.

Biscuits and gravy (pages 276 to 277); She-Crab Soup (page 80); Jambalaya (page 114); Chicken with Drop Dumplin's (page 165). Oh, my goodness, I was like a kid in a candy shop trying to fit everything wonderful about the Southern table into this cookbook, and, y'all, I have hardly scratched the surface. I mean, what Southern cook worth her salt—or sugar—would feel content with only five dessert chapters? You'll see that beyond the Divinity (page 414), the Lemony Chess Pie (page 324), the Nutty Brittle (page 418), and the Coconut Cake (page 363), there is an infinity of other beautiful treats just waiting to be discovered.

All my recipes are big on flavor—because in the South, as my mama always told me, your seasonings need to be scared of you, not the other way around. We're not afraid to pull out that ham hock and that butter and do to a dish what needs to be done. Now, Southerners can be big, loud, and passionate, and we are never more that way than when we're talking food—cooking or eating it. Because when you come right down to it, whether you think your dumplings should be rolled or dropped, whether you make a white milk gravy or a redeye gravy, and whichever way you make your chili, your corn bread, or your barbecue, whenever you are cooking Southern food, you are cooking from the heart.

So, y'all, get cookin' and find your own favorites. And, as always, I'm sending you best dishes and best wishes from down South!

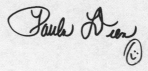

PAULA DEEN'S
Southern Cooking
BIBLE

Chapter 1

GETTIN' IT STARTED

Have y'all ever been to a party in the South? If you have, then you will surely know that a Southerner will greet you at the door with two things: a smile and a plate. No matter how big or small a gathering, a party just cannot be said to have started without the appetizer course being served—it just isn't done. And that holds true if we're talking about a cocktail bash, a sit-down dinner party, or just having the girls over for cards and conversation. Little nibbles eaten with one hand leave the other hand free for an adult beverage of some sort, and the corner of the mouth available for chitchat. They are a Southerner's way of saying, "Y'all come in and sit a spell."

At any get-together, the first bites you serve set the tone. Sure, you could cook every dainty fresh-out-of-the-oven treat you know, but the message you'd be sending when you answered the door would be something like this: "Listen, I am freaking exhausted. Y'all better enjoy this damn party. I am going to bed." You want to plan your cooking so you open that door with a big wide smile that says, "Come on in and let's get this party started!" That means having delicious, fuss-free recipes that you can serve right away.

To make things easier, I divide up my appetizers between hot and cold. You can make most cold dishes ahead and have them out as your first guests arrive, which is a big stress reliever. Then, I choose a few hot appetizers to do last-minute. And I'm not shy about grabbing friends who love to feel helpful and set them to work on those. It always goes smoother when I cook things I've made before. And I always assume there will be a vegetarian showing up (it takes all kinds, after all). Finally, I like to stick to what's fresh and available—no need to go chasing down tomatoes in January.

5

If you're making a whole meal, you need only about three different appetizers. For a cocktail party, do eight or nine. If your party is timed so folks are likely to skip dinner, serve heartier choices like the Family Reunion Deviled Eggs (page 25) and the Hot Crab Dip with Cheddar (page 8). And I always go for variety. You want only one or two bread-based appetizers, like Tomato Sandwiches (page 36), which you prep in advance, then assemble last-minute, or Benne Seed Canapés (page 24), which are so easy and out-of-this-universe delicious. Then serve some sort of fruit, like Pecan and Cream Cheese–Stuffed Dates (page 7), some sort of vegetable, maybe Bubblin' Brown Artichoke and Cream Cheese Dip (page 13), and one or two meats—and if you haven't had the Sizzlin' Jalapeño Sausage Balls (page 11), y'all just ain't from around these parts.

I always figure people will eat about ten bites of appetizers each, so there's no need to overdo the quantities. Then again, if you've got a roomful of Michael Groovers, you might want to up that a bit. Oh, and my Two Little Piggies in a Blanket (page 16)? Folks lose count with that one, so I just keep 'em coming.

Setting out a "little something" is kind of like giving somebody a hug when they walk into the house. And I like to make it a bear hug.

PECAN AND CREAM CHEESE–STUFFED DATES

■ ■

This perfect Southern party starter is as easy as one-two-three. Because if you tell any Southern cook that there are people coming over, the first thing she'll do is reach into the refrigerator and grab a block of cream cheese. The second thing she'll do is get out the bacon. And number three is she's just got to find something in the pantry to go in between the cream cheese and the bacon—in this case, plump dates. To make this an extra-memorable nibble, I mix the cream cheese filling with finely chopped pecans and a dash of freshly ground black pepper.

MAKES 12 STUFFED DATES

3 tablespoons (1½ ounces) cream cheese,
   at room temperature
3 tablespoons finely chopped pecans

¼ teaspoon black pepper (optional)
12 Medjool dates
4 slices bacon, cut crosswise into thirds

1. Preheat the oven to 400°F. Line a baking sheet with foil.

2. In a bowl, stir together the cream cheese, pecans, and black pepper (if you are using it—the pepper adds a little heat). Using a teaspoon, stuff each date with some of the cream cheese mixture. There should be enough to fill each date without the mixture spilling out and making a mess.

3. Wrap a piece of bacon around each date and secure the bacon to the date with a toothpick. Place the stuffed dates on the foil-lined baking sheet and put them in the oven for 8 minutes. Then, if you're like me and have been cooking for long enough to develop some calluses on your fingertips, go ahead and use your fingers to flip each date—otherwise, use a pair of kitchen tongs. Then return the dates to the oven and bake until the bacon is crisp, 4 to 7 minutes longer.

4. Lay the stuffed dates on a paper towel–lined plate to drain off some of the bacon fat. Serve them while they're still hot.

WHEN SELECTING DATES, BE CHOOSY!

I specify Medjool dates in this recipe because they are bigger and more tender than your average supermarket date. But if you can't find them in your area, don't fret. All you got to do is choose the plumpest dates to stuff, no matter what kind.

HOT CRAB DIP WITH CHEDDAR

■ ■

In the past twenty years since I have called Savannah, Georgia, my home, do you know how many events I have attended where a crab dish was not on the menu? Zero! Because when you have the blessing of abundant seafood, you simply have to find a way to serve it at every gathering.

This hot crab dip is a tried-and-true crowd-pleaser. Crab is such a rich-tasting shellfish, I think it goes extremely well with a little extra creaminess—and that's why I mix in cream cheese, mayonnaise, and sour cream for a smooth and decadent dip that is impressive enough to serve at even your fanciest soirees. And a little bit of hot-sauce kick lets your taste buds know that this hearty starter still has plenty of good, down-home flavor in its soul.

SERVES 10 TO 12

1 pound crabmeat, picked over to remove bits of shell (see box)

1½ cups shredded sharp Cheddar cheese (6 ounces)

8 ounces cream cheese, at room temperature

¼ cup mayonnaise

¼ cup sour cream

4 scallions, white and light green parts finely chopped, dark green tops reserved

2 cloves garlic, finely chopped

2 teaspoons fresh lemon juice

1½ teaspoons Worcestershire sauce

1 teaspoon hot sauce, or to taste

½ teaspoon mustard powder

Tortilla chips or crackers, for dipping

1. Preheat the oven to 325°F.

2. In a bowl, stir together the crabmeat, Cheddar, cream cheese, mayonnaise, sour cream, chopped scallions, garlic, lemon juice, Worcestershire sauce, hot sauce, and mustard powder.

3. Scrape the mixture into a wide baking dish—one that's pretty enough for serving. Bake until the dip is golden and bubbling, 45 to 55 minutes.

4. Chop the dark green scallion tops and sprinkle over the dip to add a little color. Serve hot, with a bowl of tortilla chips or crackers to use as dippers.

> ### NO SHELLS IN THE DIP, PLEASE
> Believe me, crunching into a stray bit of shell is no way to experience a mouthful of crab dip. Here's a little trick I learned in the restaurant business: Spread the crabmeat onto a baking sheet in an even layer and place in a low oven (about 200°F) for about 3 minutes. The heat will turn the shells red, making them so much easier to pick out of the white meat.

Loosen the peel by pressing down firmly on the garlic clove with the side of a large, heavy knife. The skin will split open, and the clove will slip easily from the peel.

SHORE IS GOOD SEAFOOD DIP

This is another wonderful bubbling-hot dip along the same lines as my Hot Crab Dip with Cheddar. This has been a mainstay on the menu of The Lady & Sons from time immemorial. In fact, it has become so popular at the restaurant that we have started selling it all across the country at Costco stores. So if you just don't have the time to make this recipe for your next party, I recommend you make a trip to your local Costco and pick some up in the frozen foods section!

SERVES 12 TO 16

2 tablespoons (¼ stick) butter

1 medium green bell pepper, diced

1 medium yellow onion, diced

2 celery stalks, diced

Half of a 10¾-ounce can condensed cream of shrimp soup (discard the top half and use the bottom part of the soup)

1 cup mayonnaise

2 cups grated Parmesan cheese (8 ounces)

6 ounces crabmeat, picked over to remove bits of shell (see box opposite)

6 ounces cooked peeled shrimp, fresh (see box, page 33) or canned

½ teaspoon white pepper

Toast points or crackers, for dipping

1. Preheat the oven to 325°F. Lightly grease a 2½- to 3-quart baking dish.

2. In a skillet, melt the butter over medium heat. Add the bell pepper, onion, and celery, and cook, stirring often, until softened, about 2 minutes.

3. In a bowl, combine the soup, mayonnaise, Parmesan, crabmeat, shrimp, and white pepper. Stir the vegetable mixture into the seafood mixture.

4. Spoon the mixture into the baking dish and bake until bubbling and golden brown, about 30 minutes. Serve with toast points or crackers for dipping.

HOT CHILI AND CHEESE DIP

■ ■

Now, sometimes a party might mean puttin' on your fancy dress and laying a table with canapés and cocktails. But other times it means having the gang over, turnin' on the game on TV, opening some cans of beer, and puttin' out the best hot chili and cheese dip in all of creation. Both kinds of parties are all right with me. Believe it or not, I keep all the fixings for this fantastic hot dip in the house just in case I can wrangle a free evening to spend with my daughter-in-law, Brooke, and my niece, Corrie. And without the boys around, we get that dip (and the clicker) all to ourselves!

SERVES 6 TO 8

1 can (15 ounces) chili with beans
8 ounces cream cheese, at room temperature
1 teaspoon chili powder

1 cup shredded pepper Jack cheese
   (4 ounces)
Tortilla chips, for dipping

1. In a medium saucepan, combine the chili, cream cheese, and chili powder. Cook over medium heat, stirring occasionally, until the mixture is smooth. Stir in the pepper Jack and cook until the cheese melts and the dip is hot, 3 to 5 minutes.

2. Very, very carefully pour the hot dip into a bowl for serving. Make sure there are plenty of tortilla chips on hand for dipping.

COUCH POTATOES

If you end up with leftover dip (hah!) or if you just love potatoes as much as I do, try this as a baked potato topping, along with sour cream, scallions, and maybe some crumbled crisp bacon.

SIZZLIN' JALAPEÑO SAUSAGE BALLS

■ ■

Now, y'all, I swear sausage balls have been around since just about the dawn of time. And can I make a confession? I have grown just the tiniest bit tired of them. But for heaven's sake, I wouldn't dare leave them off my table when I'm entertaining, because Southerners have just got to have their sausage balls with some kind of sauce for dipping right alongside. So I say if you can't beat 'em, join 'em. And my recipe for sausage balls packs such a spicy sizzle that you wouldn't ever get tired of popping one of these in your mouth—that pepper will wake you right up!

MAKES 60 SAUSAGE BALLS

Mustard-Mayo Dipping Sauce

1 cup mayonnaise

1 tablespoon Dijon mustard

SPICE THINGS UP

If you don't like chopping up chilies but still want a dip with a kick, try using hot Italian sausage here.

Jalapeño Sausage Balls

3 cups Bisquick baking mix

2½ cups shredded sharp Cheddar cheese (10 ounces)

1 pound sweet Italian sausage, casings removed

3 tablespoons cold butter, cut into small bits

1 jalapeño pepper, seeded, if desired, and finely chopped

1. Preheat the oven to 375°F. Grease two baking sheets well with butter or coat with cooking spray.

2. To make the dipping sauce: In a small bowl, whisk together the mayonnaise and mustard. Cover with plastic wrap and refrigerate until the sausage balls are ready to serve.

3. To make the sausage balls: In a large bowl, knead together all of the sausage ball ingredients until well combined. If the mixture seems dry, add 1 to 2 tablespoons water, as needed, to bring the mixture together.

4. Form the mixture into 1¼-inch balls (a little smaller than a Ping-Pong ball) and place them on the prepared baking sheets. Take care that the sausage balls don't touch, as that will make them take longer to cook through. Bake until they are golden all over, about 25 minutes.

5. Set the sausage balls on paper towels to drain off extra grease, and then place them on a pretty platter with some cocktail sticks so people don't have to eat them with their fingers. Serve warm, with the mustard-mayo sauce for dipping.

BACON AND SPINACH–STUFFED MUSHROOMS

■ ■

Every good Southern bride has her secrets, and I am about to share one of mine with y'all. The secret of how I get my charming husband, Michael, to eat his vegetables is that I hide spinach in these tasty little stuffed mushroom caps. And with the crumbled bacon and cheesy Parmesan topping, they are so easy to eat, he doesn't even mind that he's getting a helping of leafy greens in every bite. Just one more reason to serve these beauties at your next party, or whenever your man turns up his nose at the salad course!

MAKES 20 STUFFED MUSHROOMS

20 large white mushrooms, stems removed
1 package (10 ounces) frozen chopped
    spinach, thawed
6 slices bacon, cooked and crumbled
8 ounces cream cheese, at room temperature
½ cup chopped scallion
Salt and black pepper
½ cup grated Parmesan cheese
    (about 2 ounces)

> **TWO FOR ONE**
> In a rush? Some stores stock scallion cream cheese, which will save you the step of chopping scallions. Just use a heaping ½ cup of scallion cream cheese in place of the plain.

1. Preheat the oven to 400°F.

2. Put a little water on a paper towel and wipe those mushroom caps clean. Put the spinach in a sieve, set it over the sink, and squeeze out as much liquid as you can. You don't want that extra spinach juice making your mushroom caps soggy.

3. In a large bowl, mix together the spinach, bacon, cream cheese, scallion, and salt and black pepper to taste. Fill the mushroom caps with the mixture and set them on a baking sheet. Sprinkle the Parmesan on top.

4. Bake until the topping is golden brown, about 15 minutes. Let the mushrooms cool a little bit on the baking sheet. Then, while they're still warm, arrange them on a pretty platter and serve.

> **THE SECRET TO THE CRUNCHIEST BACON IN THE UNIVERSE**
> Y'all, I have a deep-fat fryer in my home kitchen and I like to use it. Just follow the manufacturer's instructions for the crunchiest, crispiest bacon you'll ever taste.

BUBBLIN' BROWN ARTICHOKE
AND CREAM CHEESE DIP

■ ■

This is a dip I learned to make from my darling Aunt Peggy and Uncle George, who had it out at every family get-together since I was a very little girl growing up in southwest Georgia. And you know what? That very same bubbling-hot appetizer that I loved to scoop up when I was barely big enough to reach the table is still the one I like to serve to my family and friends at our Savannah table—and in my own restaurant!

SERVES 6 TO 8

8 ounces cream cheese, at room temperature

1 cup mayonnaise

1¾ cups grated Parmesan cheese
   (about 7 ounces)

1 can (14 ounces) artichoke hearts,
   drained and coarsely chopped

3 scallions, finely chopped

1 clove garlic, finely chopped

¾ teaspoon hot sauce

¼ teaspoon black pepper

⅛ teaspoon salt

Crackers, tortilla chips, or crusty bread,
   for dipping

1. Preheat the oven to 350°F.

2. Using an electric mixer, beat the cream cheese until it is smooth. Beat in the mayonnaise until combined. Add 1½ cups of the Parmesan, the artichoke hearts, scallions, garlic, hot sauce, black pepper, and salt and mix with a spatula until combined.

3. Scrape the mixture into a wide, shallow gratin or baking dish that's pretty enough for serving and top with the remaining ¼ cup Parmesan. Bake until the dip is bubbling and the top is golden, 30 to 40 minutes. Serve hot, with crackers, tortilla chips, or crusty bread for dipping.

DIPPING DETAILS

Here is something I used to make to serve with artichoke dip when I first started out in the catering business in Savannah. Take slices of white bread, cut off the crusts, then cut each slice into four squares. Then get out your mini-muffin tins, brush the bottom of each cup with a little butter, and poke the bread squares into them. Put them in a 350°F oven for about 5 minutes, until they crisp up and form little buttery cups, the perfect party dippers.

HOT PIMIENTO CHEESE DIP

■ ■

I am always amazed when I go around the country and I hear people say, "Pimiento cheese? What's that? I've never heard of it." Well, I say y'all haven't lived until you have tasted good old homemade pimiento cheese—and for goodness' sake, if I ever left the pimiento cheese sandwiches out of Jamie's and Bobby's lunch boxes, you can be sure they would trade their tuna fish or egg salad until they got their hands on one of their classmates' pimiento cheese. It is a classic Southern ingredient.

This is the perfect way of serving it up hot and ready for a party. Why, it's just like dipping into the melted insides of one of my all-time favorite grilled pimiento cheese sandwiches. Yum.

SERVES 6 TO 8

2 cups shredded sharp Cheddar cheese
   (8 ounces)
2 cups shredded Monterey Jack cheese
   (8 ounces)
1 jar (4 ounces) chopped pimientos,
   well drained
½ cup mayonnaise

1½ teaspoons grated yellow onion
¼ teaspoon garlic powder
¼ teaspoon salt
¼ teaspoon black pepper
½ cup diced tomato
Tortilla chips or crackers,
   for dipping

1. Preheat the oven to 350°F.

2. In the bowl of an electric mixer, stir together the cheeses by hand. Measure out ½ cup of the cheese mixture for the topping and set aside.

3. Pat the pimientos dry with a paper towel and add them to the mixer bowl along with the mayonnaise, onion, garlic powder, salt, and black pepper. Mix at medium speed until the ingredients are well combined. Use a spatula or wooden spoon to fold the tomato in by hand.

4. Scrape the mixture into a gratin dish or wide, shallow baking dish that's pretty enough for serving. Sprinkle the top of the dip with the reserved cheese mixture. Bake until the dip is bubbling and golden, about 25 minutes. Let cool for 5 minutes before serving with plenty of chips or crackers.

GIVE IT A WHIRL

To make quick work of dicing a tomato, I must confess I often reach for my food processor. Pulse that beauty a few times, and it's done. Plus, you can transfer it to the dip with a slotted spoon to leave behind some of the tomato juices. I say a smart cook is one who knows a good shortcut.

BAKED BRIE WITH FIG JAM

■ ■

This is one of my favorite foods in the whole world: creamy Brie cheese and figs. I just love that salty-sweet combination. And when you serve it like this, all wrapped up in a flaky, buttery puff pastry, it's not just delicious but a real beauty, too. I always serve this when I want to make an especially good impression—in fact, it's what I taught Jamie to make for his beautiful wife, Brooke, the first time he had her over to his house for dinner.

SERVES 8 TO 10

All-purpose flour, for dusting
1 sheet puff pastry (from a 17½-ounce package), thawed if frozen
1 wheel (2 to 2¼ pounds) Brie

½ cup Fig Jam (page 421)
1 cup chopped toasted walnuts
1 large egg, lightly beaten
Crackers or crusty bread, for serving

1. Preheat the oven to 375°F.

2. Sprinkle a little flour onto a work surface and gently roll out the sheet of puff pastry until it is big enough to cover the wheel of Brie, about a 9-inch square. Place the Brie in the center of the dough. Spread the jam thickly on top of the cheese and sprinkle with the nuts. Close the ends of the pastry over the cheese like a package, pinching the edges to seal, and transfer to a rimmed baking sheet.

3. Brush the pastry all over with the beaten egg and bake until golden brown with no white spots, 35 to 40 minutes. Carefully transfer the cheese to a platter and serve while still warm with crackers or crusty bread.

WRAP IT UP!

Is there anything more deliciously rich and flaky than puff pastry? And no matter how many times you shrug your shoulders and confess that you just thawed a package, folks will insist on praising you to the skies for your baking. Well, let them. This is one of those dishes that's a stunner on a holiday table. For a fun presentation, I take my kitchen twine and, instead of folding over the ends of the pastry, I bring it all up around the Brie and tie it closed so it looks like a gift bag. So pretty.

TWO LITTLE PIGGIES IN A BLANKET

■ ■

Pig in a blanket is a classic American appetizer, what I remember having at all the best parties when I was growing up. When I started making them for Jamie's and Bobby's birthday parties, I just had to put my own Paula-spin on it. So what's better than one little piggie in a blanket? Well, nothing but two little piggies in a blanket, of course! And that is the way Jamie and Brooke still make them for their sweet little boy, Jack.

MAKES 16 LITTLE PIGGIES

8 slices bacon

1 package (8 ounces) crescent rolls

16 cocktail wieners

6 tablespoons ketchup

¼ cup Dijon mustard

1. Preheat the oven to 375°F. Coat a baking sheet with cooking spray or line it with parchment paper.

2. In a large skillet, cook the bacon until golden but still pliable. Remove from the skillet and halve crosswise.

3. Separate the dough into 8 triangles. Cut each dough triangle in half lengthwise (you will end up with 16 slender triangles). Wrap each wiener in a half slice of bacon. Place each wrapped wiener on the wide end of a dough triangle and roll the dough over the wiener. Place the rolls on the prepared baking sheet, 2 inches apart. Bake until golden, about 15 minutes.

4. Meanwhile, whisk together the ketchup and mustard. Serve alongside the piggies, for dipping.

PIGGIES ON ICE

Before the holidays, do yourself a favor and roll up a double recipe of these babies. Freeze them, unbaked, on parchment-lined baking sheets, then transfer to an airtight container. They'll keep in the freezer for a few months and can be baked from frozen (just add a few minutes to the cooking time). Now, who's the hostess with the mostest?

HAM BISCUITS

■ ■

Now, I learned this recipe from the good folks in Kentucky. Ham and biscuits is a classic taste of the South, no matter where you go, but over in Kentucky they mince the ham with butter and spread it on good cream biscuits, which to me is just absolutely out of this world. I would not have a ham biscuit any other way.

MAKES 12 BISCUITS

Cream Biscuits

2 cups self-rising flour, plus more for dusting

1 tablespoon sugar

1½ cups heavy cream

Ham

½ pound cooked country ham, or any cooked ham, coarsely chopped

4 tablespoons (½ stick) butter

1. Preheat the oven to 500°F. Lightly grease a rimmed baking sheet with butter or coat with cooking spray.

2. To make the biscuits: In a large bowl, mix together the flour and sugar. Pour in the cream and fold together until a soft dough forms. Turn the dough out onto a surface that's been lightly sprinkled with more flour. With the palms of your hands, knead the dough gently 6 or 7 times, adding just enough flour as needed to keep the dough from sticking to your hands.

3. Roll or pat the dough out until it's about ½ inch thick. Dip a 3-inch round biscuit or cookie cutter in flour and cut out the biscuits, placing them at least 1 inch apart on the prepared baking sheet. Bake until golden brown, 10 to 12 minutes. Transfer to a wire rack to cool slightly.

4. Meanwhile, to make the ham filling: Place the ham and butter in a food processor and pulse until combined and the pieces of ham are finely chopped.

5. Split the hot biscuits in half and fill each with about 1 tablespoon of the ham mixture. Serve them up while they're still warm.

CUT TO THE CHASE

I know a lot of cooks who will take any old juice glass out of the cupboard to cut their biscuits, and I'm sure their biscuits rise plenty even and tall, but let me just tell you that the blunt edge of a glass can sometimes press down your dough at the edges and keep those biscuits from rising up to their lightest, fluffiest selves. So use a sharp metal cutter, or, in a pinch, grab a clean empty tin can for the job.

SWEET SALTINES WITH BACON

■ ■

If y'all are anything like me and love that sweet-salty combo, you are just going to love this recipe. In any pantry in the South you are sure to find a box of saltine crackers, and you are certainly sure to find a package of bacon in the fridge. So whenever guests drop by unexpectedly, just whip up a batch of these showstopping snacks, and believe me, those drop-in callers will be singing your praises all over town.

MAKES 24 CRACKERS

24 saltine crackers
¼ cup maple syrup
12 slices bacon, halved crosswise

> ### SWEET AS A SOUTHERN BELLE
> I call for maple syrup here because you can find it easily. But if you're in the South, go ahead and use cane syrup instead. Darker than motor oil, with a sweet molasses flavor, that is one of our finer foods, and it's only a matter of time before you start seeing it above the Mason-Dixon Line.

1. Preheat the oven to 425°F. Line a rimmed baking sheet with foil.

2. Arrange the crackers salt side up on the prepared sheet. Brush each cracker top with the maple syrup and wrap a half slice of bacon around each cracker, with the ends meeting in the middle (not at the edge) of the unsalted side. Brush the bacon with the remaining maple syrup.

3. Bake the crackers for 5 minutes, then remove the baking sheet from the oven and carefully flip each cracker. I just use my bare fingertips for this, which you can do if you're real quick, or else use a pair of kitchen tongs. Return the sheet to the oven and continue baking until the bacon is crisp, another 8 to 10 minutes.

4. Allow the crackers to cool slightly on the baking sheet, then arrange them on a platter, seam side down, and watch them go!

BATTER-FRIED COUNTRY HAM BITES

Ham steak is such a convenient way to get yourself a ham fix without having to commit to a great big country roast. I love it with a spicy-sweet glaze. Well, one thing leads to another in a Southern kitchen, and at some point I began making my ham steak in a skillet, by breading and frying it in cubes, with spicy-sweet Jezebel Sauce for dipping.

SERVES 12 TO 14

About 2 quarts vegetable oil, for deep-frying
One 2-pound ham steak (1 inch thick)
1 cup all-purpose flour

½ teaspoon baking powder
1⅓ cups buttermilk
Jezebel Sauce (page 431)

1. In a large, heavy pot, heat 1½ inches of oil to 360°F. Preheat the oven to 200°F.

2. Meanwhile, cut the ham into 1-inch cubes. In a medium bowl, whisk the flour and baking powder together and then whisk in the buttermilk.

3. Drop about 10 ham cubes into the batter. Lift out, letting any excess drip back into the bowl. Fry in the hot oil until deep golden, about 1½ minutes. Remove with tongs or a slotted spoon to a paper towel–lined baking sheet to drain.

4. Repeat with the remaining ham cubes. As you finish each batch of ham bites, they can be kept warm in a 200°F oven. Serve the ham bites with the Jezebel Sauce.

Carefully insert the thermometer into the hot oil, angling it away from the bottom of the pan so that it does not touch the pan base but remains suspended in the oil.

PUT IT TO GOOD USE

Now, remember what I keep telling you about us Southern chefs being smart and economical about our ingredients? Here's a perfect example. This is just the recipe for your leftover ham after a big family gathering.

CAJUN POPCORN ROYALE

■ ■

One of my favorite things to do with my precious grandbaby Jack is to snuggle up on the couch and watch movies. We each get out our own big bowl of popcorn—I make his with just a little butter and salt for a topping, but I like to have more flavor than that in my bowl. So I load it up with some Cajun seasoning and grated Parmesan cheese. That way even if we're watching the same Disney cartoon for the zillionth time, I will still be interested.

I've even started serving bowls of this on my party buffet table. It makes a nice change from salty mixed nuts, one of those easy little twists that will make your party a smash.

SERVES 4 TO 6

2 tablespoons vegetable oil

⅓ cup popcorn kernels

2 tablespoons (¼ stick) butter

1 teaspoon Cajun seasoning

⅓ cup grated Parmesan cheese
 (about 1½ ounces)

1. In a large skillet with a lid, heat the oil over medium-high heat. Add 2 kernels of the corn and cover the skillet. When one of the kernels pops, add the remaining popcorn to the pan. Cover and shake until the popping stops, then transfer the popcorn to a large bowl.

2. Melt the butter in a small saucepan or in the microwave, then stir the Cajun seasoning into it.

3. Toss the popcorn with the seasoned butter. Add the Parmesan, toss again, and serve in small individual bowls—or in one big bowl and have everyone dig in.

MIX IT UP

This is one of those wonderful recipes that you can adapt to almost any taste. I love to sub in different kinds of cheeses, like shredded Cheddar or blue cheese crumbles. Sometimes I'll even skip the cheese and the Cajun seasoning altogether and have myself a piping-hot bowl of cinnamon-sugared popcorn.

DR PEPPER PECANS

■ ■

Here in the South we love our soda pop, and every time I open up a bottle, I am instantly brought back to my school days when I'd stop at the corner store for an icy-cold Coke with my baby brother, Bubba. And though I do have a fondness for Coca-Cola–glazed ham, I think these Dr Pepper Pecans are my number one favorite way to enjoy a pop without sucking it through a straw. Surprisingly, they are not too sweet but have that certain peppy flavor that will have people wondering just what could be the secret ingredient in these nuts. I love to watch their eyes light up when I tell them!

MAKES 1 CUP (4 SERVINGS)

1 cup Dr Pepper

2 tablespoons (¼ stick) butter

1 cup pecan halves

Salt

1. Preheat the oven to 350°F. Line a rimmed baking sheet with foil.

2. In a small saucepan, bring the Dr Pepper and butter to a boil over medium-high heat. Simmer until the liquid reduces by half, about 15 minutes.

3. Stir in the pecans and continue to cook until the liquid becomes a sticky glaze, 3 to 4 minutes. Add a big pinch of salt, stir, and transfer the nuts to the prepared baking sheet. Bake, stirring once or twice, until toasted, about 10 minutes.

NOT EVERYBODY'S A PEPPER

If Dr Pepper is not your soda pop of choice, this recipe works just fantastically with any variety of cola or root beer.

CHEESE STRAWS

■ ■

If you lay out only one appetizer on your Southern party table, I really think it should be this one. I don't think any party should be without a glass (or basket) of these beautiful cheese straws.

My smart-as-a-whip cousin, Johnnie Gabriel (the proprietress of Gabriel's Desserts in Marietta, Georgia), serves the most fantastic cheese straws I've ever had. She was kind enough to share her recipe with me, which I have adapted slightly over the years. These straws are a true taste of the South and, for me, a true taste of family.

MAKES 12 DOZEN CHEESE STRAWS

3½ cups all-purpose flour
1 teaspoon salt
½ teaspoon cayenne pepper

4 cups shredded extra-sharp Cheddar cheese
   (16 ounces)
3 sticks (¾ pound) butter,
   at room temperature

1. Preheat the oven to 400°F. Lightly grease three baking sheets or coat with cooking spray.

2. In a large bowl, sift together the flour, salt, and cayenne pepper. In another large bowl, use an electric mixer to cream together the Cheddar and butter. With the mixer at low speed, add the flour mixture to the cheese and butter in two batches just to combine. Once the flour mixture is evenly mixed in, increase the speed and beat the dough until well combined. Scrape the dough into a cookie press or pastry bag fitted with a star tip.

3. Pipe the dough in 2- to 3-inch strips onto the prepared baking sheets and bake until lightly browned, 12 to 15 minutes. Allow the cheese straws to cool for about 5 minutes on the baking sheets before transferring them to wire racks to continue cooling. Cheese straws are best served warm or at room temperature on the day they are made, but they will keep for up to 3 days in an airtight container.

BREAKING UP IS EASY TO DO!

Cheese straws are just so darn delicate—it's part of their charm. But if you end up with a ton of broken-up pieces of cheese straws, please, for the love of cheese, do not toss them in the trash! Instead, toss them onto a baking sheet, sprinkle them with grated Parmesan cheese, and pop them into a 350°F oven until the Parmesan is golden. Let these little cheese bites cool, then serve them in a pretty bowl for nibbling. Folks will think you meant to serve them that way!

BENNE SEED COCKTAILERS

Like the Cheese Straws, these are another classic Southern nibble, and they are just right as a base for a spread or dip. They can even be enjoyed just on their own. The benne seeds (which I understand are known as sesame seeds in other parts of the country) have a subtle, nutty flavor that is so very enjoyable in this buttery cracker. In fact, I like to make up a batch of these crispy treats to have in the house just for the sake of snacking, no matter if I happen to be planning a get-together or not.

MAKES 30 CRACKERS

2 cups all-purpose flour, plus extra for dusting
1 cup sesame seeds (benne seeds), lightly toasted (see box)
Pinch of cayenne pepper

Salt
1½ sticks (6 ounces) cold butter, cut into pieces, or ¾ cup vegetable shortening
3 to 5 tablespoons ice water

1. Preheat the oven to 325°F. Lightly grease two rimmed baking sheets or coat with cooking spray.

2. Place the flour, sesame seeds, cayenne pepper, and 1 teaspoon salt in a food processor. Add the butter or shortening, and pulse until chickpea-size crumbs form. Pulse in the ice water, 1 tablespoon at a time, until the dough comes together.

3. Turn the dough out onto a lightly floured surface and roll it out to a thickness of about ¼ inch. Dip a 2-inch round biscuit or cookie cutter in flour and cut the dough into rounds. Gather the scraps and reroll to cut out more biscuits. (Do not roll a third time, because the dough will be too tough.) Transfer the dough rounds to the prepared baking sheets and sprinkle each round with a very small pinch of salt. Bake until the crackers are pale golden, 20 to 25 minutes. Transfer the crackers to a wire rack to cool completely. The crackers will keep, in an airtight container at room temperature, for up to 3 weeks.

A TOAST

To toast sesame seeds perfectly, have a large, shallow bowl ready by your elbow. Shake those seeds continuously in a large dry skillet over medium heat until they start popping and they smell nice and nutty. Then shake them right into the bowl to stop the cooking and let them cool.

BENNE SEED CANAPÉS

■ ■

Now, if for some reason you've forgotten to make your Benne Seed Cocktailers (or, more likely, if you've made them and they have gotten all eaten up), have no fear: these Benne Seed Canapés can be thrown together in no time at all. Or, if you're a benne seed lover and you just want to skip the work of the Cocktailers, this is the recipe for you! Seriously, folks, these quick and yummy canapés are so good, so salty and buttery—everyone will swoon.

MAKES 24 CANAPÉS

6 tablespoons (¾ stick) butter
1 box (5 ounces) melba toast

¾ cup sesame seeds (benne seeds)
Salt

1. Preheat the oven to 325°F. Butter one side of each melba toast generously and place them, butter side up, on a rimmed baking sheet. Sprinkle the sesame seeds on top of the toasts (they should stick to the butter) and add a small pinch of salt.

2. Bake until the seeds are golden brown, 10 to 12 minutes. Arrange the canapés on a pretty platter and serve them while they're still warm.

> ### SAY "CHEESE"
> Now, I can't be the only person who adores melba toast—it's in every supermarket I've ever checked. For a change, you can make this recipe with finely grated Parmesan or sharp Cheddar in place of the benne seeds, and you'll have yourself the tastiest little cheese toasts you could want. Just top the buttered toasts with a sprinkle of cheese and a grind of black pepper, then toast until the cheese is golden.

FAMILY REUNION DEVILED EGGS

When I was a child and we would go on family picnics, there were three things I knew I could always find in the basket. One was the tomatoes to make tomato sandwiches, two was fried chicken, and three was deviled eggs. I swear, Bubba and I just didn't know which one to eat up first!

MAKES 24 DEVILED EGGS

1 dozen large eggs
⅓ cup mayonnaise
2 teaspoons Dijon mustard

¼ teaspoon hot sauce
Salt and black pepper
Paprika, for garnish

1. Place the eggs in a large pot and cover them with cold water. Bring the water to a boil over high heat. Immediately remove the pot from the heat, cover it, and let stand for 10 minutes. Uncover the pot and let the eggs cool in the water.

2. Peel the eggs and halve them lengthwise. Pop the yolks out into a large bowl and arrange the whites on a pretty serving platter.

3. Mash the yolks with the mayonnaise, mustard, hot sauce, and salt and black pepper to taste until everything is thoroughly combined and smooth. Spoon the filling back into the egg whites and serve lightly dusted with paprika.

AVOIDING THE EGG ROLL

If you entertain much in the South, you probably have yourself a deviled egg serving dish or container: something with little oval indents to keep those stuffed eggs from sliding all around. But if you don't have one, you can keep those eggs in their place by cutting a tiny slice from the base of each halved egg white to create a flat surface (just don't slice too deep, or you'll make a hole). A bed of lettuce will also help the eggs stay put.

Create a homemade piping bag by spooning the filling into a plastic bag. Twist the top of the bag closed to the level of the filling. Snip off a corner of the bag with scissors and squeeze the filling out of the hole.

CHEDDAR, PEPPER JELLY, AND PECAN CHEESE BALL

■ ■

Y'all, this is a little variation on my friend Mr. Jimmy Carter's favorite cheese ring. His is shaped in a tube pan with strawberry jelly at the center. But mine is shaped into a ball and filled with pepper jelly. If y'all like Mr. Jimmy's favorite recipe, try this one; it's a kicked-up version that's sure to please all spicy-food lovers.

SERVES 8 TO 10

2 cups shredded sharp Cheddar cheese
  (8 ounces)
3 tablespoons (1½ ounces) cream cheese,
  at room temperature
1 cup finely chopped pecans
⅓ cup mayonnaise

2 scallions, finely chopped
1 small clove garlic,
  finely chopped
⅛ teaspoon salt
⅛ teaspoon black pepper
¼ cup red pepper jelly

1. In a food processor or with an electric mixer, blend the Cheddar, cream cheese, ½ cup of the pecans, the mayonnaise, scallions, garlic, salt, and black pepper. Scrape the mixture onto a sheet of plastic wrap. Shape it into a ball, wrap with the plastic, and chill for 2 hours.

2. Unwrap the cheese ball and cut it in half. Use your fingers to press a deep well into the bottom half and fill the well with the jelly. Top with the upper half of the cheese ball and press the edges of the ball together to seal. Roll the cheese ball in the remaining ½ cup pecans. Serve immediately or refrigerate until ready to serve (up to 3 days).

HOT STUFF

Taste your pepper jelly. Some have kick, and some taste about as spicy as a jar of grape jelly. If you like a little more bite, mix a dash of hot sauce into the jelly before you fill your cheese ball. Or try my Pepper Jelly (page 434). That one has guaranteed heat!

GETTIN' IT STARTED

EVERYONE'S FAVORITE PIMIENTO CHEESE

■ ■

This recipe was featured in my first-ever cookbook, but back then it was known as Bobby's Pimiento Cheese because it was always my youngest son's favorite. Well, since my business has grown from The Bag Lady sandwiches and catering to The Lady & Sons restaurant, I have been making this same pimiento cheese recipe all along the way and now it is *everyone's* favorite. So I reckon it was about time for a name change.

SERVES 12 TO 16

1 package (3 ounces) cream cheese, at room temperature
1 cup shredded Cheddar cheese (4 ounces)
1 cup shredded Monterey Jack cheese (4 ounces)
½ cup mayonnaise

½ teaspoon Paula Deen's House Seasoning (page 435)
2 to 3 tablespoons mashed pimientos
1 teaspoon grated yellow onion (optional)
Salt and black pepper

Using an electric mixer, beat the cream cheese until fluffy. Add the Cheddar, Monterey Jack, mayonnaise, House Seasoning, pimientos, onion (if you are using it), and the salt and black pepper to taste and beat until smooth. The cheese may be refrigerated, covered, for up to 1 week.

GRATE JOB

Finely grating onion is not only a sure way to bring tears to your eyes, it's also a little secret for adding real savory flavor to just about any dressing or spread with mayonnaise in it. Try adding a teaspoon next time you make coleslaw and you'll see what I mean.

BUTTERMILK GREEN GODDESS DIP

If you love ranch-style dressings and dips, you are going to go absolutely wild for this. All of the good, garden-fresh herbs that go into this recipe make it so tasty and fragrant, not to mention pretty and green. And the anchovies give it that certain something, a saltiness and depth of flavor that wows. Now, I wouldn't necessarily tell people that there are anchovies in this dip—go ahead and let them fall in love with this dip first, then let them in on the secret ingredient.

SERVES 4 TO 6

¾ cup mayonnaise

¼ cup buttermilk

¾ cup packed fresh basil leaves

3 tablespoons coarsely chopped fresh chives

3 tablespoons coarsely chopped fresh parsley

1¼ teaspoons fresh lemon juice

2 anchovy fillets

1 clove garlic, finely chopped

⅛ teaspoon salt

⅛ teaspoon black pepper

Baked chips or raw vegetables,
    for dipping

In a food processor or blender, combine the mayonnaise, buttermilk, basil, chives, parsley, lemon juice, anchovies, garlic, salt, and black pepper and process until smooth. Scrape the dip into a bowl and serve, with plenty of baked chips or raw vegetables for healthful dipping.

DRESS IT UP
Leftover dip can be thinned with a drizzle of buttermilk to make the most scrumptious salad dressing. It will keep for a day in the refrigerator.

EASY GUACAMOLE

■ ■

Y'all, it just does not get any easier than this. Over my many years of working in the kitchen, of throwing parties and catering, I have tried all sorts of guacamole recipes, most of them fancier than this one. But you know what? I receive just as many compliments with this simple preparation as I do with the more time-consuming and labor-intensive ones. So next time you want to serve guacamole, whip up a big bowl of this recipe, open up a bag of tortilla chips—then get yourself out of the kitchen and join the party.

SERVES 8 TO 10

4 large Hass avocados, halved and pitted
½ cup store-bought salsa

Tortilla chips, for dipping

Scoop the avocado flesh right into the serving bowl. Use a fork to mash it, then mix in the salsa. Serve with sturdy tortilla chips for dipping.

THE RIPE STUFF

Choosing avocados can be tricky. You want to buy them a day or two ahead so they have time to ripen. Find firm, dark, unblemished avocados and then let them sit out a day or two until they have just a little give. Anything soft or spotty is going to let you down. Since they're so tasty, I usually buy a few extra avocados when I'm planning to serve guacamole. That way, if I open one up and it's got too many brown spots, I don't have to send Michael running around town looking for ripe avocados right before the party starts.

CRAB AND AVOCADO DIP

■ ■

Here is a fresh take on crab dip. This is especially wonderful in the warmer summer weather, when you may not want to have a bubbling-hot crab dip on your appetizer menu. The tomato and basil are like a little taste of summertime, and the ripe avocado is creamy without being too heavy. It's delicious, pretty, and just the thing for when your guests expect crab on the table but you would prefer not to run the oven *and* the air-conditioning.

SERVES 12 TO 16

2 Hass avocados, halved and pitted

1 pound canned crabmeat

¾ cup sour cream

¼ cup mayonnaise

1 tablespoon fresh lime juice

½ cup chopped fresh basil

1 clove garlic, finely chopped

1 jalapeño pepper, seeded and chopped
   (leave the seeds in if you want more heat)
   (optional)

1 teaspoon salt

½ teaspoon black pepper

1 cup chopped tomato

Tortilla chips or crackers,
   for dipping

Scoop the avocado flesh straight into a bowl pretty enough to serve in and mash with a fork until smooth. Fold in the crabmeat, sour cream, mayonnaise, lime juice, basil, garlic, jalapeño (if you are using it), salt, and black pepper. Just before serving, gently fold in the tomato. Serve with tortilla chips or crackers for dipping.

PARTY-READY DIPPING CHIPS

As a last touch before my party guests arrive, I like to spread my tortilla chips on a baking sheet and crisp them up in a 350°F oven, just long enough to get them warm and toasty without giving any extra color. I think it's a nice touch that makes folks feel more welcome and gets everybody in the dipping mood.

SOUTH GEORGIA "CAVIAR"

■ ■

In the South we laughingly call this redneck caviar, because a lot of poor folks couldn't afford caviar spread to set out with their crackers and we just thought black-eyed peas would make a perfectly good substitute. And do you know what? I think they're even better! For one thing, fish eggs taste pretty awful on tortilla chips. But this mix of beans, spicy Ro*Tel tomatoes (a Southern staple that I am seeing more and more in supermarkets across the country), and Italian dressing makes for a dip that is classy in its own special way.

SERVES 12 TO 15

2 cans (15 ounces each) black-eyed peas,
    rinsed and drained
1 can (15 ounces) corn kernels, drained
1 can (14½ ounces) spicy diced tomatoes,
    such as Ro*Tel
2 cups chopped red bell pepper

½ cup chopped jalapeño pepper
½ cup chopped yellow onion
1 bottle (8 ounces) Italian dressing
1 jar (4 ounces) chopped pimientos, drained
Tortilla chips or crackers, for dipping

In a large serving bowl, mix together the black-eyed peas, corn, tomatoes, bell pepper, jalapeño pepper, onion, Italian dressing, and pimientos. Cover and refrigerate for at least 4 hours or overnight to let the flavors come out. Serve with tortilla chips or crackers for dipping.

DON'T FEEL THE BURN

If you're chopping fresh chilies, you want to have some respect for those little seeds and white veins inside, because that's where all the spice is, and it will burn your hand just like it burns your mouth. To play it safe, wear latex gloves to chop the chilies, then wash your knife and board right away. If you want it real hot, chop the whole chili, seeds and all; but to tone it down, first scrape the seeds and white veins away and discard them, and then chop the chili.

SAVANNAH SHRIMP DIP

We love our shrimp here in Savannah, and this shrimp dip is a real favorite. Why, I believe that shrimp was one of the very first things my husband, Michael, a long time Savannahian, ever made for me when we were first courting. So it really has a special place in my heart.

To really make this dip correctly, be sure to have a light touch with the food processor. You do not want to overchop the shrimp. In fact, you could just go ahead and chop the shrimp by hand and fold it into the dip after everything else has been mixed. That way you'll get the meaty shrimp texture and flavor in every bite, which is the way we serve it here.

SERVES 8 TO 10

8 tablespoons (1 stick) butter, at room temperature
3 tablespoons finely chopped shallot
1 clove garlic, finely chopped
1 bay leaf
1 pound large shrimp, peeled and deveined
½ teaspoon salt
¼ teaspoon black pepper

2 tablespoons sherry
6 ounces cream cheese, at room temperature
2 tablespoons finely chopped fresh chives
2 teaspoons fresh lemon juice
½ teaspoon Worcestershire sauce
Tabasco or other hot sauce
Crackers or toasted bread, for serving

1. In a large skillet, melt 2 tablespoons of the butter over medium-high heat. Add the shallot, garlic, and bay leaf. Cook until the shallot and garlic are softened, about 4 minutes. Stir in the shrimp, ¼ teaspoon of the salt, and the black pepper and keep cooking, stirring occasionally, for 2 minutes.

2. Take the skillet off the heat (you want to be sure the alcohol doesn't come into contact with the gas flame) and stir in the sherry. Return the skillet to the heat and cook until the shrimp are cooked through, about 2 minutes. Discard the bay leaf and let the mixture cool.

3. In a food processor, combine the remaining 6 tablespoons butter and the cream cheese and process until smooth. Add the chives,

FOR BIG SHRIMP LOVERS

If you adore shrimp and you don't live in a coastal place like Savannah, frozen shrimp are a very convenient option. Stock the freezer with a few boxes and thaw them overnight in the refrigerator before your party. You can get your shrimp fix any time.

lemon juice, Worcestershire sauce, remaining ¼ teaspoon salt, and hot sauce to taste, and pulse just to combine. Scrape in the shrimp mixture and pulse several times just until the shrimp is coarsely chopped.

4. Scrape the mixture into a serving crock or bowl. Cover tightly with plastic wrap. Chill for at least 1 hour. Serve with crackers or toasted bread.

SHRIMP RÉMOULADE

■ ■

This is a starter that is served everywhere along the Southern coastal region, but especially in New Orleans. What I really love about it is that special pickle-y pucker the vinegar and seasoning give to the inside of my mouth. It's such a fun way to enjoy shrimp and a wonderful addition to every Southern-style party table.

SERVES 6

½ cup vegetable oil

⅓ cup Dijon mustard

¼ cup distilled white vinegar

¼ cup mayonnaise

2 tablespoons drained pickle relish

¼ teaspoon garlic powder

Dash of hot sauce

Salt and black pepper

1½ pounds shrimp, cooked and peeled

About 3 cups shredded lettuce, for serving

1. In a medium bowl, whisk together the oil, mustard, vinegar, mayonnaise, relish, garlic powder, hot sauce, and salt and black pepper to taste. Cover and refrigerate for at least 1 hour or up to overnight.

2. Toss the shrimp with the rémoulade and serve, chilled, over the shredded lettuce.

IN THE PINK

To cook your own shrimp, toss headless, deveined shrimp in a big pot of boiling water until they just turn pink—it takes only a couple of minutes. Then transfer them to a bowl of ice water to stop the cooking. Drain well, remove the shells, and you're done. Or speed things along by spending an extra buck at the fish store to buy precooked shrimp.

PAULA'S SHRIMP COCKTAIL

■ ■

Traditionally, cocktail sauce is just ketchup mixed with horseradish and a squeeze of lemon. But I like to serve this gussied-up version, which, with the addition of mayonnaise, grated onion, and mustard, is almost a combination of cocktail sauce and tartar sauce. I find it goes just beautifully with chilled jumbo shrimp or any of the fruits of the sea.

SERVES 6 TO 8

¾ cup mayonnaise

2 tablespoons horseradish

1 teaspoon grated yellow onion

2 teaspoons Dijon mustard

Juice of 1 lemon

2 pounds jumbo shrimp, cooked and peeled

In a bowl, combine the mayonnaise, horseradish, onion, mustard, and lemon juice and mix well. Refrigerate the shrimp and cocktail sauce separately. Serve chilled.

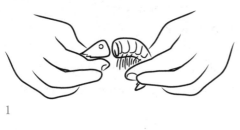

1

2

3

KEEP IT COOL

It is very important that the shrimp cocktail stays cold while it's out on the buffet table. I like to serve this in small amounts, arranging the shrimp in a pretty little bowl that's nestled inside a pretty big bowl filled with ice.

To peel shrimp, remove the head (if it's still there) and legs first, then gently pull off the shell, starting from the underside at the head end, until the entire shell is removed, leaving the tail intact if you'd like. Devein by making a shallow cut along the back with a small knife. Using the tip of the knife, remove and discard the vein.

4

GETTIN' IT STARTED

SMOKED SALMON MOUSSE

I cannot tell a lie: This is not a traditional Southern recipe—but it is so good I could not stop myself from including it. I first got to try hot smoked salmon on one of our Paula Deen Cruises that stopped in Alaska. But you can't get that kind of fish everywhere, certainly not at my local Piggly Wiggly. So I had to lock myself in my kitchen for a spell and do some experimenting with the ingredients I could get my hands on, to try to re-create that marvelous one-of-a-kind flavor. What I came up with is mighty tasty, if I do say so myself.

SERVES 6 TO 8

1 can (6 ounces) salmon, drained
2 ounces cream cheese, at room temperature
¼ cup mayonnaise
2 tablespoons fresh lemon juice
¼ teaspoon liquid smoke
Salt and black pepper
Crackers and celery sticks,
 for dipping

In a food processor, combine the salmon, cream cheese, mayonnaise, lemon juice, liquid smoke, and a pinch each of salt and black pepper and blend until smooth. Taste and add more salt and pepper if you'd like. Serve the mousse at room temperature or chilled, with crackers and celery sticks for dipping.

LIQUID SMOKE

Liquid smoke is a popular Southern flavoring. It adds a smoky barbecue flavor to your foods in just a few squirts. You can find it in large supermarkets.

DON'T STRING ME ALONG

There is nothing more bothersome than trying to deal with stringy celery while you're making small talk. If your celery stalks are big and tough, run a veggie peeler over the outside of each stalk before you slice the celery. Your guests will thank you.

TOMATO SANDWICHES

■ ■

You just don't call it a party in the South if you don't serve tomato sandwiches. But even though this recipe is easy, you do have to stick to the technique. Otherwise, a few things could really go wrong. You do not want the bread to dry out, so keep it covered while you are filling the sandwiches. You don't want the bread to get too soggy, so drain the tomatoes really well between layers of paper towels. And for the prettiest sandwiches, the tomatoes should be just a little bit smaller than the size of the bread circles so they don't hang out the sides. If you follow all these simple steps, you will be rewarded with a truly magnificent Southern treat.

SERVES 4 TO 6

4 to 6 small tomatoes, such as
   Roma (plum) tomatoes
8 slices white bread
½ cup mayonnaise, plus extra (optional)
   for garnish

Paula Deen's House Seasoning
   (page 435)
Fresh parsley leaves for garnish (optional)

1. To prepare the tomatoes, thinly slice crosswise and drain thoroughly between layers of paper towels. You can stack up the slices on top of each other with paper towels in between to soak up the moisture.

2. Use a biscuit cutter or cookie cutter (a little larger than the diameter of the tomato slices) to cut rounds from the bread. Spread the mayonnaise onto one side of each bread round.

3. Sprinkle the tomato slices with the House Seasoning to taste. Place a tomato slice on a bread round, mayonnaise side up, and top with another bread round, mayonnaise side down. (Make sure the tomato has good contact with the mayonnaise; it's the glue that keeps everything together.) For a fancy touch, place a dab of mayonnaise in the center of the top of each sandwich, then press a parsley leaf on for decoration (this is optional). The sandwiches may be prepared several hours before serving. Cover well with a damp paper towel and refrigerate until ready to serve.

DON'T BE BLUNT

To slice a ripe tomato thinly, you need to have respect—and a good knife. Otherwise, you'll end up with a bruised tomato and smushed, uneven slices. Use a very sharp knife for the task, or, better yet, choose a good serrated knife, such as a bread knife. The teeth on a serrated knife do a perfect job of cutting through the tough skin of a tomato without harming the tender and juicy insides.

GETTIN' IT STARTED

SHRIMP BUTTER AND TOMATO SANDWICHES

■ ■

This is a wonderful recipe, one that I learned to make in the years since I made my home in Savannah. When I serve these sandwiches at parties, I like to take off the crusts and cut the bread into quarters. That way you can pile them high on a pretty platter. When folks take them, they can hold the sandwich in one hand, leaving the other free for a glass of punch or a cocktail.

SERVES 12

8 tablespoons (1 stick) butter,
   at room temperature
½ teaspoon freshly grated lemon zest
1½ teaspoons fresh lemon juice
1½ tablespoons chopped fresh chives

Cayenne pepper
Salt and black pepper
½ pound shrimp, cooked and peeled
1 medium tomato, thinly sliced
12 slices white bread

1. In a food processor, combine the butter, lemon zest, lemon juice, chives, a pinch of cayenne pepper, ¼ teaspoon salt, and ⅛ teaspoon black pepper. Process the mixture until smooth. Pulse in the shrimp until it reaches the desired texture, slightly chunky to silky smooth. Taste and add more salt, black pepper, or cayenne pepper if you'd like.

2. Drain the tomato slices on several layers of paper towels. You can stack up the slices on top of each other with paper towels in between to soak up the moisture.

3. Spread 1 tablespoon shrimp butter on each slice of bread. Top half the bread slices, butter side up, with a tomato slice. Sprinkle with salt and black pepper to taste and cover with another bread slice, butter side down. (You'll have shrimp butter left over, but see the box below for great ways to use it.) Cut the crusts off the sandwiches and cut the sandwiches into quarters to serve. If you are not serving these right away, cover them with a damp paper towel and refrigerate. They will stay fresh for 2 or 3 hours.

BUTTER ME UP

I adore this shrimp butter, so of course I'm always trying to find other uses for it. I love to stuff fish with it (see Grouper with Shrimp Butter, page 200) or simply spread it on melba toast. It even makes a great filling for celery sticks—a perfect way to get some extra veggies into my boys!

Chapter 2

SALADS AND SLAWS

S alad is one of those foods that we think we need to eat because we have to eat our vegetables. Oftentimes I'll ask, "Can I fix you a salad first?" and my husband, Michael, will say, "No, actually, I'm on a diet, so I'll just have the meat and potatoes." Well, he doesn't get away with that one. When I say the word *salad,* I could be talkin' about a good old pasta salad, chicken salad, or potato salad, so I tell him don't start turnin' up your nose until you find out just what kind of salad we're talking about.

A nice salad can be the most delicious way to start a meal, whether it's my mama's simple, refreshing Iceberg Wedge with Homemade Thousand Island Dressing (page 61) or an irresistible Wilted Salad with Hot Bacon Dressing (page 57). Then there are all the heartier salads I love to make, like Black-Eyed Pea Salad (page 43), or the Fried Chicken Salad (page 44) I serve just often enough to remind Michael (and all you others like him) that you can't afford to turn down the salad, because, honey, you might miss out on the main attraction!

Down South, salad means so much more than a side plate piled with lettuce and cucumbers. We break out the great big tub of mayonnaise for picnics and suppers; we'll shred cabbage, cook macaroni or potatoes, or even open up that box of Jell-O to make a salad, slaw, or mold that'll steal the show. Southern salads stand on their own. A bowl of Warm Macaroni Salad (page 60) on a buffet table will disappear before anything else. And a nice slaw will turn your sandwich into something out of this world. Top your next barbecue sandwich with a scoop of zippy, creamy Hot Slaw (page 47) and you'll be in hog heaven!

For the cook, of course, salad is a true gift. Most salads can be made ahead, and when you have weather as hot as we do in Savannah, believe me, you'll be craving chilled recipes like Corn, Tomato, and Shrimp Salad (page 52) or 7-Layer Molded Salad (page 62) for every meal.

Fixing your own dressing makes even the simplest salad special. Now, I know that many people use fancy olive oil, but I don't particularly enjoy a real virgin-y flavor. I prefer a light, mild one, or a good fresh vegetable oil. To me, whatever else you're adding to the dressing should be the star. That's what makes salad so much fun. Pecans? Raisins? Shredded carrots? A nice healthy dollop of my favorite, Kraft mayonnaise? So to all you Michaels out there who think salad is for health nuts, I'm telling you, you do not want to miss out on these recipes.

BLACK-EYED PEA SALAD

▪ ▪

Black-eyed peas are a classic Southern ingredient that can be found all over these United States. I find this salad makes a fantastic dish to bring to potluck events. When Jamie and Bobby were young kids, I would just never know when I needed to show up with a covered dish for a school fund-raiser. Well, I say I would never know, but it was because those two rascals always forgot to tell me they needed to bring something until the very last minute! But that's what it's all about when you're a mama; you got to have a recipe like this tucked up your sleeve!

SERVES 4 TO 6

2 cans (15 ounces each) black-eyed peas,
    rinsed and drained
1 can (15 ounces) diced tomatoes, drained
1 jar (4 ounces) pimientos,
    drained and chopped
1 clove garlic, finely chopped
¼ cup olive oil

3 tablespoons balsamic vinegar
2 tablespoons finely chopped red onion
2 tablespoons chopped fresh parsley
2 teaspoons chopped pickled
    jalapeño pepper
1 teaspoon sugar
¼ teaspoon salt, plus more to taste

Place all the ingredients in a large salad bowl and toss well to combine. Taste the salad and add a sprinkle more salt if you think it needs it, then serve.

THE MIGHTY PIMIENTO

Now, you may have noticed by now that the pimiento likes to pop up in my ingredient lists. That's because it's one of the most beloved ingredients in Southern cooking. It adds tang and color to any dish, especially pimiento cheese (see Everyone's Favorite Pimiento Cheese, page 27).

FRIED CHICKEN SALAD

■ ■

This is a fun recipe I created just for my darling husband, Michael. It seems whenever I would put a big green salad on the table, you could count on Michael not being able to find room for it on his plate. Well, with this dish I believe I have fixed his wagon. Homemade fried chicken strips with tangy buttermilk dressing served on top of a garden-fresh salad—Michael (and the salad avoider in your family) will always make room for this.

SERVES 4 TO 6

Buttermilk Dressing
⅓ cup buttermilk
¼ cup olive oil
1 teaspoon fresh lemon juice
½ teaspoon salt
¼ teaspoon black pepper
3 tablespoons chopped fresh chives

Fried Chicken
1 pound boneless, skinless chicken breasts
2 large eggs, lightly beaten
1 cup self-rising flour
Black pepper
Vegetable oil, for deep-frying
Salt

Salad
12 cups mixed greens
2 plum tomatoes, chopped
½ small Vidalia onion, thinly sliced

1. To make the dressing: In a small bowl, whisk together the buttermilk, oil, lemon juice, salt, and black pepper. Whisk in the chives.

2. To make the chicken: Cut the chicken into 1-inch strips. In a wide, shallow bowl, whisk the eggs with ¼ cup water. In a separate wide, shallow bowl, whisk together the flour and ½ teaspoon black pepper.

3. In a large saucepan, heat 3 inches of oil to 350°F.

4. Coat the chicken with the eggs and let the excess drip back into the bowl. Dip the chicken in the flour and shake off any excess. Add the chicken to the hot oil and cook until it is golden and cooked through, 3 to 4 minutes. Then set it on a paper towel–lined plate to drain. Season the chicken with salt and black pepper to taste.

5. To make the salad: Toss together the greens, tomatoes, onion, and two-thirds of the dressing in a large bowl. Divide the greens among 4 to 6 serving plates, depending on how many people you want to feed. Top the greens with the fried chicken and drizzle with the remaining dressing. Serve immediately.

EASY DOES IT
Salad greens need to be treated gently! To keep the greens from wilting, be sure to dress the salad just before serving. And take care not to overdress your salad. You can always add more dressing, but you can't take it away once you pour it on.

CHICKEN, RICE, AND AVOCADO SALAD

This is such a pretty little salad and so suitable as a main course at fancy luncheons. It's a light dish, but, with all the chicken and rice, it is more filling than it looks. I think chopped avocados are so fun to use (they don't always have to make an appearance on your table as guacamole, you know), and their texture gives the salad a wonderful creaminess without being too heavy. This recipe dates back to my Bag Lady days, and it's just as good today.

SERVES 8

Dressing

1 large Hass avocado, halved and pitted
2 tablespoons fresh lemon juice
1 cup mayonnaise
½ cup sour cream
⅓ cup coarsely chopped onion
2 cloves garlic, coarsely chopped
1 teaspoon salt
½ teaspoon Worcestershire sauce
Pinch of cayenne pepper

Salad

2 Hass avocados, pitted, peeled, and coarsely chopped
1 tablespoon fresh lemon juice
3 cups chopped cooked chicken
3 cups cooked white rice
1 cup mayonnaise
¾ cup diced yellow onion
¼ cup chopped fresh parsley
1 teaspoon salt
1 teaspoon black pepper
1 lemon, cut into wedges, for serving

1. To make the dressing: Scoop the avocado flesh into a food processor. Add the remaining dressing ingredients and blend until smooth. Pour the dressing into a small bowl or a pretty little pitcher and chill until serving.

2. To make the salad: Toss the chopped avocados with the lemon juice in a large bowl. Add the chicken, rice, mayonnaise, onion, parsley, salt, and black pepper and toss just to combine. Chill the salad for at least 30 minutes or up to 4 hours before serving. Serve in individual bowls with the lemon wedges and pass around the dressing.

Quickly pit an avocado by slicing it in half lengthwise along the pit. Carefully but firmly, strike the pit with a large knife, then twist out.

IT AIN'T EASY BEING GREEN

There's nothing more unsightly than a salad with brown avocado. Keep your avocados bright green by tossing them with lemon or lime juice as soon as you cut into them. And if you're using only part of the avocado, keep the remainder fresh by wrapping plastic wrap tightly over the leftover pieces.

TACO SALAD

■ ■

Taco salad is a great example of the Southwestern flavors that we have come to love here in the South. Now, it's *called* a salad, but really this is a full meal in a bowl. You've got your meat and plenty of vegetables, plus tortilla chips for a crunch. And believe me, even the pickiest eaters at your table will not turn their noses up at this dish.

SERVES 6 TO 8

1 pound ground beef
1 packet (1¼ ounces) taco seasoning
1 head iceberg lettuce, shredded
2 cups shredded sharp Cheddar cheese
   (8 ounces)
2 plum tomatoes, chopped

1 Hass avocado, pitted, peeled, and chopped
4 scallions, chopped
2 cups crumbled tortilla chips
⅓ cup fresh or store-bought salsa
⅓ cup sour cream
2 teaspoons fresh lime juice

1. Heat a large skillet over medium-high heat. Add the beef and cook it, breaking it up with a fork, until browned, 5 to 7 minutes. Stir in the taco seasoning and ⅓ cup water; simmer until the liquid is just about gone, 3 to 5 minutes.

2. In a large salad bowl, combine the beef, lettuce, 1½ cups of the Cheddar, the tomatoes, avocado, and scallions. Toss in 1½ cups of the crumbled tortilla chips.

3. In a small bowl, whisk together the salsa, sour cream, and lime juice. Pour over the salad and toss to combine. Sprinkle the top with the remaining ½ cup Cheddar and ½ cup crumbled tortilla chips and serve. This salad tastes great hot or cold.

SWITCH IT UP

No ground beef in the fridge? Here are two more yummy options. Try this salad with some shredded cooked chicken tossed in a pan with the taco seasoning. Or open a couple cans of black or red beans and heat them with the taco seasoning.

HOT SLAW

■ ■

Here in the South we love our coleslaw, and you will certainly find it on our tables, especially in the summer months when that crunch is just what you want in the heat. But I just love the taste of a good slaw too much to eat it only when the temperature is above 70 degrees. Now, here's a recipe I like to serve when there's a chill in the air because it'll make you feel all warm and toasty. It's a nice, warm coleslaw with crispy, crumbly bacon and just a dash of hot sauce.

SERVES 4 TO 6

3 tablespoons apple cider vinegar
2 teaspoons sugar
¾ teaspoon salt
¾ teaspoon hot sauce
⅛ teaspoon black pepper
4 slices bacon

1 cup chopped yellow onion
½ cup chopped green bell pepper
½ teaspoon garlic powder
¼ teaspoon celery seed
4 cups shredded green cabbage
(½ medium head)

1. In a small bowl, whisk together the vinegar, sugar, salt, hot sauce, and black pepper.

2. In a large skillet, cook the bacon over medium-high heat until crisp, 5 to 7 minutes. Set the bacon on a paper towel–lined plate to drain.

3. Reduce the heat to medium-low and add the onion and bell pepper to the skillet. Cook, stirring, until softened, about 5 minutes. Stir in the garlic powder and celery seed. Cook for 1 minute. Add the cabbage and cook, tossing, until softened, about 5 minutes. Carefully pour in the vinegar mixture and cook until the liquid has evaporated, 2 to 3 minutes. Take the skillet off the heat and crumble in the bacon. Taste and adjust seasoning, if needed, then serve the slaw while it's hot.

> **HEADS UP**
>
> Go ahead and substitute shredded coleslaw mix if you like. It's easier, and then you won't have half a cabbage sitting around in your fridge!

EASY COLESLAW

■ ■

This classic recipe for Southern-style coleslaw is something that can be served as a side dish to almost any kind of meat. We'll put a bowl of it on the table and folks will just help themselves—as they would in just about any part of the country. But do you know the sign of a true Southerner? That'll be the one who makes up this coleslaw just to use as a condiment for sandwiches—slathered on top of some juicy pulled pork, sandwiched in a fresh roll.

SERVES 6 TO 8

¾ cup mayonnaise
¼ cup apple cider vinegar
1 tablespoon sugar

8 cups shredded green cabbage (1 small head)
Salt and black pepper

1. In a small bowl, whisk together the mayonnaise, vinegar, and sugar.

2. Place the cabbage in a large salad bowl. Pour the dressing over the cabbage and toss well to coat. Season to taste with salt and black pepper. This salad can be kept in the refrigerator for up to 3 days before serving it.

> **LET IT SIT A SPELL**
>
> Classic slaw is a complete do-ahead dish. Unlike a delicate green salad, coleslaw should definitely sit a spell. I like to make it well ahead, at least 2 hours, so that the flavors develop and the cabbage softens up a bit.

COLESLAW WITH RAISINS, DILL, AND HONEY-ROASTED PEANUTS

This is the coleslaw I make when I want to serve it all on its own in a pretty bowl on the table. It's a gussied-up version of Easy Coleslaw, and I think the extra ingredients make a world of difference. Raisins in a salad always seem to me to be an extra-special touch. And I just love to use the chopped fresh dill to give it a hint of springtime. But you know, I think it's the honey-roasted peanuts that I chop up and sprinkle on top that make this dish such a guaranteed crowd-pleaser. I swear, whenever I set it on my buffet table, I barely have to wash the bowl at the end of the meal!

SERVES 6 TO 8

½ cup mayonnaise
2 teaspoons distilled white or
    apple cider vinegar
1 teaspoon sugar
½ teaspoon salt
½ teaspoon black pepper

4 cups shredded green cabbage
    (½ medium head)
1 cup grated carrot (1 large)
¼ cup finely chopped Vidalia onion
2 tablespoons chopped fresh dill
¾ cup raisins
¼ cup chopped honey-roasted peanuts

1. In a small bowl, whisk together the mayonnaise, vinegar, sugar, salt, and black pepper.

2. In a large salad bowl that's pretty enough to serve in, combine the cabbage, carrot, onion, dill, and raisins. Stir in the dressing and toss well to combine. Let the slaw stand for 10 minutes for the flavors to develop before sprinkling with peanuts to serve.

ROCK AND ROLL

Chopping nuts can be tricky—they have a tendency to roll all around your cutting board. Your best bet is to lay them in a compact circle and rock the blade back and forth in a seesaw motion over the nuts while rotating the knife in a circle. Take care to always leave a part of the knife in contact with the board. Because you want the pieces nice and chunky, don't use a food processor.

AMBROSIA CHICKEN SALAD

Ambrosia salad is what we call our fruit salad here in these parts, which we make with cherries and tropical fruit like pineapple and coconut. Sometimes we add marshmallows, too. One day I got to thinking that ambrosia salad needed something savory in there to help it all come together. So I added some cooked chicken breast and slivered almonds just to see what would happen— I left out the marshmallows; they just didn't seem right anymore. I think it's absolutely slap-your-mama good. Some people say they have a sweet tooth, but I swear I have a salty-sweet tooth!

SERVES 4

4 cups chopped cooked chicken breast

1 can (20 ounces) crushed pineapple, drained

1 cup sweetened shredded coconut

½ cup slivered almonds, lightly toasted

¾ cup mayonnaise

1 tablespoon fresh lime juice

Salt

8 maraschino cherries, for garnish (optional)

In a large bowl, combine the chicken, pineapple, coconut, almonds, mayonnaise, and lime juice, tossing well. Add salt to taste. This salad can be served immediately or refrigerated for up to 8 hours and served chilled. Serve in individual bowls topped with pretty little maraschino cherries, if desired.

HOW EASY IS THIS?

Make this a total no-cook meal by buying yourself a rotisserie chicken from the supermarket. It is just about the handiest thing to have in the fridge. Just cut off some thick pieces of the white meat and chop them into this salad. Use the remaining chicken meat in sandwiches, tossed into rice dishes, or even just warmed up with a little gravy.

SOUTHERN SHRIMP AND RICE SALAD

■ ■

This is something I did not learn to make until I came to live in Savannah, for here shrimp is so plentiful, we always find a way to serve it at every meal. What I really love about this recipe is that you cook the rice using the same water that you've already cooked the shrimp in, so the rice comes out tasting extra delicious. That is the thing about Southern cooks—we know how not to waste one bit of flavor!

SERVES 6

2 tablespoons Old Bay seasoning
2 pounds shrimp, peeled and deveined
1 cup long-grain white rice
½ cup finely chopped yellow onion

½ cup chopped pitted green olives
1 cup mayonnaise
Black pepper

1. In a saucepan, combine the Old Bay seasoning and 4 cups water. Bring to a boil, add the shrimp, and boil for 4 minutes. Use a slotted spoon to transfer the shrimp to a cutting board, leaving the cooking water in the pot. When cool enough to handle, chop the shrimp into bite-size chunks.

2. In the reserved shrimp cooking water, boil the rice until tender, 15 to 20 minutes. Drain in a colander and allow to cool.

3. In a large bowl, combine the rice, onion, olives, mayonnaise, and black pepper to taste. Mix in the shrimp just before serving with a smile!

A PERFECT PAIR

Shrimp and Old Bay seasoning— has there ever been a more perfect pairing? The Southern shrimp boil (which is just shrimp that's been boiled in a pot of seasoned water) has featured Old Bay for the past seventy years or so. I'm not sure what they did before then, but I'm sure glad that today we've got those zesty spices and herbs to make our shrimp really sing. But don't just use it with your shrimp; it's great with all seafood, from snapper to crab. And you can't beat an Old Bay Bloody Mary for Sunday brunch.

CORN, TOMATO, AND SHRIMP SALAD

■ ■

This dish is a favorite of my beloved niece, Corrie. She is just a gorgeous girl, and even though she looks like she eats like a bird, believe me, she comes to the table hungry and expecting a hearty meal. And this salad has got it all—fresh tomatoes and good summer corn, and it's packed with shrimp in every bite.

SERVES 4

2½ teaspoons fresh lemon juice
½ teaspoon salt
½ teaspoon black pepper
2 cloves garlic, finely chopped
¼ cup olive oil
1 pound small shrimp, cooked and peeled

1 head Boston lettuce, torn into
   bite-size pieces
1⅓ cups corn kernels, cooked fresh
   or thawed frozen
2 plum tomatoes, sliced
½ small red onion, very thinly sliced
⅓ cup chopped fresh basil

1. In a small bowl, whisk together the lemon juice, salt, black pepper, and garlic. Whisk in the oil until completely combined.

2. In a large salad bowl, combine the shrimp, lettuce, corn, tomatoes, onion, and basil. Pour the dressing over the salad and toss well to combine. This salad is best served just as soon as you make it up.

A WHOLE LOTTA SHAKIN'

Keep your finished and cleaned jelly jars in the cupboard and use them to make your dressings. Just add all the ingredients to the jar, cap tightly, and shake, shake, shake. I like to make full jars of dressing and keep them in the fridge so I can pull out homemade dressing all through the week.

Core a tomato by inserting a small knife just to the side of the core on the stem end. Angling the knife away from the core, carve a 1-inch-deep circle and pop out the core with the tip of the knife.

NUTTY SHRIMP SALAD

■ ■

Typically, I'll make this salad if I am hosting a luncheon or a brunch, and serve it in small and dainty portions on a bed of lettuce as a starter course. It makes such a pretty presentation that way. And don't forget to save any leftovers to put in between two slices of toast for a shrimp salad sandwich that will knock your socks off.

SERVES 4

4 cups cooked large shrimp, peeled, deveined, and halved crosswise

½ cup corn kernels, cooked fresh or thawed frozen

⅓ cup chopped pecans

¼ cup chopped pimiento

¼ cup finely chopped celery

3 tablespoons chopped fresh parsley

2 tablespoons chopped scallion

¼ cup mayonnaise

Salt and black pepper

Lettuce leaves, for serving

In a large bowl, combine the shrimp, corn, pecans, pimiento, celery, parsley, scallion, mayonnaise, and salt and black pepper to taste. Scoop the salad onto pretty little lunch plates lined with lettuce leaves.

BUTTER ME UP

I recommend butterhead lettuce (like Boston lettuce) here. It is so pretty and bright on a plate, and the leaves are nice and big and sturdy. Romaine lettuce will work too. And, in a pinch, iceberg will do just fine. Be careful not to rip your lettuce leaves. You want them as whole and intact as possible on the plate. I like to remove the core first with a small paring knife and then gently pull the leaves apart from the base.

DOUBLE POTATO SALAD

■ ■

Potato salad is everybody's favorite. I don't care how stubborn your man is about eating salad, you can bet that potato salad will disappear practically before the bowl hits the table. And when you double your potato salad pleasure by topping it with crunchy crumbled potato chips, well, there is no potato lover I know who can resist.

SERVES 8 TO 10

3 pounds small creamer potatoes
   (see box), unpeeled
1¼ cups sour cream
1 small green bell pepper, chopped
¼ cup chopped fresh chives

1¼ teaspoons salt
½ teaspoon paprika
½ teaspoon black pepper
Potato chips, crumbled

1. Place the potatoes in a large pot and cover with salted water. Bring to a boil and cook until tender, 15 to 20 minutes. Drain the potatoes and allow them to cool before you coarsely dice them.

2. In a large bowl pretty enough for serving, combine the potatoes with the sour cream, bell pepper, chives, salt, paprika, and black pepper. Sprinkle the salad with crumbled potato chips just before serving.

YOU SAY POTATO

Creamer potatoes are generally Yukon Gold or red potatoes that are harvested early in the season. They have a low starch content that makes them just right for boiling, and they turn out small and delicate. The thin, waxy skin is perfect if left on and adds such pretty color to the salad.

PAULA'S CLASSIC POTATO SALAD

■ ■

One of the most precious memories I have from my childhood in Albany, Georgia, is Mama setting out a picnic blanket under a shade tree by the creek and Daddy pulling all these wonderful dishes out of the picnic basket. I swear my brother, Bubba, and I had eyes as big as saucers when we got a look at all the good food Mama had made for us. One of our favorites (aside from the deviled eggs and tomato sandwiches) was this simple, old-fashioned potato salad. When I tell you that this recipe is just the way Mama made it, well, you know I can't give it a higher recommendation than that.

SERVES 6 TO 8

4 pounds red potatoes, unpeeled, cut into
   ¾-inch cubes
3 large eggs
About ¾ cup mayonnaise
2½ teaspoons apple cider vinegar
½ cup chopped dill pickle relish

2 celery stalks, finely chopped
3 scallions, finely chopped
3 tablespoons chopped fresh parsley
Paula Deen Collection Silly Salt or Paula
   Deen's House Seasoning (page 435) and
   black pepper

1. In a large pot of boiling water, cook the potatoes and eggs for about 10 minutes. Drain the potatoes and eggs and allow them to cool. Peel the eggs and squish them with your hands until they crumble.

2. In a small bowl, whisk together ¾ cup mayonnaise and the vinegar.

3. In a large serving bowl, combine the potatoes, eggs, pickle relish, celery, scallions, and parsley and toss with the dressing. Season with salt and black pepper to taste. Add more mayonnaise if not creamy enough. Serve immediately or pack it up in some plastic containers for your picnic.

AS THE EGG CRUMBLES

I'd much rather crumble hard-boiled eggs in my hands instead of chasing 'em around the cutting board as they roll all over the place. Obviously you want the eggs to be cooled before you lay your bare hands on them.

HOT GERMAN POTATO SALAD WITH BACON

■ ■

This hot potato salad is surely not what you think about when you think of potato salad, but let me tell you that it is just about one of the best things you could ever put in your mouth. That's because it's got lots of bacon mixed in, and all those meaty juices really give this salad some heft, while the yellow mustard makes it zippy. Just try it once and you will find yourself making it over and over again.

SERVES 6 TO 8

3 pounds small red potatoes, unpeeled
6 slices bacon
1 to 2 tablespoons vegetable oil
⅔ cup chicken broth
2 tablespoons apple cider vinegar

4 teaspoons yellow mustard
1 teaspoon sugar
Salt and black pepper
3 or 4 scallions, chopped

1. Place the potatoes in a medium pot with water to cover. Bring to a boil and cook until just tender, 15 to 20 minutes. Drain the potatoes and allow them to cool before halving or quartering, depending on size.

2. Meanwhile, in a large skillet, cook the bacon until crispy, 5 to 7 minutes. Set the bacon on a paper towel–lined plate to drain.

3. Carefully pour the bacon fat from the skillet into a measuring cup. Add enough vegetable oil to the bacon fat to make ¼ cup, then pour the fat back into the skillet along with the broth, vinegar, mustard, sugar, and salt and black pepper to taste. Whisk the mixture in the skillet to combine and simmer for 4 minutes.

4. Place the potatoes in a large salad bowl and add the warm vinaigrette, tossing well to combine. Crumble the bacon on top of the salad and sprinkle with the scallions just before serving.

HOT POTATO

When boiling potatoes for potato salad, it's best to cook them until just tender, because even after you drain potatoes from the pan, they'll keep cooking while they cool. You want the potatoes to keep their shape, not go all mushy on you when you toss them with the other ingredients. To test for doneness, stick a fork or skewer into a potato; if the fork or skewer slides in easily, those potatoes are done!

WILTED SALAD WITH HOT BACON DRESSING

■ ■

This is the kind of warm, comforting salad you might expect to find on the menu of a good steak-house. And if you could really call any salad "romantic," well, it would be this one. The hot bacon dressing covers the greens so that every leaf just drips with flavor. Now, this is a salad you can really sink your teeth into.

SERVES 4

12 cups salad greens, such as spinach, butterhead lettuce, and red leaf lettuce, or equivalent mixed greens
3 scallions, white and light green parts only, chopped

About 2½ teaspoons apple cider vinegar
¼ teaspoon sugar
¼ teaspoon salt
4 slices bacon
Black pepper

1. In a large salad bowl, combine the greens and scallions. In a small bowl, mix together 2½ teaspoons vinegar, the sugar, and salt. Toss with the salad. Add a few more drops of vinegar if you need it to coat all those greens.

2. In a large skillet, fry the bacon until crisp, 5 to 7 minutes. Set the bacon on a paper towel–lined plate to drain. Crumble the bacon over the salad and pour the hot bacon grease over the greens. Toss well to combine. Season with black pepper to taste.

> **KEEP IT CLEAN**
>
> There's nothing worse than a salad filled with grit. Make sure you clean your salad greens thoroughly. I like to fill the sink up with a whole load of cold water (sometimes I even throw some ice cubes in there), give a generous shake of salt to the water, and submerge my leaves. The salt will take care of any critters that have stowed away in your leaves, and they will drop to the bottom of the sink. Give the leaves a swirl around in the water, then dry them thoroughly. A salad spinner is the best bet for drying, but if you don't have one, just lay the leaves out on a kitchen towel to dry.

BEET AND BLUE CHEESE SALAD

■ ■

I absolutely love a beet salad, and I will always order one when I'm at a restaurant. But I must confess, I very rarely make one at home. It's because I don't like to see my hands get stained red from all the roasting and peeling you have to do to get beets ready to eat. So I decided to just go ahead and make it easy on myself by buying canned precooked beets. I've never had another day of worry.

SERVES 4

3 tablespoons walnut pieces

2 teaspoons balsamic vinegar

¼ teaspoon salt

Black pepper

1½ tablespoons olive oil

3 cups canned sliced beets, drained

Salad greens, for serving

⅓ cup crumbled blue cheese

1. Preheat the oven to 350°F. Spread the walnuts on a rimmed baking sheet and toast until golden and fragrant, about 7 minutes. Let the nuts cool, then give them a rough chop.

2. In a small bowl, whisk together the vinegar, salt, and black pepper to taste. Whisk in the oil until completely combined.

3. In a bowl, toss the beets and walnuts with the vinaigrette. Serve on a bed of greens, topped with the blue cheese.

WRAP IT UP

To roast your own beets, place trimmed beets on a large sheet of foil. Wrap them up in a package, scrunching the edges together to seal. Place the beet package on a baking sheet to catch any juices that might leak while roasting. Roast in a 375°F oven until a knife easily pierces the beets, 30 minutes to 1 hour, depending on the size of the beets. Let cool until you can handle them without scorching your fingers, then peel the warm beets with your fingers (it will stain them red) or with a paring knife.

CREAMY RICE SALAD WITH COUNTRY HAM AND PEAS

■ ■

This creamy salad is something you'll find on many Southern tables and picnic blankets on a Sunday afternoon after church. It's a hearty dish that tastes great served either hot or cold—so it's especially convenient to make when you suspect you might have company coming later. You know nobody will go hungry when you've got this in the fridge!

SERVES 6 TO 8

2 cups long-grain white rice
½ teaspoon salt
1 cup diced country-style ham
   (¼ pound thick cut)
¾ cup frozen peas, thawed
⅓ cup mayonnaise

⅓ cup sour cream
⅓ cup chopped fresh parsley
¼ cup finely chopped red onion
1 clove garlic, finely chopped
1 teaspoon fresh lemon juice
½ teaspoon hot sauce, plus extra for serving

1. In a medium saucepan, combine the rice, salt, and 3 cups water. Bring to a boil over medium-high heat. Reduce to a simmer, cover, and cook until the liquid has evaporated and the rice is tender, about 20 minutes. Remove the saucepan from the heat and let stand, still covered, for 10 minutes. Fluff with a fork and let it cool, uncovered.

2. In a large salad bowl, toss the rice with the ham, peas, mayonnaise, sour cream, parsley, onion, garlic, lemon juice, and hot sauce. Serve with plenty of extra hot sauce to pass at the table.

HOT, HOT, HOT

We sure like our hot sauce here in the South. And no table is complete without plenty of hot sauce options laid out. From vinegary Louisiana-style sauces to Georgia sweet and spicy sauces, nothing punches up a meal like hot sauce.

WARM MACARONI SALAD

■ ■

There is one thing everybody should know about my dear son Bobby—he goes crazy for macaroni! I created this salad just for him. It's got plenty of macaroni, grated carrot for color, and just a pucker of chopped pickle that brings it all together. I like to serve it warm, but it will still be tasty if you refrigerate the leftovers to eat the next day.

SERVES 6 TO 8

2 cups elbow macaroni (about 8 ounces)
½ cup grated carrot (about 1 large)
3 tablespoons finely chopped
   Vidalia onion
1 celery stalk, finely chopped

3 tablespoons finely chopped
   bread-and-butter pickle
⅔ cup mayonnaise
½ teaspoon salt
¼ teaspoon black pepper

1. In a large pot of boiling salted water, cook the pasta according to the package directions. Drain well and transfer to a large serving bowl.

2. Add the carrot, onion, celery, and pickle to the warm macaroni. Stir in the mayonnaise, salt, and black pepper. Serve it while it's still warm.

A GEORGIA SWEET

Vidalia onions are one of the greatest prides of Georgia! They have a sweet, mild taste that reminds me of the temperament of most Georgians. Because they are never sharp or overpowering, Vidalias are perfect chopped raw into a salad.

MAMA'S ICEBERG WEDGE WITH HOMEMADE THOUSAND ISLAND DRESSING

I am just in love with these simple old-fashioned recipes! It seems like you so rarely see something with so few ingredients on a plate these days; when I was growing up it was the simplest things that were the best. This salad is nothing but a quarter of a head of lettuce placed on a plate with a drizzle of good ol' Thousand Island dressing. This is a dinner salad the way my mama used to serve it, just as elegant and as tasty as can be.

SERVES 4

Dressing
1½ cups mayonnaise
1 cup ketchup
1 hard-boiled egg, peeled and very finely chopped
¼ cup dill pickle relish
Salt and black pepper
Lemon-pepper seasoning, such as Paula Deen Collection (optional)

Salad
1 small head iceberg lettuce, cut into 4 wedges
Crumbled bacon, for serving (optional)

CHOP, CHOP
For another take, try giving this salad a good chop and adding some cooked bacon. Place it all on a hamburger on a fluffy sweet bun and you've got yourself a hearty meal.

1. To make the dressing: In a small bowl, whisk together the mayonnaise, ketchup, egg, relish, salt and black pepper to taste, and lemon-pepper seasoning, if desired.

2. To assemble the salad: Place the lettuce wedges on individual plates and drizzle generously with the dressing. Top with crumbled bacon, if you'd like.

7-LAYER MOLDED SALAD

■ ■

Now, who doesn't love a molded salad? Especially one that's got seven layers! I make this classic salad all the time, and it's always a hit at any Southern buffet or picnic.

SERVES 8 TO 10

2 packages (3 ounces each)
   powdered lemon gelatin
Pinch of salt
2 cups boiling water
1 tablespoon fresh lemon juice
½ cup full-fat cottage cheese

½ cup chopped red bell pepper
½ cup chopped celery
2 hard-boiled eggs, peeled and sliced
½ cup frozen peas, thawed
4 slices bacon, cooked and crumbled

1. In a medium heatproof bowl, mix the powdered gelatin and salt with the boiling water until completely dissolved. Stir in 1½ cups cold water and the lemon juice. Refrigerate, covered, until the gelatin is just wiggly but not firmed up (like loose jelly), about 1 hour.

2. Scoop 1 cup of the gelatin and place in a small bowl. Stir in the cottage cheese and set aside.

3. Spoon ½ cup of the gelatin into a 6-cup mold. Scatter the bell pepper evenly on top and cover with another ½ cup of the gelatin. Then scatter the celery on top, followed by another ½ cup of the gelatin. Next, layer the eggs and top with the remaining gelatin. Top this with the peas and bacon. Evenly spoon the reserved gelatin–cottage cheese mixture on top of the peas and bacon. Refrigerate until firm, about 4 hours or overnight. Unmold and serve.

BREAKING THE MOLD

Here are some tips for easily unmolding gelatin. Before filling your mold, rinse it in a little cold water. This helps prepare the sides of the mold. Then, when you are ready to unmold, dip the mold in some warm water (not too hot!) for about 5 seconds. This will help to loosen the gelatin. Lift the mold out of the water and gently pull the gelatin away from the sides with the pads of your fingers. Then place a pretty serving plate on top of the mold and invert right onto the plate, giving the gelatin a little shake back and forth as you do so.

For easy unmolding, dip the bottom of the mold into a bowl of warm (not hot) water for a few seconds. Using your fingertips, gently pull the gelatin away from the sides of the mold and invert onto a serving plate.

Chapter 3

SOUPS AND STEWS

I can't think of one thing more comforting and fulfilling than a wonderful bowl of hot soup or stew with a slab of corn bread beside it. As a child, I loved Fridays at the old country school I attended, because that was the day they served homemade vegetable soup, buttered toast, and peanut butter balls. I swear I would almost run over the child in front of me to get to that lunch line. Nothing says Mama and comfort like a soup.

Of course, down South in the summertime I'm so busy running from air-conditioned car to air-conditioned house, I wouldn't stop once to think of soup if not for my husband. But I tell you what—that man could live off soup. Michael couldn't care less if it's 100 degrees outside; he would happily eat soup three meals a day. He adores a hearty Sour Cream, Bacon, and Split Pea Soup (page 77), which has such a deep, porky flavor and is truly soul-satisfying. Michael also makes the best Ham Bone Soup (page 76) I've ever had. He's got all these ham hocks bobbing in a pot with one old sack of beans. It's so rich and delicious.

I *do* think of soup whenever the house is full of friends. A big wintertime celebration, or even just a handful of guests staying the weekend, will inspire me to pull down my stockpot and make up a big old pot of hearty The Lady & Sons Beef Vegetable Soup (page 70), one of my specialties. The beautiful thing about soup is that you can leave a pot on the stove, stack some bowls and spoons nearby, then step back. If you're having an open house, or you've got overnight guests and you know they'll all want to eat something at different times, you can just tell 'em, "Hey, y'all, soup's on—help yourself."

For the cold and sniffle season, you want to have a good chicken soup. My Cure-All Chicken Rice Soup (page 69) has special properties that come from making it with good ingredients and love. Chicken soup is a comfort that everyone the world 'round swears by, but in this chapter I also include many Southern specialties, like Burgoo (page 74). This thick stew-y soup is traditionally eaten on the day of the Kentucky Derby. Old-time versions of the recipe feature squirrel. My chicken, beef, and lamb version is much tamer, but, honey, you could give those Derby horses a run for their money after a steaming, meaty bowl of good burgoo.

The Real Deal Gumbo (page 79), She-Crab Soup (page 80), Charleston Okra Soup (page 75), Easy Shrimp Bisque (page 81), and Creamy Peanut Soup (page 84) . . . Southern soups are like a history of the South simmered in a pot. There are enough fine soup recipes here to last you the year. So ladle up a bowl of comfort, Southern style.

CURE-ALL CHICKEN RICE SOUP

■ ■

I have been a mama a pretty long time now, and I come from a long line of ladies who knew the power of soup, so I feel qualified to tell y'all that this is the best cure for whatever ails you that I know. Plenty of chicken flavor, plenty of chicken meat, tender carrots, and rice, and a sweet little surprise tarragon flavor make this just about the most comforting, healing food you can serve. I make it whenever anyone's sick—or even just thinking about it—and it has never failed to improve things.

SERVES 6 TO 8

1 whole chicken (3½ pounds), rinsed, patted dry, and cut into 8 pieces
3 celery stalks, chopped
2 large carrots, halved crosswise
1 large yellow onion, halved through the root end
3 cloves garlic, finely chopped

2 bay leaves
2½ teaspoons salt
¾ teaspoon black pepper
¾ teaspoon dried tarragon
1 cup long-grain white rice
⅓ cup chopped fresh parsley

1. In a large stockpot, combine the chicken, 12 cups water, celery, carrots, onion, garlic, bay leaves, salt, black pepper, and tarragon. Bring to a boil over high heat. Reduce to a simmer and cook until the chicken is cooked through, about 45 minutes.

2. Remove the chicken and carrots from the pot and set aside. Strain the remaining liquid and discard the solids. Return the strained broth to the pot, stir in the rice, bring to a gentle simmer, and cook until the rice is tender, 15 to 20 minutes.

3. Meanwhile, once the chicken is cool enough to handle, pick the meat off the bones, discarding the bones and skin. Cut the meat into bite-size pieces and thinly slice the carrots. Return the chicken and carrots to the pot. Simmer for 5 minutes. Adjust seasoning and stir in the parsley just before serving.

THE BONES HAVE IT

Flavor, that is. It's always best to stick with bone-in meat when preparing soups because that's where your soup gets all its richness and flavor.

THE LADY & SONS BEEF VEGETABLE SOUP

Now, I don't usually aim to write down recipes for y'all that have more ingredients than you can count on your fingers, but this soup is an exception. For one thing, many of these ingredients are just seasonings, and most can be kept on hand in the freezer or pantry, so you don't need to run out with a fresh shopping list. Second, the soup comes together fast and makes enough to feed an army. If you ever find yourself stuck in the house—say, a heavy rain caught you by surprise—get situated in the kitchen with this recipe and you can have soup in the freezer to last months.

MAKES 8 QUARTS

2½ to 3 pounds boneless chuck or beef short
   ribs (see top left box, opposite)
2 tablespoons vegetable oil
   (if using chuck roast)
3 tablespoons dried parsley flakes
1 tablespoon Italian seasoning
1 tablespoon beef bouillon granules
1 tablespoon Paula Deen's House Seasoning
   (page 435)
1 tablespoon Paula Deen Collection Seasoned
   Salt, or other seasoned salt
1 teaspoon garlic powder
1 teaspoon celery salt
½ teaspoon black pepper
2 bay leaves
1 tablespoon Worcestershire sauce

1½ cups chopped yellow onions
1 can (28 ounces) diced tomatoes
1 cup thinly sliced carrots
1 cup chopped celery
1 cup sliced green beans, fresh or rinsed
   and drained canned
1 cup black-eyed peas, frozen or rinsed
   and drained canned
1 cup butter beans, frozen or rinsed
   and drained canned
1 cup sliced okra, fresh or frozen
1 cup corn kernels, fresh, frozen,
   or rinsed and drained canned
1 cup chopped red potatoes
½ cup elbow macaroni
2 teaspoons Accent (optional)

1. If using chuck roast, in a large skillet, heat the oil over medium-high heat until shimmering. Place the roast in the skillet and cook until browned on both sides, about 5 minutes per side. Remove the roast from the skillet and cut it into 1½- to 2-inch cubes; discard the fat.

2. Place the beef in a large stockpot. (If using short ribs, you can put them right in the pot with no preparation.) Add 4 quarts water, the parsley, Italian seasoning, bouillon granules, House Seasoning, seasoned salt, garlic powder, celery salt, black pepper, bay leaves, Worcestershire sauce, onions, and diced tomatoes. Bring to a boil over high heat. Reduce to a simmer, cover, and cook until the meat is very tender, 1½ to 2 hours. If using short ribs, remove them from the pot and cut the meat from the bones, discard the bones and fat, and return the meat to the pot.

3. Add the remaining vegetables and the macaroni and bring the soup back to a boil, stirring to combine the ingredients. Reduce the heat to a simmer and cook, uncovered, for 45 minutes. Add the Accent, if you'd like. Remove the bay leaves before serving.

> ### BONE UP ON FLAVOR
> The chuck roast will yield more meat, but the bones from the short ribs give the soup an incredible flavor.

> ### CLEVER DEGREASING
> To remove excess fat that floats to the top of the soup, swirl a lettuce leaf around the surface of the soup—it will pick up a lot of the fat.

FRIED ONION SOUP

Y'all, a can of French's fried onions in my pantry is like a challenge: How can I work those delicious things into whatever I'm cooking? I've found they give my onion soup a wonderful little crunch, along with their savory flavor.

SERVES 6

8 cups beef broth

4 cups chicken broth

2 teaspoons dried thyme

3 cans (2.8 ounces each) French's fried onions

¼ cup dry sherry

6 slices day-old French bread

1½ cups shredded Swiss cheese (6 ounces)

1 tablespoon chopped fresh parsley, for garnish

1. Preheat the broiler. Arrange six 2-cup ovenproof bowls on a baking sheet.

2. In a large stockpot, combine both broths with the thyme. Bring to a boil over high heat. Reduce to a gentle simmer and cook for 10 minutes. Stir in the fried onions. Simmer for 5 minutes more. Stir in the sherry and simmer for 2 minutes. Ladle the soup into the bowls.

3. Place a slice of bread on the top of each bowl of soup and scatter the cheese over the bread. Place the soup under the broiler until the cheese is melted and bubbling and just starting to brown, 3 to 4 minutes. Garnish with parsley to pretty it up, and serve.

> ### SERVING SUGGESTION
> If you have them, this soup looks great in onion soup crocks. It's the authentic way to serve onion soup, just like the French do!

SUMMER CORN AND POTATO CHOWDER

■ ■

When corn is fresh and sweet, so many roadside stands pop up in the South that you couldn't be blamed for stopping to buy a sack of corn every few minutes. After the first few ears, which I just love to steam, then eat with sweet butter and salt, I get creative and I start adding corn kernels to just about everything. They sweeten and thicken up this nice little chowder.

SERVES 4 TO 6

3 tablespoons butter

1 large yellow onion, chopped

2½ cups fresh corn kernels (from 3 ears of corn)

1 large (¾ pound) baking potato, peeled and cut into ½-inch cubes

3 cups chicken broth

½ cup heavy cream

⅛ teaspoon cayenne pepper

Salt and black pepper

¼ cup chopped fresh chives, for garnish

1. In a medium saucepan, melt the butter over medium heat. Add the onion and cook, stirring occasionally, until softened, about 5 minutes.

2. Add the corn, potato, broth, cream, cayenne pepper, and salt and black pepper to taste. Bring the soup to a boil. Reduce to a simmer and cook until the potato is tender, about 10 minutes. Serve in pretty shallow bowls garnished with the chives.

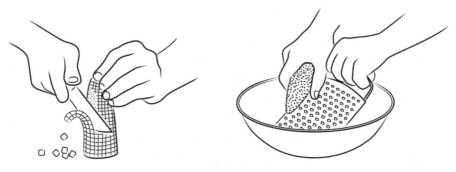

Quickly cut corn off the cob by cutting the cob in half crosswise and, using a large sharp knife, scraping in a downward motion along the cob. For added flavor, milk the corncob by coarsely grating it in a large, shallow bowl until you release all the wonderful flavor that the cob has to offer.

SOUPS AND STEWS

BRUNSWICK STEW

■ ■

Georgians and Virginians both lay claim to this rib-sticking stew. Wherever it got its start, it's a soul-satisfying combination of tangy, sweet, and smoky flavors. My version comes together quickly, since I use rotisserie chicken along with bacon and barbecue sauce, but it tastes like you've been simmering it for hours.

SERVES 4 TO 6 AS A MAIN COURSE

4 slices bacon, chopped

1 large yellow onion, chopped

1 rotisserie chicken (2½ pounds), meat removed and chopped (about 5 cups)

1 can (28 ounces) diced tomatoes

1 can (16 ounces) creamed corn

1 package (10 ounces) frozen lima beans

1 cup chicken broth

½ cup barbecue sauce

1 tablespoon distilled white vinegar

1 teaspoon Worcestershire sauce

½ teaspoon celery salt

Black pepper

1. In a large saucepan, cook the bacon over medium-high heat until almost crisp, about 5 minutes. Add the onion and cook until softened, about 5 minutes.

2. Add the chicken, tomatoes, corn, lima beans, broth, barbecue sauce, vinegar, Worcestershire sauce, celery salt, and black pepper to taste. Bring to a boil. Reduce to a simmer, cover, and cook until the lima beans are tender, 5 to 7 minutes. And that's it, folks!

VARIATIONS ON A STEW

This gorgeous stew is also delicious with butter beans instead of lima beans. And I like to throw in some okra when I've got it in the house (which is just about always).

BURGOO

■ ■

Kentucky burgoo is an old-time tradition that some claim should be served from mint julep cups after their contents are drunk at Kentucky Derby parties—a good way to ensure you don't drink yourself off to the races without any food to hold you down! Burgoo is a mix of meats and vegetables that once relied on plentiful squirrel meat but now usually contains more domestic fare: chicken, beef, and sometimes game. I use lamb along with a garden full of vegetables for a souplike version. Some prefer to keep it simmering until they have a real thick, stewlike burgoo, which you can try if you like.

SERVES 12 TO 14

3 pounds bone-in chicken thighs

2 pounds beef round steak, cut into
   3-inch chunks

2 pounds lamb shoulder, cut into
   3-inch chunks

Salt and black pepper

¼ cup vegetable oil

2 medium yellow onions, finely chopped

2 medium carrots, chopped

2 celery stalks, chopped

1 large green bell pepper, chopped

1 jalapeño pepper, seeded and finely chopped
   (leave the seeds in if you want more heat)

4 cloves garlic, finely chopped

6 cups beef broth, chicken broth, or water

1 can (28 ounces) crushed tomatoes

2 large baking potatoes, peeled and diced

1 package (10 ounces) frozen corn kernels

1 package (10 ounces) frozen lima beans

3 tablespoons Worcestershire sauce

1½ teaspoons Tabasco or other hot sauce

1. Lightly season the chicken, beef, and lamb all over with salt and black pepper. In a large Dutch oven, heat the oil over medium-high heat until shimmering. Working in batches, brown the meats on all sides, about 7 minutes per batch. Drain the meats on a paper towel–lined baking sheet.

2. Add the onions, carrots, celery, and bell pepper to the pan. Cook, stirring, until slightly softened, about 5 minutes. Add the jalapeño and

UPDATING A CLASSIC

Although a traditional burgoo uses a whole cut-up chicken, I like to use all chicken thighs. For a slow-cooking stew, the texture and flavor of dark meat really can't be beat. But if you're a white meat sort of person, bone-in chicken breasts or a mix of breasts and legs will work just fine.

garlic and cook for 2 minutes. Return the beef and lamb to the pan (cover the chicken with plastic wrap and refrigerate until ready to use). Stir in the broth or water, the crushed tomatoes, and 1 tablespoon salt. Bring the mixture to a boil. Reduce to a simmer, cover, and cook for 1½ hours.

3. Return the chicken to the pan. Cover and simmer for 45 minutes. Add the potatoes and simmer until all the meats are very tender and shred easily with a fork, 45 minutes longer.

4. Remove the chicken from the pan. Once the chicken is cool enough to handle, pick the meat off the bones, discarding the bones and skin; shred the chicken and return to the pan. Stir in the corn, lima beans, Worcestershire sauce, and hot sauce. Simmer until the vegetables are hot and the stew reaches the thickness you like, 10 to 15 minutes.

CHARLESTON OKRA SOUP

■ ■

Okra soup is traditional in Savannah as well as in Charleston. Meaty beef bones give the broth a real deep background flavor, and okra provides that lovely silky texture that Southerners crave.

SERVES 10 TO 12

3 pounds beef bones with meat
  (such as beef hindquarter shanks)
1 bay leaf
1 tablespoon salt

2 cans (28 ounces each) peeled whole
  tomatoes, coarsely broken with a fork
3 pounds fresh or thawed frozen okra, sliced
1 large yellow onion, chopped
1 large green bell pepper, chopped
Hot sauce

1. In a large pot, combine the beef bones, bay leaf, and 1 teaspoon of the salt. Cover with 12 cups water. Bring to a simmer and cook over medium-low heat for 1 hour.

2. Add the tomatoes, okra, onion, bell pepper, and the remaining 2 teaspoons salt. Simmer until the soup is thick and the meat is falling apart, 1 to 1½ hours. Remove the meat, bones, and bay leaf from the pot. When cool enough to handle, pick the meat off the bones, cut into bite-size pieces, and return it to the pot. Discard the bones and bay leaf. Stir in hot sauce to taste.

> **FREEZE OUT**
>
> This soup freezes just great. Since it's a nice big batch, freeze it in separate containers so you can pull out serving portions throughout the week. If you do choose to freeze it, stick with fresh okra instead of the frozen.

HAM BONE SOUP

■ ■

Honey, if you haven't made friends with your local butcher yet, now's the time. He'll cut you a nice ham bone for this hearty, simple soup, and chances are he'll set your heart aflutter while he's at it—I don't recall ever meeting a butcher who didn't have a certain appeal.

SERVES 6 TO 8

4 slices bacon, cut into ½-inch pieces

2 large carrots, chopped

2 celery stalks, chopped

1 large yellow onion, chopped

3 cloves garlic, finely chopped

1 smoked ham bone (about 1¼ pounds), cut into thirds by your butcher

1 bay leaf

Salt

4 cups shredded green cabbage (½ head)

2 cans (15 ounces each) kidney beans, rinsed and drained

Black pepper

1. Heat a large pot over medium-high heat. Add the bacon and cook until almost crisp, about 5 minutes. Add the carrots, celery, and onion and cook, stirring, until softened, about 5 minutes. Add the garlic and cook for 1 minute.

2. Drop in the ham bone and bay leaf. Add 8 cups water and 2 teaspoons salt. Bring the mixture to a boil over high heat. Reduce to a simmer and cook for 20 minutes.

3. Stir in the cabbage and simmer for 30 minutes.

4. Add the kidney beans and simmer for 30 minutes more. Discard the bay leaf and season with salt and black pepper to taste.

A HELPING HAM

If you've got a leftover ham bone from dinner, this is a great way to use it, making this soup a real economical treat. An added bonus is that any meat still stuck to the bone will just fall off into the soup to thicken it up.

SOUR CREAM, BACON, AND SPLIT PEA SOUP

■ ■

Bacon fat gives this comforting split pea soup a nice smoky taste in no time, and I reserve the crisped bacon to top the creamy green soup—along with a nice dollop of sour cream. We grow a pot of thyme year-round so we always have the ingredients on hand for this one. Consider planting your own herbs. They are low-maintenance and high-flavor.

SERVES 6

6 slices bacon, cut into ½-inch pieces
1 large white onion, finely chopped
1 celery stalk, finely chopped
1 clove garlic, finely chopped
1 tablespoon tomato paste
1 pound green split peas, rinsed

1½ teaspoons salt
2 sprigs fresh thyme
1 bay leaf
½ teaspoon black pepper
Sour cream, for serving
Chopped fresh parsley, for garnish

1. In a large pot, cook the bacon over medium-high heat until crisp, 5 to 7 minutes. Drain the bacon on a paper towel–lined plate, then crumble it up.

2. Add the onion, celery, and garlic to the pot. Cook, stirring, until tender, about 5 minutes. Stir in the tomato paste until blended in. Stir in the split peas, 8 cups water, the salt, thyme, and bay leaf. Bring to a boil. Reduce to a gentle simmer and cook until the peas have completely fallen apart and the soup thickens, 1½ to 2 hours. Keep an eye on the soup and add more water if the soup thickens too much while cooking.

3. Discard the bay leaf and season the soup with the black pepper. Serve the soup topped with the crumbled bacon, a hearty dollop of sour cream, and a pretty sprinkling of parsley.

PEAS, PLEASE

Split peas are so easy to prepare. They don't need to be soaked—just give them a good rinse and you're off. They are such a great source of protein that they make this (almost) vegetarian soup as hearty as a meaty concoction.

CONFEDERATE BEAN SOUP

■ ■

Now, I adore baked beans and I never let myself get down to the last can or two in my pantry before I pick up a few more. I love to eat them plain, but I especially love to boil them up into this meaty, simple, and hearty soup. It'll warm your bones. Serve it with piping-hot corn bread.

SERVES 3 TO 4

2 tablespoons (¼ stick) butter

½ pound smoked sausage, sliced into
   ¼-inch-thick rounds

2 slices bacon, chopped

1 medium yellow onion, chopped

½ medium green bell pepper, chopped

1 clove garlic, finely chopped

2 cups leftover baked beans, or 1 can
   (16 ounces) Bush's Baked Beans

1½ cups half-and-half

Hot sauce, for serving

1. In a medium pot, heat the butter over medium-high heat. Add the sausage, bacon, onion, bell pepper, and garlic. Cook, stirring, until the bacon is crisp, 5 to 7 minutes.

2. Add the beans and simmer for a few minutes over low to medium heat. Stir in 1 cup half-and-half. Add more half-and-half depending on how thick you want your soup. Pass hot sauce at the table.

A TASTE OF THE SOUTH

Don't forget the hot sauce on this one. A smoky, bacony bean soup served with corn bread and loads of hot sauce is a true taste of the South.

THE REAL DEAL GUMBO

■ ■

Cooking the okra separately before adding it to this shrimp gumbo lets you enjoy its silkiness without the sliminess. The soup—thickened with a roux (see step 2) and flavored with sausage, onion, bell pepper, garlic, and Cajun seasoning—is a real traditional Cajun recipe, full of shrimp and perfect for serving over rice.

SERVES 4 TO 6

1 tablespoon vegetable oil

1 cup chopped okra, fresh or thawed frozen

3 tablespoons butter

3 tablespoons all-purpose flour

1 large yellow onion, chopped

1 large green bell pepper, chopped

1 tablespoon chopped garlic

4 cups chicken broth

¾ pound andouille or other smoked sausage, sliced

1 teaspoon Cajun seasoning

Salt and black pepper

1 pound large shrimp, peeled and deveined

4 cups cooked rice, for serving

Hot sauce, for serving

1. In a small skillet, heat the oil over medium heat. Add the okra and cook, stirring frequently, until no longer slimy, about 3 minutes. Set aside.

2. In a large saucepan, melt the butter over medium heat. Whisk in the flour and cook, stirring constantly, until it is a light chocolate color, about 5 minutes (this is the "roux").

3. Add the onion, bell pepper, and garlic and cook for 2 minutes. Add the broth, sausage, and Cajun seasoning and bring to a boil. Reduce the heat to a simmer, cover, and cook for 20 minutes. Season to taste with salt and black pepper.

4. Add the shrimp and simmer until they are pink and cooked through. Serve over the rice. Pass hot sauce at the table.

TASTE AND ADJUST

Because soups have a tendency to cook down as the liquid evaporates, tasting and adjusting seasoning is one of the most important steps in soup making. I like to keep a spoon in a clean glass of water near my pot so I can have frequent tastes to see how my flavors are developing.

SHE-CRAB SOUP

■ ■

To find out if you're looking at a she- or a he-crab, turn it over. The belly flap part of the shell, called the apron, is wide on a she-crab, and narrow and pointed on a he. Blue she-crab was the crab of choice for this soup because the traditional garnish was crab roe, but any type of picked crabmeat will work. My version is simply garnished with chives and Parmesan (no crab roe). The base of the soup is a homemade fish broth that is enriched with cream and flavored with sherry. The crabmeat gets mixed right in along with pieces of fish, and no matter the sex of your crab, you'll have yourself a real flavorful, traditional soup.

SERVES 8

One 2-pound fish head (preferably grouper), eyes, gills, and scales removed (see top box, opposite)

1 medium yellow onion, peeled

2 celery stalks, including leaves

½ teaspoon salt

½ teaspoon white pepper

4 tablespoons (½ stick) butter

¾ cup chopped scallions, white and light green parts only

2 teaspoons finely chopped garlic

3 tablespoons all-purpose flour

1 cup heavy cream

1 cup whole milk

1 pound crabmeat, picked over to remove bits of shell (see below)

¼ cup dry sherry

½ teaspoon lemon-pepper seasoning, such as Paula Deen Collection

1 cup grated Parmesan cheese (about 4 ounces)

½ cup chopped fresh chives

1. In a large pot, combine the fish head, onion, celery, salt, white pepper, and 4½ cups water. Bring to a boil over high heat. Reduce to a simmer, cover, and cook for 30 minutes. Remove the fish from the pot. When cool enough to handle, pick the fish meat off the bones in pieces that resemble picked crabmeat. Discard the bones and skin. Remove the celery and onion from the broth and discard.

To easily find shells in crabmeat, spread out the crabmeat on a baking sheet in an even layer and place in a low oven (about 200°F) for a few minutes. The shells will turn red in the heat.

2. In a medium saucepan, melt the butter over medium-high heat. Add the scallions and garlic and cook until tender, 2 to 3 minutes. Add the flour, stirring until well blended. Slowly add 2 cups of the fish broth, continuing to cook until smooth and bubbling. Slowly add the cream and milk. Stir in the reserved fish and the crabmeat. Add the sherry and lemon-pepper seasoning. Simmer until piping hot. Taste and add more sherry, garlic, salt, or white pepper to taste. Serve in pretty bowls and top with the Parmesan and chives.

BROTH OPTIONS

You can freeze leftover fish broth for future use. It should keep in your freezer in a good airtight container for about a month, but after that it will start to lose its flavor. If you'd like, you can skip the homemade fish broth and substitute 2 cups chicken broth instead.

EASY SHRIMP BISQUE

■ ■

This soup is so elegant, no one will believe you if you tell them it took you about 5 minutes to make. So you just keep that to yourself and break out the fine china for this one. It makes a wonderfully smooth first-course soup.

SERVES 4

½ pound cooked shrimp, peeled and chopped

1 can (10¾ ounces) condensed cream of
    celery soup

2 cups half-and-half

½ cup whole milk

2 tablespoons dry sherry

2 teaspoons tomato paste

1 teaspoon paprika

Salt and black pepper

2 tablespoons chopped fresh parsley,
    for garnish

In a blender (in batches if necessary), puree the shrimp, soup, half-and-half, milk, sherry, tomato paste, and paprika. Pour into a medium saucepan and warm gently over medium-low heat, stirring often, until the bisque is heated through. Season to taste with salt and black pepper. Serve garnished with the parsley. It's easy and delicious!

BY DEFINITION

A bisque is a velvety, creamy soup traditionally flavored by shrimp, crab, lobster, or crayfish. Feel free to substitute any of these other seafood options in this easy bisque.

OYSTER STEW

Oysters are generally considered the food of love, and I have always liked to serve them for a romantic dinner. You can serve them raw, holding the half-shell for your honey to slurp down, or cook them—ever so gently—in this mild, sweet-tasting stew. Either way, you should be prepared to reap the benefits of one of the world's greatest aphrodisiacs.

SERVES 4 TO 5

2 tablespoons (¼ stick) butter
2 scallions, thinly sliced
1 pound shucked raw oysters, with
   their liquor (juices)
4 cups half-and-half or whole milk

¼ teaspoon salt
⅛ teaspoon cayenne pepper
Dash of Worcestershire sauce
Oyster crackers, for serving

In a medium saucepan, melt the butter over medium-high heat. Add the scallions and cook until tender, 1 to 2 minutes. Add the oysters, half-and-half, salt, cayenne pepper, and Worcestershire sauce. Simmer until the edges of the oysters begin to curl and the mixture is hot but not boiling. Serve the stew with, what else? Oyster crackers!

OYSTER PICKING

Choose your freshly shucked oysters wisely. They should be plump and their color should be a milky cream to various shades of gray. Make sure the liquid they are in is not cloudy. And here's something a lot of folks don't know. Freshly shucked oysters can keep in the refrigerator for 7 to 10 days. Just make sure they are kept in a real cold part of the refrigerator.

CREAMY CREOLE TOMATO SOUP

Louisiana Creole cooking can get pretty fancy—and pretty spicy. I keep it simple with this creamy tomato soup. But look out! Thanks to a hit of Cajun seasoning and a pinch of cayenne pepper, it does bite back!

SERVES 8 TO 10

4 tablespoons (½ stick) butter
2 medium yellow onions, chopped
2 cloves garlic, finely chopped
1 tablespoon Cajun seasoning
¼ teaspoon cayenne pepper

2 cans (28 ounces each)
   diced tomatoes
4 cups chicken broth
1½ cups heavy cream
1 teaspoon salt

1. In a large pot, melt the butter over medium-high heat. Add the onions and cook, stirring, until very tender, 7 to 10 minutes.

2. Stir in the garlic, Cajun seasoning, and cayenne pepper and cook, stirring, for 1 minute. Stir in the diced tomatoes and broth. Simmer, uncovered, for 15 minutes.

3. Working in batches, transfer the soup to a blender or food processor and puree until smooth. Return the soup to the pot. Stir in the cream and salt and simmer until heated through, about 3 minutes. Serve piping hot.

BLENDING IN

When blending hot soups, there's always the chance of the soup getting all filled up with air and blowing the top off your blender. So it's best to fill the blender up only halfway and blend your soup in batches. Hold the lid down firmly when blending, and drape a dish towel over it for extra protection.

CREAMY PEANUT SOUP

▪ ▪

When Southern cotton was ravaged by the boll weevil in the 1890s, George Washington Carver championed the peanut, teaching farmers to grow it and cooks to use it in as many ways as possible. Peanut soup was a keeper, and once you taste the smooth, rich, nutty flavor, you'll see why.

SERVES 4 TO 6

3 tablespoons butter
1 small yellow onion, chopped
2 celery stalks, chopped
3 tablespoons all-purpose flour
6 cups chicken broth
2 cups creamy peanut butter

1¾ cups sour cream
Salt and black pepper
1 tablespoon sliced scallions, for garnish
1 tablespoon finely chopped peanuts,
    for garnish

1. In a large pot, melt the butter over medium-high heat. Add the onion and celery and cook, stirring, until tender, about 5 minutes. Stir in the flour and cook for 2 minutes. Slowly whisk in the broth. Bring to a boil over high heat. Reduce to a simmer and cook until thickened, 10 to 15 minutes. Strain the soup and discard the solids.

2. Return the strained soup to the pot. Whisk in the peanut butter over low heat until fully incorporated and heated through. Gently stir in the sour cream. Season with salt and black pepper to taste. Ladle the soup into pretty bowls and serve hot, garnished with the scallions and peanuts.

STICKY SITUATION

To keep your peanut butter from sticking to your measuring cup, coat the cup with a little cooking spray first—the peanut butter will slide out easily.

Chapter 4

BRUNCH AND OTHER SAVORY EGG AND CHEESE DISHES

B runch is really big now in the South, but, of course, for generations, in many families, the mother cooked a great big meal every Sunday after church, whether or not you called it brunch. I adore hosting this meal. It's early in the day, the sun is shining, and you still have plenty of energy, so it can be even more fun than a dinner party. Besides, it's very family-friendly and much more economical than an evening get-together. And most brunch menus are all about one of my passions: good old farm-fresh eggs.

Now, y'all, if you've got room for a chicken coop anywhere in your yard, I highly recommend one. There is nothing like going out there every day collecting those fresh eggs. I adore my chickens. Mine are rescued from a place where they test mosquito control here in Savannah. And, oh my, they are the sweetest girls. I go out there and I pick them up, rock them, and scratch their ears, and they lie in my arms and go to sleep. I come in from being on the road for a week, and I'll say, "I bet there's nothing here to eat." And then I think, "Oh, yes, there is! My girls will have me something."

All my hens lay brown eggs. I gather them and clean them off and they can sit out on the counter for about 30 days. Most recipes call for eggs at room temperature because they beat up higher. So that basket of eggs on the counter is just a great big delicious brunch waiting to happen.

My favorite brunch dishes are the ones you can make ahead, like Sunday Morning Casserole (page 93), which I put together the night before, then pop in the oven when I wake up. That is such a great-smelling way to start the day. Artichoke and Smoked Cheddar Bake (page 92), Southern Shrimp and Pimiento Strata (page 94), and Praline French Toast Casserole (page 100) are three more of my all-time favorite do-ahead brunch dishes.

If y'all are egg lovers like me, you want to start with the basics, though: follow my instructions for Paula's Perfect Omelet (page 90) a few times and, honey, you will be turning out the lightest, fluffiest, most beautiful yellow omelets you ever saw. Once you have a gorgeous omelet in your repertoire, you can take on anything: Southern Eggs Benedict with Tasso Hollandaise (page 96), Eggs Baked with Grits and Ham (page 97), Cheesy Southern Quiche with Country Ham (page 98) . . .

So you get yourself some chickens—or a dozen farm-fresh eggs—some ham or bacon, a loaf of bread, cheese, potatoes or grits, and whatever else you've got lying around, and you're ready to whip up a meal so good, so homey, and so hearty that it counts for breakfast *and* lunch. Oh, and did I mention you should go ahead and pop a bottle of bubbly if you like mimosas?

BAKED EGG CRISPS

■ ■

Here is an individual baked egg dish that is a surefire hit. Crispy toast, runny yolks, melted cheese, and crunchy bacon—this one's got it all.

SERVES 6

6 slices bacon
6 slices white bread, crusts removed
2 tablespoons (¼ stick) butter,
    at room temperature

6 large eggs
Salt and black pepper
1 tablespoon grated Parmesan cheese

1. Preheat the oven to 425°F.

2. In a large skillet, cook the bacon over medium-high heat until crisp, 5 to 7 minutes. Drain the bacon on a paper towel–lined plate, then crumble it up.

3. Spread one side of each slice of bread with the butter. Press the slices, buttered side up, into each of six 4-ounce ramekins. Bake until pale golden, about 8 minutes. Remove from the oven and reduce the oven temperature to 350°F.

4. Crack an egg into each ramekin. Season the eggs with salt and black pepper to taste. Sprinkle each one with ½ teaspoon of the Parmesan. Bake until the whites are set but the yolks are still nice and runny, 15 to 20 minutes. Serve topped with the crumbled bacon.

POUR IT ON

It can be tricky cracking your eggs straight into your ramekins without breaking those fragile yolks. To be extra sure those yolks stay whole, try cracking your eggs into a shallow bowl or teacup before sliding them into the ramekins. Just a little extra insurance!

Break eggs into a shallow bowl or teacup and then pour into ramekins to ensure that the yolks remain intact.

PAULA'S PERFECT OMELET

■ ■

I got my first cooking lessons in my Grandmama Paul's kitchen, and the earliest, most important lessons were fixing basics like this one. Once you've mastered a light, fluffy folded omelet, you can walk into any kitchen with confidence. So, y'all, this is one to practice at home. Try this recipe once or twice and you'll be able to do it in your sleep, I promise! Then, feel free to get creative. This recipe is a perfect canvas for any filling that strikes your fancy (see top box, opposite).

MAKES 1 SERVING

1 tablespoon butter
2 large eggs

1 tablespoon whole milk
Salt and white pepper

1. In an 8-inch omelet pan or nonstick skillet with sloped sides, melt the butter over medium heat. In a bowl, give the eggs a good beat with the milk and salt and white pepper to taste. Pour into the pan. Leave it be and after about 1 minute the bottom will start to set.

2. Using a rubber spatula, move the edges of the egg mixture toward the middle and, swirling the pan, let the uncooked egg run out onto the surface of the pan along the edges. Give the pan a shake (if you are adding fillings, now is the time to do it). Let cook until just set.

3. Using the spatula, fold one-third of the omelet over the middle, and, tilting the pan over a plate, fold the omelet over one more time as it rolls out onto the plate.

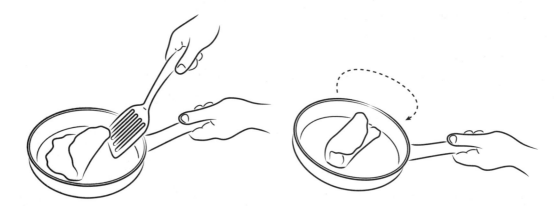

Alternatively, fold the omelet by tilting the pan away from you and, using a spatula, lifting the edge closest to the handle over the center of the omelet. Tilt the pan back toward the handle to flip the unfolded portion over the folded portion, then slide the omelet onto a plate.

BAKED HAM 'N' EGG CUPS

Brunch is the time of day when I just love to serve up dishes that have a playful presentation like this one. Baking slices of ham in muffin tins turns them into the prettiest "bowls" for baked eggs. They look like tulips and are some of the best-tasting ham 'n' eggs you ever put in your mouth.

SERVES 4

¼ pound ham, cut into 4 thick (⅛-inch) slices
4 teaspoons ketchup
4 large eggs

Salt and black pepper
1 or 2 teaspoons sliced scallions
Hot sauce, for serving

1. Preheat the oven to 375°F. Lightly grease four cups of a standard-size muffin tin or coat with cooking spray. Line the cups with the ham slices. Spread a small dollop of ketchup on each slice of ham.

2. Carefully crack an egg into each ham-lined cup. Season the eggs with salt and black pepper to taste. Bake until the whites are set but the yolks are still nice and runny, 15 to 20 minutes. Sprinkle with the scallions and serve. Pass hot sauce at the table.

A GOOD EGG

Now, you do want to be a little careful that the baked eggs don't dry out in the oven. To keep baked eggs as moist as possible, I like to spoon a little milk or cream on top of my eggs just as I'm putting them in the oven. Keeps everything nice and tender.

ARTICHOKE AND SMOKED CHEDDAR BAKE

■ ■

There's only one thing I like better than a full-on Sunday brunch, and that is a lazy morning. With this easy dish I can have both. I can put this together the night before, then pop it in the oven when I get up. When that oven timer rings, I've got a deluxe brunch on the table, and if you look close, I may still have a pillow crease on my cheek.

SERVES 6

1 tablespoon butter

1 tablespoon vegetable oil

1 yellow onion, chopped

6 cups 1-inch bread cubes (about 7 slices of bread)

3 cups shredded smoked Cheddar cheese (¾ pound)

2 jars (6 ounces each) marinated artichoke hearts, drained and chopped

7 large eggs

2½ cups whole milk

1 teaspoon salt

¼ teaspoon black pepper

1. Grease a 13 by 9-inch baking dish with butter, oil, or cooking spray.

2. In a medium skillet, melt the butter with the oil over medium heat. Add the onion and cook until it just starts to brown, about 7 minutes. Remove from the heat and let cool.

3. Evenly scatter the bread cubes in the prepared baking dish. Top with 1½ cups of the cheese, all of the cooled onion, and the artichoke hearts.

4. In a large bowl, whisk together the eggs, milk, salt, and black pepper. Pour over the bread mixture. Cover the dish with plastic wrap and refrigerate for at least 1 hour or up to overnight.

5. Let the casserole come to room temperature as you preheat the oven to 350°F.

6. Top with the remaining 1½ cups cheese and bake until puffed and golden, about 45 minutes.

FREEZE IT

Every home cook has tricks for keeping the monthly food bills down. Here's one that I think you're gonna like. Make your own croutons or bread crumbs using leftover ends of bread or whenever there's a real good sale on bread at your market. Cut the bread into cubes and toast in a 325°F oven until golden. Store as croutons or grind them in a food processor and store as bread crumbs. Then freeze them in airtight containers for several months. Pull them out as you need them.

SUNDAY MORNING CASSEROLE

You need only look down at the ingredient list to know how I feel about this recipe. I put just about everything I love into this one, and when it comes out of the oven I get so excited, I'm likely to burn my mouth. What a wonderful way to wake up your taste buds.

SERVES 6

2 slices white bread

1 pound bulk mild breakfast sausage meat (see box)

1½ cups thinly sliced cooked unpeeled red potatoes

1½ cups mixed shredded Cheddar and Monterey Jack cheese (6 ounces total)

6 large eggs, lightly beaten

2 cups whole milk

1 teaspoon mustard powder

½ teaspoon salt

Black pepper

1. Grease a 2½- to 3-quart baking dish (attractive enough to bring to the table) with butter, oil, or cooking spray. Cube the bread and place in the dish in a single even layer.

2. In a large skillet, cook the sausage, breaking it up with a spoon, until it's almost cooked through, about 5 minutes. Drain off the fat. Layer the sausage over the bread, and top with the potatoes. Sprinkle the cheese on top.

3. In a medium bowl, whisk together the eggs, milk, mustard powder, salt, and black pepper to taste. Pour the egg mixture over the sausage and potatoes in the casserole. Cover with plastic wrap and refrigerate overnight.

4. When ready to cook the casserole, preheat the oven to 350°F. Bake the casserole until set and golden, about 30 minutes. Serve hot.

GIVE IT A SQUEEZE

If you can't find bulk sausage meat in your market, just buy sausage links and squeeze the meat out of the casings. Just slice off the end of the sausage and give it a squeeze as you would do with a toothpaste tube.

SOUTHERN SHRIMP AND PIMIENTO STRATA

■ ■

Any way you serve shrimp, I'm gonna love 'em. Here I toss big pink shrimp with plenty of grated cheese, cubed bread, pimiento, and scallions to make a savory baked strata that will keep you going 'til suppertime. Oh, and if you ever did have any left over, which happens when I make this for just a few of us, it is a divine light lunch served alongside a little green salad. Almost worth holding back at brunch. Almost.

SERVES 6 TO 8

2 tablespoons (¼ stick) butter
1 pound large shrimp, peeled and deveined
About 8 cups 2-inch bread cubes (from
    ¾ pound Italian bread)
2 cups shredded Gruyère or Swiss cheese
    (8 ounces)
⅓ cup chopped scallions
1 jar (4 ounces) diced pimientos, drained

1 teaspoon salt
½ teaspoon black pepper
8 large eggs
2 cups whole milk
1 teaspoon dried thyme
Pinch of grated nutmeg
3 tablespoons chopped fresh parsley,
    for garnish

1. Grease a 13 by 9-inch baking dish with butter, oil, or cooking spray.

2. In a large skillet, melt the butter over high heat. Add the shrimp and cook until just pink, about 30 seconds per side. Transfer the shrimp to a large bowl.

3. Add the bread, cheese, scallions, pimientos, ½ teaspoon of the salt, and ¼ teaspoon of the black pepper to the bowl with the shrimp. Toss well to combine and empty the contents into the prepared baking dish.

4. In a large bowl, whisk together the eggs, milk, thyme, nutmeg, the remaining ½ teaspoon salt, the remaining ¼ teaspoon pepper, and the parsley to make the custard. Pour the custard over the bread mixture. Use the back of a spoon, or just your fingertips if you like, to press the bread so that it will absorb the custard. Cover the strata with plastic wrap and refrigerate for at least 1 hour or up to overnight.

Using your fingertips or the back of a spoon, push the bread down into the custard to ensure that the bread soaks up the liquid.

5. Let the strata come to room temperature as you preheat the oven to 350°F. Remove the plastic wrap and bake until the top is golden and the custard is set, 45 to 50 minutes. Serve sprinkled with the parsley.

SOAK IT UP

It's important that you let your strata or any other bread and egg dish (such as bread pudding) sit for at least 1 hour. That way, the bread is sure to soak up lots of the liquid from the egg and milk, so your dish doesn't end up dry and tough. You want that custard light and fluffy and wrapped around the cubes of bread.

PICKLED EGGS AND BEETS

Pickled eggs are one of those items you'll notice sitting in a jar on the counters of Southern country stores, and if you've never had the opportunity to try one, now's your chance. The eggs take on the color of the beet juice and look so festive on the table when you're having company. They make a beautiful snack on their own, but pickled along with beets they are a brunch showstopper worthy of your best china (though perhaps not your fine white linen napkins, since these beauties are fuchsia!).

SERVES 6

1 can (15 ounces) whole beets, drained,
  liquid reserved
¾ cup sugar
½ cup distilled white vinegar

½ teaspoon whole cloves
1 teaspoon salt
6 hard-boiled eggs, peeled and rinsed

1. In a medium saucepan, heat the reserved beet liquid, sugar, vinegar, cloves, and salt over medium-low heat until the sugar has dissolved.

2. Place the eggs in a large bowl with the beets. Pour in the vinegar mixture so that the eggs are fully submerged. Cover and refrigerate overnight.

3. When you're ready to serve, remove the eggs and beets from the vinegar mixture with a slotted spoon and place them whole on a pretty serving platter.

DO AHEAD

Get these eggs done ahead of time and keep them in mason jars in the refrigerator. They will keep for 3 to 5 days, if not longer.

SOUTHERN EGGS BENEDICT WITH TASSO HOLLANDAISE

■ ■

Tasso is a real traditional ham down here, and we throw some in the pot whenever we crave that special Cajun flavor. It adds just the right bit of spice to a rich, creamy hollandaise sauce here. The recipe calls for you to play short-order cook, since it should be made right before serving, so sit your loved ones down, serve a little fruit to keep them occupied, then whip up a breakfast worth waiting for.

SERVES 2 TO 4

2 ounces tasso (see top box, opposite), diced (about ½ cup)

4 slices Canadian bacon (about ¼ pound)

8 tablespoons (1 stick) butter, at room temperature

3 large egg yolks

3 tablespoons fresh lemon juice

¼ teaspoon salt

1 tablespoon distilled white vinegar

4 large eggs

2 English muffins, split and toasted

1. Preheat the oven to 350°F.

2. Place the tasso on one side of an 8-inch square baking dish and the Canadian bacon on the other side. Cover with foil and bake until the meats are cooked, about 10 minutes. If you're not finished with the rest of the recipe after the meats have been in the oven for 10 minutes, just turn the oven off and leave the meats inside to keep nice and warm.

3. In a small saucepan, combine the butter, egg yolks, lemon juice, and salt. Cook over low heat, stirring constantly with a whisk, until the sauce coats the back of a spoon, 4 to 5 minutes. Remove from the heat and keep whisking until thick (the heat from the pan will continue cooking the sauce, so make sure you keep on stirring until it cools down).

4. Fill a small, shallow saucepan with 2 inches of water and the vinegar and bring to a simmer. Break one of the eggs into a small cup and slide the egg into the water, stirring the water very gently with a spoon. Repeat immediately with the other eggs and cook until the whites are firm, about 3 minutes. Remove the eggs with a slotted spoon and drain them on paper towels.

5. Top each English muffin half with a slice of Canadian bacon, followed by one poached egg. Stir the tasso into the hollandaise and spoon over the tops of the eggs. Serve just as soon as you can.

EGGS BAKED WITH GRITS AND HAM

Y'all, I can't believe how well I ate growing up. Even if we didn't have much, and so many families from southwest Georgia had very little, we *did* have grits. Breakfast, lunch, and dinner, I never tire of grits, and this is my go-to method of serving them up with ham and eggs in the morning. It's an easy, one-pan bake that lets you feed folks like kings on even a beggar's budget.

SERVES 4

½ cup quick-cooking grits
1¼ cups shredded sharp Cheddar cheese
    (5 ounces)
¾ cup coarsely chopped country-style ham
    (3 ounces, thickly sliced)

Salt and black pepper
⅛ teaspoon garlic powder
4 large eggs
1 to 2 tablespoons sliced scallions

1. Preheat the oven to 350°F. Lightly grease an 8-inch square baking pan with butter, oil, or cooking spray.

2. In a medium saucepan, cook the grits according to the package directions. Once the grits are cooked, stir in ¾ cup of the Cheddar, the ham, ½ teaspoon salt, ¼ teaspoon black pepper, and the garlic powder and continue stirring until the cheese melts.

3. Scrape the grits mixture into the prepared pan. Using a spoon, make four egg-size indents in the grits mixture (these will be the nests for the eggs). Crack 1 egg into each nest. Season the eggs lightly with salt and black pepper. Top with the remaining ½ cup Cheddar. Bake until the whites are set but the yolks are still runny and the cheese is melted, 15 to 20 minutes. Serve sprinkled with the scallions.

QUICK STUDY

When picking up your grits at the supermarket, make sure you choose the quick-cooking grits. If you see the instant kind, just walk on by. Any Southerner worth his salt will tell you they are just not real grits.

CHEESY SOUTHERN QUICHE
WITH COUNTRY HAM

■ ■

I baked my share of quiches back before I opened the restaurant, when I was catering. Everyone adores a rich, eggy pie like this, and I think it's the prettiest thing for a brunch buffet.

SERVES 6 TO 8

Paula's Flaky Piecrust Dough (page 339) or
    store-bought piecrust
1 large egg white
3 tablespoons shredded Cheddar cheese
3 large eggs
1½ cups half-and-half

¼ teaspoon grated nutmeg
¼ teaspoon salt
¼ teaspoon black pepper
6 ounces thinly sliced fully cooked country
    ham, cut into ½-inch-wide strips
1 tablespoon butter, cut into small bits

1. Preheat the oven to 350°F. Roll the dough out to a ⅜-inch thickness and line a 9-inch pie plate. Line the dough with foil and fill with dried beans or pie weights. Bake for 20 to 25 minutes, then remove the foil and beans or weights and bake for 5 to 7 minutes longer.

2. Take the crust out of the oven, but leave the oven on and increase the oven temperature to 375°F. Brush the bottom of the crust with the egg white and sprinkle evenly with the cheese. Return the crust to the oven and bake until lightly browned, 10 to 13 minutes.

3. In a medium bowl, prepare the custard by whisking together the whole eggs, half-and-half, nutmeg, salt, and black pepper.

4. Lay the ham over the bottom of the partially baked crust and carefully pour in the custard. Dot the top with the butter pieces and return to the oven. Bake until the top of the quiche is puffed up and golden and the middle is almost set, 25 to 35 minutes. Let the quiche cool for at least 15 minutes on the counter. That middle will keep on cooking gently. By the time you cut into it, the quiche should be good and set so that your slices come out nice and clean.

BLIND BAKING

This means partially baking a piecrust before you add your filling. Blind baking ensures that your crust doesn't get all soggy from a liquid filling. The pie weights prevent the crust from puffing up when you bake it. If you don't have pie weights around your house, just use dried beans or uncooked rice on top of the foil to hold that crust in place.

KENTUCKY HOT BROWN

■ ■

Now, a Hot Brown is a historical food. It was invented at The Brown Hotel in Louisville, Kentucky, in 1926. What is it? A hot open-face turkey sandwich gilded with tomato, bacon, and plenty of melted cheese sauce. Oh my, that's just the thing to revive you after a late night.

SERVES 4

8 tablespoons (1 stick) butter

¼ cup all-purpose flour

2 cups whole milk

1½ cups shredded Monterey Jack cheese
   (6 ounces)

½ teaspoon salt

⅛ teaspoon cayenne pepper

4 slices white bread, toasted

¾ pound sliced roast turkey

4 slices tomato

¼ cup grated Parmesan cheese
   (about 1 ounce)

8 slices bacon, cooked until crisp

1. In a medium saucepan, melt the butter over medium-high heat. Whisk in the flour and cook, stirring with the whisk, for 1 minute. Add the milk, bring to a boil, and cook, stirring with the whisk, until thickened, about 3 minutes. Stir in the Jack cheese until melted. Stir in the salt and cayenne pepper.

2. Preheat the broiler. Place the toast in a baking dish large enough to fit the 4 slices in one layer. Divide the turkey and tomato among the bread slices. Pour the cheese sauce over the toasts and top with the Parmesan. Broil until brown and bubbling, about 5 minutes. Place 2 slices of the bacon (like an "X") on top of each cheesy toast and serve.

IT STARTS WITH THE ROUX

It may seem like nothing, but the most important step in this recipe is the one where you cook the flour and the butter. This is called a roux, and it's a foundation of good Southern cooking. If you don't take the time to cook it for the full minute called for, you will taste the raw flour in your finished dish.

PRALINE FRENCH TOAST CASSEROLE

I make this rich, sweet recipe for my sweet family whenever they ask. It's an old favorite that is just out of this world and it brings out everyone's sweet tooth—especially mine.

SERVES 6 TO 8

French Toast
Butter, for the baking dish
1 loaf French bread (13 to 16 ounces)
8 large eggs
2 cups half-and-half
1 cup whole milk
2 tablespoons granulated sugar
1 tablespoon vanilla extract
½ teaspoon ground cinnamon
½ teaspoon grated nutmeg
Pinch of salt

Praline Topping
2 sticks (8 ounces) butter,
  at room temperature
1 cup packed light brown sugar
1 cup chopped pecans
2 tablespoons light corn syrup
½ teaspoon ground cinnamon
½ teaspoon grated nutmeg

Raspberry Syrup
1 cup raspberry preserves
2 tablespoons raspberry liqueur,
  such as Chambord

1. To prepare the French toast: Grease a 13 by 9-inch baking dish generously with butter. Cut the bread crosswise into twenty 1-inch-thick slices. Arrange the slices in two overlapping rows.

2. In a large bowl, combine the eggs, half-and-half, milk, granulated sugar, vanilla, cinnamon, nutmeg, and salt. Beat with a rotary beater or whisk until the custard mixture is blended but not too foamy. Pour the custard over the bread slices, making sure they all are covered evenly. Spoon some of the custard in between the slices. Cover with foil and refrigerate overnight.

3. The next day, preheat the oven to 350°F.

4. Meanwhile, prepare the praline topping: In a medium bowl, combine the butter, brown sugar, pecans, corn syrup, cinnamon, and nutmeg and blend well with a fork. Spread the topping evenly over the bread slices. Bake until puffed and lightly golden, about 45 minutes.

5. Meanwhile, make the raspberry syrup: In a small saucepan, heat the preserves, liqueur, and 3 tablespoons water over medium heat. Stir until warm and thinned out to a syruplike consistency.

6. Serve the French toast casserole drizzled with the pretty raspberry syrup.

> **SYRUP SWAP-OUT**
>
> If you'd rather not use raspberry liqueur or if you can't find it, substitute orange juice.

Chapter 5

PASTA AND RICE

Y'all, I love my carbs! No Southern table is complete without a bowl of carbohydrate goodness on there. I don't care where you are in the South, you'll always find pasta, noodles, or rice on the table. In the North I have enjoyed wonderful authentic Italian food. Down here we tend to cook our pasta a bit more, then smother it with cheese, cream, and butter, and call it macaroni and cheese.

I make mac 'n' cheese crispy (The Lady's Cheesy Mac, page 105), creamy (Creamiest Mac and Cheese, page 106), or healthy (Healthier Mac and Cheese, page 107), depending upon my mood. But no matter what, it is a dish that kids and adults always come together on. My grandbaby Jack has never turned down a plate of macaroni, and I'm sure I never met a child who has.

Now, I do a lasagna, too, but I do it Southern style. A little cream cheese is my secret, and I'm sharing the recipe for My Favorite Lasagna (page 108) with y'all because it makes the best lasagna you could dream of. Cream cheese goes in my pretty Pasta with Creamy Primavera Sauce (page 112), too.

Another one of my takes on classic Italian cooking is my Smoky Southern Spaghetti Carbonara (page 111), and this is another marriage made in heaven. Italian cooks came up with this divine sauce of egg, cheese, and pork—I just make mine with good smoky bacon and a nice dash of hot sauce to sweeten the deal.

Using a bit of meat to enrich your starch is an old Southern trick. Take our rice dishes. Where I am originally from, in the southwest corner of Georgia, it was rice and brown gravy. When I made it to Savannah, I was introduced to Savannah red rice. I'll never turn my back on rice and gravy, but my Savannah red rice (page 113), packed with tomato and sausage, is truly delicious.

Around here you also see Dirty Rice (page 118), which has to have chicken livers in it if you want the real deal. The comforting flavors of that dish, full of butter, ground beef, and the Cajun combination of green pepper, scallions, and garlic, will even win over someone who swears they can't love a liver dish.

No matter how you eat it, rice is just so fast and simple, and you can make it a bed for anything, and flavor it in just about any way. Plus, leftovers are a gift that will allow you to make the best Rice Croquettes (page 120).

Historically, even the poorest Southern families ate really well because they usually had their own gardens, raised some animals, and knew how to make the most amazing dishes from simple foods like noodles and rice. Recipes like the ones in this chapter have filled so many bellies and brought such comfort and enjoyment to people over the years. And here they are for your eating pleasure.

THE LADY'S CHEESY MAC

■ ■

Do y'all have a recipe that you're just so proud to serve because you know it is absolutely the best it can be? Well, for me that recipe is The Lady's Cheesy Mac. I have made this rich and creamy macaroni and cheese so many times, I don't even need to use measuring cups anymore. I can just do it by sight. Our buffet table at The Lady & Sons is never without it, and, of course, Jamie and Bobby expect to see it on our family table!

SERVES 4 TO 6

2 cups elbow macaroni (8 ounces)
2 cups shredded Cheddar cheese, plus extra
    for topping
4 tablespoons (½ stick) butter, cut into pieces

3 large eggs, lightly beaten
1 cup whole milk or evaporated milk
½ cup sour cream
½ teaspoon salt

1. Preheat the oven to 350°F. Lightly grease a 13 by 9-inch baking dish with butter, oil, or cooking spray.

2. In a large pot of boiling salted water, cook the macaroni according to the package directions. Drain well and transfer to a large bowl. Add the 2 cups Cheddar and the butter, stirring until the pasta is coated.

3. In a medium bowl, whisk together the eggs, milk, sour cream, and salt. Add the egg mixture to the pasta and stir well to combine. Scrape the mixture into the prepared baking dish. Bake until golden, 35 to 40 minutes. Take the dish out of the oven and top with extra cheese, then return it to the oven until the cheese is melted and beginning to brown, about 5 minutes. Serve hot.

THE SECRET'S OUT

It's the sour cream that makes this mac and cheese truly special! It creates the oh-so-velvety smooth texture inside—a perfect complement to the crispy browned top. And the tangy sour notes are just the right balance for the cheesy richness.

CREAMIEST MAC AND CHEESE

■ ■

I swear there must be something in the human gene—all children everywhere love mac and cheese. And kids all seem to agree: the creamier, the better. Well, this stovetop macaroni and cheese not only comes together in the twinkle of an eye, it is the richest, the silkiest, the most yummy creamy mac and cheese you have ever tasted. Your children will beg for it, and I'll bet you'll be only too happy to oblige.

SERVES 4 TO 6

2 cups elbow macaroni (8 ounces)

3 tablespoons butter

2 large eggs

¾ cup heavy cream or evaporated milk

1 teaspoon salt

¾ teaspoon black pepper

¾ teaspoon mustard powder

Pinch of cayenne pepper (optional)

1½ cups shredded Cheddar cheese (6 ounces)

8 slices American cheese

1. In a large pot of boiling salted water, cook the macaroni according to the package directions. Drain well and return the pasta to the pot. Add the butter and stir over medium heat until the butter has melted and the pasta is coated.

2. In a medium bowl, whisk together the eggs, cream, salt, black pepper, mustard powder, and cayenne pepper, if using. Pour the egg and cream mixture into the pot and stir. Add the cheeses and continue stirring over medium heat until the sauce has thickened and is very creamy, about 3 minutes. Serve hot.

> ### CREAM OF THE CROP
> Dairy products are delicate creatures when they come across heat. There's always the risk of curdling, which makes a clumpy mess. The best protection against curdling, folks, is fat. So, regular milk, with its lower fat content, will just not cut it in this recipe. Stick with the heavy cream or evaporated milk, and this mac will be at its creamy best!

HEALTHIER MAC AND CHEESE

Now, do you know that my son Bobby is something of a health nut? He loves his salads, and his grilled chicken breast, and his tuna steaks. But no matter what kind of health regime he's on, he's just got to have macaroni and cheese—so I make this up for him to satisfy his craving and honor his health kick.

SERVES 4 TO 6

2 cups whole wheat or regular elbow
    macaroni (8 ounces)
2 cups shredded reduced-fat Cheddar cheese
    (8 ounces)
½ cup low-fat evaporated milk
2 large eggs, lightly beaten

¼ cup reduced-fat sour cream
1 tablespoon Dijon mustard
½ teaspoon salt
¼ teaspoon cayenne pepper
⅓ cup grated Parmesan cheese

1. Preheat the oven to 350°F. Coat a 13 by 9-inch baking dish with cooking spray.

2. In a large pot of boiling salted water, cook the macaroni according to the package directions. Drain well and transfer the pasta to a large bowl. Add the Cheddar and stir until the pasta is coated and the cheese has melted.

3. In a medium bowl, whisk together the evaporated milk, eggs, sour cream, mustard, salt, and cayenne pepper. Add the milk-egg mixture to the macaroni and cheese and stir well to combine. Scrape the mixture into the prepared baking dish and sprinkle the Parmesan evenly over the top. Bake until golden brown and crispy around the edges, 35 to 40 minutes.

A HEALTHY OPTION

Whole grains aren't just for breakfast cereal. When it comes to types of pasta, there are so many options on the supermarket shelves these days—from whole wheat and gluten-free pastas all the way to pastas enriched with vegetables like spinach and carrot. Well, who knew it was so easy to be healthy?

MY FAVORITE LASAGNA

■ ■

America is just one great big melting pot of cultures and cuisines, and the South is no different. Down here, we serve the classics of Italian cooking, like lasagna, and set them on our potluck buffet table right next to the fried chicken and gravy. Of course, we do put a Southern spin on it. I make it extra-special with cream cheese. I just love to bring it hot and bubbling to the table.

SERVES 8

12 ounces lasagna noodles

2 tablespoons olive oil

1 small yellow onion, finely chopped

1 clove garlic, finely chopped

1 pound ground beef

½ teaspoon salt

¼ teaspoon black pepper

1 jar (24 ounces) spaghetti sauce

5 ounces cream cheese, cut into bits

1 pound fresh mozzarella cheese,
   thinly sliced

1½ cups grated Parmesan cheese
   (about 6 ounces)

1. Preheat the oven to 375°F. Lightly grease a 13 by 9-inch baking dish with butter, oil, or cooking spray.

2. In a large pot of boiling salted water, parboil the lasagna noodles according to the package directions.

3. In a large skillet, heat the oil over medium-high heat. Add the onion and cook until translucent, about 5 minutes. Add the garlic and cook until fragrant, about 1 minute. Add the beef and cook, breaking it up with a fork, until browned, 5 to 7 minutes. Sprinkle with the salt and black pepper. Add the spaghetti sauce and cream cheese. Stir until the cheese has melted into the sauce.

4. Spoon ½ cup of the meat sauce into the bottom of the prepared baking dish. Top with a single layer of noodles, 1 cup of the sauce, one-third of the mozzarella, and ½ cup of the Parmesan. Repeat the layering two more times, until all of the ingredients have been used, ending with a layer of mozzarella and Parmesan.

5. Cover the baking dish with foil and bake for 30 minutes. Remove the foil and continue baking until golden on top and bubbling, 20 to 25 minutes.

DO AHEAD

Don't you just love a dish that tastes even better the day after you make it? Well, this is just that kind of dish—which, of course, makes it perfect for hassle-free entertaining. I even like to make up two dishes sometimes and stick one in the freezer for future midweek meals.

BUTTERNUT SQUASH RAVIOLI WITH PECAN BROWN BUTTER

■ ■

When I first started seeing this butternut squash ravioli for sale in the supermarket, I thought, "Really? Squash in ravioli?" I wasn't quite convinced I'd like it because I'm used to having meat or cheese in my ravioli, but I'm game to try anything once. And I am so glad I did, because I love it to pieces. The squash adds just a bit of sweetness to a savory dish, and, as y'all know, that salty-sweet taste is my absolute downfall. To get the full force of the flavor, you need to serve it with a butter sauce rather than a red sauce as you would other ravioli. And this brown-butter sauce is just the thing.

SERVES 4

1 pound fresh or frozen butternut squash or
    pumpkin ravioli
4 tablespoons (½ stick) butter

½ cup finely chopped pecans
¼ teaspoon salt
¼ teaspoon black pepper

1. In a large pot of boiling salted water, cook the ravioli according to the package directions. Drain well.

2. In a large skillet, melt the butter over medium-high heat. Stir in the pecans and cook, stirring occasionally, until the pecans are golden and the butter is brown and fragrant, about 2 minutes. Add the ravioli, stirring to coat in the butter, and cook until warmed through, about 30 seconds. Stir in the salt and black pepper and serve hot.

PASTA PERFECT

In a perfect world, your pasta comes out done just as you are ready to throw the sauce on it. Well, things don't always work out that way. If your pasta is done before your sauce is ready, just give it a quick rinse under some cold or cool water, never hot. Don't bother with oil to stop it from sticking—water is your best bet.

LINGUINE WITH SPICY CAJUN SHRIMP

You just can't get a better taste of the South than serving that hot and spicy Cajun seasoning with some nice, buttery shrimp. All you got to do is add some noodles and you have a meal that will please anybody who has working taste buds. My husband, Michael, who knows a thing or two about Cajun cooking, will often come home with a whole mess of shrimp and a box of pasta and ask me to fix him up some of this. Now that I've got the recipe written down, I guess he'll be making it for *me*!

SERVES 4

2 tablespoons olive oil
4 tablespoons (½ stick) butter
1 pound large shrimp, peeled and deveined
2 teaspoons Cajun seasoning
12 ounces linguine
1 tablespoon chopped garlic

½ cup chicken broth
2 dashes of hot sauce
½ cup chopped scallions, plus 1 or
   2 tablespoons for garnish
Grated Parmesan cheese, for serving

1. In a large, deep skillet, heat the oil and 2 tablespoons of the butter over medium-high heat. Dust the shrimp evenly with the Cajun seasoning and add them to the pan. Cook the shrimp, turning once, until they are just opaque and cooked through, about 3 minutes. Transfer the shrimp to a plate.

2. In a large pot of boiling salted water, cook the pasta according to the package directions. Drain well.

3. Meanwhile, as the pasta cooks, melt the remaining 2 tablespoons butter in the pan. Add the garlic and cook for 30 seconds. Add the broth and hot sauce. Bring to a simmer and stir up any browned bits from the pan. Turn off the heat and return the shrimp to the pan.

4. Toss the pasta with the shrimp sauce and the ½ cup scallions. Serve garnished with scallions. Pass the Parmesan cheese at the table.

RAGIN' CAJUN

You'll notice that I don't call for salt and pepper in this recipe. That's because it's all taken care of in the Cajun seasoning. Truly an amazing spice blend, this mix of salt, peppers, paprika, ground garlic, and onion (with a million variations in between) is a staple of Cajun cooking.

SMOKY SOUTHERN SPAGHETTI CARBONARA

■ ■

This dish has got everything I love right there in one bowl: that smoky flavor of good, crispy bacon combined with a wonderful cheesy, creamy sauce and just the right amount of hot sauce to slap some sense into your taste buds. It's the kind of dish that will make you stand up and holler a big "Thank you!" to the cook.

SERVES 4

½ pound bacon, chopped

1¼ cups grated Parmesan cheese
(about 5 ounces)

¼ cup heavy cream

2 large eggs

Salt

Tabasco or other hot sauce

Black pepper

1 pound spaghetti

1 medium yellow onion, finely chopped

1. In a large, deep skillet, cook the bacon over medium-high heat until crisp, about 5 minutes. Drain the bacon on a paper towel–lined plate. Take the skillet off the heat, but don't drain off the bacon fat.

2. In a bowl, whisk together the Parmesan, cream, eggs, ¾ teaspoon salt, ½ teaspoon hot sauce, and black pepper to taste.

3. In a large pot of boiling salted water, cook the pasta according to the package directions. Drain well.

4. While the pasta cooks, return the skillet to medium-high heat. Add the onion and cook until softened, about 5 minutes. Remove the skillet from the heat.

5. Immediately add the hot pasta, the bacon, and the egg mixture to the skillet; toss everything together to combine. The heat from the pasta and skillet will thicken the eggs into a creamy sauce. Taste and add more salt, hot sauce, or black pepper, if desired. Serve hot.

THE HEAT IS ON

Now, you may look at this recipe and say, "Paula, how in heaven's name are my eggs going to cook without any heat on them?" Don't you worry; there will be enough heat coming from that pasta and the skillet itself to make sure those eggs are good and cooked but not scrambled. If you left them on the direct heat, you'd have a scrambled egg pasta dish. I'm telling you, make sure your pasta is hot, make sure you give it a really good stir, and what you will end up with is a creamy, beautiful sauce. And we'll just leave the scrambled eggs for breakfast.

PASTA WITH CREAMY PRIMAVERA SAUCE

■ ■

This dish is a real beauty, plain and simple. All of those gorgeous fresh vegetables are so colorful and inviting, I swear it just makes you want to dive right into the bowl! And because it is so easy to prepare (the vegetables and the pasta cook in no time), it's a wonderful dish to serve for a luncheon or a party where you may have other things to put your mind to. I like to serve this in a clear glass bowl and place it right in the center of the table.

SERVES 6

1 small head broccoli (½ pound),
   cut into bite-size florets
1 medium carrot, thinly sliced
1 medium zucchini, quartered lengthwise
   and thinly sliced crosswise
⅓ cup frozen green peas
1 pound penne pasta
1 tablespoon olive oil
1 clove garlic, finely chopped

¾ cup halved cherry tomatoes
¾ cup heavy cream
2 ounces cream cheese, cut into bits
¾ cup grated Parmesan cheese
   (about 3 ounces)
½ teaspoon salt
¼ teaspoon black pepper
¼ cup chopped fresh basil

1. Bring a large pot of salted water to a boil. Have a bowl of ice water at the ready. Add the broccoli and carrot to the boiling water and cook until crisp-tender, about 2 minutes. Transfer the vegetables with a slotted spoon to the ice water. Add the zucchini and peas to the boiling water and cook for 1 minute. Transfer with a slotted spoon to the ice water. Drain the vegetables and transfer to a large bowl that's pretty enough to serve in.

2. Bring the vegetable cooking water back to a boil. Add the penne and cook according to the package directions; drain well.

3. Meanwhile, in a large skillet, heat the oil over medium-high heat. Add the garlic and cook until fragrant, about 15 seconds. Add the tomatoes and cook until just soft, 1 to 2 minutes. Scrape the garlic and tomatoes into the bowl of vegetables.

> **'TIS THE SEASON**
>
> *Primavera* means "spring" in Italian. Traditionally, this pasta was made with the fresh bounty of vegetables harvested in the springtime. But my pasta primavera is too good to have just in the springtime! Since you can get these vegetables any time of the year, you can serve primavera any time you crave it.

4. Return the skillet to the heat. Add the cream and bring to a simmer. Whisk in the cream cheese until smooth. Whisk in ½ cup of the Parmesan, the salt, and the black pepper.

5. Add the pasta to the bowl of vegetables. Pour the hot cream sauce over the mixture. Stir in the basil and the remaining ¼ cup Parmesan and toss well. Taste and adjust seasoning, if necessary.

SAVANNAH RED RICE

Now, in the inland areas of Georgia, people do up their rice with brown gravy, but out on the coast, they are all about their red rice. This is how I make rice for my husband, Michael, and his two children, Michelle and Anthony. Though I admit it's taken me a few years of living in Savannah to come around to their way of eating, now this is how I love it, too. Serve with crusty bread to sop up that good sauce.

SERVES 4 TO 6

3 tablespoons butter
1 cup chopped yellow onion
1 cup chopped green bell pepper
1 cup chopped andouille or other
   smoked sausage
1 cup long-grain white rice
1 can (15 ounces) crushed tomatoes
1 cup chicken broth
1 teaspoon hot sauce
Pinch of salt
Pinch of black pepper

RELAXED ENTERTAINING

This is another great dish for entertaining. Baked rice is so easy and foolproof, and when you've got guests stopping by, it's a surefire hit. There are two ways you can prep this up ahead of time. One way is to just get the dish ready to the point that everything is in the baking dish waiting to be baked. Then, bake it off when guests start arriving and it'll be ready when you sit down to supper. Or, in a pinch, go ahead and bake it off earlier and just reheat it, covered, when your guests show up.

1. Preheat the oven to 350°F. Lightly grease a 13 by 9-inch baking dish with butter, oil, or cooking spray.

2. In a medium saucepan, melt the butter over medium heat. Add the onion, bell pepper, and sausage and cook until the vegetables soften, 5 to 7 minutes. Stir in the remaining ingredients and bring to a simmer. Cook until the sauce begins to thicken, about 10 minutes.

3. Scrape the mixture into the prepared baking dish and cover with foil. Bake until the rice is tender and the sauce is bubbling, 40 to 45 minutes. Serve hot.

JAMBALAYA

■ ■

To me, jambalaya is another testament to what a Southern cook can do, even on a tight budget. This classic dish seems to have just a little bit of everything in it, and all those odds and ends sure do make one delicious meal. Now, if shellfish are not so readily available in your area, this tastes just as fantastic with shredded rotisserie chicken tossed through, in place of the shrimp.

SERVES 4 TO 6

1 cup long-grain white rice

3 tablespoons dried minced onion

1 tablespoon dried parsley flakes

1 tablespoon beef bouillon granules

½ teaspoon dried thyme

½ teaspoon garlic powder

½ teaspoon black pepper

¼ teaspoon cayenne pepper

¼ teaspoon salt

1 bay leaf

1 can (14½ ounces) diced tomatoes

1 can (8 ounces) tomato sauce

½ pound fully cooked smoked sausage, such as andouille, cut into ¼-inch slices

¾ pound large shrimp, peeled and deveined

1. In a medium bowl, combine the rice, onion, parsley flakes, bouillon, thyme, garlic powder, black pepper, cayenne pepper, salt, and bay leaf. (This seasoned rice may be used immediately or stored in an airtight container at room temperature for up to 6 months.)

2. In a Dutch oven, combine the rice mixture, 2½ cups water, the diced tomatoes, tomato sauce, and sausage. Bring to a boil over medium-high heat. Reduce to a simmer and cook, stirring occasionally, until the rice is tender, about 20 minutes.

3. Add the shrimp and cook until just opaque, 5 to 7 minutes; discard the bay leaf. Dish it up while it's hot.

DUTCH TREAT

I love to make my jambalaya in a Dutch oven. It's just the right cooking vessel for a dish like this because of its thick walls and ability to conduct and hold heat evenly throughout, especially during long simmers. If, however, you don't have a Dutch oven, you can use a wide, deep saucepan. Just make sure the base has a heavy bottom, to prevent sticking and burning and to make sure the rice is cooked evenly and gently.

RED BEANS AND RICE WITH ANDOUILLE SAUSAGE

■ ■

Oh, Lord, do I love my red beans and rice! That is something my son Jamie and I can absolutely agree upon—we could have red beans and rice for just about every meal and you'd never, ever hear us complain. I love to make mine with spices and herbs that deepen the flavor without overpowering it. And of course I've got to add a dash or two of hot sauce because I love some heat in most dishes. This one always takes me back to my Southern kitchen, no matter what part of the world I'm eating it in.

SERVES 8

3 tablespoons bacon fat, lard, or olive oil

1¾ cups chopped andouille sausage
   (about ½ pound)

1 yellow onion, chopped

1 green bell pepper, chopped

2 celery stalks with leaves, chopped

3 cloves garlic, finely chopped

2 teaspoons ground cumin

1 teaspoon dried thyme

1 pound dried red beans

1½ teaspoons salt

1 teaspoon hot sauce

3 bay leaves

6 cups cooked rice

¼ cup sliced scallions

3 tablespoons chopped fresh parsley,
   for garnish

1. In a large pot or a Dutch oven, heat the fat, lard, or oil over medium-high heat. Add the sausage and cook until golden, 5 to 7 minutes. Add the onion, bell pepper, celery, and garlic. Cook, stirring, until softened, 5 to 7 minutes. Stir in the cumin and thyme and cook for 1 minute.

2. Add the beans, salt, hot sauce, bay leaves, and enough water to cover the beans by 2 inches. Bring the mixture to a boil. Immediately reduce to a simmer, cover, and cook for 1½ hours. Uncover and simmer until the beans are tender and the sauce has thickened, 30 to 45 minutes, adding more water if necessary. Remove and discard the bay leaves. Serve over the rice, topped with the scallions. Garnish with the parsley.

SMOKIN' SAUSAGE

Andouille sausage came to the American South from France, via Louisiana, of course. It's a smoked-pork sausage flavored with pepper, onion, and all sorts of yummy seasonings. If you can't find it near you, though, you can substitute a nice smoked kielbasa.

PERLOW

Did y'all know that Charleston, South Carolina, was built on rice? That lovely little grain was grown on Low-Country plantations and even used as currency there during the eighteenth century. (Can y'all imagine getting paid in rice?) Perlow, a variation on the word *pilau* or *pilaf* (as in rice pilaf), is the way they cook rice in that region to this day. The dish almost always includes some ham or bacon, and scallions, and usually tomato as well. But the key ingredient is good old rice, baked up to a tender, fluffy, glorious dish. I make mine with bacon and a smoked turkey wing for flavor, and then plenty of tender turkey pieces to become a main course.

SERVES 4 AS A MAIN DISH

1 tablespoon butter

2 slices bacon, chopped

1 cup chopped yellow onion

1 clove garlic, chopped

½ pound turkey cutlets, cut into ¾-inch
 pieces

1½ cups long-grain white rice

1 cup chopped tomato

One ½-pound smoked turkey wing

1 teaspoon salt

Black pepper

⅓ cup chopped scallions,
 dark green tops only

1. Preheat the oven to 350°F.

2. In a Dutch oven, melt the butter over medium heat. Add the bacon and cook until crisp, 5 to 7 minutes. Add the onion and cook until soft, about 5 minutes. Add the garlic and cook for 1 minute.

3. Add the turkey pieces and cook until the turkey loses its raw color, about 2 minutes. Add the rice, tomato, smoked turkey wing, salt, black pepper to taste, and 3 cups water. Bring to a boil, cover, and bake until the rice is tender and the liquid has been absorbed, about 30 minutes.

To chop a peeled onion, halve the onion lengthwise and lay cut side down. Hold one half steady while slicing the onion lengthwise in parallel strokes up to but not through the root. Make horizontal cuts across these cuts to create pieces of desired size. Repeat with the other half.

PASTA AND RICE

4. Remove the smoked turkey wing from the pot. When cool enough to handle, pull the meat from the bones and finely chop. Stir the meat into the perlow along with the scallion greens and dig in.

SMOKY FLAVOR

The smoked turkey wing here gives this perlow a really deep, rich flavor. And the meat on the turkey wing is sure to be juicy because the smoking process locks in all the moisture. If you can't find smoked turkey wings in your market, you can substitute a smoked ham hock or, if you're feeling ambitious, smoke your very own turkey!

SOUTHERN BROWN RICE WITH MUSHROOMS

This is the way we made our rice when I was growing up in Albany, Georgia, in the southwest corner of the state. I guess Bubba and I would get this for dinner at least twice a week, which, believe me, was just fine with us. It's the kind of dish that'll fill you up right without emptying out your pocketbook.

SERVES 4

3 tablespoons butter
¾ cup chopped yellow onion
1 cup long-grain white rice
1 can (4 ounces) sliced mushrooms, drained

1¾ cups beef broth
¼ teaspoon salt
Chopped fresh parsley, for garnish

1. In a medium saucepan, heat the butter over medium heat. Add the onion and cook until soft and golden, 10 to 12 minutes.

2. Add the rice and mushrooms and cook, stirring to coat with the butter, for about 2 minutes. Pour in the broth and add the salt. Bring to a boil over high heat. Reduce to a simmer, cover, and cook until most of the liquid has been absorbed and the rice is tender, 17 to 20 minutes. Remove from the heat and let stand, covered, for 5 minutes. Fluff with a fork. Serve garnished with parsley.

THE FLUFFIEST RICE

Long-grain rice is my favorite rice. Its grains are slender and lower in the type of starch that shorter-grain rice types have. So for rice dishes like this, stick with long-grain and they won't end up all gluey and sticky. Instead, your rice will cook fluffy, with separate grains.

DIRTY RICE

■ ■

What did I tell you about how good Southern cooks can get every bit of flavor out of any ingredient? Well, you don't think we'd let the chicken livers go to waste, do you? Truth be told, I love to eat chicken livers. They are so tender and rich and economical, I just feel like a richer and smarter person with every bite. This is a traditional Southern dish that blends great taste with great home economics.

SERVES 6 TO 8

1 cup long-grain white rice	8 tablespoons (1 stick) butter
1¼ teaspoons salt	½ cup chopped green bell pepper
2 tablespoons vegetable oil	4 scallions, chopped
¾ pound ground beef	1 clove garlic, finely chopped
¾ pound chicken livers, finely chopped	¾ teaspoon hot sauce
½ teaspoon black pepper	Chopped fresh parsley

1. In a medium saucepan, combine the rice, 1¾ cups water, and ¼ teaspoon of the salt. Bring to a boil over medium-high heat. Reduce to a simmer, cover, and cook until most of the liquid has been absorbed and the rice is tender, 17 to 20 minutes. Remove from the heat and let stand, covered, for 5 minutes.

2. Meanwhile, in a large skillet, heat the oil over medium-high heat. Add the beef and cook, breaking it up with a fork, until well browned, 5 to 7 minutes. Add the chicken livers and cook, turning once, until no longer pink, 2 to 3 minutes. Season with ½ teaspoon of the salt and ¼ teaspoon of the black pepper. With a slotted spoon, transfer the mixture to a paper towel–lined plate to drain.

To remove the bitter-tasting connective tissue between the lobes of chicken liver, place the liver on a cutting board and gently spread the lobes apart. Hold one lobe steady while pressing the side of a small sharp knife against the other lobe. The stringy tissue should release from the lobe being held down. Gently scrape the tissue from the lobe to which it is still attached. Rinse the lobes and pat dry.

3. Return the skillet to the heat. Add the butter and let it melt. Add the bell pepper, scallions, and garlic. Cook until the vegetables have softened, 5 to 7 minutes. Stir in the cooked rice and the meat mixture. Cook until warmed through. Season with the hot sauce, and the remaining ½ teaspoon salt and ¼ teaspoon black pepper. Stir in the parsley just before serving.

ANOTHER SOUTHERN CLASSIC

My other favorite thing to do with chicken livers is to fry them up! We Southerners may have started out cooking up those chicken livers because they were inexpensive, but as soon as we started frying them, we realized how much possibility they had. Check out my Cajun Chicken-Fried Livers with Cream Gravy (page 181).

RICE CROQUETTES

■ ■

Do I need to argue with anyone about this one? Frying leftover rice into crisp little breaded cakes full of Parmesan cheese is just a no-brainer. Make extra rice so you won't have to go without this delicious dish.

MAKES 16 CROQUETTES (8 SERVINGS)

2 cups cooked rice
Salt and black pepper
1 large egg, lightly beaten
1 teaspoon onion powder

1 cup grated Parmesan cheese
  (about 4 ounces)
½ cup dry bread crumbs
Vegetable oil, for frying

1. In a medium bowl, toss the rice with salt and black pepper to taste. Stir in the egg, onion powder, and Parmesan, and mix well.

2. Working with moistened hands, scoop 2 tablespoons of the rice mixture into your palm and give it a squeeze, then shape it into a fat little patty. Coat with the bread crumbs and repeat with the rest of the rice.

3. In a large skillet, heat ¼ inch of oil over medium-high heat until hot but not smoking. Working in batches (don't crowd the pan), cook the croquettes until browned on both sides, about 1½ to 2 minutes total. Drain on a paper towel–lined plate for a minute, then serve warm.

STICKY FINGERS

Keep a small dish of water nearby while you're shaping the croquettes. You'll need to lightly dampen your hands now and again to make sure the rice doesn't stick to your hands as you handle it.

Chapter 6

MEAT

There's no denying I love meat. Nothing will fill you up and satisfy you like a good steak or a nice roast. I crave it. If we go a long time without eating steak, I'll call home to say, "Tonight is the night. I have just got to put me a steak on the grill." I can't think of a meat that I don't like. I like liver and onions. I love gizzards. And I would not want to live in a world without fried pork chops.

Now, putting meat on your table does not have to be a big splurge. You just got to make the most of your cheaper cuts. One of the tastiest is one of the cheapest: bone-in chuck roast. We use it for The Lady & Sons Pot Roast (page 125) that we serve on Friday nights, and everyone just loves that dish. I have found that when you take your time cooking them until they're truly tender, those more economical cuts of meat become especially moist and full of flavor. Another one of my favorites is also a bargain: Chicken-Fried Steak with Cream Gravy (page 127). You take a round steak so tough you couldn't bite it with wooden teeth, your butcher runs it through the cuber, and, oh, my goodness, what a lot of flavor!

When you're buying beef, you've got Select, Choice, and Prime. I generally go middle of the road with Choice because I can count on that to be a good tender cut. Unless I'm going to cook it a good long while, I stay away from Select, and I don't buy Prime often—it has to be a special occasion.

I insist on having steak medium-rare. It just kills me to hear somebody order a steak well-done. They're missing out on the richest flavor! On the other hand, I was taught as a young bride to cook pork to death. You don't need to cook it so much for safety's sake anymore—as long as it's 140°F, you know it's all right—but in many of my recipes, like my Pulled Pork BBQ (page 140) or my Fried Pork Chops with Tomato Gravy (page 142), that pork is good and cooked.

Then there's ham. Hallelujah! Some of my earliest memories were of watching my grandmother pulling great big hams out of the oven. I swear by those Southern hams, which are raised and cured to precise, time-honored standards, and give off a wonderful salty-sweet flavor. Try my Batter-Fried Country Ham Bites (page 19) and tell me if that right there isn't pork candy!

Now, you don't have to be Southern to make meat taste good. Some of the recipes I adore are just good ol' American favorites like my Cheeseburger Meat Loaf and Sauce (page 138), and others get their inspiration from different cuisines. On chilly nights I make a Red Wine Beef Stew (page 128) that I just had to share with y'all, and every St. Paddy's Day we love to have our St. Paddy's Day Corned Beef and Cabbage (page 133). For entertaining, I love me a real big cut of meat. Whether it's Rack of Lamb with Rosemary (page 148), a Baked Sugared Ham (page 146), or my Famous Foolproof Standing Rib Roast (page 129), one of the great glories of cooking meat is how simply you can produce a showstopper of a meal.

THE LADY & SONS POT ROAST

This has to be one of my favorite roasts in the whole entire world (and it happens to be one of the most economical, too). We order chuck roasts to do our Friday Pot Roast each week at The Lady & Sons and folks line up out the door for that dinner. It truly is an occasion, so why not make it at home? It could hardly be simpler, since this is a set-it-and-forget-it type of meal made in a slow cooker. You just ask your butcher to tie the roast so it cooks evenly, then plan on cooking it low and slow—you can't rush a good thing—and by the time you're ready for dinner, well, that meat has just about melted and it is so full of flavor. This dish packs more taste than your fancier cuts, and is divine with a plate of noodles or in a sandwich the next day.

SERVES 6

One 3-pound boneless chuck roast
1½ teaspoons Paula Deen's House Seasoning
    (page 435)
Salt and black pepper
¼ cup vegetable oil
1 yellow onion, thinly sliced
3 bay leaves

3 or 4 beef bouillon cubes, crushed
2 cloves garlic, minced
1 can (10¾ ounces) condensed cream of
    mushroom soup
½ cup Chardonnay or other
    full-bodied white wine

1. Sprinkle the roast on all sides with House Seasoning. Season all over with salt and black pepper. In a large skillet, heat the oil over medium-high heat until it shimmers. Add the roast and brown on all sides, about 5 minutes per side.

2. Place the roast in a slow cooker. Place the onion, bay leaves, crushed bouillon cubes, garlic, and soup on top of roast. Pour in the wine. Add just enough water to cover the roast. Cook on low for 8 hours; remove and discard the bay leaves before serving. I tell you, it doesn't get much easier than that, folks.

MAKE IT SLOW

Now I know most of you know how truly wonderful the slow cooker is, but I just have to sing its praises, y'all! It has got to be one of the most convenient kitchen appliances there is. Just place your ingredients in the pot, turn it on, and there's not much more to be done. You can leave that slow cooker going even when you're out all day.

SMOTHERED STEAK AND ONIONS

■ ■

How many times did I yell "Put a lid on it, y'all" as my boys ran wild through the house shouting at the top of their lungs back when they were in school? Well, now they're perfect gentlemen, to my pride. And I chuckle about those days whenever I make my smothered steak. Putting a lid on your pot—a way of cooking we Southerners call "smothering"—makes for tender, juicy meat and plenty of flavorful sauce. I smother my top round steak strips with a big old tangle of onions, and those onions keep the meat moist at the same time that they turn the cream gravy sweeter than syrup.

SERVES 4 TO 6

2 pounds thin boneless top round steaks, sliced into ¼-inch-thick strips

Salt and black pepper

1 teaspoon dried oregano

3 tablespoons all-purpose flour

4 tablespoons (½ stick) butter

4 large Vidalia or other sweet onions, sliced

¼ teaspoon cayenne pepper

2½ cups beef or chicken broth

½ cup heavy cream

6 cups cooked noodles or white rice, for serving

1 to 2 tablespoons chopped fresh parsley, for garnish

1. Place the meat in a bowl. Season lightly with salt and black pepper. Add the oregano and flour and toss to coat well.

2. In a very large skillet, melt 3 tablespoons of the butter over medium-high heat. Working in batches, brown the meat until dark golden on all sides, 5 to 7 minutes per batch. Transfer the meat to a paper towel–lined plate to drain.

3. Add the remaining 1 tablespoon butter to the skillet. Add the onions and cook, stirring, until wilted and softened, about 10 minutes. Stir in 1 teaspoon salt, ½ teaspoon black pepper, and the cayenne pepper.

4. Return the meat to the skillet and pour in the broth. Scrape up any browned bits from the bottom of the pan. Bring to a boil. Reduce to a simmer, cover, and cook until the meat and onions are very tender and the gravy is thick, about 1 hour.

5. Pour in the cream and simmer until hot, about 5 minutes. Serve over buttered noodles or white rice. Garnish with the parsley to pretty it up.

FULL FLAVOR

Now, why do I keep telling you to scrape up those brown bits from the bottom of your pans? Because that's where the flavor is! When you get at those brown bits and distribute them into your stews and gravies, you're getting all the flavor released when you browned the meat.

CHICKEN-FRIED STEAK WITH CREAM GRAVY

■ ■

Chicken-frying is nothing fancy. You just tenderize a tougher cut of steak (or have your butcher cube it, which means partly cutting through the meat in a checkerboard pattern to tenderize it by breaking tough fibers), then you treat it like chicken: a buttermilk dip, a coating of seasoned flour, and a nice hot fry. But whoa, Mama, is that a tasty way to cook meat! What you end up with in your skillet are the makings for one of the finest sauces in the whole wide world: cream gravy. It's nothing more than pan drippings, broth, and cream, but it comes together like magic.

SERVES 4

4 boneless top round steaks (½ pound each, ½ inch thick)

2½ teaspoons Paula Deen's House Seasoning (page 435), plus extra as needed

1½ cups plus 3 tablespoons all-purpose flour

1 cup buttermilk

1 large egg

½ cup vegetable oil

1 cup beef broth

1 cup heavy cream

1. With the flat side of a meat pounder or a small, heavy skillet, pound the steaks until ⅓ inch thick. Season all over with 1 teaspoon of the House Seasoning.

2. In a shallow bowl, mix together the 1½ cups of the flour and the remaining 1½ teaspoons House Seasoning. In a separate shallow bowl, beat together the buttermilk and egg.

3. Dredge the steaks in the seasoned flour, shaking off any excess, then dip into the buttermilk mixture, letting any excess drip off, and then dip again into the flour to coat.

4. In a large skillet (I like to use cast iron), heat the oil over medium-high heat until it shimmers. You want it real hot. Cook the steaks until browned, about 3 minutes per side. Transfer to a paper towel–lined plate to drain.

5. Drain all but 3 tablespoons of the oil from the skillet. Add the 3 tablespoons flour and stir until browned, about 2 minutes. Add the broth and cream and bring to a boil. Stir until thickened, about 2 minutes. Taste and add some House Seasoning to the gravy, if desired. Serve up the steaks smothered in the cream gravy. It doesn't get much more Southern than this, folks.

THE SKILLFUL SKILLET

The cast-iron pan is a kitchen tool I could not do without, y'all. It conducts heat evenly across your food, and if the pan is seasoned just right, you'll never have to worry about the meat sticking. Plus, they don't cost much and chances are you've got one your mama passed on down to you.

RED WINE BEEF STEW

When you live in a warm place like I do, you really savor those nippy nights when you can get cozy, and nothing is cozier than simmering a beef stew. I made so many beef stews for the boys when they were growing—it was a surefire way to make sure they didn't end up back in the kitchen an hour later claiming to be hungry again. These days, I make this classic red wine and herb-flavored stew when I want to serve something special for a crowd, whether it's friends or family. Serve the stew with Buttery Buttermilk Mashed Potatoes (page 248).

SERVES 8 TO 10

3 pounds beef stew meat, cut into
   2-inch chunks

2¼ teaspoons salt

2¼ teaspoons black pepper

⅓ cup all-purpose flour

3 tablespoons butter

Olive oil

½ pound cremini mushrooms, quartered

2 large carrots, cut into ¼-inch rounds

1 large yellow onion, finely chopped

1 large clove garlic, finely chopped

2 tablespoons tomato paste

1 bottle (750ml) cabernet sauvignon or other
   full-bodied red wine

2 sprigs fresh thyme

2 sprigs fresh rosemary

1. Season the meat all over with 2 teaspoons each of the salt and black pepper. Dip the meat in the flour, then shake off any excess.

2. In a large Dutch oven, melt 2 tablespoons of the butter in 2 tablespoons oil over medium-high heat until very hot. Working in batches, brown the beef until golden all over, about 10 minutes. Transfer the meat to a paper towel–lined platter to drain. Add more oil, a tablespoon at a time, as needed, if the pan starts to dry up.

3. Add the remaining 1 tablespoon butter and 1 tablespoon oil to the pan. Stir in the mushrooms, carrots, onion, and garlic. Cook until the vegetables have softened, about 7 minutes. Stir in the remaining ¼ teaspoon each salt and black pepper. Stir in the tomato paste and cook for 1 minute. Transfer the vegetables to the platter with the meat.

OVEN BRAISE

If you'd like, you can also make this stew in the oven. Just preheat the oven to 300°F, and after you've returned the meat and vegetables to the Dutch oven and brought it back up to the boil, go on ahead and cover the pan, pop it into the oven, and bake for 2 to 3 hours. But do take care, if you're not using a Dutch oven, that your pan is ovenproof.

4. Pour the wine into the pan. Simmer, scraping up any browned bits from the bottom of the pan, until the wine has reduced by half, 15 to 20 minutes.

5. Return the meat and vegetables to the pan. Tie the thyme and rosemary together with kitchen string (so you can fish them back out easily before serving the stew) and drop the bundle into the pan. Bring the mixture to a boil. Immediately reduce to a simmer, cover, and cook until the meat is very tender, 2 to 2½ hours.

PAULA'S FAMOUS FOOLPROOF STANDING RIB ROAST

■ ■

If there is a simpler way to wow a big party than with a beautiful rib roast, I would like to hear about it. This recipe is nothing more than good meat done right. Perfectly medium-rare, nice and pink at the center, the roast slices up so pretty. And since all you've got to do is season it and leave it in the oven, you're freed up to make a few nice sides—maybe spoon bread or mashed potatoes, plus asparagus or green beans.

SERVES 6 TO 8

One 5-pound bone-in standing rib roast

1 tablespoon Paula Deen's House Seasoning (page 435)

1. Allow the roast to stand at room temperature for at least 1 hour. Meanwhile, preheat the oven to 375°F. Place a roasting rack in a large roasting pan.

2. Rub the roast all over with the House Seasoning. Place on the prepared roasting rack with the rib side down and the fatty side up. Roast for 1 hour. Turn the oven off. Leave the roast in the oven but do not open the oven door for at least another 3 hours (it can sit in the oven for up to 6 hours after roasting). About 30 to 45 minutes before serving time, preheat the oven to 375°F. Reheat the roast until a meat thermometer inserted in the center of the meat reads 120°F. The result? The most perfectly cooked rib roast you have ever tasted!

STAND AND DELIVER

It's important to let your roast stand at room temperature for a bit before you cook it so that it cooks nice and evenly. So be sure you don't skip that step! And I mean it about keeping that oven door closed. You don't want to release any of the radiant heat that cooks the roast so perfectly.

STUFFED CABBAGE

■ ■

I have such fond memories of my grandmama's stuffed cabbage that I decided to start making it myself. And wouldn't you know, it is surprisingly easy: something about the shape of cabbage leaves just makes them roll right up around your filling. I stuff mine with rice and meat mixed with sweet raisins and tender cooked onion. After it all simmers together in a nice tomato-based sauce, you wind up with such a wonderful old-timey flavor.

SERVES 4 OR 5

2 tablespoons vegetable oil

1 cup chopped yellow onion

1 medium head (about 2 pounds)
   green cabbage

1 pound ground beef

½ cup cooked rice

¼ cup raisins

¾ teaspoon salt

1 can (16 ounces) tomato sauce

½ cup beef broth

½ teaspoon paprika

About ½ cup sour cream, for serving

1. Preheat the oven to 350°F. Grease a 13 by 9-inch baking dish with butter, oil, or cooking spray.

2. In a medium skillet, heat the oil over medium-high heat. Add the onion and cook until softened, about 5 minutes. Set aside to cool.

3. Meanwhile, bring a large pot of salted water to a boil. Using a small, sharp knife, cut in a circle all around the stem of the cabbage and remove the core. Place the cabbage in the boiling water. After about 2 minutes an outside leaf will come loose—pull it off and out of the water using tongs. After another minute the next leaf will come loose. Remove and repeat until you have 8 to 10 nice leaves. Pat the leaves dry with paper towels. Cut out the thick part of the rib from the bottom of each leaf, but don't cut more than a third of the way into the leaf. (Unused cabbage can be made into my Easy Coleslaw (page 48) and Coleslaw with Raisins, Dill, and Honey-Roasted Peanuts (page 49).

> **KEEP IT COVERED**
>
> Make sure that the cabbage rolls are fully covered by the sauce. This will keep them from drying out and will ensure that they cook nice and evenly.

4. In a bowl, mix together the beef, cooled onion, rice, raisins, and salt. With the stem side of the cabbage leaf facing you, place a scant ⅓ cup of the beef mixture in the center of each cabbage leaf. Fold the bottom edge over the mixture and then fold the sides over and roll into a tidy packet. Place the cabbage rolls, seam side down, in the prepared baking dish.

5. In a bowl, mix together the tomato sauce, broth, and paprika and pour over the cabbage. Cover the baking dish with foil and bake for 1 hour. Serve the cabbage rolls with a big dollop of sour cream.

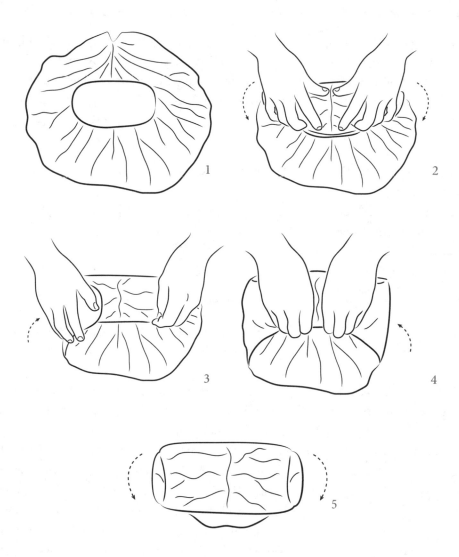

Place a small amount of filling in the center of a cabbage leaf and fold the leaf over from each side, then roll up to form a packet. Place in the pan seam side down.

FRIED BEEF TENDERLOIN WITH GRITS AND GRAVY

■ ■

Grits are such a comfort to a Southerner; you can't go too long without a bowl. I whip up this recipe for hearty, full-on flavorful gravy and good, satisfying beef to serve over my grits whenever we want real food fast. Don't forget to put out a bottle of hot sauce on the table for folks who like a little more warmth. This is stick-to-your-ribs comfort food.

SERVES 4 TO 6

1½ pounds beef tenderloin tips, cut into 1-inch chunks

Salt and black pepper

1½ tablespoons Wondra flour,
    plus extra for dusting the meat

8 tablespoons (1 stick) butter

1 large yellow onion, finely chopped

2 cloves garlic, finely chopped

1½ cups whole milk

Hot sauce

6 cups cooked grits

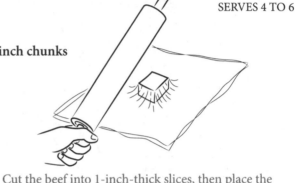

Cut the beef into 1-inch-thick slices, then place the slices between two sheets of plastic wrap. Strike them firmly with a rolling pin until the desired thickness is reached.

1. With the flat side of a meat pounder or a small, heavy skillet, pound each chunk of meat between two sheets of plastic wrap until ¼ inch thick. Season the meat generously all over with salt and black pepper. Dust the pieces with the flour, shaking off any excess.

2. In a very large skillet, melt 3 tablespoons of the butter over medium-high heat until foamy. Place half the beef in the skillet and cook, without stirring, until golden brown, 1 to 2 minutes per side. Transfer the beef to a plate. Add another 3 tablespoons of the butter to the skillet and cook the remaining beef. Keep the beef warm by tenting some foil over it. Don't cover it tightly or it will keep on cooking and stewing under that foil.

3. Add the onion to the skillet. Cook, stirring, until softened, about 5 minutes. Add the garlic and cook for 1 minute. Add the remaining 2 tablespoons butter and stir until melted. Stir in the 1½ tablespoons flour and cook for 1 minute. Slowly whisk in the milk. Simmer over medium heat

INSTANT SUCCESS

Well, I just think that Wondra is a wonderful product! It's the best way to keep your gravy from getting all lumpy on you. Basically, it's flour that's been treated to dissolve in liquid quickly and fully without any lumps!

MEAT

until the gravy has thickened, about 2 minutes. Season the gravy to taste with salt and hot sauce. Serve the beef tips over the grits with plenty of gravy poured over, and hot sauce to pass at the table.

ST. PADDY'S DAY CORNED BEEF AND CABBAGE

■■■

Quite a few Irish Catholics live here in Savannah, and the town puts on one of the largest St. Patrick's Day celebrations in the country, second only to New York City. The whole town takes pride in its Irish heritage that day, and at The Lady & Sons we serve this corned beef and cabbage to all of our guests. It's a savory, hearty meal that comes together fast and tastes like you spent all day on it. Serve this with Turnip Mashed Potatoes (page 249) and Corn Sticks (page 274).

SERVES 8

One 3-pound corned beef brisket
1 large head (about 2½ pounds)
   green cabbage

6 tablespoons (¾ stick) butter
1 to 2 teaspoons Paula Deen's House
   Seasoning (page 435)

1. Place the corned beef in a large stockpot and cover it with cold water to nearly fill the pot. Bring to a boil. Reduce to a simmer, cover, and cook until the beef is firm but tender to the fork, 2½ to 3 hours. Remove the beef from the pot. (Save the broth, if desired; see step 3.)

2. When the corned beef is almost done, core the cabbage. Then pull off any dark green outer leaves from the head of cabbage, chop, and set aside. Chop the rest of the cabbage and keep separate from the dark green leaves. Place the lighter-colored cabbage in a colander and rinse with cool water. In a separate large pot, melt the butter over medium-high heat. Immediately add the rinsed cabbage to the pot, leaving as much water as possible on the leaves. Cook, stirring, until the cabbage is well coated with butter. Sprinkle with the House Seasoning. Cover the pot and simmer until the cabbage is tender but still somewhat crisp, 7 to 10 minutes.

3. Slice the corned beef thinly across the grain. Place the cabbage in a serving dish and place the sliced corned beef on top. Drizzle a spoonful or two of broth from the stockpot over the corned beef and cabbage, if you like.

THE SKILL OF THE IRISH
You want to make sure you choose your corned beef brisket well so you get the best end result. There are basically three different brisket cuts you'll find: point, flat, and round. I recommend flat cut because it has enough fat to give good flavor to your corned beef but not so much that your braise comes out greasy and with precious little meat to go around.

SOUTHERN CHILI IN A BISCUIT BOWL

■ ■

What could be more festive than these adorable little biscuit bowls full of chili? I love to set them out in a basket on the buffet next to a big old Crock-Pot of chili. This is my classic chili, and it's got your ground beef, your good chili spices, and your beans, peppers, and tomatoes. But what really does it up special is the fixin's: it's amazing what some scallions, sour cream, and shredded cheese can do for a nice bowl of chili—just like a nice new purse will pull together your outfit, or a pretty vase of flowers will dress up your decor. Throw in a green salad, and something sweet after, and you're good to go.

SERVES 6

Biscuit Bowls

2 cups Bisquick baking mix

⅔ cup whole milk

½ teaspoon cayenne pepper

All-purpose flour, for dusting the work
    surface

Chili

1 tablespoon vegetable oil

1 pound ground chuck

1 medium yellow onion, chopped

1 green bell pepper, chopped

2 cans (14 ounces each) Mexican-style
    stewed tomatoes

1 can (15 ounces) kidney beans,
    rinsed and drained

2 tablespoons chili powder

1 teaspoon salt

Fixin's

Shredded sharp Cheddar cheese

Sour cream

Sliced scallions, white and light green
    parts only

Tortilla chips

Hot sauce

> ### DO AHEAD
> Make this meal as easy as can be by making up your biscuit bowls ahead of time. They will keep in an airtight container at room temperature for up to a week. The chili can be made a day or two before, as well.

1. Make the biscuit bowls: Preheat the oven to 450°F. Invert a standard-size muffin tin and coat the underside with cooking spray. In a bowl, stir together the baking mix, milk, and cayenne pepper to make a stiff dough. Shape into a ball. Dust a work surface with a small handful of flour and knead the dough 3 or 4 times. Divide the dough into 6 pieces and flatten each piece into a 6-inch round. Place 1 dough round over the back of each muffin cup and press around the cup to form a

bowl shape. Bake until lightly browned, 10 to 12 minutes. Let cool slightly on the pan, then remove the biscuit bowls and set aside while you make the chili to fill them with.

2. Make the chili: In a Dutch oven, heat the oil over medium heat. Add the beef and cook, breaking it up with a spoon, until most of the pink is gone, about 3 minutes. Add the onion and bell pepper and cook until the beef is completely browned and the vegetables are tender. Drain off any fat. Stir in the tomatoes, beans, chili powder, and salt. Bring the mixture to a boil. Reduce to a simmer, cover, and cook for 35 minutes.

3. To serve, spoon the hot chili into the biscuit bowls. Top with shredded Cheddar, sour cream, sliced scallions, and tortilla chips. And be sure to pass around extra toppings and hot sauce at the table.

TEXAS-STYLE CHILI

■ ■

Y'all, I love all kinds of chili. But traveling in Texas, especially around San Antonio, I got good and schooled in the matter. Texans take their chili seriously and don't go in for extra ingredients: just peppers, spices, and pieces of meat. Ground chuck will not cut it, and beans are not invited to the party. I came home with some new chili recipes and a ten-gallon hat. Well, y'all, I'm not from Texas, but I do love to tinker, so this is the Paula Deen salute to Texas chili.

SERVES 6 TO 8

3 tablespoons vegetable oil
3 pounds beef stew meat, cut into
   1½-inch chunks
Salt and black pepper
1 large yellow onion, chopped
2 cloves garlic, finely chopped

1 fresh jalapeño pepper, finely chopped
   (leave the seeds in if you want more heat)
3 tablespoons chili powder
2 teaspoons dried oregano
1½ teaspoons ground cumin
1 can (28 ounces) diced tomatoes
About ½ cup sour cream, for serving

1. In a large Dutch oven, heat the oil over medium-high heat until it shimmers. You want that oil good and hot. Lightly sprinkle the meat with salt and black pepper. Working in batches, cook the meat until well browned on all sides, 7 to 10 minutes per batch. Transfer the meat to a paper towel–lined plate to drain.

2. Add the onion, garlic, and jalapeño to the pan. Cook, stirring until softened, about 5 minutes. Stir in the chili powder, oregano, and cumin and cook for 1 minute. Stir in the tomatoes, 4 cups water, and 1 teaspoon salt and bring to a boil over high heat. Reduce immediately to a

simmer and cook, uncovered, until the meat shreds easily with a fork, 2½ to 3 hours. While it simmers, add extra water, as needed, to keep the meat covered with liquid.

3. Ladle into bowls and serve topped with a hearty dollop of sour cream.

CHOOSING CUTS

When shopping for stew meat, look for economical cuts like chuck or rump. Because they tend to be tougher, with lots of connective tissue that needs to be broken down, they take well to long, slow cooking. And that's exactly what you need for your stews and chilis. All that slow breaking down adds loads of flavor to the broth. You can go buy precut stew meat, but I prefer to cut my own from a whole piece of chuck.

CRUNCHY WIENER SCHNITZEL

■ ■

I like to think of Wiener schnitzel as Austria's answer to chicken-fried steak. The recipe is simple—the secret is to use real thin cutlets and fry them nice and hot. You'll wind up with the crispiest breaded coating that way. Veal is so tender and delicate, all these need to embellish them is a squeeze of lemon. I love to serve my Wiener schnitzel over potato salad with a green salad on the side for a fast meal that feels special.

SERVES 4

¾ cup all-purpose flour
1½ teaspoons Paula Deen's House Seasoning
   (page 435)
2 large eggs
1 cup dry bread crumbs

1½ pounds veal cutlets, ⅛ to ¼ inch thick
Vegetable oil, for frying
1 lemon, cut into wedges

1. In a shallow bowl, mix together the flour and ¾ teaspoon of the House Seasoning. In a separate shallow bowl, lightly beat the eggs. Put the bread crumbs in a third shallow bowl and season with the remaining ¾ teaspoon House Seasoning.

FLOUR POWER

You may wonder, why do I need to dip my meat in flour right before dipping it in egg? If you want your bread coating to stick to the meat, you have to do the flour first, then the egg, and then the bread. The flour acts as a sticky base to keep the egg and bread on the meat.

2. Dredge the veal in the seasoned flour, shaking off any excess, then dip into the egg, letting any excess drip off, and then coat well with the bread crumbs.

3. In a large skillet, heat ¼ inch of oil over medium-high heat. To make things a little easier on yourself, use two skillets at the same time if you have them. Working in batches, cook the veal until browned on both sides, 1½ to 2 minutes per side. Transfer to a paper towel–lined plate to drain. Serve as soon as possible, with the lemon wedges.

BASIC MEAT LOAF

■ ■

My dear sweet Aunt Peggy has done so much to help bring me and the boys along, supporting us financially when The Lady & Sons was just a dream I never thought I'd live to see, and showing us what family and love truly mean. She's also taught me just about as much about good cooking as anyone. This meat loaf is absolutely one of her classics. She wrote down the recipe for me when I first started my bag lunch business, The Bag Lady, way back when. Every time I make it now, it brings me back to all the wonderful meals we've enjoyed around our family table.

SERVES 4

Meat Loaf
1 pound ground beef
½ cup chopped yellow onion
½ cup chopped green bell pepper
1 large egg, lightly beaten
1 cup canned diced tomatoes, with juice
½ cup quick-cooking oats

1¼ teaspoons salt
¼ teaspoon black pepper

Topping
⅓ cup ketchup
2 tablespoons light brown sugar
1 tablespoon yellow mustard

1. Preheat the oven to 375°F. In a large bowl, combine the beef, onion, bell pepper, egg, tomatoes, oats, salt, and black pepper. Mix well with your hands. Place the mixture in a baking dish big enough to hold the meat loaf. Shape the meat mixture into a loaf about 8 by 3 inches.

2. In a small bowl, combine the ketchup, brown sugar, and mustard. Spread over the loaf. Bake for 1 hour, until well browned. Serve hot.

> **LEFTOVERS THAT DON'T LET YOU DOWN**
>
> I tell you, a meat loaf sandwich could give the hamburger a run for its money. My favorite way to enjoy leftover meat loaf is to place it between halves of a bun and top it with spicy ketchup or barbecue sauce, cheese slices, and lots of chopped iceberg lettuce.

CHEESEBURGER MEAT LOAF AND SAUCE

Cheeseburger Meat Loaf is one of those Paula Deen specialties that has taken on a life of its own. Adding cheese to your meat loaf is a no-brainer, and I just keep making it because it is so darn delicious that if I took it off the menu at the restaurant, there'd be a revolt. Oh, and get in there with your hands when you're mixing up a meat loaf. It's easier that way, so don't be shy.

SERVES 6 TO 8

Meat Loaf
2 pounds ground beef
2 teaspoons Paula Deen's House Seasoning (page 435)
1 teaspoon Lawry's Seasoned Salt
1 medium yellow onion, chopped
1 bell pepper, chopped
1 cup shredded Cheddar cheese (4 ounces)
1 cup crushed Ritz crackers

1 cup sour cream
¼ cup Worcestershire sauce
8 slices white bread

Sauce
1 can (10¾ ounces) condensed cream of mushroom soup
1 soup-can measure of milk
1½ cups shredded Cheddar cheese (6 ounces)

1. Make the meat loaf: Preheat the oven to 325°F. In a large bowl, combine the beef, House Seasoning, Lawry's salt, onion, bell pepper, Cheddar, cracker crumbs, sour cream, and Worcestershire sauce. Use your hands and make sure you mix the ingredients really well so they are thoroughly combined. Shape into a loaf about 8 by 3 inches.

2. Line a rimmed baking sheet with the bread slices and place the loaf on top. Bake the loaf until well browned, 45 minutes to 1 hour. Remove from the oven and discard the bread slices.

3. Meanwhile, make the sauce: In a medium saucepan, heat the soup and milk over medium heat. Add the Cheddar and stir until the cheese is melted.

4. Slice the meat loaf and serve topped with the sauce or pass the sauce at the table.

SOAK UP THE GREASE

If there's one thing I don't like, it's when my meat loaf comes out of the oven swimming in grease. The white bread slices in this recipe are an ingenious way of soaking up that grease as the meat loaf cooks.

Clockwise from top left: Family Reunion Deviled Eggs (page 25); Hot Pimiento Cheese Dip (page 14); Cheese Straws (page 22); Ham Biscuits (page 17); Baked Brie with Fig Jam (page 15).

Fried Chicken Salad (page 44).

Brunswick Stew (page 73) with Fluffy Sweet Potato Biscuits (page 279).

She-Crab Soup (page 80).

Baked Ham 'n' Egg Cups (page 91).

Praline French Toast Casserole (page 100).

My Favorite Lasagna (page 108).

Chicken-Fried Steak with Cream Gravy (page 127).

Red Wine Beef Stew (page 128) with Buttery Buttermilk Mashed Potatoes (page 248).

Paula's Famous Foolproof Standing Rib Roast (page 129).

Southern Chili in a Biscuit Bowl (page 134).

Turnip Mashed Potatoes (page 249) and Cheeseburger Meat Loaf and Sauce (page 138).

Easy Chicken and Dumplin's (page 167).

The Lady & Sons Chicken Pot Pie (page 168).

Skillet Chicken and Sausage Jambalaya (page 171).

Country Captain Chicken (page 174).

Savannah Crab Cakes (page 197).

Catfish Po' Boy (page 205) and Coleslaw with Raisins, Dill, and Honey-Roasted Peanuts (page 49).

THE LADY & SONS
SMOKED BOSTON BUTT ROAST

■ ■

I love cooking a big hunk of pork like this—it feeds so many people and comes out so moist and flavorful. All you need to do is season it a bit and then give it time in the oven so the fat inside starts to render out. Serve it sliced for a sit-down dinner, or chop some to pile on rolls with barbecue sauce for a picnic lunch. Heck, this recipe feeds so many, you could do both!

SERVES 12 TO 15

One 8-pound bone-in pork butt roast (also sold as shoulder)
4 tablespoons Paula Deen's House Seasoning (page 435)

2 tablespoons Paula Deen Collection Seasoned Salt, or other seasoned salt
¼ cup liquid smoke
1 medium yellow onion, sliced
3 bay leaves

1. Sprinkle one side of the roast with 2 tablespoons of the House Seasoning, rubbing it in well. Flip the roast over and sprinkle with the remaining 2 tablespoons House Seasoning, rubbing it in well. Repeat this process with the seasoned salt and the liquid smoke and let the meat rest, covered, in the refrigerator for at least 2 hours or overnight.

2. Preheat the oven to 350°F. Place the roast in a large roasting pan. Add the onion, bay leaves, and 1 cup water. Cover with foil and bake until an instant-read meat thermometer inserted in the center of the roast registers 170°F, 2½ to 3 hours. Let the roast rest for 15 to 20 minutes before slicing.

SIT AND SOAK

To get the full flavor of this roasted pork butt, make sure you give it ample time to sit in the seasonings: a minimum of 2 hours, though overnight is always best. This pork butt is such a large hunk o' meat, it needs the time to soak up all that flavorful goodness.

PULLED PORK BBQ

■ ■

Good old white bread buns piled with pulled pork and barbecue sauce, some mayo or coleslaw, all topped off with dill pickles: my idea of heaven in a sandwich. Michael does this recipe in the smoker we have in our backyard, and if you've got one, try it. The extra smoke flavor is wonderful. But, y'all, I do mine in the oven so I can enjoy this heavenly sandwich year-round. You got to cook your pork till it just about melts. And invite friends to join in pulling the pork! Hand everyone a couple forks and show them how to shred the meat up instead of cutting it, so you get nice strands that hold on to the tangy sauce.

SERVES 8

Pulled Pork
2 tablespoons dark brown sugar
2 tablespoons paprika
1½ tablespoons salt
1½ tablespoons black pepper
1 tablespoon ground cumin
1½ teaspoons cayenne pepper
1 teaspoon garlic powder
1 teaspoon mustard powder
One 4-pound boneless pork butt
   or shoulder roast
2 cups apple juice

1 cup apple cider vinegar
1½ tablespoons Worcestershire sauce

BBQ Sauce
1½ cups ketchup
⅓ cup molasses
¼ cup fresh lemon juice
1½ tablespoons Worcestershire sauce
1½ teaspoons mustard powder
1 teaspoon onion powder
½ teaspoon cayenne pepper

8 hamburger buns (optional)

1. To make the pulled pork: In a small bowl, combine the brown sugar, paprika, salt, black pepper, cumin, cayenne pepper, garlic powder, and mustard powder. Place the meat in a large bowl and rub the mixture all over. Cover with plastic wrap and refrigerate for at least 2 hours or overnight.

2. When you are ready to cook the pork, preheat the oven to 325°F. Pour the apple juice, vinegar, and Worcestershire sauce into a large Dutch oven. Place the pork in the pot and tightly cover it with foil, then the lid. Bake until the meat is fork tender and shreds easily, about 4 hours, basting the roast with the cooking juices about every hour.

3. Meanwhile, make the barbecue sauce: In a small saucepan, combine the ketchup, molasses, lemon juice, Worcestershire sauce, mustard powder, onion powder, and cayenne pepper. Bring to a simmer over medium-low heat and cook for 15 minutes, then remove from the heat.

4. Remove the meat from the oven and let stand until cool enough to handle. Shred the pork into strands with a fork or tongs. Toss with the barbecue sauce and serve, sandwiched in buns if you'd like.

Use your fingers to pull apart and shred the pork.

HANDS ON

While a fork or tongs will do just fine, I prefer to pull my pork by hand. That way, I can fish out any remaining fat or gristle that I sure don't want to serve up to my guests. But no matter which way you choose to do it, make sure you pull the pork. Slicing or dicing with a knife will only make it dry out.

HAM STEAKS WITH REDEYE GRAVY

I love stories about cowboys pouring black coffee into a skillet to make redeye gravy, but I take my coffee with cream and sugar, so this is redeye gravy Paula style, smoothed out with a little cream and just a kiss of brown sugar. It is such a fine, tasty sauce, I just have to serve my ham over grits for soaking up every bit.

SERVES 2 TO 3

1 tablespoon butter
One 1-pound ham steak (½ inch thick)
1 cup brewed coffee

¼ cup heavy cream
1 teaspoon light brown sugar

1. In a large skillet, melt the butter over medium-high heat. Add the ham steak and cook until browned on both sides, about 2 minutes per side. Transfer to a warm platter.

2. Add the coffee, cream, and brown sugar to the skillet and bring to a boil, scraping up any browned bits from the bottom of the pan. Serve the ham topped with the gravy. I tell you, this is a real pick-me-up!

THE HAM BISCUIT

You know another way I love to serve this dish? Take a biscuit, cut it in half, and soak each side with plenty of that redeye gravy. Then put slices of that ham steak between those biscuit sides and, well, you have yourself a meal.

FRIED PORK CHOPS WITH TOMATO GRAVY

■ ■

Is there one dinner that you can just make with your eyes closed? Well, for me it would have to be fried pork chops along with red beans and rice. I sit down to that meal and I know all is right.

SERVES 4

4 bone-in center-cut pork chops (1 inch thick, ½ pound each)
Salt and black pepper
¼ teaspoon garlic powder
3 tablespoons olive oil
4 tablespoons (½ stick) butter

2 tablespoons finely chopped onion
¼ cup all-purpose flour
1½ cups whole milk
½ cup chicken broth or water
1 can (14½ ounces) diced tomatoes, drained

1. Lightly sprinkle the chops on both sides with salt and black pepper, then sprinkle with the garlic powder. In a large skillet, heat the oil over medium-high heat. Add the chops and cook, without moving, until a dark golden crust forms on the bottom of each, 5 to 6 minutes. Flip the chops and cook for 5 minutes more. Transfer to a paper towel–lined plate to drain.

2. Add the butter to the skillet and melt. Add the onion and cook, stirring, until softened, about 5 minutes. Go ahead and reduce the heat if the onion starts to brown too quickly. Sprinkle the flour over the onion and cook, stirring, for 1 minute. Slowly whisk in the milk, then the broth or water. Simmer the mixture until thickened, about 5 minutes. Whisk in the tomatoes, ½ teaspoon salt, and ¼ teaspoon black pepper. Spoon the sauce over the pork chops and serve up to a hungry family.

SEAL IN THE FLAVOR

Searing meat is a really important step in producing the juiciest meat possible. When the meat first hits the pan, make sure you leave it be as it develops a nice crust in that oil or butter. This will lock in all the flavor and moistness and leave you with just the nicest texture—a little crunch on the outside and tenderness on the inside. Doesn't that just make your mouth water thinking about it?

BBQ PORK RIBS

Y'all, there are few things simpler to make than oven-barbecued ribs, and they come out so succulent you won't believe it. You can use other cuts of pork ribs here, but I love to sink my teeth into big, meaty country-style ribs. Just count on seasoning them the night before (or at least a few hours ahead) so the meat is seasoned all the way through before you pop them in the oven. I love to serve my ribs with warm Angel Biscuits (page 275) and a little bowl of extra barbecue sauce.

SERVES 6

5 pounds bone-in country-style pork ribs
Salt and black pepper
1 teaspoon garlic powder

Daddy's Tangy Grilling Sauce (page 212),
for basting

1. Remove the white membrane from the bony side of the rack of ribs. Season the ribs generously all over with salt and black pepper. Sprinkle all over with the garlic powder. Cover the ribs and refrigerate for at least 4 hours or overnight.

2. When you are ready to cook the ribs, preheat the oven to 300°F. Pour half the sauce into the bottom of a roasting pan. Add the ribs to the pan, turning them to coat evenly with the sauce. Cover the pan tightly with foil and bake for 1½ hours. Uncover the ribs and pour the remaining sauce over them. Replace the foil and continue baking until the meat is nearly falling off the bone, 1 to 1½ hours longer. Let rest for 5 minutes before slicing into individual ribs. Serve up to a hungry crowd and be sure to pass around plenty of extra napkins!

DO IT ON THE GRILL

If you feel like gettin' outside, you can do this barbecued pork on the grill. Same idea as the oven. Cook it in the pan over indirect heat with the grill cover on. To create indirect heat, start the charcoal as usual and then push the coals to either side of the grill, creating an area in the middle that does not have coals burning directly underneath. If using a gas grill, leave the center burner unlit, but light burners to each side of this burner on medium. Place the pan with the ribs over the center and grill until done.

ROASTED PORK RIBS
WITH SAUERKRAUT AND APPLES

■ ■

The flavors of apple and cabbage are so delicious with pork ribs, and this recipe falls into one of my favorite categories: set-it-and-forget-it. After a few hours, your whole house will smell like heaven and you'll have a comforting meal that will satisfy even the heartiest meat-and-potato types. In fact, I love to serve potatoes—mashed, baked, or in a salad—alongside these ribs. Call it Oktoberfest, Paula style.

SERVES 4

5 pounds bone-in, country-style
    pork ribs
Salt and black pepper
2½ teaspoons paprika
3 tablespoons olive oil
4 tablespoons (½ stick) butter

2 Granny Smith apples (¾ pound),
    unpeeled and cut into ¼-inch-thick slices
1 yellow onion, thinly sliced
½ cup white wine
1 bag (32 ounces) sauerkraut, drained
1 bay leaf

1. Preheat the oven to 325°F.

2. Remove the white membrane from the bony side of the rack of ribs. Season the ribs generously all over with salt and black pepper. Sprinkle the paprika over the ribs. Coat the ribs evenly with the oil.

3. In a large skillet, melt the butter over medium heat. Add the apples and onion and cook, stirring, until both are golden, about 10 minutes. Season with ½ teaspoon salt and ½ teaspoon black pepper. Pour in the wine and simmer for 2 minutes, scraping up any browned bits from the bottom of the pan.

4. Transfer the apple-onion mixture to a large roasting pan. Add the sauerkraut and bay leaf; toss the mixture well to combine. Nestle the ribs on top of the sauerkraut. Cover the pan with foil. Bake until the ribs are very tender and falling off the bone, 2½ to 3 hours. Remove and discard the bay leaf. Serve immediately, alongside the sauerkraut.

STICK TO YOUR RIBS

Country-style pork ribs are cut from the shoulder blade end of the pork rib. They are packed with meat and have plenty of fat that will break down during this long cook to give the sauerkraut loads of flavor.

CROWN ROAST OF PORK

■ ■

Now, I don't think of myself as a drama queen, but I sure do love to put on a show, and few dishes that I make get quite as many "Ooh's" and "Ahh's" as this one. A crown roast is made up of two rib sections tied (your butcher will take care of this; just ask) into a standing ring just like a crown. Stuffed in the middle with a true Southern corn bread dressing, it is a meal fit for royalty, and I look for occasions to serve it.

SERVES 6 TO 8

Pork

3 tablespoons olive oil

4 cloves garlic, finely chopped

1 tablespoon dried thyme

1½ teaspoons salt

1 teaspoon black pepper

One 5-pound crown roast of pork, rib ends
 frenched (see box, page 148)

Stuffing

4 tablespoons (½ stick) butter

1 large green bell pepper, chopped

¾ cup sliced scallions

1 celery stalk, chopped

2 cloves garlic, finely chopped

1 fresh jalapeño pepper, finely chopped
 (include some seeds if you want more heat)

6 cups crumbled corn bread

2 large eggs, lightly beaten

½ cup chopped fresh cilantro

½ teaspoon cayenne pepper

½ teaspoon salt

¼ teaspoon black pepper

2 cups chicken broth, plus more if needed

1. To prepare the pork: In a bowl, combine the oil, garlic, thyme, salt, and black pepper. Rub the mixture all over the roast, making sure to cover the areas between the chops. Transfer to a roasting pan. Cover well with plastic wrap and refrigerate for at least 4 hours or overnight.

2. When you are ready to cook the roast, preheat the oven to 450°F. Turn the roast upside down (rib bones down) in the roasting pan. Roast for 15 minutes. Reduce the oven temperature to 350°F and roast until an instant-read meat thermometer registers 155°F when inserted 2 inches into the center of the meat, about 1½ hours longer.

3. Meanwhile, prepare the stuffing. In a large skillet, melt the butter over medium-high heat. Add the bell pepper, scallions, celery, garlic, and jalapeño. Cook until the vegetables are softened, 5 to 7 minutes. Transfer to a large bowl.

4. Add the crumbled corn bread to the sautéed vegetables. Add the eggs, cilantro, cayenne pepper, salt, and black pepper; stir to combine. Stir in the 2 cups broth. Stir in more broth, if needed, so

the stuffing is moistened. Grease a shallow 2-quart baking dish with butter, oil, or cooking spray. Press the stuffing into the baking dish. Thirty minutes before removing the roast, place the stuffing in the oven and bake until golden, about 45 minutes.

5. When the roast is done, remove it from the oven, tent with foil, and let stand for at least 15 minutes. Cut the string. When the stuffing is done, mound half of it on a serving platter. Flip the roast upright on top of the stuffing. Fill the center of the roast with the remaining stuffing. Slice at the table to a chorus of "Ooh's" and "Ahh's."

GIVE IT A REST

Resting meat is one of the most important steps in serving it perfectly cooked. By resting the meat, you ensure that all the meat juices stay locked in and don't come spilling out all over your cutting board when you slice into it. I like to tent foil over my roast when it's resting so that it stays nice and warm. Never cover it tightly, or it will stew under there and lose the nice crust it's formed.

BAKED SUGARED HAM

■ ■

Baked ham may be the food that gives Southerners their taste for salty-sweet foods. I adore the combination and consider a beautiful baked ham to be the perfect centerpiece for Christmas, a New Year's buffet, an open house, or any other festive occasion.

SERVES 10

One 10-pound whole cured ham
¾ cup packed light brown sugar
3 tablespoons brown or Dijon mustard

1½ tablespoons apple cider vinegar
1 teaspoon black pepper

1. Preheat the oven to 350°F. Place a roasting rack in a large roasting pan. Score the fat of the ham in a diamond pattern (see box opposite). Place the ham on the roasting rack. Bake for 2 hours.

2. Meanwhile, in a small bowl, whisk together the brown sugar, mustard, vinegar, and black pepper.

3. Remove the ham from the oven and spread the glaze all over the ham. Return the ham to the oven and bake until the glaze is thick and slightly caramelized, 30 to 40 minutes longer.

4. Transfer the ham to a cutting board and let it rest for 15 minutes before slicing and serving.

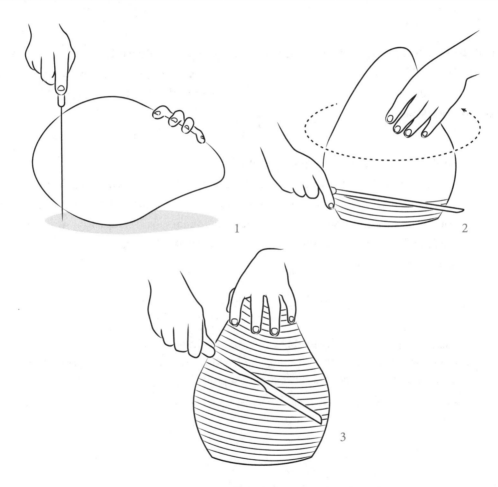

To carve a whole ham, create a flat surface by cutting a few slices from one of the long sides of the ham, then place that side flat on the cutting board. Starting at the shank end, make even cuts perpendicular to the bone using a long, sharp knife, working your way around the bone in a spiral fashion. Cut parallel to the bone to free the slices.

RACK OF LAMB WITH ROSEMARY

■ ■

Down in parts of Georgia, some folks never did quite take to serving ham on Easter. If sheep grazed in the area, you could just as easily see lamb on the menu. These days, most butchers can sell you a beautiful rack of lamb. I love rosemary's herby fresh flavor, which goes so beautifully with the taste of lamb.

SERVES 4

Two 14- to 16-rib racks of lamb (1½ pounds
    each), rib ends frenched (see box)
1½ teaspoons salt
1 teaspoon black pepper

2 tablespoons olive oil
¼ cup chopped fresh rosemary
4 cloves garlic, finely chopped

1. Preheat the broiler. Line a baking sheet with foil.

2. Sprinkle the lamb all over with the salt and black pepper. Rub it with the oil, then the rosemary and garlic. Transfer the lamb, fatty side up, to the baking sheet. Broil, turning over once halfway through the cooking time, until it reaches the doneness you like, 7 to 8 minutes total for medium-rare (125°F on a meat thermometer). Let the meat rest for 5 minutes before carving into individual chops and serving.

FRENCH CUT

Ask your butcher to french your racks of lamb. He will cut into the meat at the end of the bone and scrape it off so that the bone is exposed. Your lamb will look so much prettier at the table. It's all in the presentation, folks!

GRILLADES AND GRITS

■ ■

You know you're cooking Louisiana style when you've got celery and peppers in your pan and a thick dark roux made with flour and fat. All together, this is one heck of a flavorful mess of sliced pork and deep, rich sauce. It was just made to serve over steaming-hot grits, with a bottle of hot sauce on the side. If you want to, serve Cheese Straws (page 22) as a garnish.

SERVES 8

Grillades

One 3-pound boneless pork butt or pork
    shoulder, cut into ½-inch pieces
Paula Deen's House Seasoning (page 435)
⅓ cup plus ¼ cup all-purpose flour
4 tablespoons bacon fat
8 tablespoons (1 stick) butter
1 large bell pepper, chopped
1 medium yellow onion, chopped
1 cup chopped celery
3 large cloves garlic, finely chopped
4 cups beef broth or water
3 bay leaves
1 teaspoon dried thyme
2 tablespoons hot sauce

1 tablespoon Worcestershire sauce
1 teaspoon dried basil
1 teaspoon salt
1 teaspoon black pepper
1 can (10 ounces) extra-spicy tomatoes (such
    as Ro*Tel)
4 large fresh tomatoes, peeled and quartered
½ cup chopped fresh parsley

Grits

1¼ cups whole milk
1 teaspoon salt
1 cup quick-cooking grits (not instant)
4 tablespoons (½ stick) butter

    1. To prepare the grillades: Sprinkle the meat with the House Seasoning. Dust with the ⅓ cup of the flour and toss together lightly.

    2. Heat the bacon fat and 4 tablespoons of the butter over medium-high heat in a Dutch oven until very hot. Working in batches, add the meat and brown all over, 5 to 7 minutes. Transfer to a large bowl using a slotted spoon.

    3. Add the bell pepper, onion, celery, and garlic to the Dutch oven and cook, stirring, until softened and just beginning to brown, 8 to 10 minutes. Transfer the vegetables to the bowl with the meat using a slotted spoon, leaving a total of 3 tablespoons of fat in your Dutch oven.

    4. Add the ¼ cup flour to the Dutch oven and cook over medium heat, stirring constantly and slowly, until the flour is a nice deep brown, about 5 minutes; take care not to burn the flour. Slowly

MEAT   149

add the broth or water and stir. Bring to a simmer. Return the meat and vegetables to the pan. Add the bay leaves, thyme, hot sauce, Worcestershire sauce, basil, salt, and black pepper and stir. Add the canned tomatoes and simmer, stirring occasionally, until the pork is tender, about 1½ hours.

5. Meanwhile, make the grits: In a small saucepan, combine the milk, salt, and 2 cups water. Bring to a boil and add the grits in a slow stream, stirring constantly until well mixed. Let the mixture return to a boil, cover, reduce to a simmer, and cook for about 30 minutes, stirring from time to time. Add more water, if it needs it. Grits are done when they have the consistency of smooth cream of wheat. Stir in the butter.

6. Just before serving, discard the bay leaves from the grillades. Stir in the fresh tomatoes and parsley.

7. Ladle the grits into bowls and top each with 1½ teaspoons of the butter and the grillades.

YOU SAY TOMATO

If you can't get your hands on the extra-spicy Ro*Tel tomatoes, have no fear. Just substitute the same amount of other spicy diced tomatoes, or use regular diced tomatoes and add some minced jalapeños or hot sauce for some heat.

MICHAEL'S FAVORITE OXTAIL STEW

I believe I've already shared with y'all the secret to my steamy marriage and it is this soup. Chocolate-covered strawberries and Champagne may be sweet, but this simple, slow-cooked ox-tail soup will melt any man. It is a proven aphrodisiac, in my experience—not to mention a darn good bowl of tender, beefy soup to serve with rice. And what you do with yourselves while it's cooking in the slow cooker is up to you.

SERVES 4 TO 6

2½ pounds beef oxtails, cut into 1½-inch-thick slices

1 tablespoon Paula Deen's House Seasoning (page 435)

4 teaspoons soy sauce

2 large Spanish onions, thinly sliced

2 bay leaves

4 cups cooked rice, for serving

Sprinkle the oxtails with the House Seasoning and toss with the soy sauce. Place the oxtails in a slow cooker and add the onions and bay leaves. Cover and cook on high for 5 to 6 hours, until tender. Discard the bay leaves. Serve over a fluffy bed of rice.

MORE ABOUT OXTAILS
This beef cut has a large bone and is very gelatinous, making it just the right cut for long, slow stews.

Chapter 7

POULTRY

There have been chickens scratching around front yards and backyards for most of Southern history. You'll spot fewer yard birds these days, but Southern tables still regularly feature a beautiful platter of fried or baked chicken. Sunday suppers, revival dinners, church suppers, covered-dish dinners . . . there is no end of occasions that call for chicken in the South, and I do believe that Southern cooks have created some of the best chicken recipes in the world. Make a batch of my Best Ever Southern Fried Chicken (page 159) if you're looking to decide the matter.

Folks used to argue over who was going to have the preacher over after Sunday service. And you knew that wherever you ate, whatever else was served, at the center of that table was fried chicken. It was common for the woman of the house to run out, catch the chicken, bring it back, and prepare the meal right then. Thank goodness we don't have to do that today, but you do want a good fresh bird. Nowadays they grow some big, fat hens, but the sweetest chicken in the world is a 2½-pound bird. They're called fryers for a reason. Smaller birds get nicely and evenly browned, and they have such good flavor.

Big old stewing hens that weigh 4 pounds and up have a purpose, too. I like a nice big chicken for my Chicken and Dumplin's (page 164). That is one of the most important chicken dishes to me, because it was my daddy's favorite. I was nineteen when he died, and I remember calling my grandmama and saying, "I want to come get you and go to the grocery store and have you teach me how to make those chicken and dumplings." Tasting it brings his memory back.

I also like those great big chickens for any slower-cooking recipe, such as The Lady & Sons Chicken Potpie (page 168) or Chicken Bog (page 169), which is a soupy South Carolina rice dish and one of earth's greatest comfort foods. You know, with so many wonderful ways to enjoy chicken, I have never once grown tired of it. I don't expect I will. But I do mix things up from time to time by cooking up a turkey instead. Michael and I adore turkey too much to wait until Thanksgiving, so I'll do Pot-Roasted Turkey Breast with Vegetables (page 175). And then for Thanksgiving I'll make my Classic Roast Turkey and Dressing (page 177).

Beyond raising chickens and turkeys, folks down South always hunted birds in the fall. I remember as a child that it was not unusual at all for President Eisenhower to fly into Darden County, Georgia, for quail and dove. We love our game birds. And for holidays and other special meals, I occasionally cook Molasses Game Hens (page 179) for something out of the ordinary. And you know, the number one dish at my sweet niece Corrie's wedding was Quails in Gravy (page 180).

Whether you cook up a dainty little quail or just a big mess of Skillet Chicken and Sausage Jambalaya (page 171), I never met a person who's tired of poultry.

BAKED CHICKEN AND PINEAPPLE CASSEROLE

If you're like me, the combination of sweet and salty, along with a dash of spice, is just so good you can hardly stand it. That's what I was aiming for when I whipped up this casserole, along with a nice crunch from a cheesy Ritz cracker topping, and oh, boy, let me tell you, it is all that. I find that children love to hold on to a drumstick, so I make these with a mix of thighs for the knife-and-fork set and legs for the ankle biters.

SERVES 4

1½ tablespoons vegetable oil
2 to 2½ pounds whole chicken legs
    (drumsticks and thighs)
Salt and black pepper
2 cans (8 ounces each) crushed pineapple,
    drained

1½ teaspoons hot sauce
1 cup crushed Ritz or saltine crackers
4 tablespoons (½ stick) butter,
    melted
1 cup shredded Cheddar cheese
    (4 ounces)

1. Preheat the oven to 375°F. Grease a 13 by 9-inch baking dish (attractive enough to come to the table) or coat with cooking spray.

2. In a large skillet, heat the oil over medium-high heat. Lightly season the chicken all over with salt and black pepper. In batches if necessary, place the chicken in the hot oil and cook, turning once, until golden brown, about 8 minutes. Transfer the chicken to a paper towel–lined plate to drain.

3. In a small bowl, toss together the pineapple and hot sauce. Spread evenly on the bottom of the prepared baking dish. Place the chicken on top of the pineapple. In a small bowl, combine the crackers, butter, and Cheddar. Scatter the mixture over the top of the chicken and pineapple.

4. Bake until the topping is melted and golden and the chicken is just cooked through, about 45 minutes. Bring straight to the table in the baking dish.

SOME FRESH IDEAS
Try adding a little freshly squeezed lemon juice to this casserole, about a tablespoon or so, to give it a sweet-and-sour flavor. And give it some extra crunch and color by scattering sliced scallions over the top just before setting it on the table.

GLAZED BACON-WRAPPED CHICKEN

■ ■

I had been serving bacon-wrapped chicken bites as an appetizer for years, and one day, well, I just wanted more. So I said to myself, "Paula, why not make these the main course?" Then I jumped into my kitchen and adjusted my recipe to turn it into these beauties. That slightly spicy orange-soy glaze, along with your salty bacon and a kiss of garlic, hits just about every flavor note you could need, and the bacon keeps the chicken nice and moist. I figured this one would be a winner right off the bat, but I recall the boys were over at the house when I made it, so I let them try it. When I turned around and the plate was empty, I had my proof.

SERVES 4

⅓ cup soy sauce

¼ cup orange juice

1 tablespoon hot sauce

1½ tablespoons finely chopped garlic

8 boneless, skinless chicken thighs (about
  2 pounds), halved

8 slices bacon, halved crosswise

1 cup packed light brown sugar

1. In a medium bowl, combine the soy sauce, orange juice, hot sauce, and garlic. Add the chicken to the bowl and toss to coat well with the marinade. Cover with plastic wrap and refrigerate for 2 hours.

2. Preheat the oven to 375°F. Line a rimmed baking sheet with foil and grease a wire cooling rack or coat with cooking spray. Place the rack on the baking sheet.

3. Remove the chicken from the marinade, letting any excess drip off. Wrap a bacon slice around each piece of thigh. Secure the bacon with a toothpick.

4. Crumble the brown sugar into a bowl. Dip each bacon-wrapped thigh into the sugar, taking care to coat evenly. Place the chicken on the prepared rack. Bake, turning once, until the bacon is crisp, the chicken is cooked through, and the house smells of sweetness, about 30 minutes.

> **TRY ANOTHER WRAP**
> If you're serving this to someone who doesn't eat pork, you can substitute turkey bacon.

BEST EVER SOUTHERN FRIED CHICKEN

■ ■

In my book, a well-fried chicken is among life's greatest accomplishments, and I can truthfully claim that I wouldn't be where I am without the fried chicken recipe I'm sharing with y'all here. You could say I am practically made of Southern fried chicken—certainly I grew up eating and cooking it. I use some hot sauce to season the crust, and I love to fry in shortening, which gives the crust a particularly crunchy texture. But I don't see the need for any other tricks and frills with a skillet of fried chicken: some things in life cannot be improved upon.

SERVES 4

3 large eggs
2 cups self-rising flour
Black pepper and salt

1 whole chicken (1 to 2½ pounds), rinsed,
    patted dry, and cut into 8 pieces
Solid vegetable shortening, for deep-frying

1. In a shallow bowl, lightly beat the eggs with ⅓ cup water. In a separate shallow bowl, combine the flour and 1 teaspoon black pepper. Lightly season the chicken all over with salt and black pepper. Dip the chicken pieces in the egg mixture, letting any excess drip off, and then coat well in the flour mixture.

2. In a large skillet, heat the shortening over medium-high heat until it melts and reaches 350°F on a deep-fry thermometer; you'll want a depth of 2 inches. Add the chicken and cook until browned and crisp, 13 to 14 minutes for the dark meat and 8 to 10 minutes for the white meat. And just like that, you've got yourself the best ever Southern fried chicken.

TAKING THE TEMPERATURE

Be extra careful when using a deep fry thermometer. And make sure it doesn't have any moisture on it that can make the oil spatter. Insert it into the melted shortening, angling it away from the bottom of the pan so you get an accurate read on the temperature of the oil—not the bottom of the pan!

EASY OVEN "FRIED" CHICKEN

■ ■

Take it from Auntie Paula, no matter how much you adore fried chicken, you just can't eat it every day. This oven "fried" version is another matter, though. It's not only perfectly healthy and simple enough for a weeknight (you can start it marinating in the morning), it is also darn crispy outside and moist inside. No need to deny yourself here! And if you want to make this even healthier, just peel off the skin right before eating.

SERVES 4

1 whole chicken (3 to 3½ pounds), rinsed, patted dry, and cut into 8 pieces
Salt and black pepper
¾ cup buttermilk
1½ tablespoons Dijon mustard

2 cloves garlic, finely chopped
1½ teaspoons hot sauce
1 cup self-rising flour
Cooking spray, for coating the chicken

1. Lightly season the chicken all over with salt. Season the chicken generously with black pepper (at least ½ teaspoon). In a large bowl, combine the buttermilk, mustard, garlic, and hot sauce. Add the chicken to the marinade, turning to coat evenly with the mixture. Cover with plastic wrap and refrigerate for at least 30 minutes or up to 8 hours.

2. When you are ready to cook the chicken, preheat the oven to 425°F. Place a wire rack on top of a large rimmed baking sheet.

3. In a large resealable plastic bag, combine the flour and ½ teaspoon black pepper. Remove the chicken from the marinade, letting the excess drip off, and transfer to the bag. Close it up tightly and give it a good shake until the chicken is coated all over with the flour mixture.

4. Transfer the chicken to the wire rack. Coat the chicken generously all over with cooking spray. Bake, turning every 15 minutes or so, until the chicken is crispy, browned, and cooked through, 40 to 50 minutes.

BUTTER ME UP

For fixing my oven "fried" chicken, a buttermilk marinade is the way to go. It's the buttermilk that prevents the chicken from going dry on you when you cook it and gives it a tangy flavor.

PECAN-CRUSTED CHICKEN BREASTS

With their crunchy, nutty coating, these breasts are my version of chicken fingers and nuggets. My grandbaby Jack will tell you he's a big boy now, but he has adored this recipe since the day he was old enough to eat it. Then again, grown-ups love it, too, thanks to the sweet pecan and panko bread crumb crust. I keep this recipe fairly lean by baking the chicken, so go ahead and add this to your weekly rotation if your family loves it as much as mine does.

SERVES 4

4 boneless, skinless chicken breasts
   (½ pound each)
1½ teaspoons salt
½ teaspoon black pepper

4 teaspoons mayonnaise
¾ cup pecans, crushed
¾ cup panko bread crumbs

1. Place an oven rack in the upper third of the oven and preheat to 350°F. Lightly grease a baking dish or coat with cooking spray.

2. Sprinkle the chicken with 1 teaspoon of the salt and the black pepper. Coat each breast with 1 teaspoon mayonnaise. In a shallow dish, toss the pecans and bread crumbs together. Dredge the chicken in the bread crumb mixture, pressing firmly to make sure it sticks well to the chicken. Season with the remaining ½ teaspoon salt and place in the prepared baking dish. Bake until the crust is nicely browned and the chicken is cooked through, 30 to 40 minutes.

GO NUTS

This recipe works well with all kinds of nuts. Change it up by using cashews, almonds, or even macadamias if you're feeling really rich.

Place the pecans between two paper towels and crush by rolling a rolling pin back and forth over the paper towels.

SUNDAY BAKED CHICKEN

■ ■

Sunday supper is a chicken meal in most Southern homes. This recipe for a simple, bronze-skinned bird offers the added bonus of veggies—carrots and potatoes—cooked right alongside it. The pan juices make those sweet carrots and tender potatoes out of this world. All you need to fix while the chicken is roasting is something green, maybe a salad or a plate of simmered green beans. And sop up those pan juices with my Skillet Corn Bread (page 273) for the ultimate Sunday supper!

SERVES 4

4 tablespoons (½ stick) butter,
   at room temperature
1 teaspoon black pepper
1 teaspoon dried thyme
½ teaspoon paprika

1 whole chicken (3½ pounds),
   rinsed and patted dry
2 teaspoons salt
1 pound Yukon Gold potatoes, halved
½ pound carrots, halved crosswise
4 cloves garlic, unpeeled

1. Preheat the oven to 375°F.

2. In a bowl, mash together the butter, ½ teaspoon of the black pepper, the thyme, and paprika. Sprinkle the chicken inside and out with the salt and the remaining ½ teaspoon black pepper. Rub the chicken all over with the butter mixture, spreading it as evenly as possible so the chicken will brown evenly.

PREPPING YOUR BIRD

To get a nice crisp on the chicken skin, make sure you pat that bird good and dry before you season and cook it. Then, tuck the wings under the bird and tie the legs together with kitchen string. This little trick turns the bird into a tight little package so that it cooks evenly all over.

Pierce the chicken in the thickest part of the thigh. If the juices run clear (no pink or red), then the chicken is done.

3. Scatter the potatoes, carrots, and garlic in the bottom of a large roasting pan. Top the vegetables with a roasting rack. Place the chicken on the rack, breast side up. Roast, stirring the vegetables occasionally, until the chicken is golden, the thigh juices run clear when pierced with a knife, or the temperature registers 180°F in the thigh, about 1½ hours.

4. Transfer the chicken to a cutting board to rest for 5 minutes before carving. Serve with the vegetables and pan juices.

OLD-FASHIONED CREAMED CHICKEN

■ ■ ■ ■ ■ ■ ■ ■ ■ ■ ■ ■ ■ ■ ■ ■ ■ ■ POULTRY ■ ■ ■ ■ ■ ■ ■ ■ ■ ■ ■ ■ ■ ■ ■ ■ ■ ■

When someone says "creamed," my ears perk right up. Oh, how I adore old-timey dishes like this one. I jump up to make this whenever we've got leftover chicken breasts. The lovely white sauce keeps the meat tender and moist. Serve this classic over egg noodles, toast, or waffles (or see the box for other suggestions).

SERVES 4

1 tablespoon butter
1 tablespoon all-purpose flour
½ cup chicken broth
½ cup half-and-half
1 tablespoon dry sherry

2 cups chopped cooked chicken breast
½ teaspoon dried thyme
Salt and black pepper
1 to 2 tablespoons chopped fresh parsley
   or scallions, for garnish

1. In a medium saucepan, melt the butter over medium heat. Whisk in the flour and cook, stirring constantly, until bubbling, about 1 minute. Whisk in the broth, half-and-half, and sherry. Bring to a boil, whisking frequently. Reduce to a simmer and cook, stirring, until nice and thick, 3 to 5 minutes.

2. Stir in the chicken, thyme, and salt and black pepper to taste, and warm through. Serve garnished with parsley or scallions.

A SOUTHERN COMFORT
You can serve this comfort food on just about anything. Try it in baked frozen pastry shells or over homemade biscuits, corn bread, or rice.

PAULA'S CHICKEN AND DUMPLIN'S

I never saw a dumplin' I didn't like. And I especially love chicken and dumplin's because it was my daddy's favorite dish. When he passed and I asked my grandmama for the recipe, she taught me how to do rolled dumplin's like these. To make them correctly, you mix your dough with ice water, then roll it out real thin on the kitchen table. It takes some elbow grease: What you want is a dough that puts up a little bit of a fight, so you end up with a real thin, tough dumplin' you have to cut with a fork. That gives you a nice chew, and it's the secret to this recipe.

SERVES 4 TO 6

Chicken
1 whole chicken (2½ pounds), rinsed, patted dry, and cut into 8 pieces
3 celery stalks, chopped
1 large yellow onion, chopped
2 bay leaves
2 chicken bouillon cubes
1 teaspoon Paula Deen's House Seasoning (page 435)

1 can (10¾ ounces) condensed cream of celery or cream of chicken soup

Dumplings
2 cups all-purpose flour, plus extra for dusting
1 teaspoon salt
1 cup ice water

1. To prepare the chicken: In a large pot, combine the chicken, celery, onion, bay leaves, bouillon cubes, House Seasoning, and 16 cups water. Bring to a simmer over medium heat and cook until the chicken is tender and the thigh juices run clear when pierced with a knife, about 40 minutes. Remove the chicken from the pot and discard the bay leaves. When the chicken is cool enough to handle, pick the meat off the bones, discarding the bones and skin. Return the chicken meat to the pot. Add the canned soup to the pot and simmer gently over medium-low heat.

2. To make the dumplings: In a medium bowl, mix the flour with the salt and mound together. Beginning at the center of the mound, drizzle about 2 tablespoons of ice water over the flour. Using your fingers, and moving from the center to the sides of the bowl, gradually drizzle the flour with about ¾ cup ice water and incorporate. Knead the dough and form it into a ball.

3. Dust a small handful of flour onto a work surface. Roll out the dough (it will be firm), working from the center, until it is ⅛ inch thick. Let the dough relax for several minutes.

4. Once the dough is nice and relaxed, cut it into 1-inch squares. Pull each piece in half and

drop the halves into the simmering soup. Do not stir the pot once the dumplings have been added or they may break apart. Instead, gently move the pot in a circular motion so the dumplings become submerged and cook evenly. Cook until the dumplings float and are no longer doughy, 3 to 4 minutes.

5. To serve, ladle the chicken, gravy, and dumplings into warm bowls.

THICK AND THIN

If the chicken stew is too thin, it can be thickened up before the dumplings are added. Simply mix together 2 tablespoons cornstarch and ¼ cup water, then whisk this mixture into the stew and cook until it reaches the desired consistency.

CHICKEN WITH DROP DUMPLIN'S

Oftentimes I prefer the simplicity of a dropped dumpling to one you roll out on your kitchen table. This version of chicken and dumplin's comes together pretty easily, but it tastes like it took all afternoon. I pour a good old glug of fresh cream into the sauce at the last minute to give it a sweet, rich flavor. Sometimes I like to leave the chicken pieces whole on the bone like my grandmama and mama used to, but Michael likes it this way, pulled into bite-size pieces. I wake things up with the tiniest bit of cayenne pepper in the dumplin's. The end result is pure old-fashioned comfort food.

SERVES 6 TO 8

1 whole chicken (3 to 4 pounds), rinsed, patted dry, and cut into 8 pieces

8 cups chicken broth

2 celery stalks, finely chopped

1 bay leaf

2 cups plus 1 tablespoon all-purpose flour

4 teaspoons baking powder

1¼ teaspoons salt

¾ cup whole milk

¼ cup finely chopped scallions

Pinch of cayenne pepper

1 tablespoon butter

½ cup heavy cream

2 to 3 tablespoons chopped fresh parsley, for garnish

1. In a stockpot, combine the chicken, broth, celery, and bay leaf. Bring to a boil over medium-high heat. Reduce to a simmer and cook until the meat is falling off the bone, 45 minutes to 1 hour. Remove the chicken from the pot and reserve the broth; discard the bay leaf. When the chicken is cool enough to handle, pick the meat off the bones, discarding the bones and skin.

2. In a medium bowl, whisk together the 2 cups flour, the baking powder, and 1 teaspoon of the salt. Stir in the milk and mix well. Add the scallions and cayenne pepper and mix again. Bring the broth that you cooked the chicken in back to a slow boil and drop the batter by tablespoonfuls into the broth until all the batter is used up. Gently shake the pot. (Don't ever stir the dumplings with a spoon! This will only make them break apart and become a big mess.) Reduce to a simmer, cover, and cook gently until the dumplings are just cooked through, about 15 minutes.

3. While the dumplings are cooking, in a small saucepan, melt the butter over medium heat until frothy and bubbling. Whisk in the 1 tablespoon flour and cook for 1 minute. Slowly whisk in the cream and the remaining ¼ teaspoon salt. Let the mixture bubble until it thickens up slightly, about 2 minutes.

4. When the dumplings are done, carefully pour the cream mixture into the dumpling pot. Shake the pot gently. Return the chicken to the pot and shake the pot one more time, this time in a rotating motion until the cream and chicken are incorporated into the dumpling mixture. Serve up nice and hot, garnished with the parsley.

Scoop up spoonfuls of the dumpling dough, then put them into the pot by pushing the dough off the spoon with a second spoon.

DUMPLIN' DOS AND DON'TS

Dumplings are delicate creatures, so take care cooking them. Never stir them or let your simmer get going too fast, or they may break apart. If you're not sure your dumplings are done, try sticking a toothpick in them. If the toothpick comes out clean, it's time to serve.

EASY CHICKEN AND DUMPLIN'S

■ ■

Some good Southern dishes are a labor of love. Then there are ones like this little number that come easier. Any good cook will tell you there is no shame in putting a beautiful pot of chicken and dumplin's on the table in 45 minutes. Canned soup and Bisquick make this not only possible, but so flavorful. I have always believed that good cooking is all about taking some smart shortcuts from time to time, and I know many busy Southerners who eat well every night thanks to family favorites like this one.

SERVES 4 TO 6

Chicken and Gravy
1 can (10¾ ounces) condensed cream of chicken soup
1 can (10¾ ounces) condensed cream of celery soup
1½ cups whole milk
2 pounds boneless, skinless chicken breasts, cut into 1-inch chunks
1 cup frozen peas and carrots

¼ teaspoon grated nutmeg
Salt and black pepper

Dumplings
1 cup Bisquick baking mix
⅓ cup whole milk
Pinch of paprika
1 to 2 tablespoons chopped fresh parsley, for garnish

1. To make the chicken and gravy: In a medium saucepan, combine the soups and milk. Bring to a simmer over medium-high heat and whisk to a smooth consistency. Stir in the chicken, reduce the heat to medium, and simmer until just cooked through, about 15 minutes. Stir in the peas and carrots and cook for 2 minutes to heat through. Season with the nutmeg and salt and pepper to taste.

2. To make the dumplings: In a medium bowl, stir together the baking mix, milk, and paprika. Drop the dough by tablespoonfuls into the simmering chicken mixture; do not stir the dumplings into the mixture or you'll wind up with a big mess. Cook the dumplings, uncovered, over medium-low heat for 10 minutes. Cover and cook until the dumplings are firm to the touch and cooked through, about 10 minutes longer. Make sure to stay at a gentle simmer, or the dumplings may start to break up. Serve hot, sprinkled with the parsley.

> **CHICKEN CHOICES**
>
> This dish can also be prepared with boneless thigh meat if you prefer. Just cook the meat a few minutes longer to ensure it's done. Or, for an even easier option, toss in some shredded cooked rotisserie chicken after the dumplings have cooked through. Then all you need to do is warm the chicken through.

THE LADY & SONS CHICKEN POTPIE

For this beautiful potpie, I fill the crust with tender chicken in a creamy sauce with carrots and peas, and top it with a pastry lattice. That sauce bubbling up through the lattice is so pretty, and the finished pie is just absolutely full of chicken flavor and so satisfying, you could put it on the table with nothing else and you'd be serving up one of the tastiest, most complete meals I know. I think of this recipe whenever I'm asked to bring along a main-course dish for a potluck supper.

SERVES 6 TO 8

Filling
1 cooked chicken (store-bought rotisserie chicken is fine)
1 can (10¾ ounces) condensed Cheddar cheese soup
1 can (10¾ ounces) condensed cream of celery soup
½ cup whole milk
1 medium yellow onion, chopped
1 package (10 ounces) frozen green peas or 1 can (8 ounces) peas, drained
3 carrots, sliced, cooked, and drained
Salt and black pepper

Pastry
3 cups all-purpose flour, plus extra for dusting
1 teaspoon salt
¼ teaspoon baking powder
¾ cup solid vegetable shortening
About ¼ cup ice water
Butter

1. To make the filling: Pull the skin off the chicken and separate the meat from the bones. Coarsely chop the chicken meat. Discard the bones and skin.

2. In a large saucepan, heat the soups and milk. Stir in the chicken, onion, peas, carrots, and salt and black pepper to taste and bring to a boil. Remove from the heat and set aside to cool slightly.

3. To make the pastry: Preheat the oven to 350°F. In a large bowl, sift together the flour, salt, and baking powder. Cut in the shortening with a pastry blender, your hands, or two knives until the pieces of shortening are the size of small peas. Sprinkle 1 to 2 tablespoons of ice water over half of the mixture. Gently toss with a fork, then push to the side of the bowl. Repeat with another 1 to 2 tablespoons ice water until all of the mixture is moistened. Form the dough into 2 balls.

4. Dust a work surface with a small handful of flour. Flatten a ball of dough by pressing with the palm of your hand three

A CUTUP

"Cutting in" is the term for combining shortening (or butter) with dry ingredients. If you don't have a pastry blender, a pair of (not too warm) hands or two knives do the job just as well (see illustration, page 277).

times across in both directions. With a floured rolling pin, roll the dough out, rolling from the center to the edges, to a rectangle ⅛ inch thick and big enough to line a 13 by 9-inch baking pan. Fit the dough into the pan.

5. Pour the chicken filling into the pastry-lined pan. Roll out the second ball of dough to a 13 by 9-inch rectangle and cut into ½-inch strips. Lay over the pie filling in a lattice style (see illustration, page 314). Dot the top with butter. Bake until golden brown on top and all bubbling on the inside, about 45 minutes.

CHICKEN BOG

■ ■

It's hard to beat a good pot of chicken and rice. In South Carolina, folks add smoked sausage and call it chicken bog. This is simple, hearty, full-flavored food that you can fix for a crowd. You'll see Carolina cooks simmering up a bog big enough to feed an army—or a large family reunion. I don't think anyone knows why it's called chicken bog, but you don't dwell on the details when you've got a soupy plate of chicken, sausage, and rice steaming in front of you.

SERVES 10 TO 12

1 whole chicken (3 pounds), rinsed, patted dry, and quartered

1 pound smoked link sausage, like andouille or kielbasa, cut into ½-inch-thick slices

1 cup chopped yellow onion

8 tablespoons (1 stick) butter

2 teaspoons Paula Deen Collection Seasoned Salt, or other seasoned salt

1 teaspoon cayenne pepper

1 teaspoon black pepper

3 bay leaves

3 cups long-grain white rice

1. In a stockpot, combine the chicken quarters, sausage, onion, butter, seasoned salt, cayenne pepper, black pepper, bay leaves, and 8 cups water. Bring to a boil. Reduce to a simmer, cover, and cook for 40 minutes. Remove the chicken from the pot, reserving the cooking broth. When the chicken is cool enough to handle, pick the meat off the bones, discarding the bones and skin.

2. Meanwhile, add the rice to the pot of broth and bring to a boil, stirring well. Boil for 10 minutes, then reduce to a simmer, cover, and cook until the rice is done, about 10 minutes longer. Discard the bay leaves. Return the chicken to the pot, give it all a good stir, and serve.

BETTER WITH BACON

That could be my motto! For nice texture and added flavor, here's a dish that's even better topped with crispy crumbled bacon.

CHICKEN AND RICE CASSEROLE

■ ■

One of my favorite ways to eat chicken is with rice, and here in Georgia every cook seems to have her own opinion about how to combine them. For my casserole, I add water chestnuts for crunch, which I just love, and green beans and pimientos for color. The recipe couldn't be simpler. You just stir your chicken and vegetables all together with a box of mixed wild and white rice, a can of cream of celery soup, and plenty of Cheddar cheese, then bake until the whole thing is bubbling and smells like you just went to casserole heaven.

SERVES 6 TO 8

2 tablespoons vegetable oil

1 medium yellow onion, chopped

1 box (6 ounces) Uncle Ben's long-grain and wild rice or another quick-cooking long-grain and wild rice mix

3 cups chopped cooked chicken

1 can (8 ounces) water chestnuts, drained and chopped

2 cans (14½ ounces each) French-style green beans, drained

1 jar (4 ounces) pimientos, rinsed and drained

1 can (10¾ ounces) condensed cream of celery soup

1 cup mayonnaise

1 cup shredded sharp Cheddar cheese (4 ounces)

1. In a medium saucepan, heat the oil over medium heat. Add the onion and cook until softened and translucent, 7 to 10 minutes. Transfer to a large bowl to cool.

2. Cook the wild rice blend according to the package directions. Let cool and stir into the onion.

3. Preheat the oven to 300°F. Add the chicken and all the remaining ingredients to the rice mixture and stir to combine. Scrape into a 3-quart baking dish. Bake for 25 minutes and you have yourself a great midweek meal.

> **DO AHEAD**
> This is a dish I like to do ahead on the weekend so I have it ready for the busy workweek. It will keep in the fridge for up to 3 days.

SKILLET CHICKEN AND SAUSAGE JAMBALAYA

■ ■

Y'all, jambalaya comes from the Creole-Cajun tradition of Louisiana cooking and it is a party in a pot. You can make yourself a big old pot of rice and other goodies, and as long as it's got sausage, bell pepper, and a hint of celery (I use celery seeds), I call it jambalaya. I keep mine simple and straightforward, with plenty of chicken to make it a square meal.

SERVES 4 TO 6

2 tablespoons vegetable oil

1 tablespoon butter

¾ pound andouille or other smoked sausage, cut into ¼-inch-thick slices

1 large yellow onion, chopped

1 large green bell pepper, chopped

1 pound boneless, skinless chicken thighs, cut into 1½-inch pieces

Salt and black pepper

1 clove garlic, chopped

1 teaspoon dried thyme

1 teaspoon paprika

½ teaspoon cayenne pepper

½ teaspoon celery seeds

2 bay leaves

3 cups chicken broth

1 can (14½ ounces) diced tomatoes

1½ cups long-grain white rice

1. In a large skillet with a lid, heat the vegetable oil and butter over medium-high heat. Add the sausage and cook until browned on both sides, about 5 minutes. Transfer the sausage to a bowl. Add the onion and bell pepper to the skillet and cook until just beginning to soften, 2 to 3 minutes.

2. Lightly sprinkle the chicken all over with salt and black pepper. Add the chicken and garlic to the skillet. Cook, stirring, until the chicken loses its raw color, about 3 minutes. Add the thyme, paprika, cayenne pepper, celery seeds, and bay leaves and cook for 30 seconds, or until fragrant. Add the broth and tomatoes, bring to a boil, and taste for seasoning. Return the sausage to the pan with any accumulated juices and sprinkle in the rice (make sure you sprinkle the rice evenly all over the skillet).

3. Cover the pan, reduce the heat to low, and cook until all the liquid has been absorbed and the rice is tender, about 15 minutes. Remove from the heat and let stand, covered, for 10 minutes. Remove and discard the bay leaves. Serve it up right from the skillet.

EVEN STEVEN

By sprinkling the rice all over your skillet when you add it, you ensure that all the grains cook evenly. You want to make sure you don't crowd the pan in any one area.

SMOTHERED CHICKEN

■ ■

We started turning fried chicken into smothered chicken at the restaurant and I brought the habit home with me. To make a traditional Southern smothered dish, you take your meat—I use chicken pieces, but you can do the same thing with pork chops—and you bread it, fry it in a skillet, then make a thick milk gravy and cook your meat down in that gravy, covered, until it's completely tender and the sauce is just too delicious and the whole house smells so good you can't stand it. To keep yourself busy while the chicken is cooking, make a big pot of rice and a salad, then sit down at the table and watch everyone in sniffing distance turn up.

SERVES 4

1 cup all-purpose flour
½ teaspoon garlic powder
Salt and black pepper
1 whole chicken (3½ pounds), rinsed, patted
　dry, and cut into 8 pieces

4 tablespoons (½ stick) butter
1 small yellow onion, chopped
1 small green bell pepper, chopped
1½ cups whole milk

1. In a wide, shallow bowl, whisk together the flour, garlic powder, and ½ teaspoon each salt and black pepper. Lightly sprinkle the chicken all over with salt and black pepper. Dip each piece of chicken in the flour mixture, shaking off any excess flour. (Set any leftover flour aside to use in step 3.)

2. In a large skillet with a lid, melt the butter over medium-high heat. Add the chicken and cook, turning occasionally, until golden brown all over, 8 to 10 minutes. Transfer the chicken to a paper towel–lined plate to drain.

3. Add the onion and bell pepper to the skillet and cook, stirring, until softened, about 5 minutes. Stir in 3 tablespoons of the reserved flour mixture and cook, stirring, for 1 minute. Slowly whisk in the milk and ½ cup water. Simmer until the sauce has thickened and is nice and creamy, about 5 minutes.

4. Return the chicken to the pan. Cover the pan and simmer on low heat until the chicken is tender, about 30 minutes. Bring to the table right there in that skillet.

A BIRD IN HAND

Instead of using a whole bird cut up, you can go ahead and use 3½ pounds of whatever chicken pieces your family likes best. That way, if everyone likes drumsticks, there'll be enough to go around.

HOT BUFFALO WINGS

■ ■

Now, everyone and their football bud loves chicken wings. Frying them and dunking those babies in buttery hot sauce makes them perfect for one thing: the dip. Blue cheese, sour cream, cream cheese, mayonnaise—all the good stuff! And there's nothin' better than cooling that Buffalo-wing burn with blue cheese dip on a stick of celery. While my boys are rooting for the Bulldogs, you'll find me swiping every last bit of goodness from the dip bowl.

SERVES 4 TO 6

Creamy Roquefort Dip
½ cup crumbled Roquefort cheese (2 ounces)
1 package (3 ounces) cream cheese, at room
   temperature
½ cup mayonnaise
½ cup sour cream
1 tablespoon fresh lemon juice
1 tablespoon white wine vinegar

Wings
About 4 quarts vegetable oil, for deep-frying
12 chicken wings, disjointed (see box)
8 tablespoons (1 stick) butter
1 cup Paula Deen Collection Hot Sauce, or
   any hot sauce you like

1. To make the dip: In a medium bowl, cream the Roquefort and cream cheese with a wooden spoon until well combined. Mix in the mayonnaise, sour cream, lemon juice, and vinegar and blend well. Cover with plastic wrap and chill for 2 hours.

2. To make the wings: Using a deep-fat fryer or a large, heavy pot, heat 3 inches of oil until it reaches 350°F on a deep-fry thermometer. Deep-fry the wings in batches until golden and crispy, about 10 minutes, and transfer them to a paper towel–lined plate to drain.

3. In a small saucepan, melt the butter, stir in the hot sauce, and heat thoroughly. Then quickly pour the butter sauce into a large bowl and toss the hot wings in the sauce. Serve the wings on a pretty platter along with the creamy Roquefort dip.

> **WING IT**
>
> If you buy your wings whole (which is the most economical way to buy them), you'll need to cut them into three pieces at the joints. It's fast and easy to do. Save the wing tips for broths or just discard. The other meaty portions of the wing are what you want for these Hot Buffalo Wings.

COUNTRY CAPTAIN CHICKEN

■ ■

This Southern curry has been a favorite for entertaining for the better part of a century and I see no reason to retire it now. It's an easy and beautiful stew of chicken with curry powder, tomatoes, bell pepper, and sweet little currants that you serve over rice and sprinkle with almonds. A little old-fashioned, perhaps, but then again, so am I.

SERVES 4

2 tablespoons vegetable oil

1 tablespoon butter

1 whole chicken (3½ pounds), rinsed, patted dry, and cut into 8 pieces

Salt and black pepper

1 large yellow onion, chopped

1 large green bell pepper, chopped

1 clove garlic, chopped

1 tablespoon curry powder

1 can (28 ounces) diced tomatoes

⅓ cup dried currants

3 cups cooked rice

½ cup slivered almonds, toasted

1. Preheat the oven to 350°F.

2. In a large ovenproof skillet, heat the oil and butter over medium-high heat. Lightly sprinkle the chicken all over with salt and black pepper. Add to the skillet, skin side down. Cook, turning once, until browned on both sides, about 8 minutes. Transfer the chicken to a plate.

3. Add the onion and bell pepper to the skillet and cook until softened, about 5 minutes. Add the garlic and curry powder and cook for 30 seconds, until fragrant. Add the tomatoes and currants and bring to a boil. Taste and add some salt and/or black pepper if you think it needs it.

4. Return the chicken and any accumulated juices to the pan, skin side up, and transfer to the oven. Bake, uncovered, until the chicken is cooked through, about 40 minutes. Serve over the rice and sprinkle with the slivered almonds.

SWEET SUBSTITUTIONS

The currants in this dish add a nice sweet flavor that pairs up perfectly with the curry. Currants are a type of dried sweet berry, a little smaller than raisins. If you can't get your hands on currants, you can substitute dark raisins, golden raisins, or even dried cranberries.

POT-ROASTED TURKEY BREAST
WITH VEGETABLES

■ ■

This is my everyday version of Thanksgiving dinner, which is fitting because I do give thanks every day. I like roasting the breast with plenty of veggies, then using the pan juices for a rich-tasting gravy.

SERVES 6

1 bone-in turkey breast (6 pounds), rinsed and patted dry

2 tablespoons (¼ stick) butter, at room temperature

Salt and black pepper

2 teaspoons dried sage

1 large Vidalia or other sweet onion, cut into chunks

2 large sprigs fresh rosemary

3 cups turkey or chicken broth

2 carrots, chopped

2 baking potatoes, peeled and chopped

1 celery stalk, chopped

3 tablespoons all-purpose flour

1. Preheat the oven to 325°F. Rub the turkey breast inside and out with the butter. Generously sprinkle salt and black pepper all over. Sprinkle the sage all over.

2. Heat a large Dutch oven over high heat. Add the turkey, breast side down, and cook until the skin is dark golden on all sides, 7 to 10 minutes. Using tongs, lift out the turkey breast and scatter the onion and rosemary on the bottom of the pan. Return the turkey, breast side up, to the pan. Pour ¾ cup of the broth into the pan. Cover and bake for 1 hour.

3. Stir the carrots, potatoes, and celery into the pan juices, coating well. Cover and continue baking until the vegetables are tender and an instant-read thermometer inserted into the thickest part of the breast registers 160°F, 1 to 1½ hours longer. Transfer the turkey to a cutting board and tent loosely with foil. Let rest for 20 minutes. (The breast temperature will continue to rise to 170°F as it rests.) Transfer the vegetables to a bowl and cover with foil.

4. Pour the pan juices from the Dutch oven into a measuring cup or gravy separator. Let stand until the fat rises to the top, 1 to 2 minutes. Skim off the fat and reserve 3 tablespoons, discarding the rest (or, if using a separator, carefully pour the juices into a measuring cup and reserve 3 tablespoons of the fat remaining in the separator). Add the pan juices to the remaining 2¼ cups broth. Return the 3 tablespoons of fat to the pan and place on a burner over medium-high heat. Scrape up any browned bits from the pan with a wooden spoon. Stir in the flour and cook for 2 minutes, stirring constantly. Whisk in the broth mixture and bring to a boil, stirring. Cook until

thickened, about 3 minutes. Strain the gravy. Taste and add more salt and/or black pepper if you think it needs it. To serve, carve the breast and lay it out on a pretty platter with the vegetables scattered around. Pass the gravy at the table.

YOU'VE GOT OPTIONS

You can change up this dish in so many ways. Try it with different vegetables like parsnips or turnips. Or fiddle with the herbs. Switching out sage and rosemary for thyme, lemon thyme, or parsley makes it a whole new dish.

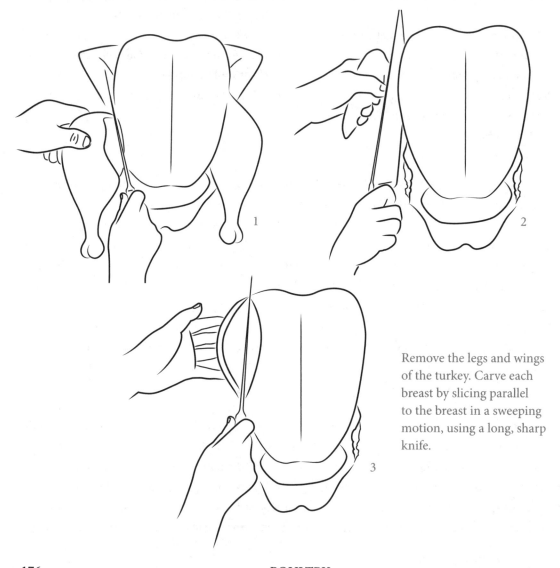

Remove the legs and wings of the turkey. Carve each breast by slicing parallel to the breast in a sweeping motion, using a long, sharp knife.

CLASSIC ROAST TURKEY AND DRESSING

I don't save turkey just for Thanksgiving Day—Michael and I love it too much. But I do love to make this traditional recipe for the holiday (or any other big buffet dinner). The dressing is cooked out of the bird, and the turkey itself gets an onion, a head of garlic, and some herbs in the cavity to give the meat that much more flavor. I brush the bird with butter as it roasts until it is bronze and ready to serve. Along with the dressing and gravy, you've got a meal that takes me right back to every Thanksgiving table I ever sat at, from my Grandmama Paul's to the little turkeys I roasted back when we were a small family of three, just me and my boys.

SERVES 8 TO 10

Turkey Broth
Neck and giblets from the turkey (liver discarded)
2 cups chicken broth
1 medium yellow onion, finely chopped

Dressing
8 tablespoons (1 stick) butter
1½ cups chopped celery
1 bunch scallions, chopped
8 cups large chunks day-old bread (1½ pounds)
1 sleeve saltine crackers (about 40 crackers), coarsely crushed
2 cups chicken broth

2 large eggs, lightly beaten
2 teaspoons chopped fresh sage
1 teaspoon salt
½ teaspoon black pepper

Turkey
1 whole turkey (8 to 10 pounds)
Salt and black pepper
1 medium yellow onion, quartered
1 head garlic, halved crosswise
1 small bunch (about 10 sprigs) fresh sage
8 tablespoons (1 stick) plus about 3 tablespoons butter, melted
¼ cup all-purpose flour

1. To make the broth: In a large saucepan, combine the turkey neck, giblets, chicken broth, and onion. Bring to a simmer and cook over low heat for 1 hour. Strain the broth into a bowl. Discard the neck, giblets, and onion. Let cool completely, then refrigerate, covered, until ready to use.

2. To prepare the dressing: Grease a 13 by 9-inch pan with butter, oil, or cooking spray. In a large skillet, melt the butter. Add the celery and scallions and cook until softened, 5 to 7 minutes. In a large bowl, combine the bread, cracker crumbs, and celery mixture. Stir in the chicken broth, eggs, sage, salt, and black pepper. Transfer the dressing to the prepared pan.

3. To prepare the turkey: Preheat the oven to 350°F. Place a roasting rack in a large roasting pan. Rinse the turkey and pat it dry. Season the inside of the turkey with 1 teaspoon each of salt and black pepper; season the outside with 2 teaspoons salt and 1 teaspoon black pepper. Stuff the onion, garlic, and sage into the cavity.

4. Place the turkey, breast side up, on the roasting rack. Brush the turkey with ¼ cup of the melted butter. Tent the turkey with foil. Transfer the turkey and the pan of dressing to the oven. Bake the dressing, uncovered, until golden, about 45 minutes. Remove and set aside. Continue roasting the turkey for 1 hour and 15 minutes longer.

5. Remove the foil, brush the turkey with another ¼ cup of the melted butter, and increase the oven temperature to 425°F. Roast until an instant-read thermometer inserted into the thickest part of the thigh registers 170°F, 25 to 30 minutes longer. Let the turkey rest for 15 minutes before carving. (The temperature will continue to rise while the meat rests.)

6. Reduce the oven temperature to 250°F. Cover the dressing with foil and return it to the oven to warm through while you make the gravy.

7. Pour the pan juices out of the roasting pan into a measuring cup or gravy separator. Let stand until the fat rises to the top, 1 to 2 minutes. Skim off the fat and reserve (or, if using a separator, carefully pour the juices into a measuring cup and reserve the fat remaining in the separator). Measure the turkey fat, adding enough of the remaining melted butter to equal ¼ cup.

8. Straddle the roasting pan across two burners over medium-high heat. Add the fat and heat until bubbling. Whisk in the flour and cook for 1 minute. Slowly whisk in the reserved turkey broth and the degreased pan juices, scraping up any browned bits from the bottom of the roasting pan. Simmer until the gravy is slightly thickened, about 5 minutes. Taste and see if it needs more salt and/or black pepper. Proudly serve the turkey with the dressing and gravy alongside!

STRESS-FREE ENTERTAINING

I know, I know, this recipe may look a little daunting. But, I promise you, folks, it's all in the preparation. To make your entertaining fun and easy, go ahead and make the turkey broth and the dressing a day ahead. The dressing can then be warmed up 45 minutes before you're ready to serve, leaving you more time for family and friends on the special day.

MOLASSES GAME HENS

■ ■

Many Southern men love to hunt small game birds, and some Southern wives are obliging enough to dress and cook their haul. For the rest of us who might not hunt, the good, hearty, chicken-like flavor of Cornish game hen is easy enough to order from a good butcher. I love to give these little birds a sweet, tangy glaze. They make for a very elegant main course.

SERVES 4 TO 6

¾ cup molasses

6 tablespoons (¾ stick) butter

1 tablespoon plus ½ teaspoon
 apple cider vinegar

¼ teaspoon plus ⅛ teaspoon cayenne pepper

Salt

3 Cornish game hens (1½ pounds each),
 rinsed and patted dry

Black pepper

1. Preheat the oven to 375°F. Place a roasting rack in a roasting pan.

2. In a small saucepan, combine the molasses, butter, vinegar, cayenne pepper, and 1½ teaspoons salt. Simmer over medium heat for 5 minutes.

3. Lightly sprinkle the hens all over with salt and black pepper. Brush each hen with about 2 tablespoons of the molasses mixture and place them on the roasting rack. Roast the hens, basting them two or three times with more of the glaze, until the juices run clear when the hens are pierced with a knife in the thickest part of the thigh, about 1 hour.

GOOD THINGS IN SMALL PACKAGES

Cornish game hens, sometimes called Rock Cornish hens, are young chickens that have a really wonderful flavor. For the prettiest presentation, I like to place them on a platter either whole or halved.

QUAILS IN GRAVY

■ ■

Back in Albany, Georgia, when I was a little girl, I remember that our claim to fame was how President Eisenhower would come to the nearby plantations to do his quail hunting. Quail is a fairly fancy food to serve these days, but it was not so rare when I was growing up, and we always enjoyed eating a down-home dish like this one while thinking to ourselves that the president might be having the same thing for supper.

SERVES 4

2 tablespoons (¼ stick) butter

1 tablespoon vegetable oil

8 quail (preferably semiboneless), rinsed and
  patted dry

1 teaspoon Paula Deen's House Seasoning
  (page 435)

2 tablespoons all-purpose flour

2 cups chicken broth

2 tablespoons heavy cream

2 tablespoons dry sherry

2 dashes of Worcestershire sauce

1 bay leaf

Salt and black pepper

1. In a large skillet with a lid, heat the butter and oil over medium-high heat. Season the quail with the House Seasoning. Add to the skillet and cook until browned, about 2 minutes per side. Transfer to a plate.

2. Whisk the flour into the skillet and cook, stirring constantly, for 1 minute. Add the broth, cream, sherry, Worcestershire sauce, and bay leaf and bring to a boil, stirring constantly. Return the quail and any accumulated juices to the pan. Reduce to a gentle simmer, cover, and cook until the quail are cooked through, about 10 minutes. Discard the bay leaf. Taste the gravy and add salt and black pepper if you think it needs it.

> ## QUALITY QUAIL
> When buying quail, look for those with a creamy yellow skin. Make sure they don't have blemishes and that they smell fresh. Quail are very lean and have a lovely, delicate flavor.

CAJUN CHICKEN-FRIED LIVERS
WITH CREAM GRAVY

■ ■

I adore chicken livers, and when it comes to folks who aren't so sure about them, I consider myself an expert: all you've got to do is fry something and dunk it down in some cream gravy, and folks will come around to it. And, hey, if I can't convince everybody, well then, that's more for me!

SERVES 4

Spicy Chicken Livers
½ cup all-purpose flour
1 tablespoon Cajun seasoning
2 teaspoons salt
2 pounds chicken livers
⅓ cup vegetable oil

Cream Gravy
1 cup milk
1 cup heavy cream
3 tablespoons all-purpose flour
Salt and black pepper

1. To prepare the spicy chicken livers: In a medium bowl, combine the flour, Cajun seasoning, and salt. Dredge the livers in the flour mixture, tapping off the excess.

2. In a large skillet, heat the oil over high heat until very hot. Fry the livers, turning them once, until golden on both sides and still slightly pinkish inside, 1 to 2 minutes per side. Transfer the livers to a paper towel–lined plate to drain. Pour off all but about ¼ cup of the oil from the skillet.

3. To make the cream gravy: In a small saucepan, combine the milk and cream. Slowly heat until hot to the touch, 5 to 10 minutes.

4. Return the skillet with the reserved oil to medium-high heat, add the flour, and stir until pale golden, about 2 minutes. Slowly whisk in the cream and milk and cook, stirring constantly, until thick and bubbling, 2 to 3 minutes. Stir in 1 teaspoon salt and black pepper to taste. Taste and add more salt if you think it needs it. Serve up the chicken livers and pass the cream gravy around.

THE GRAVY TRAIN
Getting gravy to just the right consistency takes some good old TLC. Don't worry if your gravy comes up too thick. You can fix that by adding hot water to it in small teaspoonfuls until it reaches the right consistency.

Chapter 8

FISH AND SHELLFISH

I have always said I don't care for uppity food and I can't cook it. When I was opening my restaurant, I knew I needed to stick with the down-home cooking I grew up with, and I've been so glad I did. But the funny thing is, when I really think about my childhood, the things we were eating back then would be considered fancy today! I remember as a child having fish roe with grits for breakfast. And here in the South, we've always been able to enjoy beautiful crab cakes, oysters, and the sweetest, freshest shrimp, just the kinds of foods restaurants charge a lot for these days.

Folks can eat like royalty when fresh fish and seafood are swimming outside the door. Here in Georgia, you've got rivers like the Flint and the Savannah full of freshwater, and saltwater from the Atlantic Ocean, too. I went from Saturday-night catfish fries growing up in Albany, Georgia, to picking crab and shelling shrimp off the beach in Savannah. I recall one of the first things Michael taught me to cook was shrimp, which I love because you can make it a hundred different ways, from BBQ Shrimp (page 191) to Easy Shrimp Bake (page 189), and you can serve it morning, noon, and night. When Michael goes out back to fish or crab, the first thing he does is cast right down where we're standing and pull up a big old net of shrimp to use for bait. Well, honey, I don't see the point of that! I head straight into the house with that bait to make my Shrimp and Grits (page 193).

Even living the high life here where I can fix Creamy Charleston Crab Casserole (page 196) and Creamy Scallop Bake (page 199), I started to miss freshwater fish. So I told Michael I was going to have a pond put in our front yard. Of course he said, "What are you doing that for? You got an ocean in your backyard!" But I don't know from the tides and the bait you use on the saltwater side, so I got my pond put in. And every so often I catch me some catfish. I like to slide a few into the fryer to make the freshest, crispiest Catfish Po' Boy (page 205) you ever had. And since farmed catfish is sold in most parts of this country, there's no reason you can't cook up some Cajun Blackened Catfish (page 203) no matter where you live.

One of our true glories down here is Low-Country Boil (page 206), which is one of those fabulous one-pot wonders. It's got everything: sausage, starch, protein, and a whole bunch of flavor. I love the ease of it: we'll just throw a little of whatever we've got in there. You can even add some firm types of fish and crab, plus add sausage for richness and potato, then simmer it together with plenty of sweet shrimp. Y'all, just one taste of Low-Country Boil is enough to remind you that down South even if you're poor in the pocket, you're rich in the belly.

SHRIMP ÉTOUFFÉE

■ ■

I couldn't call this book a Southern bible without including étouffée. This flavorful New Orleans classic—full of stewed tomatoes along with the "trinity" of bell peppers, onions, and celery—really showcases the sweet Gulf shrimp and has a nice spicy kick to it. Served over rice, it's a true feast.

SERVES 6 TO 8 AS A MAIN COURSE

½ cup vegetable oil

½ cup all-purpose flour

1 cup chopped yellow onion

½ cup chopped green bell pepper

1 cup chopped celery

3 cloves garlic, finely chopped

½ teaspoon black pepper

½ teaspoon white pepper

½ teaspoon cayenne pepper

1 teaspoon Cajun seasoning

½ cup finely chopped scallions, plus extra for garnish

½ cup finely chopped fresh parsley

2 to 3 dashes of hot sauce

1 bottle (8 ounces) clam juice

1 can (14½ ounces) diced tomatoes with green chilies

Salt

2 pounds small or medium shrimp, peeled and deveined

4 tablespoons (½ stick) butter

6 cups cooked rice, for serving

AN OIL-BASED ROUX

For an étouffée full of flavor, you want to cook that roux for a good long time. That's why I go with oil in this roux. If you cook butter for as long as I cook the oil, you'll wind up with a burned mess.

1. In a large, heavy-bottomed saucepan, combine the oil and flour over low heat to prepare the roux. Whisk the flour into the oil to form a paste. Continue cooking over low heat, whisking constantly, until the mixture turns a caramel color and gives off a nutty aroma, 15 to 20 minutes.

2. Add the onion, bell pepper, celery, and garlic and cook over low heat until the vegetables are tender, about 5 minutes. Add the black pepper, white pepper, cayenne pepper, Cajun seasoning, ½ cup scallions, the parsley, and hot sauce. Pour in the clam juice and diced tomatoes, stirring to blend. Add salt, starting with 1 teaspoon, then add more if you'd like. Bring the mixture to a boil. Reduce to a simmer and cook for 10 to 15 minutes.

3. Add the shrimp and stir. It will take only about 3 minutes for the shrimp to cook, so be sure you don't overcook them. Remove the saucepan from the heat and stir in the butter. The heat from the dish will melt the butter. Place the étouffée in a pretty tureen or serving bowl. Serve it over rice, garnished with scallions.

BEAUFORT SHRIMP PIE

Situated on one of South Carolina's Sea Islands is the beautiful town of Beaufort, where old Southern mansions overlook the gorgeous coastline. The town has a long-standing shellfish industry, which is celebrated yearly at the Beaufort Shrimp Festival. But you can celebrate it anytime, anywhere, with this delectable bacon-topped shrimp casserole.

SERVES 6 TO 8

2 tablespoons (¼ stick) butter
½ cup chopped yellow onion
¼ cup chopped green bell pepper
Salt
3 cups cooked, peeled, and deveined
   large shrimp

2 cups fresh bread crumbs
2 cups whole milk
2 large eggs
¼ teaspoon black pepper
3 slices bacon, cut into 2-inch lengths

1. Preheat the oven to 325°F. Lightly grease an 8-inch square baking pan or coat with cooking spray.

2. In a large skillet, melt the butter over medium-high heat. Add the onion, bell pepper, and a pinch of salt. Cook, stirring, until the vegetables have softened, about 5 minutes.

3. In the prepared pan, layer the shrimp, bread crumbs, and vegetable mixture. In a small bowl, beat together the milk, eggs, ½ teaspoon salt, and the black pepper. Pour the egg mixture into the pan. Lay the bacon across the top. Bake until the filling is set, 30 to 40 minutes. If you like bacon the way I sure do, just before serving, run the pie under the broiler to make it extra-crispy.

SHRIMP SHORTCUT
Buying already cooked, peeled, and deveined shrimp is a great time-saver. You'll pay a little more per pound for the work that's been done at the shop, but it'll save you some precious minutes.

EASY SHRIMP BAKE

■ ■

This sweet, cheesy casserole full of mushrooms and shrimp comes together so fast, you can have it in the baking dish in minutes. Better yet, you can refrigerate it in the baking dish for up to a day, then pop it in the oven just before serving. Y'all, isn't life sweet?

SERVES 6

2 tablespoons (¼ stick) butter

1 cup sliced white mushrooms

4 scallions, chopped

2 cups cooked, peeled, and deveined
  large shrimp

6 to 8 slices day-old bread, trimmed,
  buttered, and cubed

2 cups shredded sharp Cheddar cheese
  (8 ounces)

3 large eggs

½ teaspoon salt

¼ teaspoon black pepper

½ teaspoon mustard powder

Pinch of paprika

1½ cups whole milk

1. Grease a shallow 2-quart baking dish with butter, oil, or cooking spray.

2. In a large skillet, melt the butter over medium-high heat. Add the mushrooms and scallions and cook, stirring, until the vegetables are tender, 3 to 5 minutes.

3. Place the shrimp, the mushroom mixture, half of the bread, and 1 cup of the Cheddar in the prepared baking dish and stir gently. Top with the remaining bread and 1 cup Cheddar. Lightly beat the eggs with the salt, black pepper, mustard powder, and paprika. Stir the milk into the eggs and pour it all into the baking dish. Cover the dish with plastic wrap and let it sit in the fridge for 30 minutes or up to overnight (see box below).

4. When you're ready to bake it, preheat the oven to 325°F. Bake until the casserole is set and golden brown, 40 to 50 minutes.

THE BIG FREEZE

Did you know that almost all shrimp you can get your hands on has been frozen at some point since it was caught? So go ahead and feel free to buy that frozen shrimp for your next shrimp dinner.

A GOOD SOAKING

Not only will it make your morning easier if this casserole is ready the night before you bake it, but if you ask me, it tastes better, too. Letting the bread soak in the egg custard overnight lets it get good and flavorful—and you can go off to dreamland knowing you've got one less item on your to-do list for tomorrow.

CRUNCHY FRIED SHRIMP

■ ■

Oh, my, but everything is better fried! These little shrimp are so good, you won't find yourself with any leftovers.

SERVES 4

2 cups self-rising flour
Salt
½ teaspoon black pepper
2 cups buttermilk
3 tablespoons hot sauce

1 tablespoon fresh lime juice
About 2 quarts peanut oil,
   for deep-frying
2 pounds medium shrimp,
   peeled and deveined

1. In a wide, shallow bowl, whisk together the flour, 1 tablespoon salt, and the black pepper. In a separate wide, shallow bowl, whisk together the buttermilk, hot sauce, and lime juice.

2. In a medium saucepan, heat 2 inches of oil over medium-high heat until it reaches 375°F on a deep fry thermometer. Pat the shrimp dry and dredge them in the flour mixture first, then coat with the buttermilk mixture, and finally dredge in the flour mixture again. Give the shrimp a good shake after each coating to shake off any excess flour or batter.

3. Working in batches, fry the shrimp until golden brown, about 2 minutes. With a slotted spoon, transfer the shrimp to a paper towel–lined baking sheet to drain. Sprinkle with extra salt, if you'd like, and serve warm for maximum crunch.

> ## DON'T GO UP IN SMOKE
> When deep- or shallow-frying, it's best to use a mild-flavored oil like peanut or vegetable oil. Lard is also a good option. But stay away from butter and olive oil—they burn at a lower temperature than peanut and vegetable oils.

BBQ SHRIMP

Shrimp cook in no time flat, and they are so readily available here in Savannah that I find myself making this whenever we need supper on the table fast. I love to serve these saucy shrimp over grits or else alongside a nice big slice of corn bread to soak up all the good, buttery juices. Get out your paper napkins and enjoy, y'all!

SERVES 4

8 tablespoons (1 stick) butter

2 teaspoons Creole seasoning

Pinch of cayenne pepper

12 jumbo shrimp, with heads and tails
   (see box)

½ cup lager-style beer

Freshly squeezed juice of ½ lemon

½ teaspoon Worcestershire sauce

2 teaspoons chopped fresh thyme

Chopped fresh parsley, for garnish

1. In a large skillet, melt 4 tablespoons of the butter over medium-high heat. Sprinkle the Creole seasoning and cayenne pepper over the shrimp. Add the shrimp to the pan and cook for about 1 minute per side.

2. Stir in the beer, lemon juice, Worcestershire sauce, and thyme. Let the sauce bubble vigorously for 30 seconds. Reduce the heat to low, cover the pan, and cook until the shrimp are pink and opaque, about 2 minutes. Stir in the remaining 4 tablespoons butter and garnish with parsley. Serve bubbling hot.

HEADS AND TAILS

You'll notice this recipe calls for shrimp with heads and tails on. Now, don't be scared by that! The heads and tails bring a load of flavor to this dish. It can be made without them, but you'll be sacrificing some of that intense shrimp taste.

BUTTERY CAJUN SHRIMP

■ ■

The smell of these shrimp in the oven is enough to just make a person weak in the knees. Full of seasoning and, of course, plenty of butter, it's the sauce that makes this dish. Whenever I serve shrimp in the shell, it's an occasion all on its own—just rolling up your sleeves and peeling them with your fingers turns a tasty supper into a bit of a party.

SERVES 4

1½ sticks (6 ounces) butter, melted
3 tablespoons Worcestershire sauce
3 tablespoons fresh lemon juice
2 tablespoons Cajun seasoning
1½ teaspoons Paula Deen's House Seasoning
   (page 435)

¾ teaspoon hot sauce
3 scallions, finely chopped
2 cloves garlic, finely chopped
2 pounds medium shrimp, with shells
1 lemon, thinly sliced
French bread, for dipping

1. Preheat the oven to 400°F.

2. In a medium bowl, combine the butter, Worcestershire sauce, lemon juice, Cajun seasoning, House Seasoning, hot sauce, scallions, and garlic. Pour half this sauce into a 2-quart baking dish. Layer half the shrimp and half the lemon slices in the dish; then make a second layer with the remaining shrimp and lemon slices. Pour the remaining sauce into the dish.

PEEL APPEAL

Sometimes I like to keep my shrimp unpeeled, especially in a recipe like this one that cooks at a high heat for a fairly long time. With the peel on, I know my shrimp has its protective shell to keep it nice and moist.

3. Bake, uncovered, stirring occasionally, until the shrimp are pink, about 20 minutes. Ladle the sauce into pretty individual serving dishes. Serve the shrimp with plenty of French bread for dipping in the tangy, buttery sauce.

SHRIMP AND GRITS

■ ■

Creamy grits topped with sweet, succulent shrimp cooked with ham and vegetables: no wonder folks were tripping over themselves to get to the shrimp and grits we served at our wedding. Michael is a shrimp guy, and I'm a grits gal, so I felt it was fitting that our friends and family ate those shrimp and grits together. I could feel the love, y'all.

SERVES 2

Salt

1 cup quick-cooking grits (not instant grits)

2 tablespoons olive oil

½ cup chopped tasso ham (see box, page 97)

2 tablespoons chopped leek, white part only

2 tablespoons chopped yellow onion

2 tablespoons chopped green bell pepper

20 medium to large shrimp, peeled and deveined, with tails

2 tablespoons white wine (see box)

1 cup heavy cream

¼ teaspoon black pepper

1 scallion, chopped, for garnish

1. In a small saucepan, combine 2 cups water and ¾ teaspoon salt. Bring to a boil over medium-high heat. Slowly stir in the grits and stir thoroughly until the grits are well mixed. Return to a boil, then reduce to a simmer, cover, and cook, stirring from time to time, until the grits have the consistency of smooth cream of wheat, about 20 minutes.

2. Meanwhile, in a large skillet, heat the oil over medium-high heat. Add the tasso and cook, stirring once, until crisp, 7 to 9 minutes. Add the leek, onion, and bell pepper and cook, stirring, until tender, about 5 minutes. Add the shrimp and cook until pink, 30 to 45 seconds. Remove the shrimp from the pan and set aside.

3. Add the wine to the pan and cook for 30 seconds. Slowly add the cream and let reduce until thickened, 5 to 10 minutes. Season with ½ teaspoon salt and the black pepper.

4. Divide the grits between two plates. Line the edges of each plate with 10 shrimp. Pour the sauce over the grits and garnish with a scattering of scallion.

GLAZE OVER

Pouring wine or another liquid into a skillet after you've sautéed meat or seafood in it is called deglazing. That little bit of wine picks up all the rich flavor that the shrimp leaves on the bottom of the pan. And this is the flavor foundation for the sauce. If you don't have white wine handy, you can substitute fish or chicken broth or, in a pinch, a little water.

SHRIMP GUMBO CASSEROLE

■ ■

If you ever want to feel like you're cooking on TV, fix a dish like this casserole: it's just so pretty when you pull it out of the oven that you'll feel like shouting, "Ta da!" This is my lighter version of gumbo, with plenty of colorful veggies, including red pepper and green okra, plus a real hit of flavor from the thyme. It is a bright change of pace from heavier gumbos, and while it's in the oven, you'll have time to run, change into a nice clean apron, fix your hair, and make it all look easy.

SERVES 4

4 tablespoons (½ stick) butter
1 cup crushed Ritz crackers
1 teaspoon dried thyme
1 tablespoon vegetable oil
1 cup coarsely chopped yellow onion
1 cup coarsely chopped celery
1 cup coarsely chopped red bell pepper
1 clove garlic, chopped

1½ tablespoons all-purpose flour
1½ cups chicken broth
½ cup bottled clam juice
1 cup sliced fresh or thawed frozen okra
¼ teaspoon hot sauce
1 bay leaf
1½ pounds large shrimp, peeled and deveined

1. Preheat the oven to 400°F. Grease a baking dish with butter, oil, or cooking spray. In a small saucepan, melt 2 tablespoons of the butter. Pour the melted butter into a medium bowl. Add the cracker crumbs and thyme and toss together. Set aside.

2. In a medium saucepan, heat the remaining 2 tablespoons butter and the oil over medium heat. Add the onion, celery, and bell pepper and cook until softened, 5 to 7 minutes. Add the garlic and cook for 1 minute. Sprinkle with the flour and cook, stirring constantly, for 1 minute. Add the broth, clam juice, okra, hot sauce, and bay leaf and bring to a boil. Reduce the heat a tiny bit and simmer until thickened, about 2 minutes. Remove and discard the bay leaf.

3. Add the shrimp to the pan and stir to coat all over. Transfer to the prepared baking dish. Top with the cracker crumb mixture. Bake until the top is golden brown and the shrimp are cooked through, about 15 minutes. You won't believe your eyes. This is just the prettiest gumbo dish ever.

> **CLAM UP**
> You'll find clam juice bottled in most supermarkets. It's a great thing to have in the fridge, as it adds huge amounts of flavor to fish stews, sauces, and chowders. And try adding a few drops to your next Bloody Mary—y'all won't believe how good it is.

GOLDEN FRIED OYSTERS

Maybe it's got something to do with my marrying a seafaring man, but I have always considered oysters among my tools in the romance department. They're the food to make for your lover when you want to really savor the textures of a sensual feast. And frying oysters just puts me right over the edge. I do it fast, so they stay moist and succulent inside that crisp coating. Then we dip those honeys in a cool, sweet tartar sauce and—oh, baby.

SERVES 4

Tartar Sauce
¼ cup mayonnaise
1 tablespoon pickle relish
¼ teaspoon finely chopped fresh tarragon

Fried Oysters
About 2 quarts vegetable oil, for deep-frying
¼ cup finely ground cornmeal
½ pound shucked fresh oysters, drained and patted dry
Salt and black pepper

1. To make the tartar sauce: In a small bowl, stir together the mayonnaise, relish, and tarragon. Refrigerate until ready to use.

2. To prepare the oysters: In a medium saucepan, heat 2 inches of oil over medium-high heat until it reaches 375°F on a deep-fry thermometer.

3. Place the cornmeal in a wide, shallow bowl. Lightly sprinkle the oysters with salt and black pepper. Dip each oyster in the cornmeal, turning to coat evenly. Shake off any excess coating.

4. Working in batches, use a slotted spoon or a spider (see illustration) to lower half the oysters into the hot oil. Be extra careful, as that oil may splatter a bit. Fry, stirring occasionally, until crisp and golden, about 2 minutes per batch. Transfer to a paper towel–lined plate to drain. Serve with the crunchy, creamy, tangy tartar sauce for dipping.

A spider is a strainer used in deep-frying. It has a round basket at the end of a long handle for scooping food out of the hot oil.

A LITTLE SIZZLE
I strongly recommend having a deep-fry thermometer in the house, but if you don't have one on hand, you can flick a drop of water into the oil to see if the oil is ready to fry. If it's ready, it should sizzle. Just be careful with this test. The hot oil may spatter, and you don't want to get any of it on you.

CREAMY CHARLESTON CRAB CASSEROLE

■ ■

When life events—good or bad—take place, I like to bring a casserole dish to a friend's house ready for baking. "Honey, preheat your oven," I'll say. "I'm bringing you a casserole." This deliciously creamy, crisp-topped crab number has been to more births and funerals than I can count. Of course, it's so delicious, there's no cause to wait for something important to happen. Just pick up some crab and enjoy it anytime.

SERVES 4

4 tablespoons (½ stick) butter
2 tablespoons all-purpose flour
2 cups whole milk
3 tablespoons dry sherry
¾ cup shredded sharp Cheddar cheese
   (3 ounces)

1 pound crabmeat, picked over to
   remove bits of shell (see box, page 8)
½ teaspoon salt
¼ teaspoon black pepper
¼ cup dried bread crumbs
¼ cup grated Parmesan cheese
   (about 1 ounce)

1. Preheat the oven to 350°F. Grease an 8-inch square baking pan or coat with cooking spray.

2. In a large skillet, melt 2 tablespoons of the butter over medium heat. Whisk in the flour. Cook, stirring, for 1 minute. Slowly whisk in the milk and sherry and cook for 2 minutes. Whisk in the Cheddar until the mixture is smooth. Remove from the heat and stir in the crab, salt, and black pepper. Pour the mixture into the prepared pan.

3. In a small bowl, toss together the bread crumbs and Parmesan. In a small saucepan, melt the remaining 2 tablespoons butter over medium heat. Pour over the bread crumb mixture and toss to combine. Scatter the mixture over the casserole.

4. Bake the casserole until golden and bubbling, 25 to 30 minutes. Let sit a few minutes, then serve it up.

> ## TOP CHOICE
> Instead of bread crumbs, you can try crushed-up Ritz crackers or saltines or fresh bread cubes.

SAVANNAH CRAB CAKES

When it comes to crab cakes in Savannah, you'd better be ready for everyone to be a critic: few foods are as contested in these parts. I load my cakes with crab, go easy on the bread crumbs, and use only Kraft mayonnaise and a nice hit of Old Bay seasoning, which is just so perfectly delicious with seafood. Peanut oil, nice and hot, gives the crab cakes a nice clean-tasting fry. A squeeze of lemon is all they need after that!

SERVES 4 TO 6

1 pound crabmeat, picked over to remove bits of shell (see box, page 8)
½ cup dried bread crumbs
⅓ cup mayonnaise
¼ cup finely chopped scallions
1 large egg, lightly beaten

1 tablespoon Old Bay seasoning
1 teaspoon mustard powder
½ teaspoon Worcestershire sauce
¼ teaspoon hot sauce
Peanut or vegetable oil, for frying
1 lemon, cut into wedges, for serving

1. In a large bowl, combine the crab, bread crumbs, mayonnaise, scallions, egg, Old Bay seasoning, mustard powder, Worcestershire sauce, and hot sauce. Shape into six 3-inch patties.

2. In a large skillet, heat ¼ inch of oil over medium heat. When the oil is hot, carefully place the crab cakes, in batches, in the pan and fry until the undersides are golden, 4 to 5 minutes. Carefully flip the crab cakes and fry on the other side until golden brown, about 4 minutes. Serve warm, with pretty lemon wedges.

> ### TAKE A DIP
> I love to pair these crab cakes with tartar sauce. And it doesn't get much easier or much more delicious than the tartar sauce from my Golden Fried Oysters (page 195).

DEVILED CRAB

■ ■

Well, I just can't pass up anything deviled. I devil fresh crabmeat by folding it into my usual mayo and mustard combination along with some half-and-half to loosen up the mixture. Then I add some spice. But you know what really makes the difference here? Potato chips. Crush 'em over the top, bake the whole thing, and you're golden: a crab dish that no mortal can resist.

SERVES 4 TO 6

1 pound crabmeat, picked over to remove bits of shell (see box, page 8)

2 cups fresh bread crumbs (from 4 to 5 slices bread)

1 cup mayonnaise

1 cup half-and-half

2 teaspoons Dijon mustard

1 teaspoon onion powder

1 teaspoon salt

⅛ teaspoon cayenne pepper

1 cup lightly crushed potato chips

¼ teaspoon paprika

1. Preheat the oven to 350°F. Grease a shallow 1-quart baking dish with butter, oil, or cooking spray.

2. In a medium bowl, toss together the crab and bread crumbs. In a separate medium bowl, mix together the mayonnaise, half-and-half, mustard, onion powder, salt, and cayenne pepper. Add to the crab mixture and gently stir to combine.

3. Transfer the crab to the prepared dish. Top with the potato chips and sprinkle the paprika over the top. Bake until golden and bubbling, about 45 minutes. Just wait until you try this deviled crab. It tastes like it came straight from heaven.

CRAB PICKING

You'll find a wide variety of crabmeat options on the store shelves. Steer clear of "sea legs" or imitation crabmeat, since it's not true crab. Your best bet is the grade of real crab called white meat "lump," but you'll pay a little extra for it. You can save a little money with claw meat, which is dark meat from the claws and legs, or back fin, which is flakes of lump and other white crabmeat.

CREAMY SCALLOP BAKE

■ ■

A scallop is a beautiful thing. Like so many of the recipes I love, this one has very few ingredients and tastes like you slaved over it. I love to serve this elegant dish over wild rice—or even with just a crusty loaf of bread—to catch the wonderful sauce. Skinny little green beans are a nice way to round out the plate if you're using your fancy china.

SERVES 4

1 cup heavy cream

1 tablespoon dry sherry

1 clove garlic, lightly crushed

Salt and white pepper

1½ pounds sea scallops

¼ cup grated Parmesan cheese

1 tablespoon chopped fresh basil

Crusty bread, for serving

1. Preheat the oven to 400°F.

2. In a small saucepan, combine the cream, sherry, and garlic and bring to a gentle boil over medium heat. Cook, stirring occasionally, until reduced to ¾ cup. Discard the garlic clove and season to taste with salt and white pepper.

3. Meanwhile, lightly sprinkle salt and white pepper over the scallops. Divide them among 4 individual baking dishes pretty enough to serve in. In a small bowl, toss the Parmesan with the basil.

4. Pour the sauce over the scallops and top with the cheese mixture. Bake until the scallops are opaque, about 15 minutes. Serve with the crusty bread to sop up the creamy sauce.

SCALLOP COUSINS

The two types of scallops you'll come across are bay and sea. The sea scallops used here are the larger of the two. I like them in this recipe because they tend to stand up to oven heat better than their bayside cousins.

GROUPER WITH SHRIMP BUTTER

■ ■

Well, I'd eat shrimp butter off a spoon if no one was looking, but you really must try it on grouper, a firm, moist, slightly sweet fish that I absolutely adore.

SERVES 4

4 grouper fillets (8 ounces each), skin removed
Salt and black pepper

½ batch Shrimp Butter (page 37)
1 lemon, cut into wedges, for serving

1. Preheat the broiler. Line a baking sheet with foil.
2. Lightly sprinkle each fillet with salt and black pepper. Place on the baking sheet and spread the top of each fillet with a generous 2 tablespoons of Shrimp Butter. Broil until the fish is just cooked through, 5 to 8 minutes. Serve hot, with pretty lemon wedges.

A PERFECT PAIR

What is it about lemon and fish that make them so amazing together? The acidy flavor and smell of lemon have just the perfect effect on fish, bringing out all the wonderful flavors that fish has to offer. Try another citrus like orange or lime for some variety.

DRESS UP

When I call a fish "dressed," what I mean is that a whole fish has been scaled and cleaned of its innards and is ready to be stuffed. If you choose to take it home without the head, make sure you take a look at the eyes before the head is removed; they should be clear, not cloudy. That is the best sign of a fresh fish.

CRAB-STUFFED FLOUNDER

When I want to serve an impressive fish dish, I get a nice big whole fish and stuff it. To really up the ante—and make sure the fish won't dry out in the oven—I lay bacon over it. This is such a beautiful and festive dish, a perfect centerpiece for a dinner party.

SERVES 8

1 whole dressed flounder (see bottom box
    opposite), at least 7 pounds
Salt and black pepper
Garlic powder
Onion salt
2 pounds crabmeat, picked over to
    remove bits of shell (see box, page 8)
2 large eggs, lightly beaten
1 medium yellow onion, chopped
1 sleeve saltine crackers, crushed
6 slices bacon
2 slices lemon
¼ teaspoon dried dill, or 1 tablespoon
    chopped fresh dill

Stuff the fish with the crab filling, then lay the bacon and lemon slices on the fish and sprinkle lightly with the dill.

1. Preheat the oven to 350°F. Line a rimmed baking sheet with foil. Grease the foil with oil or coat with cooking spray.

2. Place the fish on the prepared baking sheet and sprinkle liberally inside and out with salt, black pepper, garlic powder, and onion salt. Make two slits on the side of the fish facing up but do not slice through.

3. In a large bowl, combine the crab, eggs, onion, cracker crumbs, and salt and black pepper to taste. Stuff this mixture into the cavity of the fish. If it is more than the fish will hold, that's just fine. Just place it all around the cavity. Lay the bacon and lemon slices over the fish and sprinkle lightly with the dill.

4. Cover the fish with foil and bake for 50 minutes. Remove the foil and bake until lightly golden, 10 minutes longer.

CRISPY TORTILLA-CRUSTED TILAPIA

■ ■

Tilapia is such a nice, light fish, with a firm, flaky texture and a nice, mild sweetness. I give it zing by coating the fillets with tortilla chip crumbs, butter, and lime zest. Then I bake it until crispy.

SERVES 4

1 cup crushed tortilla chips
4 tablespoons (½ stick) butter, melted
2 teaspoons finely grated lime zest
½ teaspoon dried basil

4 skinless tilapia fillets (4 ounces each)
1 teaspoon Paula Deen's House
    Seasoning (page 435)

1. Preheat the oven to 425°F. Line a baking sheet with foil.

2. In a medium bowl, combine the crushed chips, melted butter, lime zest, and basil.

3. Place the fish on the prepared baking sheet and season with the House Seasoning. Spread the tortilla mixture over the fish, pressing down to make it stick. Bake until the fish is opaque and just cooked through and the tortilla crumbs are golden around the edges, 12 to 15 minutes.

QUICK COOK

Always go for a quick-cooking, high-heat method when you're using fish fillets. That way, you'll be sure to get a nice crust on the outside while keeping the fish tender and moist on the inside.

FISH AND SHELLFISH

CAJUN BLACKENED CATFISH

When chef Paul Prudhomme made Cajun blackened fish all the rage at his Louisiana restaurant, K-Paul's, back in the '80s, my own restaurant dreams were still almost a decade away. The secret of his recipe is to cook the fish in a skillet so hot, the butter darkens and the spices toast—and to do it pretty fast so nothing burns. The result is a nice crust and a ton of flavor. Turn on the fume hood, y'all, and cook up some Louisiana love.

SERVES 4

2 tablespoons paprika
2 teaspoons ground thyme
1 teaspoon onion powder
½ teaspoon garlic powder
½ teaspoon salt

½ teaspoon black pepper
4 skinless catfish fillets
   (5 to 6 ounces each)
8 tablespoons (1 stick) butter, melted
1 lemon, cut into wedges, for serving

1. In a small bowl, mix together the paprika, thyme, onion powder, garlic powder, salt, and black pepper.

2. Dip the fish into the melted butter, letting any excess drip off, then dip into the spice mixture to coat thoroughly.

3. Heat a large, preferably cast-iron, skillet over medium-high heat until very hot. Add the fillets and cook, turning once, until a fork slides easily through the thickest part of the fish, 3 to 4 minutes per side. Serve with lemon wedges on the side.

> ## FISH SWITCH
> If you aren't a catfish fan, this recipe will work with any nice white fish fillet. Try tilapia or flounder if that's what you've got.

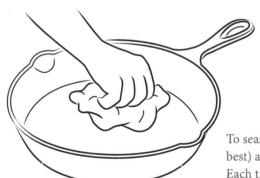

To season a new cast-iron pan, coat with oil (lard is best) and heat in a low oven (300°F) for up to 1 hour. Each time the pan is washed, season it again by wiping it with an oil-soaked paper towel and heating it on the stovetop over low heat until it begins to smoke.

FRIED CATFISH

■ ■

Living in Savannah, you'd think crab boils were the only way to enjoy life. But in landlocked southwest Georgia, where I grew up, it was all about the fish fry. We love our lake fish fried with a spicy cornmeal coating, and you will, too.

SERVES 4 TO 6

**About 4 quarts peanut or vegetable oil, for
deep-frying**
1½ cups all-purpose flour
1½ cups cornmeal

½ teaspoon cayenne pepper
8 skinless catfish fillets (5 to 6 ounces each)
Paula Deen's House Seasoning (page 435)

1. Fill a large, deep pot halfway with oil (there should be at least 3 inches) and heat over medium-high heat until it reaches 350°F on a deep fry thermometer.

2. In a wide, shallow bowl, combine the flour, cornmeal, and cayenne pepper. Generously sprinkle both sides of each fillet with House Seasoning.

3. Working in batches, dredge the catfish in the flour mixture and carefully lower into the hot oil. Fry until the fish is golden and just cooked through, 7 to 8 minutes. Set on a paper towel–lined baking sheet to drain.

FISH FLIP

Unless you've got yourself a good, flat spatula, getting that catfish out of the hot oil can prove a little tricky, so I recommend having one of these simple kitchen tools in your drawer. Sometimes called an egg flipper, it is a long-handled, broad, slotted metal spatula that is flexible.

CATFISH PO' BOY

■ ■

Oh, my goodness, there is nothing so spectacular as a fried fish po' boy. You get your creamy mayonnaise, your sweet pickles, your hot sauce, your crusty toasted French bread, and your lettuce, tomato, and onion all set up to fix the world's best sandwich. Then you fry up a batch of catfish, put it all together, and, oh, honey.

SERVES 4

½ cup mayonnaise

2 tablespoons chopped sweet pickles

1½ teaspoons liquid from the pickle jar

¼ teaspoon Paula Deen's House Seasoning (page 435)

Dash of hot sauce

1 to 2 baguettes (French bread)

4 Fried Catfish fillets (opposite)

2 medium beefsteak tomatoes, sliced

1 cup shredded iceberg lettuce

1 red onion, thinly sliced

1. Preheat the broiler.

2. In a small bowl, combine the mayonnaise, pickles, pickle liquid, House Seasoning, and hot sauce to make a homemade tartar sauce.

3. Cut the bread crosswise into four 7-inch sections, then split each section horizontally. Place the bread cut side up on a baking sheet. Broil until toasted, about 1 minute.

4. Spread the cut surfaces of the toasted bread with the tartar sauce. For each serving, sandwich the fish, tomato, lettuce, and onion between 2 bread halves. Serve while the fish is hot.

DIY SAUCE

Homemade tartar sauce is real easy. It's just a mayonnaise sauce with a coarsely chopped pickled vegetable stirred through. I like to add some liquid from the pickle jar for a little extra zing, and maybe some herbs like tarragon, dill, basil, or parsley to fancy it up.

LOW-COUNTRY BOIL

■ ■

At its simplest, a good old Low-Country boil can be cooked up in a big pot on a fire on the beach, then poured out onto newspapers to enjoy right there. But you can create the same carefree beach feeling in your home, too—just get out your biggest pot, pick up some summer corn and new taters along with your fresh shrimp and smoked sausage, and put it all together. While it's cooking, lay newspapers down on a big table, put on your flip-flops, chill some drinks, and call in everyone around. Wherever you make it, Low-Country boil is a party in a pot!

SERVES 6

Crab boil seasoning (see box)

12 small red potatoes

6 pieces (4 inches long) good smoked
    sausage, such as andouille

6 ears corn

3 pounds large shrimp, with shells

Butter, for serving

Toasted bread, for serving

1. Fill a large pot with enough water to cover all the ingredients. Add 2 teaspoons crab boil seasoning for every quart of water and bring to a boil over medium-high heat. (Add more crab boil if you like a lot of spice.)

2. Add the potatoes and sausage to the boiling water and cook over medium heat for 20 minutes. Add the corn and cook for 10 minutes. Add the shrimp and cook for no more than 3 minutes. You do not want to overcook the shrimp!

3. Drain and serve with plenty of butter for the corn, piping-hot toast, and ice-cold beer.

ON THE BOIL

There are two ways you can go with the crab boil seasoning for your Low-Country boil: the spicier Louisiana style (like Zatarain's) or the milder Maryland style (like Old Bay).

Chapter 9

GRILLING AND BARBECUE

Down South, we cook outside just about year-round, so folks get creative. The way I see it, there are two great reasons to grill and barbecue outside: the flavor is incredible, and it's just about the most fun you can have making dinner. When I fire up our outdoor kitchen, I intend to cook a no-mess, no-fuss meal, and to stay out there while I do it—chatting and enjoying the view. I tell you, there is no better appetizer in the world than smelling those good smells and waiting for your food to be cooked just right.

Whether you have a full outdoor kitchen or a tabletop grill, there are so many things you can do. Go out there with your rib eye on a plate and your bowl of mustard glaze, or your fresh salmon and some maple glaze. Then sear the meat or fish good on both sides, brush on your sauce, and, honey, that's all she wrote. Give your steak or seafood a hit of big flavor, like I do for my Cajun Flank Steak with a Kick (page 218). Don't move the meat around too much or you won't get a nice brown crust. I love my Perfect Char-Grilled Filet Mignon (page 217) for that reason. And I don't think you'll need to be convinced about my grilled Butter Burgers (page 219): they're so darn good they'll make you wanna slap your mama!

Anytime I run out of ideas in my kitchen, I head out back to make Beer Can Chicken (page 211). When you stand the bird up on that can of beer, the entire chicken gets so beautifully browned. I stick rosemary sprigs in the beer and it just permeates the whole thing. Another go-to recipe is Quick BBQ Chicken (page 213) with my Daddy's Tangy Grilling Sauce (page 212). For the last 15 minutes of cooking he would swab his grilled chicken with that sauce until it was cooked to perfection.

If grilling is the speedy hare, Southern barbecue is the good old tortoise: the low, slow cooking that folks take so seriously on the barbecue circuit. To me, you can't get any more Southern than smoking a whole pig over wood. Where I come from, that is barbecue. And nothing fills my heart like sticking my head out the door to check up on Michael while he's trying out some type of wood in his smoker, keeping his eye on a few racks of Memphis Dry-Rub Ribs (page 225).

Here in Georgia we're mainly pig eaters, but when I was shooting one of my shows, I had the opportunity to do some traveling along the barbecue belt, and some of the finest 'cue that I tasted was in San Antonio, Texas. I met this cowboy with a real old-timey chuck wagon, and he had a big fire going, making his own charcoal and cooking brisket. That cowboy slow-cooked that meat and worked that fire for 10 hours. And it was out of this world. I hardly knew the man, but when he cut me a piece of that brisket I said, "I'm sorry, but I'm in love with you. That is the best thing I've ever tasted!" There's something so powerful about cooking outside, y'all, it could make you kiss a man you just met!

These days most people have gas grills, but if you have a charcoal grill, proceed as usual with the recipes here. Just be sure to watch those flames!

BEER CAN CHICKEN

When you stand that bird up on a can of beer, you achieve two things: You expose every bit of that skin to the heat of your oven, so it has the chance to get browned and crispy all over. And your can of beer is going to turn into steam as it heats, giving off great flavor and cooking the chicken from the inside out. I use a rotisserie chicken–style spice rub on the skin and a real traditional barbecue sauce, and I tell you, it is just a revelation every time we make this.

SERVES 4

Dry Rub

2 teaspoons salt
2 teaspoons paprika
2 teaspoons light brown sugar
1 teaspoon celery salt
1 teaspoon dried oregano
1 teaspoon mustard powder
1 teaspoon black pepper
1 teaspoon ground cumin
1 teaspoon garlic powder
1 teaspoon chili powder
Pinch of cayenne pepper

NEAR BEER

If you'd rather not use a regular beer, go ahead and substitute a nonalcoholic beer. Your chicken won't know the difference!

Barbecue Sauce

2 tablespoons vegetable oil
¾ cup finely chopped yellow onion
2 teaspoons finely chopped garlic
½ teaspoon salt
¼ teaspoon black pepper
2 tablespoons light brown sugar
1 teaspoon cayenne pepper
½ cup ketchup
2 tablespoons yellow mustard
½ cup apple cider vinegar
2 tablespoons fresh lemon juice
Dash of Worcestershire sauce

Chicken

1 whole chicken (5 pounds), rinsed and
   patted dry
1 can (12 ounces) light beer
3 sprigs fresh rosemary (optional)

1. Preheat the grill to medium.

2. To make the dry rub: In a medium bowl, combine all the ingredients. (The dry rub can be stored in an airtight container and kept for 6 months.)

3. To make the barbecue sauce: In a medium saucepan, heat the oil over medium-high heat. Add the onion and garlic and cook until soft, about 5 minutes. Stir in remaining ingredients and ¼ cup water and bring to a boil. Reduce the heat and simmer for 10 minutes. Remove from the heat. Reserve some of the barbecue sauce for serving.

4. Rub the chicken all over with 2 to 3 tablespoons of the dry rub, making sure to get some around the cavity opening as well. Open the beer can and pour out about ¼ cup. Stick the rosemary sprigs, if using, in the can, then place the can, keeping it upright, into the rear cavity of the chicken. Carefully place the chicken, standing up on the can, in the center of the grill. Try not to spill any beer.

5. Cover the grill and cook the chicken for about 1 hour, turning as necessary to get an even color. The chicken is done when its juices run clear when pierced with a fork. Carefully remove the beer can from the chicken using oven mitts and let the chicken rest 10 minutes before carving. The chicken will be crispy-crunchy on the outside and falling off the bone on the inside. Serve with the reserved barbecue sauce on the side and just watch them dig in.

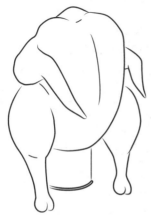

Hold the cleaned and seasoned chicken, neck side up, over a beer can and insert the can into the cavity of the chicken. Pull the chicken legs forward to form a tripod so the chicken stands upright.

DADDY'S TANGY GRILLING SAUCE

My daddy's sauce endeared him to many of the people in our little community in Albany, Georgia. I remember a fine lady named Ms. Plant—she was the Dean of Girls at my school, a member of our church, and a sponsor of our cheerleading team—and she once attended one of our family's chicken barbecues. Ms. Plant just went crazy for Daddy and his sauce, and I think she fell in love with them both! You'll see why when you taste this buttery, tangy sauce. There's nothing better.

MAKES 1½ CUPS

1 cup Worcestershire sauce
4 tablespoons (½ stick) butter

Juice of 2 lemons

In a medium saucepan, combine all the ingredients and simmer for 10 minutes. And just like that, you've got the most wonderful grilling sauce for all types of meat.

QUICK BBQ CHICKEN

This is your weeknight, feed-everyone-fast barbecue chicken, and it cannot be beat. Children and adults adore this recipe, so you might want to pick up an extra pack of legs and thighs just in case everyone eats twice their share. It has happened.

SERVES 4

1½ cups bottled barbecue sauce
½ teaspoon freshly grated orange zest
¼ cup orange juice
1 clove garlic, finely chopped

2 dashes of hot sauce
1 whole chicken (3½ pounds), rinsed,
    patted dry, and cut into 8 pieces

1. In a large bowl, combine the barbecue sauce, orange zest, orange juice, garlic, and hot sauce. Remove ½ cup of the sauce and set aside to use as a baste. Add the chicken to the sauce remaining in the bowl and toss to coat. Let the chicken sit in the marinade while you preheat the grill.

2. Lightly grease the grate by brushing with oil. Preheat the grill to medium. Place the chicken skin side up on the grill, cover, and cook for 10 minutes. Turn the chicken, baste with half of the reserved basting sauce, cover, and cook for another 10 minutes. Turn the chicken skin side up, brush with the remaining sauce, cover, and cook until an instant-read thermometer registers 170°F when inserted into the breasts and 180°F when inserted into the thighs, about 10 minutes more. Let rest for 5 minutes before serving. And don't forget to pass around plenty of napkins!

ALMOST HOMEMADE

Just because you're short on time doesn't mean you have to be short on flavor. Using store-bought sauce as a starting point for homemade dinners is a great time-saver. But if you happen to have some leftover homemade barbecue sauce, you can use that instead.

SHRIMP KEBABS

Folks love kebabs—they're fun to put together and they look so pretty on the plate. Well, that's fine by me, as long as they cook fast and have a ton of flavor. This shrimp number fills the bill on all counts.

SERVES 6

1 tablespoon fresh lemon juice
1½ teaspoons Paula Deen's House Seasoning
   (page 435)
¼ cup sliced scallions
3 tablespoons vegetable oil
1 pound large shrimp, peeled and deveined

1½ cups cherry tomatoes
2 teaspoons chopped fresh parsley, for
   garnish

12 metal skewers

1. In a small bowl, whisk together the lemon juice and House Seasoning. Whisk in the scallions and oil. In a large bowl, combine the shrimp and tomatoes. Pour the lemon marinade over the shrimp mixture. Cover with plastic wrap and refrigerate for 1 hour.

2. Thread the shrimp and tomatoes onto the metal skewers; pierce each shrimp with two skewers and the tomatoes with one.

3. Grease the grate by brushing with oil. Preheat the grill to high.

4. Place the kebabs on the grill, cover, and cook, turning once halfway through the cooking time, until the tomatoes are lightly charred and the shrimp are just cooked through and pink, about 2 minutes per side. Serve sprinkled with the parsley.

KNOCK ON WOOD

If you don't have metal skewers in your kitchen drawer, you can always substitute wooden ones. Just be sure to give them a good soak in water for about 30 minutes before you thread them—that way they won't burn on the grill.

Thread the shrimp onto two skewers to prevent them from spinning when you turn them on the grill.

MUSTARD-GLAZED RIB EYES

■ ■

I believe that you should let your meat taste like meat. I never douse my steak in steak sauce, and it always makes me a little sad to see a nice thick steak cooked past medium-rare. But give it a little something, like this delicious glaze of mustard, bourbon, and brown sugar, and you're just saying, "Here you go, y'all, my special rib eye steaks, treated respectfully, with a light hand on the seasonings to just celebrate how stinkin' delicious this beef is."

SERVES 2 TO 4

2 boneless rib eye steaks (1 pound each, 1½ inches thick)
Salt and black pepper
2 teaspoons olive oil

1 teaspoon plus 2 tablespoons Dijon mustard
1 tablespoon bourbon
1 tablespoon plus 2 teaspoons light brown sugar

1. Generously sprinkle the steaks all over with salt and black pepper. Rub them with the oil and the 1 teaspoon mustard.

2. In a small bowl, whisk together the bourbon, brown sugar, ½ teaspoon salt, ½ teaspoon black pepper, and the 2 tablespoons mustard to make the glaze.

3. Grease the grate by brushing with oil. Preheat the grill to medium-high. Place the steaks on the grill, cover, and cook for 3 minutes. Flip the steaks, cover, and cook for 3 minutes longer. Brush the tops with half the glaze, flip the steaks, cover, and cook for 2 minutes. Brush the tops with the remaining glaze, flip once more, and cook uncovered until the steaks reach the doneness you like, 2 minutes more for medium-rare. Let rest for 5 minutes before slicing and serving up with all their yummy juices.

HIGH STEAKS

Rib eye is the true steak lover's steak. With its excellent marbling of fat, it is just jam-packed full of good beef flavor. And talk about tender! In my opinion, this is the ultimate grilling steak.

GRILLED RIB EYE WITH GARLIC BUTTER

■ ■

I recall the first time I came face-to-face with a snail in a fancy French restaurant. All I could do was wiggle my nose over the little things. What was that wonderful smell? Well, to my relief, it was garlic butter, which y'all can make anytime and serve over just about anything. It makes one heck of a partner for a nice steak. I just love my beef buttery.

SERVES 2 TO 4

4 large cloves garlic, finely chopped
Salt
6 tablespoons (¾ stick) butter, at room
   temperature

2 teaspoons dried thyme
½ teaspoon black pepper
2 boneless rib eye steaks
   (1 pound each, 1½ inches thick)

1. Using a mortar and pestle or the flat side of a knife, mash the garlic with a large pinch of salt until it forms a paste. In a medium bowl, combine the garlic paste, butter, thyme, black pepper, and 1 teaspoon salt. Smear half the mixture on both sides of the steaks. Cover with plastic wrap and let stand for 30 minutes at room temperature to soak up all that flavor.

2. Grease the grate by brushing with oil. Preheat the grill to medium-high. Place the steaks on the grill, cover, and cook, turning occasionally, until the steaks reach the doneness you like, about 5 minutes per side for medium-rare. Place on a plate and drop the remaining garlic butter on the hot steaks. Let rest for 5 minutes before slicing and serving. The garlic butter will melt on the hot steak and give it a rich buttery sauce.

COMPOUND INTEREST

Compound butter is just a fancy term for a butter that has been softened and then mixed with a flavoring, like the one above. Compound butters can be combined with anything from dried spices to fresh herbs, from citrus zest to spirits. Wrap the butter tightly in plastic wrap and keep it in your fridge for up to a month.

PERFECT CHAR-GRILLED FILET MIGNON

■ ■

Tenderloin is so buttery that cooking it right is the name of the game. Here, you give it a boost of flavor with a flavorful dressing, then you wrap those steaks in bacon and cook them on the grill until they have a perfect char and a great smoky flavor from the bacon. If you've got yourself a meat-and-potatoes type of man, this is a great start for a romantic evening. Start the meat marinating, light the grill, then slip into something more comfortable.

SERVES 2

1 bottle (8 ounces) zesty Italian salad dressing
2 beef tenderloin fillets (10 ounces each,
   1½ to 2 inches thick)

2 slices bacon
2 tablespoons Lea & Perrins steak sauce

1. Pour the salad dressing into a shallow pan. Place the steaks in the pan and coat all over with the marinade. Cover with plastic wrap and let marinate in the refrigerator for 3 to 4 hours.

2. Grease the grate by brushing with oil. Preheat the grill to medium-high. Wrap a strip of bacon around each steak, securing it with a toothpick. Place the steaks on the grill, cover, and cook, turning only once, until the steaks reach the doneness you like, about 8 minutes per side for medium-rare. Transfer the steaks to a platter. Combine the steak sauce with 2 teaspoons water and baste the steaks on each side. Let rest for a few minutes, then serve it up.

WAIT YOUR TURN

For perfectly cooked fillet mignon, you've got to leave them be. Turn them only once during cooking and they will come out evenly cooked on both sides.

To create direct heat when using a charcoal grill, mound charcoal into the center of the grill. Light the coals, and when they are white hot, cook the meat directly over the hottest spot.

CAJUN FLANK STEAK WITH A KICK

■ ■

I love a piece of beef with a little chew, and flank steak is perfect in that regard. It also has a real beefy flavor, which is so satisfying. This recipe delivers with a nice hit of fire thanks to hot sauce, cayenne pepper, and spicy Cajun seasoning. Chill some drinks to put out the flames and get out your steak knives.

SERVES 4

1½ pounds flank steak
Salt
2 tablespoons olive oil

4 teaspoons Cajun seasoning
½ teaspoon hot sauce
Pinch of cayenne pepper

1. Generously sprinkle both sides of the steak with salt. In a wide, shallow bowl, combine the oil, Cajun seasoning, hot sauce, and cayenne pepper. Rub the mixture all over the steak. Cover with plastic wrap and refrigerate for at least 2 hours or overnight.

2. Grease the grate by brushing with oil. Preheat the grill to medium-high heat. Place the steak on the grill, cover, and cook until the steak reaches the doneness you like, 4 to 5 minutes per side for medium-rare. Let rest for 5 minutes before slicing and serving. This one packs a punch, folks!

FABULOUS FLANK

Flank steak is a wonderful grilling meat, and it is one of the less expensive beef cuts, so it can be on the tough side if it's not marinated. But once you've slapped a marinade on a flank steak, the grill is where it ought to be cooked.

BUTTER BURGERS

■ ■

Here's a story about my butter burgers, y'all: One night I had all the family over for hamburgers. Now, I was in the mood for a good ol' char-grilled hamburger, and I took my real cold butter and cut it up in little cubes. And I salted and peppered my burger meat, and then I worked those cubes of butter up in that meat. And my nephew Jeremy came over and said, "What's that in the hamburgers?" So my niece, Corrie, leaned over and told him, "Jeremy, that's garlic!" "It's garlic?" I said. Then she whispered, "He won't eat it if he knows there's butter in there because he's workin' on his diet." So after dinner he came up and said, "Aunt Paula, that garlic was so good in those burgers. It gave them such flavor!" Corrie and I just busted out laughin' and we finally told him. There is nothin' better than a butter burger, and sometimes deception is the most delicious policy.

SERVES 4

2 pounds ground beef

4 tablespoons (½ stick) butter, cut into small
  cubes

1 teaspoon salt

1 teaspoon black pepper

4 hamburger buns, split

Tomato slices, onion slices, and lettuce,
  for serving

1. In a large bowl, mix together the beef, butter, salt, and black pepper. Form into 4 patties about 1 inch thick. Place on a baking sheet.

2. Grease the grate by brushing with oil. Preheat the grill to medium. Place the burgers on the grill, cover, and cook, turning once, until the burgers reach the doneness you like, 7 to 9 minutes for medium-rare. Just before the burgers are done, put the buns on toward the back of the grill to toast.

3. Sandwich the burgers in the buns and top with tomato, onion, lettuce, and whatever other delicious toppings y'all like on your burgers.

> ### BBQ TOAST
> When I'm grilling up burgers, I like to go ahead and toast my hamburger buns right there on the grill toward the last minute or so, so they're ready when my burgers are!

GRILLED RED PEPPER SCALLOPS

■ ■

To me, a good grilled scallop is so delicious and buttery—few things taste better! And this is such a pretty way to dress one up. I char my red bell peppers, peel 'em, then cut strips of that smoky red pepper flesh to wrap around the scallops. You can grill or broil the scallops, and count on "Ooh's" and "Aah's" either way.

SERVES 6

1½ pounds large sea scallops
2 tablespoons olive oil
Grated zest of 1 lemon
Black pepper

4 large red bell peppers

6 metal skewers

1. In a medium bowl, combine the scallops, oil, lemon zest, and black pepper to taste. Cover tightly with plastic wrap and refrigerate while you prepare the bell peppers.

2. Preheat the broiler or grill to high heat. Halve the bell peppers lengthwise and remove the stems, seeds, and ribs. If broiling, place the bell peppers skin side up on a baking sheet; if grilling, place the peppers skin side down. Broil or grill, without turning, until the skin is charred, 6 to 10 minutes. Place in a paper bag, close the top up tight, and let the bell peppers steam for 10 minutes. Remove the charred skins and cut the bell peppers lengthwise into ¾-inch-wide strips.

3. Wrap a bell pepper strip around each scallop to cover completely, overlapping the pepper ends. Secure the strips by running a 10-inch metal skewer through the scallop and the bell pepper. Divide the scallops among 6 skewers.

4. If the grill is not already on, grease the grate and preheat. Place the skewers on the grill, cover, and cook, turning once, until the scallops are almost firm to the touch, 1 to 2 minutes on each side. (Or cook under the broiler for about 3 minutes per side.) Then serve them up just as soon as you can.

> ## DO AHEAD
>
> When I broil or grill red bell peppers, I like to do a big batch so that I have them on hand in the fridge. After they're cooked, just cover them in olive oil, close them up tightly, and they will keep in the fridge for up to a week. Those leftover peppers can be added to sandwiches and salads.

MAPLE-GLAZED SALMON

To my taste, a nice rich piece of salmon needs just a little lift—like this tangy-sweet glaze, which has a pinch of mustard powder and a nice splash of vinegar in it to pep up the syrup. The glaze caramelizes as you grill the fish, and it is just a lovely everyday (or special-occasion) way to serve this popular fish.

SERVES 4

4 skin-on salmon fillets (6 to 8 ounces each)
Salt and black pepper
2 teaspoons olive oil
4 tablespoons (½ stick) butter, melted

3 tablespoons maple syrup
1½ teaspoons apple cider vinegar
¾ teaspoon Worcestershire sauce
¾ teaspoon mustard powder

1. Generously sprinkle the salmon all over with salt and black pepper. Rub each fillet with ½ teaspoon of the oil.

2. In a small bowl, whisk together the butter, syrup, vinegar, Worcestershire sauce, mustard powder, and ¾ teaspoon black pepper to make the glaze.

3. Grease the grate by brushing with oil. Preheat the grill to medium-high. Place the salmon skin side down on the grill, cover, and cook for 4 minutes. Brush the tops generously with the glaze, flip the salmon, cover, and cook until they reach the doneness you like, about 5 minutes for medium-rare. Carefully remove the fish from the grill and place skin side down on a pretty serving platter.

UNDER THE SKIN
Keeping the skin on this salmon is important for a couple reasons. First, under the skin is a layer of fat next to the meat that keeps the fish moist and flavorful. The skin also provides stability for flipping the fillet, ensuring that the salmon won't curl up and flake apart.

BENNE SEED GRILLED TUNA STEAKS

▪ ▪

My Bobby grills him some tuna about five nights out of the week, so when I make him a meal, either I'll go whole hog and serve that boy up some fried pork chops or I'll get with his program and pick up some tuna steaks. But I like to jazz up grilled tuna with a soy-bourbon marinade and a nice coating of benne seeds, which are also known as sesame seeds.

SERVES 4

2 tablespoons soy sauce

2 tablespoons bourbon

¾ teaspoon black pepper

2 tablespoons vegetable oil

1 tablespoon sesame oil

4 tuna steaks (8 ounces each)

¾ cup benne seeds (sesame seeds)

1. In a wide, shallow bowl, whisk together the soy sauce, bourbon, and black pepper, then whisk in the oils. Add the tuna steaks and toss to coat well with the mixture. Cover tightly with plastic wrap and refrigerate for 1 hour.

2. Grease the grate by brushing with oil. Preheat the grill to medium-high. Place benne seeds in a shallow bowl or pie plate and place next to the grill. Place the tuna steaks on the grill, cover, and cook, turning once, for 2 minutes per side. Remove the steaks from the grill and quickly press each side of the steaks in the benne seeds. Return to the grill to cook, turning once, until the seeds are lightly browned, about 1 minute per side.

A HAPPY MEDIUM

If you like your tuna cooked more than medium-rare, add 1 to 2 minutes to the cooking time before coating the tuna with the benne seeds. That way, the seeds won't burn. Once you've got those seeds on your tuna, you want to cook it only another minute or two.

BOBBY'S GRILLED TUNA BURGERS

Bobby will eat a Butter Burger (page 219) if I stare him down, but he's happier fixing these healthy patties made with fresh tuna as a lighter alternative. You can't compare—it's apples to oranges—but these are mighty satisfying and flavorful, I must say.

SERVES 4

1½ pounds yellowfin tuna, finely chopped
¼ cup finely chopped Vidalia or other
   sweet onion
3 tablespoons Dijon mustard
2 teaspoons finely chopped garlic
2 teaspoons finely grated lemon zest

1½ teaspoons salt
¾ teaspoon black pepper
4 hamburger buns, split
Mayonnaise, tomato slices, and
   shredded lettuce, for serving

1. In a medium bowl, combine the tuna, onion, mustard, garlic, lemon zest, salt, and black pepper. Mix gently and shape the mixture into 4 patties 1 inch thick. Cover tightly with plastic wrap and refrigerate until cold and firm, about 30 minutes.

2. Grease the grate well by brushing with oil. Preheat the grill to medium-high.

3. Place the burgers on the grill, cover, and cook, turning once, until well browned all over and just cooked through, 2 to 3 minutes per side. Place the buns on the grill, cut side down, for the last minute of cooking and toast lightly.

4. Spread the cut sides of the buns with a little mayonnaise. Sandwich the burgers in the buns, and top with tomatoes and lettuce. I'm telling you, these burgers are so good, they'll give my Butter Burgers a run for their money!

PUT THE CHILL ON

Try not to overhandle the tuna while you're getting your patties ready. And give the patties 30 minutes in the fridge after you've formed them so that they hold together nicely on the grill.

GRILLED VEGGIE BASKET

■ ■

There's always something to be said for grilling your whole meal outside, once you're out there, so I love a side like this that comes together easy and cooks right next to your main protein. I use a dressing-type marinade to soften the veggies and give them a nice flavor before I cook them, and I just love the sweet, blackened bits that appear on their edges.

SERVES 4

2 tablespoons red wine vinegar
½ teaspoon salt
¼ teaspoon black pepper
¼ teaspoon dried oregano
1 clove garlic, finely chopped
3 tablespoons olive oil

8 ounces white mushrooms, stems trimmed
   and caps halved
1 zucchini or summer squash, cut crosswise
   into ¼-inch-thick slices
1 green bell pepper, cut into ¼-inch-wide
   strips
1 red onion, cut into ¼-inch-thick rings

1. In a small bowl, whisk together the vinegar, salt, black pepper, oregano, and garlic. Whisk in the oil to make the marinade. Combine the mushrooms, zucchini, bell pepper, and onion in a shallow dish. Pour the marinade over the vegetables and let stand while the grill heats up.

2. Grease the grate by brushing with oil. Preheat the grill to medium-high. Place the vegetables in a grill basket. Cover and cook, turning once, until the vegetables are slightly charred and cooked through, about 20 minutes. Serve the vegetables hot and just wait and see—even the meat lovers will flock to this one.

GRILL GADGET

A grill basket is a big help when you're grilling foods that could easily slip through the spaces in the grill grate. There are open grill baskets that look just like flat-bottomed colanders and enclosed grill baskets with long handles. With a grill basket, you can turn your food without worrying that it will slip through the grate as you're flipping it over.

MEMPHIS DRY-RUB RIBS

■ ■

You can just do so much with ribs. As long as you give them time to cook, you will be very happy you bothered. I love doing ribs on the grill or in the oven, and I like to use a dry rub to really infuse them with flavor all through. This particular blend of seasonings—brown sugar, paprika, and a host of other spices—is my tribute to the fine barbecue of Memphis, Tennessee. Michael teases me about my habit of gnawing on bones, but you just try to use a knife and fork on these babies—you'd be missing out!

SERVES 4

OVEN VARIATION

Try cooking these ribs in the oven if the weather outside is rotten. Simply preheat the oven to 325°F, pour a few tablespoons of water into the bottom of a roasting pan, and place the ribs in the pan. Cover the pan and cook until the ribs are very tender, about 2½ hours. Run the ribs under the broiler for a few minutes to brown them up before serving.

2 racks (1½ pounds each) baby back ribs
2 teaspoons salt
2 teaspoons light brown sugar
2 teaspoons paprika
1½ teaspoons garlic powder
1½ teaspoons chili powder
1½ teaspoons ground cumin
1 teaspoon black pepper
1 teaspoon dried oregano
½ teaspoon cayenne pepper

1. Place the ribs in a large roasting pan. In a small bowl, combine all the remaining ingredients to make the spice rub. Rub the spice mixture all over the ribs. Get in there real good and make sure you don't miss any spots. Cover tightly with plastic wrap and refrigerate for at least 2 hours or overnight.

2. Grease the grate by brushing with oil. When you are ready to cook the ribs, preheat the grill. Adjust the heat for low, indirect grilling. Place the ribs over indirect heat, cover, and cook, turning occasionally, until the ribs are tender and just about falling off the bone, 3 to 3½ hours. These ribs are certainly worth the wait.

If using a charcoal grill, start the charcoal as usual, then push the coals to either side of the grill, creating an area in the middle that does not have coals burning directly underneath. If using a gas grill, leave the center burner unlit but light the side burners. Place the ribs over the center.

SMOKY STEAK FAJITAS

■ ■

Making fajitas is always a fiesta. You know it's all about the fixings, from the guacamole and salsa and sour cream to that indispensable squeeze of fresh lime juice. I marinate flank steak with lime and spices before grilling to give it extra flavor.

SERVES 4 TO 6

1½ pounds flank steak
¼ cup olive oil
1 tablespoon fresh lime juice
1 jalapeño pepper, finely chopped (leave in the seeds if you want more heat)
1½ teaspoons ground cumin
¾ teaspoon garlic powder
Salt and black pepper

1 green bell pepper, cut lengthwise into ¼-inch-wide strips
1 Vidalia or other sweet onion, cut into ¼-inch-thick slices
6 flour tortillas (8 inches)
Guacamole, salsa, and sour cream, for serving

1. Place the steak in a shallow bowl. In a small bowl, whisk together the olive oil, lime juice, jalapeño, cumin, garlic powder, 1 teaspoon salt, and ½ teaspoon black pepper. Pour the marinade over the steak, turning to coat all over. Cover the bowl with plastic wrap and refrigerate for at least 1 hour or overnight. Let the steak come to room temperature for 30 minutes before grilling.

2. Grease the grate by brushing with oil. Preheat the grill to medium-high.

3. Brush the bell pepper and onion with some olive oil and sprinkle lightly with salt and black pepper. Place the onion in a single layer in a grill basket. Place the basket on the grill, cover, and cook, turning, until the onion is soft and slightly charred, 4 to 5 minutes per side. Set the onion on a plate.

4. Place the bell pepper in a single layer in the grill basket. Place the basket on the grill, cover, and cook, turning, until the bell pepper is tender and slightly charred, 2 to 3 minutes per side. Set on a plate separate from the onion.

5. Increase the grill heat to high. Remove the steak from the marinade, place on the grill, cover, and cook, turning once, until the steak reaches the doneness you like, 4 minutes per side for medium-rare. Let the steak rest for 5 minutes on a cutting board before slicing thinly.

> ### FILL 'ER UP
> Why stop with just steak? Fajitas are such a great party food! I like to set out grilled shrimp, chicken, portobello mushrooms, you name it. You can use the same marinade for shrimp, chicken, and vegetables as you use for the steak in this recipe.

6. Place the tortillas on the grill and cook, uncovered, until lightly colored, about 1 minute per side.

7. Set everything out on a big table and let your guests fill the tortillas with steak, bell peppers, and onion and top with guacamole, salsa, and sour cream. Roll up the tortillas and let the fun begin.

BBQ PORK LOIN

Cooking a pork loin on the grill is a healthy way to get your grilled pork fix. I slather on plenty of my daddy's sauce, and that hunk of meat ends up just tender, juicy, and full of flavor. It satisfies carnivores and health kickers, and you know I've got both in my family!

SERVES 6 TO 8

4 cloves garlic, finely chopped
Salt
¼ cup olive oil
1½ teaspoons black pepper

1 boneless pork loin roast (3 pounds)
Daddy's Tangy Grilling Sauce (page 212)
 or 1½ cups of your favorite sauce

1. Using a mortar and pestle or the flat side of a knife, mash the garlic with a pinch of salt until it forms a paste. In a medium bowl, whisk together the garlic paste, oil, 1½ teaspoons salt, and the black pepper. Place the pork in a large bowl and rub the mixture all over the pork. Cover with plastic wrap and refrigerate for at least 2 hours or overnight.

2. When you are ready to cook the pork, preheat the grill. Adjust the heat for low, indirect grilling. Place the pork over indirect heat, cover, and cook, turning occasionally, for 30 minutes. Remove from the heat and brush the pork with half the grilling sauce. Return the pork to indirect heat on the grill, cover, and cook, turning occasionally, until an instant-read thermometer registers 155°F when inserted into the pork, about 30 minutes. Place on a cutting board and brush with the remaining sauce. Let rest for 10 minutes before slicing and arranging on a pretty platter.

GENTLE HEATING

Large pieces of meat that need longer cooking on the grill are best cooked using indirect heat, meaning not directly over a flame. To create indirect heat in a charcoal grill, you need to bank all the coals to either side of the grill, leaving an area in the center that has no hot coals directly beneath. Then, I put a pan with a little water in it under the grate in the space where there aren't any coals. When the grill cover is closed, this creates a nice and steamy environment for the meat to cook gently. If you're using a gas grill, just turn on the burners to either side of the area where your meat is placed.

Chapter 10

VEGETABLES AND BEANS

Southern food takes some bad hits, y'all: people say it's not very healthy. Well, I happen to know a lot of old Southerners who have lived long, long lives eating the Southern staples down here. And since I've had the opportunity to travel around the United States, I have deduced that there's something to this: The South eats more vegetables than any other region I've been in. We eat more cucumbers, tomatoes, butter beans, black-eyed peas, fresh corn, and okra, not to mention our pickles, and our collards, turnip greens, and mustard greens.

Southerners don't just buy vegetables at the store, we also grow our own, so we know the glory of freshly harvested corn and peas from the garden. When I was a girl, my Aunt Peggy and Uncle George would let me plant a bit of their garden. I grew okra, peas, and tomatoes. Grandmama Paul and I would go out there and harvest, and make all kinds of pickles. Gardening brought my grandmama so much pleasure. Even after she could hardly walk, she would put down a piece of cardboard, get on her hands and knees, and scoot along her rows, then get back up holding on to her walker.

While I don't have much land (or time) for it, I do garden year-round. In cold weather I grow broccoli, cauliflower, lettuces, mustard greens, and collards. I mix together all my cooking greens in one big pot, simmer them down till they're tender and silky, then add some butter at the end, and they are so stinkin' outrageous. People rave over those greens. In the spring we plant our cucumbers, tomatoes, and all the herbs that I love. To just have an opportunity to have a few things from my own garden is a reward that I look forward to. Making Fried Green Tomatoes (page 254), Fried Cabbage (page 266), Sautéed Summer Squash (page 263), and Southern-Style Green Beans with Bacon and Tomato (page 262) from my very own garden allows me to stay in touch with where I came from.

In addition to the bounty of the garden, grits are one of the biggest Southern staples. That's because corn was one of those crops that we could count on down here, and grits are nothing but ground-up dried hominy corn. I swear, we have found a way to eat it four times a day—at breakfast, lunch, and dinner, and in a pie for dessert. I remember Mama would pour any leftover grits into a glass and put it in the refrigerator, and the next day she'd take her knife, run it around her glass so this cylinder came out, and slice that up to fry into grits cakes. I do my grits plain, or I do Cheese Grits (page 234) or even Cheesy Tomato Grits (page 235). Grits are very inexpensive, so they're a great way to fill up a hungry family for almost no money. But you can't convince me that they're not worth a million dollars.

ORIGINAL GRITS

■ ■

Grits are such a staple down South, you'd be hard-pressed to find a household that doesn't have them in the pantry. This recipe is so easy—you could just do it in your sleep! It's a true Southern classic that can be dressed up or down, depending on the occasion.

SERVES 4

1 cup stone-ground grits
   (not instant or quick-cooking)
½ teaspoon salt

¼ teaspoon black pepper
4 tablespoons (½ stick) butter

In a medium saucepan, bring 4 cups water to a boil. Slowly whisk in the grits, salt, and black pepper. Whisk constantly for 1 minute. Reduce the heat to the lowest possible setting and cook the grits until all the water is absorbed and the grits are thick and creamy, about 40 minutes or a bit longer. Take the grits off the heat and stir in the butter until it melts. Keep the grits covered until you're ready to serve them so that a hard skin doesn't form on the top of the grits.

TODAY'S GRITS, TOMORROW'S GRITS CAKES
To make a day-after treat out of leftover grits, spoon warm grits into a clean can or wide-mouthed jar. Cover with the lid or just use some plastic wrap and refrigerate until fully chilled, at least 3 hours or overnight. When you're ready to make up your cakes, run a thin, flexible knife or an offset spatula around the edge of the can to loosen the grits and pop them out of the can. Slice the grits log crosswise into ½-inch slabs and fry them in hot butter until golden brown and heated through. Now, that is a true taste of the South!

CHEESE GRITS

■ ■

I enjoy plain old grits so much, I might neglect to make these delicious cheesy baked grits. But cheese makes these simple grits so luxurious and silky, I could eat the whole mess if I didn't have to share 'em. Stone-ground grits are wonderful, but because they take so long to cook, I usually go with quick-cooking grits—which I also love. But I never make the instant kind—some things a Southerner just won't do!

SERVES 6

1 cup quick-cooking grits
1½ teaspoons salt
2 large eggs
8 tablespoons (1 stick) butter, cut up

1½ cups shredded combined Monterey Jack
    and Cheddar cheese (6 ounces total), plus
    extra for topping
2 cloves garlic, finely chopped
Dash of cayenne pepper

1. Preheat the oven to 350°F.

2. In a medium saucepan, bring 4 cups water to a boil. Slowly whisk in the grits and salt. Whisk constantly for 1 minute. Reduce the heat, cover, and cook for 20 minutes, or until the grits are thick and creamy.

3. In a small bowl, lightly beat the eggs. Take about 1 tablespoon of the hot cooked grits and whisk it into the eggs. Stir the warmed eggs back into the pan of grits and stir well to combine. Stir in the butter, cheese, garlic, and cayenne pepper.

4. Spoon the mixture into a 2-quart baking dish. Bake for 45 minutes. And go ahead and top the casserole with some extra shredded cheese in the last 5 minutes of baking, because you just can't get enough of a good thing.

TEMPER, TEMPER

I tell you, eggs are a temperamental food! They have a nasty habit of scrambling on you when you're adding them to something that's hot. In order to avoid that mess, you need to "temper" them before adding them to a hot food. That's what you're doing in this recipe when you add that tablespoon of hot grits to the eggs before pouring the eggs into the pan. You're just bringing the temperature of the eggs closer to the temperature of the hot food. Then, when you add the "tempered" eggs to the pan of hot grits, be sure to stir well and constantly so the eggs can get used to the hotter temperature.

CHEESY TOMATO GRITS

■ ■

I think of this as being a bit like the Deep South's answer to lasagna. With cheese, spicy tomatoes, and plenty of seasonings, this is a grits casserole for folks who like a lot of flavor. I don't like to make generalizations, but aren't those always the most interesting people to have around?

SERVES 8

1¼ cups whole milk
1 cup quick-cooking grits
1 teaspoon salt
2 tablespoons (¼ stick) butter
⅓ cup finely chopped scallions

4 ounces cream cheese spread with garlic
  and herbs
2½ cups shredded Cheddar cheese
  (10 ounces)
1 can (10 ounces) Ro*Tel, or other spicy
  diced tomatoes
2 large eggs, lightly beaten

1. Preheat the oven to 350°F. Grease a 9-inch square baking dish with butter, oil, or cooking spray.

2. In a medium saucepan, combine 2 cups water and the milk and bring to a boil over medium-high heat. Slowly whisk in the grits and salt. Whisk constantly for 1 minute. Reduce the heat, cover, and cook for 3 minutes. Uncover and stir in 1 tablespoon of the butter, stirring until the butter is melted. Cover and cook for 20 minutes, or until the grits are thick and creamy. Then take those grits off the heat and let them sit a minute.

3. In a large skillet, melt the remaining 1 tablespoon butter over medium heat. Add the scallions and cook for 1 minute.

4. Add the cream cheese spread, ½ cup of the Cheddar, and the grits to the skillet and stir until the cheese is melted. Add the tomatoes and mix well. Stir in the eggs. Pour the grits mixture into the prepared baking dish and bake for 35 minutes. Sprinkle the remaining 2 cups Cheddar over the top and bake until the cheese has melted, about 5 minutes longer.

STIR CRAZY

The secret to preparing good grits is the initial stirring of the pot. So go ahead and get yourself a workout when you're making grits. Some good hearty stirring will make your final dish the creamiest and silkiest possible—so your Southern grandma can be proud.

MAPLE BACON AND HOMINY

■ ■

When I talk about pork candy, I'm talking about this: crispy, maple-glazed pieces of golden-brown bacon. It gives plump hominy corn such a nice salty-sweet contrast. Everyone will love this even if they never saw a kernel of hominy corn in their sweet life. That's the beauty of bacon.

SERVES 4

6 slices bacon, patted dry

⅓ cup maple syrup

3 tablespoons butter

2 cans (15 ounces each) hominy, rinsed
    and drained

¼ teaspoon salt

½ teaspoon black pepper

1. Preheat the oven to 375°F. Line a baking sheet with parchment paper and coat the paper with cooking spray.

2. Arrange the bacon in a single layer on the prepared baking sheet. Coat the bacon evenly with the syrup. Bake until the bacon is golden and caramelized, about 25 minutes. When the bacon is cool enough to handle, chop it into bite-size pieces.

3. In a large skillet, melt the butter over medium heat. Add the hominy and cook, stirring, until heated through, about 5 minutes. Stir in the salt, black pepper, and bacon and serve up.

AMAZING MAIZE

I like to say, before you can have grits, you've got to have hominy. That's because hominy is the dried white or yellow corn kernels that are ground up to produce grits. But, believe me, they are delicious whole, too! You can find hominy frozen, dried, or canned. Just remember that for dried hominy you need to soak it overnight and then boil it to soften it up. The canned and frozen hominy are already cooked and soft.

NEW YEAR'S HOPPIN' JOHN

My Granddaddy Paul was so superstitious. He would not allow me to have goldfish as a child because they were bad luck; we could not open an umbrella in the house because that just brought on an early death; we could not walk underneath a ladder; and we could not have New Year's Day come and go unless we had collard greens to represent the money we were going to make during the year and hoppin' John made with black-eyed peas to bring us good luck. Go figure. Hoppin' John is really just a mean recipe for rice and beans and it's delicious any day of the year.

SERVES 6 TO 8

3 tablespoons butter

2 celery stalks, chopped

1 small green bell pepper, chopped

1 small yellow onion, chopped

2 cloves garlic, finely chopped

1 ham hock, rinsed and patted dry

2 cups black-eyed peas, frozen or rinsed and drained canned

2 cups cooked white rice

½ teaspoon salt

Hot sauce

1. In a large pot, melt the butter over medium heat. Add the celery, bell pepper, onion, and garlic and cook, stirring, until the vegetables are very tender, 7 to 10 minutes.

2. Add the ham hock, pour in enough water to just cover the ham hock, and bring to a boil. Reduce to a simmer and cook, uncovered, for 30 minutes.

3. Stir in the black-eyed peas and rice and simmer for 15 minutes longer. Season with the salt and hot sauce to taste and be sure to invite some friends around for this one.

DOWN THE DRAIN

Be sure to rinse your canned beans free of their canning liquid to avoid making the dish too salty. It's especially important to rinse in recipes that have a ham hock or bacon in them, because those meats bring a lot of salt to the pot, too.

YAM CASSEROLE WITH PECAN CRUMBLE

■ ■

Well, if there is a more Southern combination than yams and pecans out there, I don't need to know about it. This casserole comes together like a dessert crisp, with a crunchy, buttery topping of nuts, cheese, and cracker crumbs scattered over creamy sweet potatoes. I love this too much to serve it only at Thanksgiving, but it does make a perfect side for a holiday meal.

SERVES 8 TO 10

2 cups heavy cream

¼ teaspoon cayenne pepper

3 to 4 medium yams or orange sweet potatoes
   (2½ pounds), peeled and cut into ⅛-inch-
   thick rounds

1½ teaspoons salt

¾ teaspoon black pepper

¾ teaspoon dried thyme

1 cup crushed saltine crackers
   (about 20 crackers)

⅔ cup grated Parmesan cheese

½ cup chopped pecans

4 tablespoons (½ stick) butter,
   melted

1. Preheat the oven to 375°F. Lightly grease a 13 by 9-inch baking dish with oil or coat with cooking spray.

2. In a small bowl, whisk together the cream and cayenne pepper.

3. Arrange one-third of the yams in an even layer on the bottom of the prepared dish. Season with ½ teaspoon salt and ¼ teaspoon each of the black pepper and thyme. Pour in ⅔ cup of the cream mixture. Repeat for 2 more layers.

4. In a small bowl, combine the cracker crumbs, Parmesan, pecans, and melted butter. Give it a good stir so the butter coats the crackers and pecans. Scatter the mixture over the top of the casserole.

5. Cover the dish with foil and bake for 15 minutes. Uncover and bake until the top is golden brown, the yams are tender, and the house is filled with the most wonderful sweet and buttery smells, 30 to 45 minutes longer.

> **AIN'T IT SWEET**
>
> Now, don't let me confuse you with my Southernism here. The yams I call for may be called sweet potatoes where you live. When I say yams, I'm talking about the orange-fleshed potato that cooks up nice and sweet.

        VEGETABLES AND BEANS

HOMEY TOMATO CASSEROLE

■ ■

Southern cooks have been making meals out of a little bit of barely anything from the garden forever, and this is the kind of good, down-home cooking that gives me so much respect for that tradition. All you need are a few tomatoes and some sweet, juicy Vidalia onions, and you've got the makings for a real satisfying cheesy casserole. Try it alongside a few ears of steamed corn and a steak or a piece of grilled fish for a beautiful summertime meal.

SERVES 6

2 tablespoons olive oil

4 large Vidalia or other sweet onions, cut into
    ¼-inch-thick rings

1¼ teaspoons plus a pinch of salt

4 tomatoes (1¾ pounds), cut into
    ½-inch-thick slices

½ teaspoon dried oregano

¼ teaspoon black pepper

1½ cups shredded Cheddar cheese (6 ounces)

½ cup stale bread crumbs

2 tablespoons butter (¼ stick), melted

1. Preheat the oven to 375°F. Lightly grease a shallow 2-quart baking dish (pretty enough to bring to the table) with butter, oil, or cooking spray.

2. In a large skillet, heat the oil over medium-high heat. Add the onions and cook until golden and soft, 5 to 7 minutes. Sprinkle with the pinch of salt.

3. Layer half the tomatoes in the prepared baking dish and top with half the onions, ½ teaspoon of the salt, ¼ teaspoon of the oregano, and ⅛ teaspoon of the black pepper. Scatter ¾ cup of the Cheddar on top. Repeat with the remaining tomatoes and onions, another ½ teaspoon of the salt, and the remaining ¼ teaspoon oregano, ⅛ teaspoon black pepper, and ¾ cup Cheddar.

4. In a small bowl, combine the bread crumbs, melted butter, and the remaining ¼ teaspoon salt. Sprinkle over the casserole. Bake the casserole until the top is golden brown and the tomatoes are tender, 30 to 35 minutes. Bring that pretty casserole right to the table.

TOP TOMATO

I like to stick with good old trusty beefsteak tomatoes for this casserole because they are fleshy and meaty and will stay intact during the cooking process. More important, though, look for nice ripe tomatoes so that you get all the sweetness you can in this dish. They'll be red all over and will yield a bit when pressed close to the stem.

BEST BRAISED SOUTHERN GREENS

■ ■

As far as I'm concerned, in order to cook good greens, you have to grease 'em a little with bacon or butter, or—y'all know me—both! I love how after a nice braise, this traditional mess o' greens gives you that delicious pot liquor—the tastiest, healthiest broth at the bottom of the braising pot. You can serve that broth with corn bread or hoecakes to soak it up, or just slurp it up in the kitchen all by itself in a cup. I had an elderly gentleman who came into the restaurant regularly and never needed to order. I would just bring him a coffee mug full of pot liquor. It'll cure whatever ails you.

SERVES 4 TO 6

8 slices bacon, cut crosswise into
   ½-inch pieces
1 medium Vidalia or other sweet onion,
   thinly sliced
8 tablespoons (1 stick) butter

2 pounds collard greens, stems removed
   and leaves cut into ½-inch strips
Salt
Hot sauce

1. In a large saucepan, cook the bacon over medium-high heat until crisp, about 5 minutes. Add the onion and butter and cook until the onion is tender, about 5 minutes longer.

2. Add 2 cups water and bring to a boil. Reduce the heat to medium-low and simmer for 10 minutes. Add the collard greens and cook, uncovered, until very soft, about 20 minutes. Season with salt and hot sauce to taste. Place the greens in a pretty serving bowl along with the pot liquor and set out on the table.

GREEN IS GOOD

Like most Southerners, I cannot get enough of hearty greens like collards, turnip greens, and mustard greens. Here's a quick way to prep 'em. First, use this trick to trim out the thick stem (sometimes called a rib) in the center of the leaves: Fold the leaves in half and, starting from the top, at its thinner end, pull the stem away from the leaf. Or lay the leaves down flat on a cutting board, make a cut down either side of the stem, and cut out the stem. Roll the leaves up (the long way) like a cigar and then slice them crosswise to create strips.

VEGETABLES AND BEANS

VERY VEGGIE BRAISED GREENS

I have got to have my pot greens, and I usually like to cook them down forever with some bacon or ham hocks. But these days we just never know when we'll have a vegetarian among us, so I started doing my greens with just some butter, onion, and vegetable broth, and you know what? They're absolutely delicious!

SERVES 6 TO 8

8 tablespoons (1 stick) butter
1 medium yellow onion, finely chopped
2 cups vegetable broth
¾ teaspoon salt

2½ pounds mixed greens (such as turnip greens, collards, and mustard greens), stems removed and leaves coarsely chopped
Black pepper

1. In a very large skillet, melt the butter over medium-high heat. Add the onion and cook, stirring, until softened, about 5 minutes.

2. Add the broth and salt and bring to a gentle simmer. Add the greens, a handful at a time, letting each batch wilt a little bit before adding more. Once all of the greens have been added, cover the pan and reduce the heat to low. Cook, tossing from time to time, until the greens are tender, about 20 minutes. If you like them silken and Southern, continue cooking the greens for 20 to 30 minutes longer. Sprinkle with a pinch of black pepper before serving.

> ## GO GREEN
> Collard greens have broad, fanlike, dark green leaves with a thick stem, and they've got a nice nutty flavor to them. Mustard greens are a lighter green with a frilly edge to the leaves and have a sharper flavor than the collards. And turnip greens are a shade of green somewhere between the collards and the mustards and can be a little bitter if they're not cooked through.

Remove the ribs from greens by stripping the leaves from the hard, inedible center stem. Alternatively, cut along both sides of the stem with a small sharp knife to release the leaves.

TURNIPS AND GREENS

■ ■

I always say, "Don't turn up a turnip till you've tried it." Children are sometimes suspicious of these big old round root vegetables, but they are a true comfort food, and with a little braising or roasting, they become tender, sweet, and, oh, just divine! And they are so, so good for you, too! I look for a bunch of turnips with nice greens so I can cook it all down together.

SERVES 4

4 cups chicken broth
1 smoked turkey neck or wing
8 tablespoons (1 stick) butter
1½ teaspoons salt
½ teaspoon sugar

1 bunch turnip greens (about ¾ pound),
   stems removed and leaves coarsely
   chopped
2 large turnips (about 1 pound), coarsely
   chopped
Hot sauce (optional)

1. In a large pot, combine the broth and smoked turkey neck or wing. Bring to a boil over medium-high heat. Reduce to a gentle simmer and cook, uncovered, for 20 minutes. Stir in the butter, salt, and sugar. Add the greens and turnips and simmer, uncovered, until the vegetables are tender, about 30 minutes.

2. Remove the greens and turnips with a slotted spoon and place in a shallow serving dish. Season with hot sauce, if you'd like, and serve.

> **BITTERSWEET**
>
> To reduce the natural bitterness of turnip leaves, be sure to cook them with something salty like a smoked turkey neck or a ham hock. And be sure to add some sugar to the pan to complement that bitterness with a touch of sweetness. That should win 'em over!

OL' NO. 7 YAMS

■ ■

I love pulling out all the ingredients for this festive wintertime dish: whiskey, orange peel, nutmeg, cinnamon, brown sugar, and butter. What's better than all that? We often make this for Christmas supper and all those good smells just put us into the right frame of mind. You could convince yourself it was a white Christmas in June if you fixed a pan of these yams.

SERVES 4

4 large yams or orange sweet potatoes
   (3½ to 4 pounds)
⅓ cup Jack Daniel's Old No. 7 whiskey
1 cup packed light brown sugar

4 tablespoons (½ stick) butter
¼ teaspoon grated nutmeg
1 cinnamon stick (3 to 4 inches)
1 long strip orange peel

1. Preheat the oven to 400°F. Bake the yams until they are tender when pierced with a fork, about 1 hour. Reduce the oven temperature to 350°F. Remove the yams but leave the oven on. When the yams are cool enough to handle, peel them and cut crosswise into ½-inch-thick rounds.

2. Meanwhile, in a large saucepan, combine 3 cups water, the whiskey, brown sugar, butter, nutmeg, cinnamon stick, and orange peel. Bring to a boil over medium-high heat. Reduce to a simmer and cook until the sauce is slightly thickened and syrupy, 30 to 45 minutes.

3. Place the yams in a medium baking dish. Pour the syrup over them and return to the oven to bake until the yams are fork-tender, about 30 minutes. Your house will smell so good while this is baking, you'll be holding them back from the table!

> **DO AHEAD**
>
> To make this dish faster, bake the yams the night before, leave the skin on, and pop them in the refrigerator. When you're ready to bake your casserole, peel and slice the yams while the syrup is simmering. Great for entertaining!

CANDIED YAM SOUFFLÉ

■ ■

This is how we make our yams with mini marshmallows, and you know it's not just the children who adore this holiday favorite. You can assemble this dish in advance, so all you have to do is bake it right before dinner. Watch out, though: those caramelized marshmallows get scorching hot, and if you try to sneak a little of it off the top when you pull it out of the oven, you'll wish you had waited. I ought to know; I still haven't learned.

SERVES 6 TO 8

3 cans (15 ounces each) candied yams, drained

8 tablespoons (1 stick) butter, melted

½ cup whole milk

3 large eggs

1 teaspoon ground cinnamon

½ teaspoon grated nutmeg

½ teaspoon salt

4 cups mini marshmallows

1. Preheat the oven to 325°F. Grease a 13 by 9-inch baking dish with butter, oil, or cooking spray.

2. In a food processor or blender, puree the yams until smooth. Add the melted butter, milk, eggs, cinnamon, nutmeg, and salt. Continue to puree until smooth and well combined. Scrape the mixture into the prepared dish and bake for 20 minutes.

3. Increase the oven temperature to 400°F. Top the yams with the marshmallows and bake until the marshmallows are golden and melted, 10 to 15 minutes. Serve piping hot.

LIGHT AS AIR

This is not one of those soufflés that you see in a French restaurant, but it's a soufflé nonetheless, because "soufflé" simply means that it's all puffed up. And that's exactly what you do to these yams when you puree them with the eggs. They come out so light and airy, just like a fancy French soufflé.

SWEET POTATO BALLS

I've been makin' these tasty fellows for years—they are just perfect around holiday time. The orange juice, brown sugar, cinnamon, and marshmallows are familiar friends, but just wait till you taste how delicious coconut is in a sweet potato dish. These are wonderful served with turkey or ham.

SERVES 4 TO 6

4 large sweet potatoes (about 2½ pounds)
⅔ cup packed light brown sugar
1 tablespoon orange juice
½ teaspoon grated nutmeg

2 cups sweetened shredded coconut
½ cup granulated sugar
1 teaspoon ground cinnamon
8 large marshmallows

1. Preheat the oven to 400°F.

2. Place the sweet potatoes in a medium baking dish and bake until they are soft to the touch, about 1 hour. Remove the sweet potatoes but leave the oven on. Reduce the oven temperature to 350°F and line a baking sheet with foil. (The potatoes can be baked the day before and kept covered in the fridge with their skins on.)

> **ZIP IT UP**
> For a zestier flavor, use lemon or lime juice instead of orange juice.

3. When the sweet potatoes are cool enough to handle, peel them. Place them in a large bowl and mash well. Stir in the brown sugar, orange juice, and nutmeg.

4. In a medium bowl, toss the coconut with the granulated sugar and cinnamon. Press the sweet potato mixture around each marshmallow to create 8 balls, then roll the balls in the coconut mixture. Place on the prepared baking sheet.

5. Bake until browned and bubbling, 15 to 20 minutes. Watch carefully for the last few minutes of cooking; the expanding marshmallows can cause the potato balls to burst open.

Shape the balls by pressing the mashed potato mixture around the marshmallows. Roll with the palm of your hand to create a 2- to 3-inch-diameter ball.

BAKED ACORN SQUASH WITH PINEAPPLE

■ ■

A baked acorn squash is just about the prettiest thing you can put on your dinner plate in the autumn and winter months. I love the sweet and tart taste of pineapple with the mellow, silky baked squash.

SERVES 4

1 can (8½ ounces) crushed pineapple,
   drained
2 tablespoons (¼ stick) butter
2 tablespoons light brown sugar

¼ teaspoon salt
⅛ teaspoon black pepper
2 medium acorn squash, halved lengthwise,
   seeds and pulp removed

1. Preheat the oven to 400°F. Line a baking sheet with foil.

2. In a small saucepan, combine the pineapple, butter, brown sugar, salt, and black pepper. Simmer over medium heat until syrupy, about 5 minutes.

3. Place the squash halves, cut side up, on the prepared baking sheet. Spoon the pineapple mixture into the cavities, making sure to cover all the cut surfaces with the syrup. You don't want to miss 1 square inch with this delightful syrup. Bake until the squash is tender and golden brown, about 1 hour.

THE FIRST CUT

Use a strong, sharp knife when cutting your acorn squash because it's real tough. To make it easier to slice through, make a few cuts in the skin of the squash so it won't explode, and place it in the microwave for a minute or two. The outside should soften up just a little bit.

To prevent hard squash from slipping while cutting, cut on a dish-towel-lined cutting board using a serrated knife.

CREAMED POTATOES

■ ■

I love to serve this elegant recipe for tiny round potatoes in cream sauce at a spring dinner party. They're classy and remind me of a delicious chive-flavored potato chip.

SERVES 4

1½ pounds medium creamer potatoes, unpeeled, halved
1 tablespoon butter
½ small yellow onion, finely chopped
1 tablespoon all-purpose flour

1 cup whole milk
1 teaspoon salt
¼ teaspoon black pepper
2 tablespoons finely chopped fresh chives

1. In a large pot, cover the potatoes with cold salted water. Bring to a boil over medium-high heat and cook until the potatoes are almost tender, 15 to 20 minutes; drain well.

2. In a medium pot, melt the butter over medium heat. Add the onion and cook until almost soft, about 5 minutes. Sprinkle with the flour and stir for 1 minute. Slowly whisk in the milk, salt, and black pepper. Bring to a boil, reduce to a simmer, and cook until thickened, about 5 minutes. Add the potatoes and cook until they are tender, about 5 minutes. Serve sprinkled with the chives to give it some pretty color.

> **SIZED UP**
>
> When cooking potatoes, pay attention to the size of the potatoes called for in your recipe in relation to the cooking time, especially in a recipe like this one. Y'all want to make sure you don't overcook the potatoes in the first step, or you'll just end up with a mushy mess when you cook them again in the second step.

BUTTERY BUTTERMILK MASHED POTATOES

■ ■

Buttermilk is indispensable in the South because of its rich, creamy flavor. It makes these potatoes smooth and tangy at the same time.

SERVES 4

1¾ pounds baking potatoes, peeled and cut
    into chunks
½ cup buttermilk
4 tablespoons (½ stick) butter

2 teaspoons salt
½ teaspoon black pepper
⅛ teaspoon grated nutmeg

1. In a large pot, cover the potatoes with cold salted water. Bring to a boil over medium-high heat and cook until the potatoes are very tender, 20 to 25 minutes; drain well and transfer to a bowl.

2. While the potatoes are still hot, using a potato masher, mash in the buttermilk, butter, salt, black pepper, and nutmeg. Mash until the potatoes are the consistency you like. Serve piping hot.

CRÈME DE LA CRÈME
If you really want to go all out, substitute sour cream for the buttermilk—it will make your dish even richer and creamier.

For smooth and fluffy mashed potatoes, use a ricer or food mill. Fill the ricer with drained boiled potatoes and press out through the holes. Alternatively, fill a food mill with the potatoes and turn the crank in a circular motion to press them through the perforated disk.

VEGETABLES AND BEANS

TURNIP MASHED POTATOES

Let the turnips be your little secret if you're cooking for picky eaters. These underrated root veggies just make your mashed taters so light and silky and delicious—anyone will be a convert! Especially if you don't tell them until after they've cleaned their plate.

SERVES 4

1 pound small red potatoes, halved
½ pound turnips, cut into chunks
½ cup hot heavy cream

4 tablespoons (½ stick) butter, at room temperature
Salt and black pepper

1. In a large pot, cover the potatoes and turnips with cold salted water. Bring to a boil over medium-high heat and cook until the vegetables are tender, 15 to 20 minutes; drain well.

2. Transfer the vegetables to a large bowl and, using a potato masher or an electric mixer, mash in the hot cream and butter until the mash is the consistency you like. Mix in salt and black pepper to taste, starting with 1 teaspoon of salt and ¼ teaspoon of pepper. Mound into a pretty serving bowl.

HIGH AND DRY

For the smoothest, silkiest mash, be sure your potatoes are as dry as possible after you've boiled them. To prevent them from absorbing too much water while they boil, cut the potatoes into big pieces; don't make them small. And after you drain your potatoes, pop them into the hot pot and put them back over low heat for a minute to get rid of any excess moisture.

SHRIMP MASHED POTATOES

■ ■

I've been making this fun, tasty shrimp-and-tater mash for at least as long as I've lived in Savan-nah, and it never fails to give folks a pleasant surprise. The shrimp are so sweet and the whole dish is pretty and pink.

SERVES 4

4 pounds red potatoes (8 to 10 medium), cut
    into ¼-inch-thick rounds
½ cup hot whole milk, plus more if needed
8 tablespoons (1 stick) butter

½ cup sour cream
Salt and black pepper
1 cup chopped cooked shrimp
1 teaspoon paprika

1. In a medium pot, cover the potatoes with cold salted water. Bring to a boil over medium-high heat and cook until the potatoes are tender, 15 to 20 minutes; drain well and transfer to a large bowl.

2. Using a potato masher or an electric mixer, mash the potatoes with the ½ cup hot milk, the butter, and the sour cream until the mash is the consistency you like. Mash in salt and black pep-per to taste. Don't overbeat the potatoes, now; a few lumps are nice. Add the shrimp and mash again until mixed. You can adjust the thickness by adding more hot milk if it needs it. Stir in the paprika for flavor and some pretty color. Feel free to make this dish a little ahead of time and re-heat in a 375°F oven if you need to.

> **CAN'T BEAT THAT**
>
> The electric mixer is the fastest way to mash your potatoes, but you'll need to keep an eye on them while you're beating. Potatoes can turn gluey if you beat them too far. Keep checking the potatoes in the mixer.

TWICE-BAKED POTATOES

When my boys were growing and nothing ever seemed to fill them up, I could always count on a good, hearty twice-baked potato. You can stuff these simply or really do them up, and either way they're bound to please.

SERVES 6

6 large baking potatoes (as large and oval as possible) (about 5 pounds)
Vegetable oil, for coating the potatoes
8 tablespoons (1 stick) butter, cut into small bits

2 cups sour cream
Salt and black pepper
1 teaspoon dried parsley flakes
Paprika

1. Preheat the oven to 350°F. Line a baking sheet with foil. Prick the potatoes lightly in several places with a fork. Coat each potato entirely with the oil. Place on the prepared baking sheet and bake until the potato skins are very crisp and the insides are very soft, 1 to 2 hours. Remove the potatoes but leave the oven on.

2. Drop the butter into a large bowl. Carefully, as the potatoes will be hot, slice off the top one-third of each potato lengthwise. Gently scoop out the insides of the potatoes with a spoon (leaving enough so the potato skin will stay intact and not tear) and add to the bowl with the butter. Using a potato masher, mash in the sour cream and salt and black pepper to taste, mashing until it's the consistency you like. (Be careful not to overmash.)

3. Stir in the parsley flakes. Gently stuff the mixture back into the potato skins, being careful not to break them. Pile the potato mixture as high as you can above the tops of the potato skins. Sprinkle lightly with paprika. The potatoes can be frozen at this point for serving later.

4. Return the potatoes to the baking sheet and bake until the potato tops are golden brown, 20 to 30 minutes. The potatoes will be crunchy on the outside and creamy and buttery on the inside.

> **STUFFED**
> Sometimes I like to make my stuffed potatoes a meal of their own, especially when I've got leftovers in the fridge. I mix in bacon and broccoli or cut-up cooked shrimp with fresh herbs, or cubes of ham and grated Cheddar. You can get creative and clean out the fridge in one fell swoop.

ROASTED POTATOES WITH ROSEMARY

■ ■

I use two different potatoes, yellow and red, to make this dish look pretty and because I love how different they taste. The garlic in the pan is a real treat—you can serve it right along with the rosemary potatoes for everyone to peel and eat, or you can consider it the cook's reward and have yourself a little appetizer course in the kitchen.

SERVES 4

¾ pound Yukon Gold potatoes, cut into
  1¼-inch chunks
¾ pound red potatoes, cut into 1¼-inch
  chunks
3 tablespoons extra-virgin olive oil

4 cloves garlic, unpeeled
2 sprigs fresh rosemary
¾ teaspoon salt
½ teaspoon black pepper

Preheat the oven to 425°F. Spread the potatoes on a large rimmed baking sheet and toss with the oil, garlic, rosemary, salt, and black pepper. Roast the potatoes, turning occasionally, until they are golden and tender, 30 to 35 minutes. It's that easy, folks.

GOOD OLD BAY

If you don't have any fresh rosemary on hand, you can throw a couple of bay leaves onto the baking sheet instead, but be sure to remove them before you serve.

CHEESY ASPARAGUS

■ ■

I don't know why they don't serve roasted cheesy asparagus at the movies instead of popcorn. With the thin crust of golden baked cheese, it is just so darn good.

SERVES 4

1 pound asparagus, woody ends snapped off
1 tablespoon olive oil
¼ teaspoon salt

¼ teaspoon black pepper
½ cup grated Parmesan cheese

Preheat the oven to 400°F. Spread the asparagus on a baking sheet and toss with the oil, salt, and black pepper. Sprinkle generously with the Parmesan. Bake until the asparagus is tender and the cheese is melted and slightly golden, 10 to 12 minutes. Serve just as soon as you can.

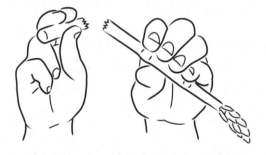

Snap off the woody stems of asparagus by holding the spear with one hand at the base of the stalk and the other hand 1 or 2 inches toward the tip. Bend the spear to break the asparagus at the woody point.

ALL SIZED UP

Some folks swear that skinny asparagus stalks have the most flavor, and others say the same about the thick, meaty stalks. I say they're both as tasty as can be. The important thing is to get asparagus stalks that are all roughly the same size. That way they'll all cook and become tender (but not mushy) at just the same time.

FRIED GREEN TOMATOES

■ ■

This is how my Grandmama Paul used up her straggler tomatoes—the ones hanging on the vine at the end of the season. Firm and green and tangy, they were perfect for frying. Grandmama Paul always breaded them with cornmeal so they'd be real crunchy, and she had a heavy hand with the black pepper. I use her method but prefer flour. I salt the tomatoes and let them sit; this gets rid of the extra moisture so they fry up nice and crisp.

SERVES 6

4 large, firm green tomatoes
Salt
About 2 quarts vegetable oil, for deep-frying

2 cups self-rising flour or self-rising
cornmeal
1 teaspoon black pepper

1. Slice the tomatoes to the thickness you like (I like mine thin). Lay out on a baking sheet and sprinkle lightly with salt. Place in a colander set in the sink and let sit for 30 minutes so the salt can pull water out of the tomatoes.

2. In a large skillet, heat 2 inches of oil until it reaches 350°F on a deep-fry thermometer.

3. In a shallow bowl, mix the flour with the black pepper. Coat the tomatoes in the flour mixture, shaking off any excess. Add to the hot oil and deep-fry until golden brown, about 2 minutes per side. Serve right away so they're nice and crunchy.

A SOUTHERN STAR

Just make sure the green tomatoes you buy at the store are actually *un*ripe. Some tomatoes stay green even after they've ripened, and you definitely don't want any of those because the texture won't be right.

STEWED TOMATOES

■ ■

This is another garden-fresh recipe that brings me back to a time when my Aunt Peggy grew the most wonderful tomatoes. Since you cook them forever to get a reduced, sweet, and saucy dish, you can also use a can of diced tomatoes. Butter, sweet onion, and a bit of sugar round out the tomatoes' tangy edge, making a real comforting dish.

SERVES 4

4 tablespoons (½ stick) butter
1 medium yellow onion, finely chopped
2 cloves garlic, finely chopped

4 cups peeled (see box) and chopped fresh tomatoes, or 1 can (28 ounces) diced tomatoes
½ teaspoon salt
½ teaspoon black pepper
2 tablespoons sugar
3 tablespoons chopped fresh parsley

PEEL AWAY

If you use fresh tomatoes here, you'll need to peel them first. Bring a pot of water to a boil. Set up a bowl filled with ice and water. With a small knife, make a little X through the skin at the blossom end of each tomato. Lower the tomatoes into the boiling water for about 15 seconds. Using a slotted spoon, lift the tomatoes out and place them directly in the ice water. Let them cool a few seconds and peel!

1. In a medium skillet, melt the butter over medium heat. Add the onion and cook, stirring, until softened, 7 to 10 minutes. Stir in the garlic and cook for 1 minute. Stir in the tomatoes, salt, and black pepper. Simmer, covered, over medium-low heat for 30 minutes.

2. Stir in the sugar and simmer, uncovered, until the liquid reduces by about half, about 15 minutes. Stir in the parsley just before serving to add some pretty green to the dish.

CHEESY CORN PUDDING

This is my cheesy version of spoon bread, a traditional Southern cornmeal pudding that you can serve with just about anything. Muffin mix makes the recipe a cinch, and sour cream makes it so moist and tender you could cry!

SERVES 6 TO 8

1 box (8½ ounces) corn muffin mix
1 can (15 ounces) cream-style corn
1½ cups shredded sharp Cheddar cheese
    (6 ounces)
¾ cup sour cream

½ cup finely chopped scallions
4 tablespoons (½ stick) butter,
    melted
2 large eggs, lightly beaten
¼ teaspoon black pepper

1. Preheat the oven to 400°F. Grease a 9-inch square baking pan with oil or coat with cooking spray.

2. In a large bowl, stir together the muffin mix, corn, ¾ cup of the Cheddar, the sour cream, scallions, melted butter, eggs, and black pepper. Scrape the mixture into the prepared pan. Scatter the remaining ¾ cup Cheddar over the top.

3. Bake the pudding until golden and firm, 25 to 30 minutes. Let the pudding cool for 10 minutes or so before cutting into squares so that it has a chance to set, and your squares will come out nice and clean.

STIR IT IN

While it's great as is, I like to get creative with this pudding. If I've got some leftover ham in the fridge, I just cube it up and stir it through. There's nothing like the flavor of smoked ham with sweet creamy corn. Or cut up some red bell peppers and stir them in to give this pudding amazing color.

SOUTHERN SPOON BREAD

■ ■

I love simple Southern food so much that I don't see the need to gussy up an old-fashioned, bare-bones recipe like this one. Spoon bread is just that: a corn bread so custardlike, you serve it with a spoon. Oh, how I love it with a good old plate of greens, tomatoes from the garden, and maybe some grilled fish or chicken.

SERVES 6

1 cup stone-ground cornmeal
1½ teaspoons salt
4 tablespoons (½ stick) butter, cut into
   small bits

1 cup cold whole milk
2 large eggs, lightly beaten

1. Preheat the oven to 375°F. Grease an 8-inch square baking pan with butter, oil, or cooking spray.

2. In a small saucepan, combine the cornmeal, salt, and 1½ cups water. Bring to a simmer over medium-high heat and cook until most of the liquid has been absorbed, about 10 minutes. Whisk in the butter until melted. Remove the pan from the heat and whisk in the milk. Slowly whisk in the eggs.

3. Scrape the mixture into the prepared pan. Bake until golden and almost firm, 45 to 50 minutes. Spoon out onto plates while hot.

> ## CHEESY SPOON BREAD
> If you like a richer spoon bread, you might try stirring a cup or so of grated cheese into the batter. Cheddar is my favorite, but y'all can use whatever you like.

LOUISIANA FRIED CORN

When it comes to good sweet corn, the simpler, the better. This is a farmhouse-style recipe that I just love. The corn stays juicy and fresh tasting, and the bits of bacon and scallion give it a real zing. This is one of those side dishes that I make just for myself if I'm eating solo, and I don't need anything else.

SERVES 4 TO 6

4 ears corn

2 slices bacon, cut crosswise into
   1-inch pieces

2 tablespoons (¼ stick) butter

4 scallions, finely chopped

½ teaspoon salt

¼ teaspoon black pepper

Large pinch of sugar

1. Cut the kernels from the cobs with a sharp knife and place them in a medium bowl. Run the back of the knife down the cobs to extract any corn milk, and add it to the bowl of corn.

2. In a large skillet, cook the bacon over medium-high heat until crisp, about 5 minutes. Set the bacon on a paper towel–lined plate to drain.

3. Add the butter to the skillet and melt over medium-high heat. Add the corn (and corn milk) and scallions. Reduce the heat to medium, cover, and cook for 10 minutes. Uncover and cook until tender, 5 to 10 minutes longer. Season with the salt, black pepper, and sugar and cook for 2 minutes longer. Top with bacon pieces and serve.

AW, SHUCKS

We like to shuck outside so that we don't make a big old mess in my kitchen. To shuck the corn, grab the outermost pieces of the husk from the top of the corn and pull down. Break the husk off at the other end, then scrape off as much of the silk as you can while the corn is still dry. Give it a rinse and you're done.

FRIED OKRA

■ ■

Don't sell okra short; it may look humble, but it's a real Southern treat and is surprisingly hearty, too. I fry mine like my mama did, tossed with buttermilk, then cornmeal, and deep-fried. Oh honey, it's so good—it'll make you see Jesus!

SERVES 4

About 2 quarts vegetable oil, for deep-frying
⅓ cup buttermilk
½ cup fine cornmeal

½ teaspoon salt
6 ounces okra (about 20 pods), sliced
   into ½-inch rounds

PUT YOUR COAT ON

I find that the best way to coat these pieces of okra in the wet and dry batter is to use two slotted spoons to dip, one for the wet buttermilk and one for the dry cornmeal. This method is less fiddly and your hands won't get all covered in coating as you're dipping and dredging.

1. In a medium pot, heat 2 inches of oil until it reaches 350°F on a deep-fry thermometer.

2. Pour the buttermilk into a shallow bowl. In another shallow bowl, mix the cornmeal with the salt. Dip the okra in the buttermilk, letting the excess drip off. Dredge the okra in the cornmeal mixture, shaking off any excess. Working in two batches, fry the okra until golden and crisp, 1 to 2 minutes; do not overcrowd the pot. Set on a paper towel–lined plate to drain. Serve hot and just tell me who can stop popping these little goodies into their mouth.

STEWED OKRA AND TOMATOES

Frozen sliced okra is a real convenience and it gives this saucy side dish just enough body. I love eating this over grits with a nice dash of hot sauce to give it a punch.

SERVES 6

3 tablespoons butter

1 medium yellow onion, finely chopped

3 cloves garlic, finely chopped

2 cans (14½ ounces each) diced tomatoes

2 cups sliced fresh or frozen okra

1 teaspoon salt

Black pepper

1. In a large skillet, melt the butter over medium-high heat. Add the onion and cook, stirring, until softened, 5 to 7 minutes. Add the garlic and cook for 1 minute.

2. Pour the tomatoes into the skillet, reduce to a simmer, and cook until the mixture becomes a thick, hearty sauce, about 20 minutes.

3. Stir in the okra and simmer for 20 minutes longer. Add the salt and spice it up with black pepper to taste.

OKAY OKRA

If you're buying fresh okra, look for pods about 3 to 4 inches in size and bright green in color. They should be firm enough that they'd snap in half if you bent them, and their coat should be fuzzy and soft without any dark blemishes.

MAQUE CHOUX

■ ■

Here is a real traditional recipe for one of Louisiana's finest culinary creations, pronounced "mock shoe." It's got all the favorite ingredients of that region—corn, bell pepper, celery, scallions, and tomatoes—simmered down with a touch of cream. Top this side off with something simple, like grilled shrimp, and make it into a lovely summertime meal.

SERVES 6

3 tablespoons butter
1 medium yellow onion, chopped
½ medium red bell pepper, chopped
1 celery stalk, chopped
Kernels from 3 ears corn (about 2 cups)
3 scallions, chopped, dark green tops
   kept separate for garnish

1 large tomato, chopped
1 tablespoon chopped fresh thyme leaves
Pinch of cayenne pepper
½ cup heavy cream
½ teaspoon salt
¼ teaspoon black pepper

1. In a large skillet, melt the butter over medium-high heat. Add the onion, bell pepper, and celery. Cook, stirring, until the vegetables are softened, 5 to 7 minutes. Stir in the corn and chopped scallions. Reduce the heat to medium and cook, covered, for 5 minutes.

2. Uncover the skillet and stir in the tomato, thyme, and cayenne pepper. Cook until the tomato is soft, about 3 minutes. Stir in the cream and cook until slightly reduced, about 2 minutes. Season with the salt and black pepper. Sprinkle with the reserved chopped dark green scallion tops. I tell you, the reds, yellows, and greens in this dish are such a pretty sight to see on your table.

MAKE IT A MAIN
Make this a one-pot dinner by adding cooked shredded chicken or cooked crawfish or shrimp toward the end of the cooking time. Or serve over a fluffy bed of rice. That's Southern comfort food.

SOUTHERN-STYLE GREEN BEANS WITH BACON AND TOMATO

If you served a Southern cook a bowl of crisp steamed green beans, she'd probably march them right back into the kitchen and cook them again. We love how soft and sweet vegetables get when you really cook them through, and this dish is a fine example. Bacon, tomato, and onion in the sauce take those beans to a whole new level.

SERVES 4 TO 6

4 slices bacon
1 small yellow onion, finely chopped
1 pound green beans

2 medium tomatoes, chopped
½ teaspoon salt
½ teaspoon black pepper

CAN DO
Go ahead and switch out canned tomatoes for fresh tomatoes in this recipe. A 28-ounce can of diced tomatoes should do, but make sure you drain the tomatoes of their juices first.

1. In a large skillet, cook the bacon over medium-high heat until crisp, 5 to 7 minutes. Set the bacon on a paper towel–lined plate to drain.

2. Add the onion to the skillet and cook, stirring, until very soft, 7 to 10 minutes.

3. Toss in the green beans, tomatoes, salt, and black pepper. Reduce the heat to medium-low, cover, and cook, tossing occasionally, until the beans are very tender and the tomatoes are falling apart, about 30 minutes.

4. Serve with the bacon crumbled all over the top.

To quickly remove the stem ends of green beans, line up the beans on a cutting board parallel to you with the stem ends even. With one cut, slice off the stem ends of all the beans with a large, sharp knife.

SAUTÉED SUMMER SQUASH

■ ■

If you turn your back on a Southern garden, you'll wind up with zucchini and summer squash so big you might trip on them. I keep tabs on my vines because I love to harvest the real thin, firm summer squash before they grow as big as my arm. Little squash just taste so sweet in this fresh, simple recipe.

SERVES 4

2 tablespoons (¼ stick) butter
½ medium yellow onion (halved lengthwise), thinly sliced crosswise
½ teaspoon plus a pinch of salt

2 small yellow summer squash or zucchini (about 6 ounces each), cut crosswise into ¼-inch-thick rounds
2 teaspoons chopped fresh thyme leaves
¼ teaspoon black pepper

1. In a large skillet, melt the butter over medium-high heat. Add the onion and the pinch of salt and cook, stirring, until the onion is soft and light golden, about 7 minutes.

2. Add the squash to the pan in a single layer. Sprinkle evenly with the ½ teaspoon salt, the thyme, and black pepper. Cook, stirring from time to time, until the squash is tender and the onion is caramelized, 5 to 7 minutes.

A SEASONAL DISH

Although you can usually find summer squash and zucchini in the dead of winter, save this dish for late spring and summer when you can get nice, locally grown, in-season squash. It's worth the wait.

THE LADY'S INDIAN SUCCOTASH

We serve this colorful, high-flavor succotash at the restaurant. Don't leave out the ham hock, y'all—that smoky-salty meat gives a real nice flavor to the sweet corn—and that salty-sweet combination will just knock you right off your feet.

SERVES 6 TO 8

1 ham hock (about ½ pound)
½ teaspoon Paula Deen's House Seasoning (page 435)
¼ teaspoon Paula Deen Collection Seasoned Salt, or other seasoned salt
1 package (16 ounces) frozen green butter beans or lima beans, or 2½ cups fresh green butter beans
6 tablespoons (¾ stick) butter

½ teaspoon Paula Deen Collection Hot Sauce, or another hot sauce or 1 small chili pepper, finely chopped
4 slices bacon, chopped
1 package (16 ounces) frozen shoepeg corn (or 1⅔ cups fresh if you can get it)
2 cups sliced fresh or frozen okra
⅓ cup chopped fresh parsley
1 teaspoon chicken bouillon granules
4 tomatoes, cut into chunks

1. Put the ham hock in a large stockpot with 2 quarts water. Bring to a boil over medium-high heat. Reduce to a simmer, then add the House Seasoning and seasoned salt. Cover and cook for 1½ hours. Add water as needed (up to 2 more cups) to keep the meat covered as it cooks. Remove the ham hock and reserve it for another purpose.

2. Add the beans, 2 tablespoons of the butter, and the hot sauce and return to a boil. Reduce the heat, cover, and cook over low heat until the beans are tender, about 20 minutes. Remove the beans from the pot and reserve the cooking liquid.

3. In a large skillet, cook the bacon over medium-high heat until crisp, about 5 minutes. Add the corn, okra, cooked beans, and about 1½ cups of the cooking liquid from the bean pot. Simmer for 10 minutes. Add the parsley and chicken bouillon; cover and simmer, stirring occasionally, for 20 minutes.

4. Throw in the tomatoes and the remaining 4 tablespoons butter at the last minute. Simmer until the tomatoes are hot. This dish delivers with its beauty and its flavor!

> **SWEET CORN**
> Shoepeg corn is a Southern favorite that is related to white sweet corn and highly prized for its sweetness. It features smaller, more tightly packed kernels than the corn you're used to. It's probably most readily available these days in frozen form, but if you can get your hands on some fresh shoepeg, you'll be ever so happy.

VIDALIA ONION PIE

■ ■

Did y'all know that the Vidalia onion is Georgia's official state vegetable? Well, in this dish it hardly seems like a vegetable at all, but it is surely a divine savory-sweet side dish to set out on a buffet. The cheesy Ritz cracker crust is a real favorite of mine.

MAKES ONE 9-INCH PIE

1½ cups crushed Ritz crackers

1½ cups shredded sharp Cheddar cheese
  (6 ounces)

7 tablespoons butter, melted

2 large eggs

3 tablespoons all-purpose flour

1½ cups sour cream

½ cup whole milk

1 teaspoon plus a pinch of salt

3 cups thinly sliced Vidalia onion
  (about 2 small)

¼ teaspoon paprika

1. Preheat the oven to 350°F.

2. In a large bowl, combine the cracker crumbs, 1 cup of the Cheddar, and 4 tablespoons of the melted butter until they form a moist, crumbly mixture.

3. In another large bowl, whisk together the eggs and flour. Whisk in the sour cream, milk, and the 1 teaspoon salt.

4. Pour the remaining 3 tablespoons melted butter into a large skillet and heat over medium-high heat. Add the onion and cook, tossing, until very soft and golden, about 15 minutes. Season with the pinch of salt and the paprika.

5. Press the cracker mixture evenly onto the bottom and sides of a 9-inch pie plate. Scatter the onion over the piecrust. Pour the sour cream mixture over the onion and scatter the remaining ½ cup Cheddar over the top. Bake the pie until just firm (it will have a custardy appearance even when it's done), 30 to 35 minutes. Let cool completely before slicing and serving.

PRESSED FOR TIME

The press-in crust is such an easy way to make homemade crusts. Just mix melted butter with crushed-up crackers (if you are going for a sweet crust, use crushed graham crackers) and press it into your pie plate with the tips of your fingers. The melted butter holds it all together and saves you the time of rolling and cutting.

FRIED CABBAGE

■ ■

The last time I grew a nice big green cabbage, I was so proud. We ate that thing for about a week, every which way, including this one. Frying it with garlic and red pepper brings out everything I love about cabbage—its heartiness, crunch, and flavor.

SERVES 6

¼ cup vegetable oil
2 cloves garlic, finely chopped
Red pepper flakes

16 cups shredded green cabbage
  (1 small head)
Salt

1. In a large skillet, heat the oil over medium heat. Add the garlic and ¼ teaspoon red pepper flakes and cook, stirring, until fragrant, about 1 minute.

2. Increase the heat to medium-high. Add the cabbage, a handful at a time, letting each handful wilt a little bit before adding more. Sprinkle with 1 teaspoon salt and cook, tossing the cabbage, until tender, about 10 minutes. Taste and add more salt or red pepper flakes if you think it needs it.

THE BITTER END

When you sauté garlic and red pepper flakes, it's important to stir constantly and make it a quick cook. If you overcook garlic by even a few seconds, it becomes bitter, and that flavor gets into the whole dish.

Chapter 11

BREADS, QUICK BREADS, AND BISCUITS

Baking is big in the South—whether it's a biscuit or a roll, we love something in our hand to put some butter on, or to sop up pot liquor. My Grandmama Paul, for instance, baked well into her old age. I was at her house one day when she was in her eighties, and she was just standing there in the kitchen, rapping a tube of canned biscuits on the edge of the counter to pop it open. She looked at me and said, "I was so damn glad when they came out with these!" Those were her words exactly.

Because, you know, down South we just revere biscuits, and I guess Grandmama Paul never thought she had mastered the art. Southerners just adore our canned biscuits and crescent rolls, and I use them all the time. But I do love to roll my own homemade dough from time to time, especially since you can improvise more that way, whether you want to make Fluffy Sweet Potato Biscuits (page 279), Chive and Cheddar Biscuits (page 280), or your standard Buttery Buttermilk Biscuits (page 277).

Corn bread, right along with biscuits, is a reliable favorite of the Southern breadbasket. There aren't many days at home when I don't bake corn bread in a big hot greased skillet. Corn bread, corn sticks, hush puppies, and biscuits are such a quick, satisfying way to put food on your table, and they are such an important Southern tradition.

Of course I do slow down from time to time to bake a nice loaf of Old-Fashioned White Bread (page 281), say, if I'm planning a real special sandwich. But soda-raised muffins and breads are more popular down here than yeast breads are. Why, for my niece Corrie's wedding gift bags, she and her mother and I got in the kitchen and made over one hundred pumpkin breads! Now, I can't bake a loaf of my Streusel

Pumpkin Bread (page 286) without getting a little choked up thinking on how beautiful my Corrie was in her wedding gown.

Banana bread is another real favorite of mine. Whenever I make my banana bread with chocolate chips for Corrie, I have to make another loaf chock-full of toasted walnuts for Michael. He won't put up with a chocolate chip in his banana bread. That man's got strong opinions about scones as well. "Why would anyone want to eat a big dry biscuit?" he'll say. But, you know, I do a tender, flaky sour cream scone that is so yummy. Back in my catering days, if I was doing something casual, I'd whip up biscuits for a breakfast or brunch, but for the fancy ladies who were coming to town, I always made sure I had Sour Cream Tea Scones (page 287) on the platter.

All the breads in this chapter make such a nice snack, and children adore helping to bake them. They don't have to be sweet, either. I make an herbed cream cheese to top my Zucchini Bread (page 285) that is just the thing when your stomach starts growlin' in the afternoon. Of course, the basic ingredients in these items are things you'll find in every Southern pantry: butter, shortening, cornmeal, and self-rising flour. What's amazing is how many different ways Southern bakers have developed for combining them. I view it as another case of limitations inspiring creativity.

JALAPEÑO HUSH PUPPIES

■ ■

Well, there are just about as many stories about how hush puppies got their name as there are Southerners with opinions, but the most popular view is that the name derived from hunters or fishermen who would fry something in cornmeal, and toss a piece or two to their dogs to "hush" them up. In any case, these fried corn bread balls are too darn good to throw to the dogs. I like to spice mine up good with fresh jalapeño, and they are just addictive. Serve them as a side with everything from eggs to chili, or pop a few of these with a cold drink and put your feet up. And since I can't get enough of spicy food, sometimes I serve these with a sweet and spicy dipping sauce to really knock their socks off!

MAKES ABOUT 22 FRITTERS

About 4 quarts vegetable oil, for deep-frying
1 cup yellow cornmeal
1 cup all-purpose flour
1 tablespoon sugar
2 teaspoons salt
1 teaspoon baking powder

1 teaspoon baking soda
1 cup buttermilk
1 large egg
¼ cup finely chopped jalapeño pepper
    (leave some seeds if you want
    more heat)

1. In a deep pot, heat 3 inches of oil until it reaches 350°F on a deep-fry thermometer.

2. While the oil is heating, in a medium bowl, whisk together the cornmeal, flour, sugar, salt, baking powder, and baking soda. In another medium bowl, whisk together the buttermilk, egg, and jalapeño. Add the wet ingredients to the cornmeal mixture and fold to combine.

3. Using a small ice cream scoop or a large spoon, drop the batter into the oil and fry, in batches of 4 at a time, until golden and crisp, 2 to 3 minutes per batch. Set on a paper towel–lined plate to drain. Serve hot.

> ## THREE'S A CROWD
> Don't crowd your hush puppies when you're deep-frying them. By frying them up in batches, you'll ensure that the oil temperature in your pot stays nice and hot. The key is to cook them hot and fast.

BRUNCHTIME POPOVERS

■ ■

Recipes like this one feel as if you're cheating: popovers rise up like they were baked by a fancy pastry chef, when all you did was whisk four ingredients together and throw them in the oven. Get your brunch guests ready and bring the popovers out warm. They're delicious plain or spread with your favorite jelly.

MAKES 12 POPOVERS

2 tablespoons (¼ stick) butter, melted, plus
   more for greasing the pan
1 cup all-purpose flour

1 teaspoon salt
1 cup whole milk
3 large eggs

1. Position a rack in the center of the oven and preheat to 450°F. Generously butter a 12-cup popover pan or muffin tin.

2. In a medium bowl, whisk together the flour and salt. In another medium bowl, whisk together the milk and eggs until combined. Add the milk mixture to the flour mixture and stir to combine. Don't go too crazy with the mixing; a slightly lumpy mixture is okay, as long as all the flour has been incorporated. Fold in the melted butter.

3. Divide the batter evenly among the cups of the prepared pan. Bake until the popovers are puffed and dark golden brown, about 25 minutes. Serve warm.

FULL STEAM AHEAD

The secret to making these popovers puff up is the high liquid content in the batter—no baking soda or baking powder needed! Combined with a very hot oven, the steam trapped inside the popovers pushes the batter up, so when you cut into them, you'll see they're practically hollow.

SKILLET CORN BREAD

■■■■■■■■■■■■■■■■■■■■■■■■■■■■■■■■■■■■■■■

This is the corn bread that I make in my big, heavy skillet. First I get that thing real hot and swirl in my grease, then I pour in the batter and it forms a great, golden crust right off the bat.

MAKES ONE 9-INCH ROUND

¼ cup lard or vegetable shortening

2 cups fine yellow cornmeal

2 teaspoons baking powder

1 teaspoon baking soda

1 teaspoon salt

1 cup buttermilk

2 large eggs

1. Preheat the oven to 400°F. In a 9-inch cast-iron skillet, melt the lard or shortening over medium heat. Swirl the melted fat around the sides of the pan to coat it all over.

2. In a large bowl, whisk together the cornmeal, baking powder, baking soda, and salt. In a small bowl, whisk together the buttermilk and eggs. Using a rubber spatula, fold the buttermilk mixture and the melted lard or shortening into the flour mixture. Gently mix to combine.

3. Scrape the batter into the skillet. Bake until light golden brown and firm to the touch, about 25 minutes. Cut into wedges and serve warm or at room temperature.

SUBSTITUTE SKILLET

If you haven't got yourself a cast-iron skillet, just use a heavy-bottomed, ovenproof 9-inch skillet. If it happens to have a wooden handle, just cover that handle with foil.

CORN STICKS

■ ■

We love our corn bread in the South and have come up with a variety of ways to dress it up. I love the sour cream and chives in these, and how well they go with a bowl of tomato soup.

MAKES 12 CORN STICKS

1 cup fine yellow cornmeal

½ cup all-purpose flour

1 tablespoon sugar

1 teaspoon baking powder

½ teaspoon baking soda

½ teaspoon salt

¾ cup sour cream

2 large eggs, lightly beaten

2 tablespoons (¼ stick) butter, melted

2 tablespoons chopped fresh chives

1. Preheat the oven to 400°F. Lightly grease two 6-stick corn stick pans with butter, oil, or cooking spray. If you don't have corn stick pans, you can use muffins tins.

2. In a large bowl, whisk together the cornmeal, flour, sugar, baking powder, baking soda, and salt. In a separate bowl, whisk together the sour cream, eggs, and melted butter. Using a rubber spatula, stir the wet ingredients into the cornmeal mixture until just combined. Fold in the chives.

3. Divide the batter between the prepared pans without making too much of a mess (just wipe the sides with a paper towel if you drip). Bake until the corn sticks are golden and a toothpick inserted into the center comes out clean, 15 to 20 minutes. Let cool for 5 minutes in the pans before serving.

A CLASSIC PAN

The corn stick pan is a traditional Southern pan, but these days you can buy one just about anywhere. It's rectangular in shape, it's made of cast iron (of course), and it has anywhere from 6 to 9 wells shaped just like an ear of corn. It's great to have on hand when you're entertainin'—you can give your guests their individual corn breads!

ANGEL BISCUITS

■ ■

Is there anything better than biting into a hot, fresh buttered biscuit? And I love how biscuits can take you right through the day from sweet to savory to sweet again. You can butter that biscuit, then reach for the jam, honey, or syrup; you can toast a cold biscuit on the griddle and eat it with dip eggs or gravy; and you can use up leftovers in a shortcake, pudding, or dressing. I never get upset when I make too many biscuits: these fluffy yeast-raised beauties reheat flawlessly.

MAKES ABOUT 3 DOZEN BISCUITS

1 envelope (¼ ounce) active dry yeast
½ cup lukewarm (100° to 110°F) water
5 cups all-purpose flour, plus extra for
   dusting
2 tablespoons sugar

1 tablespoon baking powder
1 teaspoon baking soda
1 teaspoon salt
¾ cup vegetable shortening, chilled
2 cups buttermilk

1. Preheat the oven to 400°F. Grease a baking sheet with butter, oil, or cooking spray.

2. Sprinkle the yeast over the lukewarm water in a small bowl. In a large bowl, mix together the flour, sugar, baking powder, baking soda, and salt. Cut in the shortening with a pastry blender, your hands, or two knives (see illustration, page 277) until the mixture resembles coarse meal. Add the yeast mixture and buttermilk and mix well.

3. Sprinkle a small handful of flour over a work surface. Turn the dough onto the floured surface and roll out to a 1-inch thickness.

4. Using a 2½-inch round biscuit cutter, cut the dough into biscuits. Gently reroll the scraps and cut out more biscuits. Place the biscuits on the prepared baking sheet and bake until light golden brown and firm to the touch, about 12 minutes. Serve warm or at room temperature.

LUKEWARM TO THE TOUCH

The water you mix with the yeast should be lukewarm, never hot—otherwise it can kill the yeast. Even if you don't take its temperature with a thermometer, always dip a finger or knuckle in to make sure it's not too hot. And remember, your internal body temp is around 98°, so 100° to 110° won't feel too much different from the temperature of your own skin.

IT'S JUST GRAVY

It's no secret that we Southerners love gravy with our biscuits. Here are two we can't live without.

Chocolate Gravy

Makes enough for 6 to 8 servings

⅔ cup sugar

½ cup sifted unsweetened cocoa powder

2 tablespoons all-purpose flour

Pinch of salt

4 tablespoons (½ stick) butter

2 cups whole milk

1. In a small bowl, whisk together the sugar, cocoa powder, flour, and salt.

2. In a large skillet, heat the butter over low heat. Once the butter is melted, whisk in the sugar mixture. Whisk until all the dry ingredients have been incorporated.

3. Slowly pour the milk into the skillet, whisking quickly and constantly to remove lumps. Cook, whisking constantly, until the gravy has thickened, 5 to 7 minutes; take care not to scorch it. Serve hot over Angel Biscuits.

Sawmill Gravy

Makes about 1½ cups

It's not hard to understand sausage gravy: 3 ingredients, 5 minutes . . . this is the kind of hearty, savory breakfast you can throw together before you've even made the coffee. Griddle up last night's biscuits—or roll out a fresh batch—and you've got yourself one fine start on the day.

½ pound breakfast sausage links, casings removed

¼ cup all-purpose flour

1 cup whole milk

Salt and black pepper

In a large skillet, cook the sausage over medium heat, breaking it up with a spoon, until browned, about 5 minutes. Once the sausage is browned, sprinkle in the flour. Slowly pour the milk into the skillet, whisking quickly and constantly to get rid of any lumps of flour. Cook, whisking constantly, until the gravy has thickened, about 5 minutes. Season to taste with salt and black pepper. Serve hot over Angel Biscuits.

> ### WHISK IT SMOOTH
> Whether your gravy taste runs sweet or savory, I'm sure you can agree that lumpy gravy has no place on your biscuits. For the smoothest gravy, there is just no substitute for constant whisking.

BUTTERY BUTTERMILK BISCUITS

■ ■

When you want to savor the taste of butter, this is your biscuit. It just has unbeatable flavor from plenty of butter and tangy buttermilk, and those same ingredients give it a light, flaky texture as well.

MAKES 9 BISCUITS

2¼ cups all-purpose flour, plus extra for
   dusting
1 tablespoon baking powder
2 teaspoons sugar
1 teaspoon baking soda

1 teaspoon salt
8 tablespoons (1 stick) cold butter,
   cut into small bits
1 cup buttermilk

1. Place a rack in the center of the oven and preheat to 450°F. Grease a baking sheet with butter, oil, or cooking spray.

2. In a large bowl, whisk together the flour, baking powder, sugar, baking soda, and salt. Cut in the butter with a pastry blender, your hands, or two knives (see illustration) until the mixture resembles coarse meal. Using a rubber spatula, fold the buttermilk into the flour mixture until all the flour is moistened.

3. Sprinkle a small handful of flour over a work surface. Turn the dough out onto the surface and knead lightly two or three times with the palms of your hands until the mixture comes together. Pat the dough out until it's a 6-inch square. Cut the dough twice lengthwise and twice widthwise to make 9 squares.

> ### STRAIGHT FROM THE FRIDGE
> For an airy and flaky dough, make sure your butter is cold when you're cutting it into flour mixtures for biscuits, piecrusts, and the like. Work quickly so that it doesn't start to melt on you, especially if you're using your hands.

4. Place the biscuits on the prepared baking sheet and bake until light golden brown and firm to the touch, about 12 minutes. Serve warm or at room temperature.

Cut chopped chilled butter into dry ingredients by rubbing with your fingertips until the butter and dry ingredients have combined to create the texture of coarse meal. Be careful not to overwork. Alternatively, crisscross two knives across the butter and dry ingredients until the texture becomes like coarse meal.

SAUSAGE BISCUITS

These meaty, slightly peppery biscuits are a welcome appearance on a brunch buffet, and one of the most wonderful portable foods you could take along for the day.

MAKES ABOUT 8 BISCUITS

¼ pound breakfast sausage links, casings removed

2 cups self-rising flour

1 teaspoon salt

½ teaspoon black pepper

4 tablespoons (½ stick) cold butter, cut into small bits

¼ cup lard or vegetable shortening, chilled

1 cup buttermilk

All-purpose flour, for dusting

1. In a large skillet, cook the sausage over medium heat, breaking it up with a spoon, until browned, about 5 minutes. Set the sausage on a paper towel–lined plate to drain and cool.

2. Place a rack in the center of the oven and preheat to 425°F. Grease a baking sheet with butter, oil, or cooking spray.

3. In a large bowl, whisk together the self-rising flour, salt, and black pepper. Cut in the butter and lard with a pastry blender, your hands, or two knives (see illustration, page 277) until the mixture resembles coarse meal. Add the cooled sausage and stir to combine. Using a rubber spatula, fold the buttermilk into the flour mixture until all the flour is moistened.

4. Sprinkle a small handful of all-purpose flour on a work surface. Turn the dough out onto the surface and knead lightly two or three times with the palms of your hands until the mixture comes together. Pat the dough out to a ¾-inch-thick round.

5. Using a 2½-inch round biscuit cutter, cut the dough into biscuits. Gently reroll the scraps and cut out more biscuits. Place the biscuits on the prepared baking sheet and bake until light golden brown and firm to the touch, 17 to 18 minutes. Serve warm or at room temperature with gravy, for a real Southern touch.

FEEL THE KNEAD

With biscuits, it's important that you knead just enough, but not too much. If you knead too much, your dough will toughen up. But you want to make sure you get a few good kneads in there so that your biscuits end up with nice soft layers.

FLUFFY SWEET POTATO BISCUITS

You can buy a tube of darn good buttermilk biscuits if you're in a rush, but sweet potato biscuits—fluffy, delicious, slightly sweet, orange biscuits like these—are worth the extra effort. They come together fast and are perfect in the breadbasket during the fall and the holidays.

MAKES ABOUT 9 BISCUITS

¾ cup cooked, mashed sweet potato (about 1 large)
⅓ to ½ cup whole milk
1½ cups all-purpose flour, plus extra for dusting

2 tablespoons sugar
1 tablespoon baking powder
1 teaspoon salt
6 tablespoons cold butter, cut into small bits

1. Place a rack in the center of the oven and preheat to 425°F. Grease a baking sheet with butter, oil, or cooking spray.

2. In a small bowl, whisk together the sweet potato and ⅓ cup milk. Set aside.

3. In a large bowl, whisk together the flour, sugar, baking powder, and salt. Cut in the butter with a pastry blender, your hands, or two knives (see illustration, page 277) until the mixture resembles coarse meal. Add the sweet potato mixture and fold gently to combine. Add the remaining milk a little at a time until all the flour is moistened. The amount you will need will depend on the moisture of the sweet potato.

4. Sprinkle a small handful of flour on a work surface. Turn the dough out onto the surface and knead lightly two or three times with the palms of your hands until the mixture comes together. Pat the dough out to a ½-inch-thick round.

5. Using a 2½-inch round biscuit cutter, cut the dough into biscuits. Gently reroll the scraps and cut out more biscuits. Place the biscuits on the prepared baking sheet and bake until light golden brown and firm to the touch, 12 to 14 minutes. Serve these fluffy biscuits warm or at room temperature.

> **TIME-SAVER**
> Sweet potatoes freeze so well and are such a great pantry staple that I like to make up big batches and freeze them. Just boil 'em up, peeled or unpeeled, dry and cool 'em completely, and then either slice 'em up or mash 'em. They'll keep in sealed plastic bags for up to 6 months.

CHIVE AND CHEDDAR BISCUITS

■ ■

Sweet, oniony little green chives are just about the best partner to a nice sharp Cheddar cheese that I can think of. If you have a half foot of dirt to plant them in, chives will take over, growing like crazy in the ground or a pot. I love grabbing a handful to chop into my extra-cheesy biscuits.

MAKES ABOUT 12 BISCUITS

2 cups all-purpose flour

1 tablespoon sugar

2 teaspoons baking powder

1 teaspoon baking soda

1 teaspoon salt

6 tablespoons cold butter, cut into small bits

1¼ cups shredded sharp Cheddar cheese (5 ounces)

¼ cup finely chopped fresh chives

1 cup buttermilk

1. Place a rack in the center of the oven and preheat to 425°F. Grease a baking sheet with butter, oil, or cooking spray.

2. In a large bowl, whisk together the flour, sugar, baking powder, baking soda, and salt. Cut in the butter with a pastry blender, your hands, or two knives (see illustration, page 277) until the mixture resembles coarse meal. Add 1 cup of the Cheddar and the chives to the flour mixture and toss to combine. Using a rubber spatula, fold the buttermilk into the flour mixture until all the flour is moistened.

3. Using an ice cream scoop or a large spoon, scoop the mixture and place on the prepared baking sheet. Sprinkle the remaining ¼ cup Cheddar over the biscuits. Bake until light golden brown and firm to the touch, 13 to 15 minutes. Serve warm or at room temperature.

SPICE KICK

For a spicy version of these beautiful biscuits, use pepper Jack cheese instead of Cheddar. And you can experiment with different herbs like parsley or cilantro.

OLD-FASHIONED WHITE BREAD

■ ■

Now, listen, y'all, I'm a busy lady, but I'm telling you, sometimes it's time to slow down. Baking yeast bread is such a fulfilling way to get back to basics, and that first slice, with a nice pat of butter . . . it just doesn't get more satisfying than this.

MAKES TWO 8-INCH LOAVES

1 envelope (¼ ounce) active dry yeast
½ cup lukewarm (100° to 110°F) water
6 cups all-purpose flour
2 tablespoons sugar

1½ teaspoons salt
2 cups whole milk, scalded
    (see box, page 282)
2 tablespoons vegetable shortening

1. Preheat the oven to 375°F. Grease two 8 by 4 by 3-inch loaf pans with butter, oil, or cooking spray. Sprinkle the yeast over the lukewarm water in a small bowl.

2. In a large bowl, whisk together the flour, sugar, and salt. Using a rubber spatula, fold in the hot milk, shortening, and yeast mixture until all the flour is moistened. Knead the dough until it's uniform and all the ingredients are incorporated.

With floured hands, knead the dough by pressing down very firmly on it with the heels of your hands, pushing the dough away from you, then folding it back over itself. Give the dough a little turn and repeat. Continue turning and kneading until the dough has a smooth, silky consistency.

3. Divide the dough in two and shape into loaves. Place in the prepared pans. Bake until a toothpick inserted in the center of a loaf comes out clean, 45 to 50 minutes. Homemade bread. What a treat.

> ### A GOOD SCALDING
> By scalding the milk, you will ensure a nicely structured and textured finished loaf. To scald, heat the milk up almost to the boiling point, while stirring all the while so that a skin doesn't appear on the surface of the milk and a crust doesn't form on the bottom of the pan. Keep a close eye on your pan and pull it off the heat just as the milk is about to come up to a boil.

CINNAMON TOAST MUFFINS

I remember when I barely had time to sprinkle cinnamon and sugar on toast for my boys before they headed out the door to school. Well, now I like to fix 'em these delicious, tender muffins dipped in butter and cinnamon sugar whenever I get the chance. They have a flavor reminiscent of those helter-skelter mornings. Isn't it amazing the things you end up looking back on fondly?

MAKES 12 MUFFINS

Muffins

3 cups all-purpose flour

2½ teaspoons baking powder

¾ teaspoon salt

½ teaspoon grated nutmeg

¼ teaspoon baking soda

¾ cup whole milk

2 tablespoons buttermilk

8 tablespoons (1 stick) plus 2 tablespoons (¼ stick) butter, at room temperature

¾ cup plus 2 tablespoons sugar

2 large eggs

Coating

1 cup sugar

1 tablespoon ground cinnamon

8 to 12 tablespoons (1 to 1½ sticks) butter, melted

1. To make the muffins: Preheat the oven to 375°F. Grease a 12-cup muffin tin with butter, oil, or cooking spray and dust with flour.

2. In a medium bowl, sift together the flour, baking powder, salt, nutmeg, and baking soda. In a small bowl, whisk together the milk and buttermilk.

3. In the bowl of an electric stand mixer fitted with the paddle attachment, or using a handheld mixer, cream the butter and sugar together at medium speed until light and fluffy, about 5 minutes. Beat in the eggs, one at a time, beating well after each egg is added to thoroughly combine.

4. With the mixer at low speed, beat one-fourth of the flour mixture into the butter mixture. Beat in one-third of the milk mixture. Add the rest of the two mixtures, alternating the dry and wet ingredients, ending with the dry ingredients. Take care not to overmix. You just want the ingredients to come together.

5. Scrape the batter into the prepared muffin tin, filling the cups just to the rim with batter. Bake until lightly golden and firm to the touch, about 20 minutes. Let the muffins cool in the pan for 5 minutes, then remove them and transfer to a wire rack set on a baking sheet.

6. To prepare the coating: In a small bowl, combine the sugar and cinnamon. Brush each muffin top generously with the melted butter. Then sprinkle generously with the cinnamon sugar and watch them come running to the kitchen.

CREAM AND SUGAR

I reckon that creaming is pretty much the most important step in baking sweets. By whipping together your butter and sugar until they are light and fluffy, you are certain to end up with baked goods that rise well in the oven and are light and fluffy in texture. For best results, make sure the butter is nicely softened so that it incorporates easily into the sugar.

WALNUT BANANA BREAD

■ ■

This is the sweet, nutty banana bread I fix for Michael for a special treat—he just adores it. I toast my walnuts a bit to give them extra crunch, and I use some vanilla in the batter, which makes this bread smell heavenly while it is baking and gives it a real nice flavor.

MAKES ONE 9-INCH LOAF

1¼ cups mashed ripe bananas (2 large or
    3 medium)
1 cup sugar
½ cup vegetable oil
2 large eggs
1 teaspoon vanilla extract

1¾ cups all-purpose flour
1 teaspoon baking powder
1 teaspoon salt
½ teaspoon baking soda
¾ cup chopped walnuts, lightly toasted (or
    you can use chocolate chips instead)

1. Place a rack in the bottom third of the oven and preheat to 350°F. Grease a 9 by 5-inch loaf pan with butter, oil, or cooking spray.

2. In a large bowl, whisk together the bananas, sugar, oil, eggs, and vanilla. In a medium bowl, whisk together the flour, baking powder, salt, and baking soda. Using a rubber spatula, gently fold the flour mixture into the banana mixture just to combine. Stir in the walnuts. Pour the batter into the prepared loaf pan and smooth the top.

3. Bake until a toothpick inserted into the center comes out clean and the top is golden brown, 1 hour and 10 minutes to 1 hour and 15 minutes. Let cool in the pan on a wire rack for 10 minutes. Then pop the bread out of the pan and let cool completely on the rack before slicing and serving.

SAVING A BUNCH

I'm sure you've seen it time and again, a bunch of bananas browning too fast on the countertop. When this starts to happen, I peel my bananas and pop them whole into airtight plastic bags. They keep in the freezer for 2 or 3 months.

ZUCCHINI BREAD

When I made zucchini bread on my show, I whipped up an herb cream cheese to spread on top that was so darn delicious, it nearly undid me. Y'all, I ate so much cream cheese that day, I almost thought I'd overdone it! But seriously, I adore how you can take a moist, slightly sweet zucchini bread in a savory direction or just keep it sweet.

MAKES ONE 9-INCH LOAF

1 cup grated zucchini (1 medium)
1 cup sugar
½ cup vegetable oil
2 large eggs
1 teaspoon vanilla extract

1½ cups all-purpose flour
1½ teaspoons ground cinnamon
¾ teaspoon salt
½ teaspoon baking soda
½ teaspoon baking powder

1. Place a rack in the bottom third of the oven and preheat to 350°F. Grease a 9 by 5-inch loaf pan with butter, oil, or cooking spray.

2. In a large bowl, whisk together the zucchini, sugar, oil, eggs, and vanilla. In a medium bowl, whisk together the flour, cinnamon, salt, baking soda, and baking powder. Using a rubber spatula, gently fold the flour mixture into the zucchini mixture just to combine. Pour the batter into the prepared loaf pan and smooth the top.

3. Bake until a toothpick inserted into the center comes out clean and the top is golden brown, 1 hour and 5 minutes to 1 hour and 10 minutes. Let cool in the pan on a wire rack for 10 minutes. Then pop the bread out of the pan and let cool completely on the rack before slicing and serving.

FOR SPREADING

You can make herbed cream cheese by letting cream cheese come to room temperature and stirring in chopped parsley, chives, or whatever fresh herbs you may have on hand.

STREUSEL PUMPKIN BREAD

■ ■

In case you hadn't noticed, I do like to gild the lily from time to time. So I sprinkle a sweet, buttery cinnamon streusel right on top of my pumpkin bread. Why not make it that much more special?

MAKES ONE 9-INCH LOAF

Streusel

2½ tablespoons packed light brown sugar
2½ tablespoons all-purpose flour
½ teaspoon ground cinnamon
Pinch of salt
2 tablespoons cold butter

Pumpkin Bread

1 cup canned unsweetened pumpkin puree
1½ cups packed light brown sugar
½ cup vegetable oil
2 large eggs
1 teaspoon vanilla extract
1½ cups all-purpose flour
2¼ teaspoons pumpkin pie spice
1 teaspoon baking soda
1 teaspoon salt
½ teaspoon baking powder
½ cup raisins

KEEP COOL

Cool your bread in the pan for 10 minutes: any longer might make it difficult to get the bread out. Then invert it out of the pan onto a wire rack to cool completely. As it cools, the bread has time to finish cooking with the heat still trapped inside the loaf. And the wire rack lets the loaf cool on all sides so you don't end up with a sticky bottom on your bread. This cooling process ensures firm slices when it's time to cut.

1. Place a rack in the bottom third of the oven and preheat to 350°F. Grease a 9 by 5-inch loaf pan with butter, oil, or cooking spray.

2. To prepare the streusel: In a medium bowl, whisk together the brown sugar, flour, cinnamon, and salt. Cut in the butter with a pastry blender, your hands, or two knives (see illustration, page 277) until the mixture resembles coarse meal. Set the streusel mixture aside while you make the pumpkin bread.

3. To make the pumpkin bread: In a large bowl, whisk together the pumpkin puree, brown sugar, oil, eggs, and vanilla. In a medium bowl, whisk together the flour, pumpkin pie spice, baking soda, salt, and baking powder. Using a rubber spatula, gently fold the flour mixture into the pumpkin mixture just to combine. Stir in the raisins. Pour the batter into the prepared loaf pan and smooth the top. Top with the streusel mixture.

4. Bake until a toothpick inserted into the center comes out clean and the top is golden brown, 55 minutes to 1 hour. Let cool in the pan on a wire rack for 10 minutes. Then pop the bread out of the pan and let cool completely on the rack before slicing and serving.

SOUR CREAM TEA SCONES

When it comes to scones, I don't have time for those perfect-looking ones at most coffee shops, because I can just see how dry they are. But these buttery little numbers are nice and moist thanks to the sour cream, and they're full of tangy little currants. Just pat your dough out gently, and leave the scones a little rough-looking, and you'll wind up with the most tender and delicious scones you ever had. Serve with jelly and whipped cream for slathering on top.

MAKES 8 LARGE SCONES

2 cups self-rising flour
¼ cup sugar
1 teaspoon salt
1½ sticks (6 ounces) cold butter,
    cut into small bits

1 cup dried currants
1 cup sour cream
1 large egg
All-purpose flour, for dusting

1. Place a rack in the center of the oven and preheat to 425°F. Grease a baking sheet with butter, oil, or cooking spray.

2. In a large bowl, whisk together the self-rising flour, sugar, and salt. Cut in the butter with a pastry blender, your hands, or two knives (see illustration, page 277) until the mixture resembles coarse meal. Stir in the currants. In a small bowl, whisk together the sour cream and egg. Using a rubber spatula, fold the sour cream mixture into the flour mixture until all the flour is moistened.

3. Sprinkle a small handful of the all-purpose flour over a work surface. Turn the dough out onto the surface and knead lightly two or three times with the palms of your hands until the mixture comes together. Pat the dough out to an 8-inch round. Cut the round into 8 wedges.

4. Place the scones on the prepared baking sheet. Bake until light golden brown and firm to the touch, 20 to 22 minutes. Serve warm or at room temperature.

ON THE PULSE

While I prefer to cut my butter in with a pastry blender, a food processor is a fine option as well. Use the pulse button so that you don't overwork the mixture. Just like when you cut in by hand, you want to end up with a texture that resembles coarse meal.

Chapter 12

COFFEE CAKES, GRIDDLE CAKES, AND DOUGHNUTS

Life is too short to wonder where you hid your waffle maker when the urge strikes and then go looking for it, so I keep mine right up on the counter, alongside my built-in griddle, where I can make my hoecakes and buttermilk pancakes at the drop of the hat; my boys just love that. But truthfully, y'all, the majority of the recipes in this chapter are not ones I make every day. When I do, you just want to slap your mama! Homemade doughnuts, fruit fritters, and coffee cakes are simply some of the most rewarding things to cook: people cannot stop singing your praises when you set down a warm Gooey Gorilla Bread (page 305) just dripping with butter, cinnamon, and brown sugar. Pulling that warm, sweet bread apart is an event.

For all the fuss folks make, you'd think making such recipes as doughnuts would take you hours and hours. But it just depends on how long it takes you to pop open a can of biscuits! That tube of dough is just about all you need to make Gooey Gorilla Bread, and it was my mama's trick to bringing a plate of fresh Biscuit Doughnuts (page 293) into the family room after dinner when Bubba and I were watching TV and wanting something sweet.

Now, I know my mama wasn't the only woman in the South to make Biscuit Doughnuts because I talk to other people my age, and they share some of the same memories. She would take those canned biscuits, poke her finger in the middle of each biscuit, and work 'em into a doughnut. She would deep-fry 'em, with some powdered sugar ready, and oh, my goodness! Of course my Michael has a preference for filled doughnuts, and I hate to let that man go without, so I have also perfected a fluffy, plump yeast doughnut with plenty of space to fill with jelly.

Now, mind, y'all, this is not our definition of a regular breakfast. So when I get up in the morning and fry a big plate of doughnuts, you know it's a special day. And the same goes for my towering, crumb-a-licious Cherry-Almond Coffee Crumb Cake (page 303) and my Pineapple-Pecan French Toast Casserole (page 302). For a more everyday treat, say on a lazy morning, I just love to make waffles for my whole big family. They're Corrie's absolute favorite breakfast, and nothing gets folks out early like telling them I'm planning to make my Waffles with Blackberry Syrup (page 301).

You know, I still recall my feeling of wonder when I walked into my Grandmama Paul's kitchen to find her freshly fried peach, apple, or pineapple fritters just made. Oh, my, they are a delightful snack—I would never want to leave out her fruit fritter recipes. And I love to think that my grandbaby Jack might have some of the same sweet memories of his grandma. The recipes in this chapter are all so sweet and special: make them for someone you love. And don't forget to make them for yourself.

BISCUIT DOUGHNUTS

My mama's biscuit-dough doughnuts were so delicious, I never felt the need to set foot in a doughnut shop—I knew how to make my own. But once I did, I just took inspiration from all those glazes and sprinkles, and I make those now, too. There is nothing better than a fresh-made doughnut, and homemade is the freshest they get.

MAKES 16 TO 20 DOUGHNUTS AND 16 TO 20 DOUGHNUT HOLES

About 4 quarts peanut oil, for deep-frying
1 teaspoon ground cinnamon
¼ cup granulated sugar
2 cups confectioners' sugar
5 tablespoons whole milk
1 teaspoon vanilla extract

¼ cup unsweetened cocoa powder
2 cans (16.3 ounces each) refrigerated
    buttermilk biscuit dough
Colored sprinkles, for decorating
Chocolate sprinkles, for decorating

1. In a deep pot, heat 3 inches of oil until it reaches 350°F on a deep-fry thermometer. In a shallow bowl, stir together the cinnamon and granulated sugar and set aside.

2. Meanwhile, in a medium bowl, whisk together 1 cup of the confectioners' sugar, 2 tablespoons of the milk, and the vanilla. Set the vanilla icing aside. In another medium bowl, whisk together the remaining 1 cup confectioners' sugar, the cocoa powder, and the remaining 3 tablespoons milk. Set the chocolate icing aside.

3. Lay out the biscuits on a cutting board and with a 1-inch round cookie or biscuit cutter, cut out a hole from the middle of each biscuit.

4. Set a wire rack on a baking sheet and place near the pot of hot oil. Fry the doughnuts, 2 or 3 at a time, taking care not to crowd the pot, until golden brown, 2 to 3 minutes each side. Fry the doughnut holes, also in batches, about 1 minute per side. Transfer the doughnuts and doughnut holes to the rack to cool completely. Toss in the cinnamon sugar or drizzle with one of the icings and decorate the icing with sprinkles. Have fun with the decorating, y'all. This is where you can get creative.

HOLESOME FUN

Don't waste an ounce of this biscuit dough. Fry up the cut-out doughnut holes along with the doughnuts. The little ones especially love these.

RED VELVET CAKE DOUGHNUTS WITH CREAM CHEESE ICING

■ ■

Now, my cousin Johnnie Gabriel, owner of the fabulous Gabriel's Desserts in Marietta, Georgia, makes absolutely the best red velvet cupcakes I've ever put in my mouth. I got to thinking one day, why couldn't you make a cream cheese–glazed red velvet cake doughnut? Why not? I said to myself, and went right into the kitchen to make me some.

MAKES 10 TO 12 DOUGHNUTS AND 10 TO 12 DOUGHNUT HOLES

Doughnuts
2¼ cups all-purpose flour, plus
    extra for dusting
1 cup sugar
¼ cup unsweetened cocoa powder
1 teaspoon salt
1 teaspoon baking powder
½ teaspoon baking soda
¾ cup buttermilk
2 large eggs
5 tablespoons butter, melted
1 tablespoon red food coloring
1½ teaspoons vanilla extract
About 4 quarts vegetable oil, for deep-frying

Icing
1 package (8 ounces) cream cheese, at room
    temperature
6 tablespoons sugar
3 to 4 tablespoons buttermilk
1 teaspoon vanilla extract
Pinch of salt

1. To prepare the doughnuts: In a large bowl, whisk together the flour, sugar, cocoa powder, salt, baking powder, and baking soda. In a medium bowl, whisk together the buttermilk, eggs, melted butter, food coloring, and vanilla to combine. Using a rubber spatula, fold the buttermilk mixture into the flour mixture just until combined. Cover the bowl with plastic wrap and refrigerate for 1 hour.

2. Meanwhile, make the icing: In the bowl of an electric mixer fitted with the paddle attachment, or using a handheld mixer, beat the cream cheese and sugar at medium speed until soft and lump-free, about 5 minutes, scraping down the sides while you do so. Add the buttermilk, 1 tablespoon at a time, until the icing is smooth enough to drizzle. Beat in the vanilla and salt and mix until fully combined.

3. Sprinkle a generous handful of flour over a work surface. Turn the doughnut dough out of the bowl onto the surface and pat it out to a ½-inch thickness. Using a 3-inch round biscuit

or cookie cutter, cut the dough into rounds. Using a 1-inch biscuit or cookie cutter, cut out the doughnut holes. Gently gather the scraps, re-pat, and cut more doughnuts from the scraps. Re-pat these scraps just one time, folks.

4. In a deep pot, heat 3 inches of oil until it reaches 350°F on a deep-fry thermometer. Meanwhile, set a wire rack on a baking sheet and place next to the pot.

5. Add the doughnuts and doughnut holes to the hot oil, 2 or 3 at a time, taking care not to crowd the pot. Fry until golden brown, 2 to 3 minutes each side for the doughnuts and about 1 minute per side for the doughnut holes. Transfer the doughnuts to the rack to cool completely before drizzling all over with the icing.

TOUGH STUFF

Try your best to cut out as many doughnut rings as possible with each patting of the dough. But don't pat it out past the two times called for in the recipe, because the more you work the dough, the tougher it will be.

JELLY DOUGHNUTS

■ ■

My Michael just has to have his jelly doughnuts. And if you have never watched a grown man with a snow-white beard eating a homemade jelly doughnut, well, let me tell you, it is one of life's greatest pleasures. Bless him.

MAKES ABOUT 12 DOUGHNUTS

½ cup lukewarm (100° to 110°F) whole milk

1 envelope (¼ ounce) active dry yeast

1 tablespoon honey

About 2 cups all-purpose flour, plus
    extra for dusting

¼ cup sugar, plus extra for coating doughnuts

1 large egg

1 teaspoon salt

5 tablespoons butter, at room temperature,
    cut into tablespoons

About 4 quarts vegetable oil, for deep-frying

¾ cup jelly or preserves (your favorite)

1. In the bowl of an electric mixer fitted with the whisk attachment, or using a handheld mixer, whisk together the milk, yeast, and honey at medium-low speed. Cover with plastic wrap and let sit in a warm, draft-free place until bubbly, about 10 minutes.

2. Add 2 cups flour, ¼ cup sugar, the egg, and salt to the yeast mixture and, using the dough hook attachment at low speed or kneading by hand, mix until the ingredients come together. Add

the butter, 1 tablespoon at a time, beating until incorporated. Increase the speed to medium and mix the dough until smooth and elastic, about 5 minutes. The dough should be soft, but not sticky. If it is sticky, add more flour, 1 tablespoon at a time, until it's soft and silky. Grease a large bowl with oil or coat with cooking spray and turn the dough into the prepared bowl. Cover with plastic wrap and let rise in a warm, draft-free place until doubled in size, about 1 hour.

3. Sprinkle a generous handful of flour over a work surface. Sprinkle a small handful of flour over a baking sheet. Turn the dough out onto the surface and pat into a ½-inch-thick round. Using a 3-inch round biscuit or cookie cutter, cut the dough into rounds. Gently gather the scraps, re-pat, and cut more doughnuts from the scraps. Re-pat these scraps just one time, folks. Place the doughnuts on the prepared baking sheet, cover with plastic wrap, and let rise until doubled in size, 20 to 30 minutes.

4. In a deep pot, heat 3 inches of oil until it reaches 350°F on a deep-fry thermometer. Meanwhile, set a wire rack on a baking sheet and place next to the pot. Set up a plate with sugar at the ready.

5. Add the doughnuts to the hot oil, 2 or 3 at a time, taking care not to crowd the pot. Fry until golden brown, 2 to 3 minutes each side. Transfer the doughnuts to the rack to cool for 1 minute, then roll in granulated sugar to coat all sides. Return to the rack.

6. Once all the doughnuts have cooled completely, cut a pocket in the side of each doughnut. Using a spoon, stuff 1 tablespoon of jelly inside each doughnut. Reroll in sugar if you think it needs more. I guarantee you these doughnuts are worth the wait.

LIVING PROOF

When you set your dough aside to rise, it's called proofing. It needs a nice, warm, not-too-hot spot to do its best, or the yeast will die. If you're having trouble finding just the right spot in your house, here's a neat tip: cover the bowl (without touching the dough itself) with a towel that has just been through the dryer, just like tucking it under a warm blanket. Now, doesn't that sound cozy?

THE LADY & SONS HOECAKES

At the restaurant we serve hoecakes all day. Folks love to eat these little round drop corn breads alongside their meal. Then for dessert, they'll reach for the cane syrup and have another hoecake drizzled in syrup. I've heard that the name came about because farmers originally cooked these rustic little griddled breads on the back of a flat planting hoe over a fire out in the field.

MAKES ABOUT 16 CAKES

1 cup self-rising flour
1 cup self-rising cornmeal (see box)
1 tablespoon sugar
¾ cup buttermilk

¼ cup vegetable oil or bacon fat
2 large eggs, lightly beaten
Oil or butter, for frying

1. In a large bowl, combine the flour, cornmeal, and sugar. Stir in the buttermilk, oil or bacon fat, eggs, and ⅓ cup plus 1 tablespoon water.

2. In a large skillet, heat 1 inch of oil over medium heat. Drop the hoecake batter into the hot oil, using about 2 tablespoons of batter per hoecake. Cook until browned and crisp on one side, then turn and brown on the other side, about 5 minutes per side. Set on a paper towel–lined plate to drain. If you somehow manage to have leftover batter, it will keep in the refrigerator for up to 2 days.

MIX BLESSING

If you're having problems getting your hands on self-rising cornmeal, go ahead and substitute the same amount of corn bread mix for the self-rising cornmeal. That should do the trick.

LACE HOECAKES

My Grandmama Paul's hoecake pan is one of the most treasured pieces in my kitchen, and it allows me to fry up the hoecakes with crisp, lacy edges. Y'all can order yourself a hoecake pan from my website to make this simple treat at home or even take the pan along next time you go camping. Serve lace hoecakes hot with butter and syrup for breakfast, have them alongside soups and chilis, or try my okra lace cakes (see box) with fried chicken or ribs.

SERVES 8

2 cups cornmeal

1½ teaspoons salt

¼ cup vegetable oil

1. Heat a hoecake pan over medium-high heat until very hot.

2. Meanwhile, combine the cornmeal and salt in a bowl. Stir in 2½ to 3 cups water until the mixture forms a thin batter about the consistency of heavy cream.

3. Reduce the heat under the hoecake pan to medium; add 1½ teaspoons of the oil and pour ⅓ cup batter onto the center of the pan, allowing it to spread to the sides. When the edges are golden and lacy, about 2 to 3 minutes, place a heatproof plate over the pan. Flip the pan and hoecake onto the plate, then slide the hoecake off of the plate and back into the pan so that the opposite side is now on the bottom of the pan. Cook until the underside is golden brown. Repeat with the remaining oil and batter. Keep an eye on your batter as it sits, since it has a tendency to thicken up. If it thickens, add more water to keep the proper consistency.

OKRA LACE CAKES

One of my favorite ways to change up these hoecakes is to add some okra to them. Simply stir ⅔ cup very thinly sliced okra (about ⅛ inch thick) into the batter. Start with whole frozen okra for easiest slicing.

Pour the batter into a hoecake pan.

Maple-Glazed Salmon (page 221).

Memphis Dry-Rub Ribs (page 225).

Hot German Potato Salad with Bacon (page 56) and BBQ Pork Loin (page 227).

Yam Casserole with Pecan Crumble (page 238).

Angel Biscuits (page 275) with Chocolate Gravy (page 276).

Buttermilk Pancakes (page 299).

Decadent Double-Chocolate Cream Pie (page 319).

Banana Cream Pie (page 317).

Blackberry Cobbler (page 337).

Clockwise from top: Chocolate Pecan Bars (page 345); Benne Seed Wafers (page 351); Brownie Pudding Puddles (page 347); Florida Lemon Bars (page 352).

Red Velvet Cake with Cream Cheese–Bourbon Frosting (page 364).

Mississippi Mud Cake (page 368).

Coconut Cake (page 363).

Cinnamon-Glazed Sour Cream Apple Bundt Cake (page 374).

Pecan Spice Layer Cake with Caramel Frosting (page 377).

Cream Cheese–Chocolate Chip Bread Pudding (page 400).

Clockwise from top: The Ultimate Easy Chocolate-Peanut Fudge (page 413);
Nutty Brittle (page 418); Popcorn Balls (page 415).

BUTTERMILK PANCAKES

■ ■

The great big griddle on my stove means I can pour out pancakes for everyone around my table, no matter how many we are. These are my go-to fluffy pancakes, and I serve them hot-hot-hot with plenty of maple syrup and a little more butter on the table.

MAKES 15 TO 18 (3-INCH) PANCAKES

2 cups all-purpose flour

¼ cup sugar

2 teaspoons baking powder

1 teaspoon baking soda

1 teaspoon salt

1¾ cups buttermilk

4 tablespoons (½ stick) butter, melted

2 large eggs

1 teaspoon vanilla extract

Maple syrup, for drizzling

1. Grease a griddle or large nonstick skillet with butter, oil, or cooking spray and place over medium heat.

2. Meanwhile, as your griddle heats up, in a large bowl, whisk together the flour, sugar, baking powder, baking soda, and salt. In a medium bowl, whisk together the buttermilk, butter, eggs, and vanilla until combined. Using a rubber spatula, fold the buttermilk mixture into the flour mixture just until combined. A few lumps are just fine.

3. Pour out the batter in ⅓-cup rounds onto the hot griddle and cook until light golden brown, 3 to 4 minutes. Flip the pancakes and cook until the undersides are golden, another 2 to 3 minutes. Repeat with the remaining batter, greasing the griddle if it seems dry. Serve hot with (what else?) maple syrup for drizzling.

FLIP FLAP

Pancakes give you a real good cue when they're ready to be flipped. Just look for tiny bubbles to pop up all over the uncooked surface of the pancake and for dryness all around the outer edge, and you'll know it's time to turn it over.

CORNMEAL BLUEBERRY PANCAKES

■ ■

Somewhere between a hoecake and a blueberry pancake, this is what I came up with when we were a little low on flour one morning. They are just the sunniest, fruitiest, sweetest morning treat.

MAKES ABOUT 18 (4-INCH) PANCAKES

1 cup plus 2 tablespoons cornmeal

1 cup all-purpose flour

1 teaspoon baking powder

1 teaspoon salt

½ teaspoon baking soda

1 cup whole milk

4 tablespoons (½ stick) butter, melted

1 large egg

¼ cup honey

2 cups blueberries, fresh or thawed frozen

Confectioners' sugar, for dusting (optional)

1. Grease a griddle or large nonstick skillet with butter, oil, or cooking spray and place over medium heat.

2. Meanwhile, as your griddle heats up, in a large bowl, whisk together the cornmeal, flour, baking powder, salt, and baking soda. In a medium bowl, whisk together the milk, melted butter, egg, and honey until combined. Using a rubber spatula, fold the milk mixture into the cornmeal mixture just until combined. A few lumps are just fine. Let the batter stand at room temperature for 15 minutes to thicken up.

3. Pour out the batter in ⅓-cup rounds onto the hot griddle, sprinkle with blueberries, and cook until light golden brown, 3 to 4 minutes. Flip the pancakes and cook until the undersides are golden, another 2 to 3 minutes. Repeat with the remaining batter, greasing the griddle if it seems dry. Serve hot, dusting with confectioners' sugar if you'd like.

A LITTLE SUNSHINE

Sometimes I like to grate a little lemon zest into my pancake batter, y'all. That sunshiny lemony flavor really perks up the blueberries and livens up the cornmeal. Just a teaspoon is all you need.

WAFFLES WITH BLACKBERRY SYRUP

■ ■

When I think back on picking blackberries as a child, I remember getting scratched, worrying about snakes, and coming home with as many bug bites as berries. Not that I ever minded at the time, but these days I am glad to have a bag of sweet-tart blackberries right in my freezer. I simmer them into this special syrup for our buttery, crispy waffles.

MAKES 7 TO 8 WAFFLES

Blackberry Syrup
1¾ cups (7 ounces) frozen blackberries
½ cup sugar
Juice of ½ lemon

Waffles
2⅔ cups all-purpose flour
2½ tablespoons sugar
1 tablespoon baking powder
1¼ teaspoons salt
2 cups whole milk
2¾ sticks butter, melted
4 large eggs

1. To make the blackberry syrup: In a medium saucepan, combine the blackberries, sugar, and 2 tablespoons water. Bring to a boil over medium heat. Reduce the heat to a simmer and cook for 15 minutes to reduce slightly. Add the lemon juice. You can refrigerate the syrup, but warm before serving.

2. To make the waffles: In a large bowl, whisk together the flour, sugar, baking powder, and salt. In a medium bowl, whisk together the milk, melted butter, and eggs until combined. Using a rubber spatula, fold the milk mixture into the flour mixture just until combined.

3. Preheat a standard-size electric waffle iron according to the manufacturer's instructions. To make extra sure your waffles don't stick, give it a spray with cooking spray.

4. Pour a scant 1 cup of batter into the waffle iron; cook until golden brown and crispy on both sides, 5 to 6 minutes. Serve hot, topped with warm blackberry syrup.

> **PATIENCE IS A VIRTUE**
> Don't open the waffle iron before the waffle is thoroughly cooked, or the waffle may break apart. Some waffle irons have an indicator light that changes color when the waffle is ready. If yours doesn't have one, just look for the steam to stop escaping from the sides of the waffle iron.

PINEAPPLE-PECAN FRENCH TOAST CASSEROLE

Make this fruit-filled, rich bread pudding for your next buffet brunch and stand nearby so you can hear folks talking. The combination of cinnamon, pecans, brown sugar, and pineapple will just bowl them over. This is a real fun recipe to make and to eat, and you can assemble it the night before, so it's very convenient for entertaining.

SERVES 6 TO 8

Casserole
8 large eggs
2 cups whole milk
2 cups half-and-half
1½ cups granulated sugar
1 tablespoon ground cinnamon
2 teaspoons vanilla extract
1 teaspoon salt
1 loaf French bread (1 pound), cut into
    1-inch cubes
1 can (20 ounces) pineapple chunks,
    drained

Pecan Topping
1¼ cups pecan halves
⅓ cup packed light brown sugar
½ teaspoon ground cinnamon
Pinch of salt

Confectioners' sugar, for serving

> **THE REAL DEAL**
> When shopping for vanilla, keep a lookout for pure vanilla extract as opposed to bottles marked vanilla essence or imitation vanilla extract. Essence and imitation vanilla are chemical formulations that taste like vanilla, whereas pure extract is the real McCoy, actual vanilla suspended in a mix of alcohol and water.

1. Grease a 13 by 9-inch baking dish (pretty enough to bring to the table) with butter, oil, or cooking spray.

2. To prepare the casserole: In a large bowl, whisk together the eggs, milk, half-and-half, granulated sugar, cinnamon, vanilla, and salt. Add the bread cubes and pineapple and give it a good mix so that the bread is fully coated in the custard. Place in the prepared baking dish, cover with plastic wrap, and refrigerate overnight.

3. The next day, when you are ready to bake the casserole, preheat the oven to 325°F.

4. To make the pecan topping: In a small bowl, combine the pecan halves, brown sugar, cinnamon, and salt. Remove the plastic wrap from the casserole and top with the pecan mixture. Bake until golden brown and a knife inserted into the center comes out clean, 1 hour and 10 minutes to 1 hour and 20 minutes. Dust with confectioners' sugar sifted through a fine-mesh sieve and serve warm.

CHERRY-ALMOND COFFEE CRUMB CAKE

I don't bother with a crumb-topped coffee cake unless it has enough sweet, buttery crumbs, and this one delivers with a real nice thick layer. The combination of juicy cherries and crunchy sliced almonds is one of my favorites.

SERVES 10 TO 12

Topping

1½ cups all-purpose flour
1 cup packed light brown sugar
¼ cup granulated sugar
2 teaspoons ground cinnamon
½ teaspoon salt
¾ cup sliced almonds
8 tablespoons (1 stick) butter, cut into small
   bits, at room temperature

BERRY FRESH

If you can get some nice fresh berries—blueberries, blackberries, or raspberries—you can use them here in place of the cherries. You can also use fresh cherries if you don't mind pitting them.

Cake

1 cup whole milk
1 cup sour cream
8 tablespoons (1 stick) butter, melted
2 large eggs
¾ teaspoon almond extract
3 cups all-purpose flour
1⅔ cups packed light brown sugar
1½ teaspoons baking powder
1 teaspoon baking soda
1 teaspoon salt
1¾ cups (11 ounces) frozen cherries, thawed
   and halved

1. Preheat the oven to 325°F. Grease a 13 by 9-inch baking dish with butter, oil, or cooking spray.

2. To prepare the topping: In a medium bowl, whisk together the flour, both sugars, the cinnamon, and salt. Stir in the almonds. Cut in the butter with a pastry blender, your hands, or two knives (see illustration, page 277) until the mixture resembles coarse meal and large, walnut-size clumps are formed, then set aside.

3. To make the cake: In a medium bowl, whisk together the milk, sour cream, melted butter, eggs, and almond extract. In another medium bowl, whisk together the flour, brown sugar, baking powder, baking soda, and salt. Using a rubber spatula, fold the sour cream mixture into the flour mixture just until combined. Gently fold in the cherries and pour into the prepared baking dish.

4. Spread the topping over the cake and bake until a toothpick inserted into the center comes out clean and the topping is nicely browned, about 50 minutes. Let cool in the pan on a rack. Serve at room temperature.

ULTIMATE COFFEE CAKE

■ ■

If you love coffee cake, keep a few cans of crescent rolls on hand and you're halfway there. This easy, wonderful coffee cake is just full of sweet cream cheese, with a crisp sprinkle of sugar and pecans on top.

SERVES 12 TO 15

2 cans (8 ounces each) refrigerated crescent rolls

2 packages (8 ounces each) cream cheese, at room temperature

1 cup sugar

1 teaspoon vanilla extract

1 large egg, separated

½ cup chopped pecans

1. Preheat the oven to 350°F.

2. Press the dough from 1 can of the crescent rolls into the bottom of a 13 by 9-inch baking dish. In the bowl of an electric mixer fitted with the paddle attachment, beat the cream cheese, ¾ cup of the sugar, the vanilla, and the egg yolk at medium speed until soft and lump-free, about 5 minutes, scraping down the sides as you do so. Spread this mixture over the dough. Top with the second can of crescent roll dough.

3. In a medium bowl, beat the egg white with a whisk just until frothy and brush on top of the cake. Sprinkle the cake with the remaining ¼ cup sugar and the pecans. Bake until a toothpick inserted into the center comes out clean and the cake is nicely golden, 30 to 35 minutes. Let cool in the pan. Serve warm.

> **GLAZE OVER**
> The egg white brushed on top of the dough produces a beautiful shiny glaze and helps the sugar and nuts stick. It's that extra-special touch that really wows them.

GOOEY GORILLA BREAD

Now, biscuit dough is delicious in many forms, but when you roll balls of dough in cinnamon sugar, brush them with butter and brown sugar, and tuck them all next to each other in a pan, they puff together when they bake. You turn them out onto a plate and pull the warm sticky buns apart and, y'all, they just taste like heaven.

SERVES 6 TO 8

½ cup granulated sugar
2 teaspoons ground cinnamon

3 cans (12 ounces each) refrigerated
   biscuit dough
8 tablespoons (1 stick) butter
1 cup packed light brown sugar

1. Preheat the oven to 350°F. Grease a 12-cup Bundt or tube pan with butter, oil, or cooking spray.

2. In a medium bowl, whisk together the granulated sugar and cinnamon. Cut each biscuit round into 4 wedges and dredge each wedge in the cinnamon sugar. Layer the wedges in the prepared pan.

3. In a small saucepan, melt the butter over low heat. Add the brown sugar and stir until melted. Pour over all the biscuit pieces. Bake until golden brown, 45 to 55 minutes. If you see the gorilla bread beginning to brown too quickly, loosely cover it with some foil. Let the bread cool in the pan for 5 minutes, then invert onto a plate. This is best served warm so that it's nice and gooey.

Fill a greased Bundt pan with sugared biscuit pieces until the pan is full.

IN THE RING

The Bundt pan and the tube pan are both ring-shaped baking pans. Unlike the tube pan, the Bundt pan is fluted, giving anything baked in it a pretty decorative look.

APPLE FRITTERS

▪ ▪

Grandmama Paul's fruit fritters were so light and crisp, you wouldn't believe it. I use her technique, stirring my sour cream–rich batter as little as possible before dipping apples in it and tossing them right into the fryer. Just warn greedy fingers to be patient, since the fritters have to cool a bit before you bite in.

MAKES ABOUT 20 FRITTERS

½ cup whole milk

½ cup sour cream

1 large egg

1 cup all-purpose flour

1 teaspoon baking powder

1 teaspoon granulated sugar

½ teaspoon salt

¼ teaspoon ground cinnamon

About 2 quarts vegetable oil, for deep-frying

3 apples, peeled, cored (see box), and sliced into ¼-inch-thick rings

Confectioners' sugar, for dusting

1. In a medium bowl, whisk together the milk, sour cream, and egg. In a separate medium bowl, whisk together the flour, baking powder, granulated sugar, salt, and cinnamon. Add the milk mixture to the flour mixture and stir gently with a whisk until smooth, getting out all the lumps but being careful not to overmix.

2. Meanwhile, in a large, heavy-bottomed pot, heat 1½ inches of oil until it reaches 375°F on a deep-fry thermometer.

3. Working in batches of 4 or 5, dip the apple rings into the batter, shaking off the excess. Add to the hot oil and fry until golden brown, 1 to 2 minutes per side. Set on a paper towel–lined plate to drain. Dust the fritters with confectioners' sugar sifted through a fine-mesh sieve to pretty them up.

THEM APPLES

Make your life easier, y'all, and get yourself an apple corer for these little fritters. Without one, coring an apple for apple rings can be a bit treacherous and time-consuming.

PEACH FRITTERS

There is just something about peach season that sends me to the store for a tub of vanilla ice cream. Served à la mode, these fritters are just summer in a bowl—even if you make them in February with a couple cans of peaches!

MAKES ABOUT 20 FRITTERS

½ cup whole milk

½ cup sour cream

1 large egg

1 cup all-purpose flour

1 teaspoon baking powder

1 teaspoon granulated sugar

½ teaspoon salt

About 2 quarts vegetable oil, for deep-frying

3 fresh peaches, peeled (see box, page 422), pitted, and cut into ½-inch wedges

Confectioners' sugar, for dusting

Vanilla ice cream, for serving

1. In a medium bowl, whisk together the milk, sour cream, and egg. In a separate medium bowl, whisk together the flour, baking powder, granulated sugar, and salt. Add the sour cream mixture to the flour mixture and stir gently with a whisk until smooth, getting out all the lumps but being careful not to overmix.

2. Meanwhile, in a large, heavy-bottomed pot, heat 1½ inches of oil until it reaches 375°F on a deep-fry thermometer.

3. Working in three batches of 4 or 5 fritters, dip the peaches into the batter; add to the hot oil and fry until golden brown, 1 to 2 minutes per side. Set on a paper towel–lined plate to drain. Dust the fritters with confectioners' sugar sifted through a fine-mesh sieve. Serve with a scoop of ice cream, because there's nothing quite like peaches and cream.

PEACHY KEEN

If you can't find good fresh peaches, substitute two 20-ounce cans of sliced ones. Be sure to drain and pat them dry before battering and frying them.

PINEAPPLE FRITTERS

We always keep canned pineapple on hand so I can fix up these wonderful fritters at a moment's notice. They fill the bill when we want something special for dessert.

MAKES ABOUT 20 FRITTERS

½ cup whole milk
½ cup sour cream
1 large egg
1 cup all-purpose flour
1 teaspoon baking powder
1 teaspoon granulated sugar
½ teaspoon salt

¼ teaspoon grated nutmeg
About 2 quarts vegetable oil, for deep-frying
2 cans (20 ounces each) pineapple slices, drained
¼ cup dark rum
Confectioners' sugar, for dusting

1. In a medium bowl, whisk together the milk, sour cream, and egg. In a separate medium bowl, whisk together the flour, baking powder, granulated sugar, salt, and nutmeg. Add the sour cream mixture to the flour mixture and stir gently with a whisk until smooth, getting out all the lumps but being careful not to overmix.

2. Meanwhile, in a large, heavy-bottomed pot, heat 1½ inches of oil until it reaches 375°F on a deep-fry thermometer.

3. In a medium bowl, toss the pineapple and rum together; let stand for 10 minutes. Pat the fruit dry with paper towels. Working in batches of 4 or 5, dip the pineapple into the batter; add to the hot oil and fry until golden brown, 1 to 2 minutes per side. Set on a paper towel–lined plate to drain. Dust the fritters with confectioners' sugar sifted through a fine-mesh sieve and serve up this tropical treat.

OIL CHANGE

Don't be too hasty in throwing out your frying oil, since it can often be used more than once. Always let the oil cool down completely in the pan. If you think you can use it again, strain it into a clean container. If you can't use the oil, just pour it into a sealable container and toss it in the garbage. Unless you're planning on having the plumber around for dinner, never pour the oil down the drain.

Chapter 13

PIES, COBBLERS, AND CRISPS

Next time you're in the home of a true Southern pie baker, you just poke around in kitchen drawers and you'll turn up the old tablecloth she rolls out her piecrusts on. That cloth will keep your crust from sticking to the counter when you roll—even when it's hot and humid out, like it gets around here. And when you're done, you just take it outside, shake it, and fold it up again. Everyone should have one.

To me, nothing is more comforting than a piece of pie—it knocks a piece of cake in the dirt. Sadly, in today's times, pies are an endangered dessert. Growing up, we just always had pie: I remember as a teenager, we had a restaurant right next to our house, and we'd just walk over and get us a piece of pie and a Coke. It could be chocolate meringue, lemon meringue, or coconut cream—it always hit the spot. Most pies now come from some industrial food purveyor, so when you find a homemade one, savor it because it can be hard work. And when you develop a craving, your best bet is to make your own.

I have perfected my piecrust over the years so it is just as flaky and buttery as I like, with enough salt to make itself known. But whenever I decide to roll up my sleeves and make piecrust, I have a hard time deciding what to fill it with. My favorite would have to be my Dreamy Coconut Cream Pie (page 315). But then there's Banana Cream Pie (page 317), too. Oh, those custard-type pies with a rich, creamy filling and a crunchy crust are just so insanely delicious! And of course if there's a bowl of fruit on the counter, I may just have to make an Apple Pie (page 313), a Blueberry Crumb Pie (page 332), a Peaches and Cream Pie (page 333), or even a Green Tomato Pie (page 330)—y'all, don't knock it till you've tried it; tomatoes are a fruit and I'm real proud of how tasty that one turns out.

From Down-Home Grits Pie (page 327) to Butterscotch Pretzel Pie (page 318) to Kentucky Walnut Pie (page 323), I've dedicated a pie to just about every delicious ingredient I could. You can make pie with almost nothing, like my Vanilla Buttermilk Pie (page 329), which is so simple and refreshing. Or you can throw in the kitchen sink: try out a Sweet Potato Praline Crunch Pie (page 321) on your family next Thanksgiving and watch how fast folks forget about plain old pumpkin.

Of course, pies can be a production, and you don't just need a little time and space to roll out your crust, you also need folks around to eat it up. On those occasions when I'm tight on time, I love to make a cobbler. My cobbler recipe never fails me—I don't even measure; I just mix it up and have it in the oven in no time. Oh, and then there's hand pies. My Grandmama Paul always fried these little half-moon pies instead of baking a full one. Crisp, flaky, and rich outside, with sweet, juicy fruit on the inside, those fried pies were such a treat that I've continued the tradition. I find myself making little Fried Peach Pies (page 334) an awful lot these days.

That's the thing about pie. Eating one is such a beautiful, pure tradition, it just takes you right back to all the delicious-smelling kitchens you've been in and all the delicious moments in life.

APPLE PIE

■ ■

Some occasions call for a perfect apple pie: flaky crust and tender, sweet-tart slices of apples spiced with cinnamon, nutmeg, and ginger. I use brown sugar and vanilla to give the filling more richness, and I sprinkle the top crust with cinnamon sugar, which gives the pie such a pretty glitter—and a preview of the delicious filling. Serve à la mode with big scoops of vanilla ice cream!

MAKES ONE 9-INCH PIE

3 tablespoons all-purpose flour, plus extra
    for dusting
2 batches Paula's Flaky Piecrust Dough
    (page 339), or two 9-inch unbaked
    prepared piecrusts
6 apples (about 3 pounds), peeled,
    cored, and thinly sliced
¾ cup packed light brown sugar
2 teaspoons ground cinnamon

2 teaspoons grated nutmeg
2 teaspoons vanilla extract
1 teaspoon ground ginger
Pinch of salt
2 tablespoons cold butter,
    cut into small bits
Whole milk, for brushing
Cinnamon sugar, for sprinkling

1. Dust a work surface with a small handful of flour. Roll each disk of dough into a 12-inch round about ¼ inch thick (skip this step if using prepared crusts). Use 1 round to line a 9-inch pie plate and chill in the refrigerator for 30 minutes or up to overnight (cover lightly with plastic wrap if chilling for more than 2 hours). Place the other on a baking sheet, cover with plastic wrap, and chill until you need it.

2. When you are ready to bake the pie, preheat the oven to 375°F. Line the dough in the pie pan with parchment paper or foil and fill with dried beans or pie weights. Bake for 20 minutes.

3. While the piecrust is in the oven, prepare the filling: In a large bowl, mix together the apples, brown sugar, 3 tablespoons flour, the cinnamon, nutmeg, vanilla, ginger, and salt. Go on ahead and use your hands to make sure those apples are well coated with the other ingredients.

A IS FOR APPLE

Y'all, I like to put together a mix of tart and sweet apples to give my apple pie a nice complexity. And I always look for apples that won't break down too much when you cook them. My favorites? That would have to be a mix of Golden Delicious with Granny Smith.

4. Take the crust out of the oven, but leave the oven on. Remove the beans or pie weights and paper or foil from the crust and fill with the apple mixture. Dot the apple mixture with the butter pieces. Cut the reserved round of dough into ½-inch-wide strips and use to make a lattice crust on top of the pie (see illustration). Brush the lattice top with the milk and sprinkle with cinnamon sugar. Bake until the juices are bubbling and the crust is golden brown, 45 to 50 minutes. Place the pie on a wire rack to cool for 30 minutes before serving.

Using a pastry cutter, cut an even number of ½-inch strips of the piecrust dough. Place half the strips on top of the filled pie. Weave in the remaining strips by folding every other strip back onto itself and laying another strip perpendicular to it, to create a crisscross pattern. Fold the strips back across and repeat until completed.

DREAMY COCONUT CREAM PIE

■ ■

There are few things I enjoy more than a slice of good coconut cream pie. The creamy, sweet filling, full of shredded coconut with a hint of nutmeg, is pure pleasure any time of year. A cloud of whipped cream with nutty, golden toasted coconut sprinkled on top and a crunchy, slightly salty crust underneath just puts this combination over the edge.

MAKES ONE 9-INCH PIE

Pie
All-purpose flour, for dusting
Paula's Flaky Piecrust Dough (page 339), or
    one 9-inch unbaked prepared piecrust
1½ cups whole milk
½ cup heavy cream
½ cup shredded sweetened coconut
Pinch of salt
3 large eggs

⅔ cup sugar
2 tablespoons dark rum (optional)
1 teaspoon vanilla extract
¼ teaspoon grated nutmeg

Topping
1 cup cold heavy cream
3 tablespoons sugar
Shredded sweetened coconut, toasted

1. To prepare the pie: Dust a work surface with a small handful of flour. Roll the dough into a 12-inch round about ¼ inch thick (skip this step if using a prepared crust). Use it to line a 9-inch pie plate and chill in the refrigerator for 30 minutes or up to overnight (cover lightly with plastic wrap if chilling for more than 2 hours).

2. When you are ready to bake the pie, preheat the oven to 375°F. Line the dough with parchment paper or foil and fill with dried beans or pie weights. Bake for 20 minutes. Remove the beans or pie weights and paper or foil.

3. While the piecrust is in the oven, in a medium saucepan, combine the milk, cream, coconut, and salt. Bring just to a boil over low heat, stirring constantly. Remove from the heat and let sit for 30 minutes for the flavors to develop (see box, page 316).

4. In a medium bowl, whisk together the eggs, sugar, rum (if using), vanilla, and nutmeg. Whisking constantly, slowly pour the warm milk mixture into the eggs. Pour the warm filling into the warm piecrust. Bake until the filling is set and jiggles like jelly, about 25 minutes. Let cool completely at room temperature before refrigerating, then chill thoroughly.

5. Shortly before serving, prepare the topping: In the bowl of an electric mixer fitted with the

whisk attachment, or using a handheld mixer, whip the cream and sugar at medium-high speed until medium-firm peaks form. Spread the whipped cream over the pie and sprinkle all over with the toasted coconut.

SEE WHAT DEVELOPS

You want to get as much coconut flavor as you can into this dreamy pie. That's why I recommend steeping the milk with the coconut (step 3). By heating the milk just to the boiling point and then letting it sit off the heat for about 30 minutes, the milk will take on a deep coconut flavor, making your custard taste like it came straight out of the coconut shell.

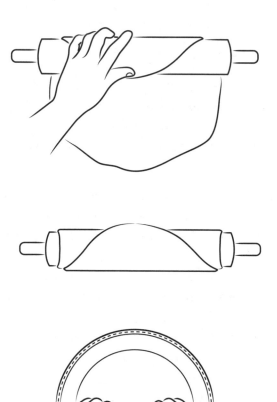

After rolling out the piecrust, place it in the pan by rolling the dough around a floured rolling pin, positioning the rolling pin over the pie pan, and unfurling the dough into the pan.

BANANA CREAM PIE

■ ■

Okay, well, this is another one of my all-time favorite pies and I have given great thought to how to layer the custard and bananas for maximum pleasure. I cannot get enough of the sweet banana flavor—don't count on this pie feeding as many people as you think it will.

MAKES ONE 9-INCH PIE

All-purpose flour, for dusting

Paula's Flaky Piecrust Dough (page 339), or one 9-inch unbaked prepared piecrust

½ cup sugar

⅓ cup cornstarch

¼ teaspoon salt

2 cups heavy cream

1 cup whole milk

3 large egg yolks

2 tablespoons (¼ stick) butter

1½ teaspoons vanilla extract

4 bananas, sliced, plus sliced bananas for serving

Whipped cream, for serving

1. Dust a work surface with a small handful of flour. Roll the dough into a 12-inch round about ¼ inch thick (skip this step if using a prepared crust). Use it to line a 9-inch pie plate and chill in the refrigerator for 30 minutes or up to overnight (cover lightly with plastic wrap if chilling for more than 2 hours).

2. When you are ready to bake the pie, preheat the oven to 375°F. Line the dough with parchment paper or foil and fill with dried beans or pie weights. Bake for 20 minutes. Remove the beans or pie weights and paper or foil.

3. While the piecrust is in the oven, prepare the filling: In a medium, heavy-bottomed saucepan, whisk together the sugar, cornstarch, and salt. Gradually whisk in the cream and milk; then whisk in the egg yolks. Place over medium-high heat and whisk until the custard thickens and boils, about 6 minutes. Remove from the heat and whisk in the butter and vanilla. Scrape the custard into a large bowl and let cool completely, whisking occasionally. This should take about 1 hour.

4. In the piecrust, alternate layers of banana slices and custard filling. Cover and chill. To serve, top with whipped cream and decorate with some more sliced bananas.

TRUE COLORS

If you slice your bananas way ahead of time, you'll wind up with brown bananas instead of the bright yellow you want for this pie. To keep them nice and yellow, go ahead and squeeze some lemon juice on them after they've been sliced.

BUTTERSCOTCH PRETZEL PIE

■ ■

I adore a nicely salted butterscotch, so I went ahead and combined bits of pretzel in the graham cracker crust. If you're like me and you can't choose between your salty tooth and your sweet tooth, this one's for you.

MAKES ONE 9-INCH PIE

Crust
¾ cup pretzel crumbs
¾ cup graham cracker crumbs
2 tablespoons granulated sugar
6 tablespoons (¾ stick) butter, melted

> ### ALL SWEET
> If you're short on time, go ahead and use a ready-made graham cracker crust for a more traditional butterscotch pie. Your pie won't be salty, but sometimes it's nice to be all sweet.

Filling
¾ cup packed dark brown sugar
¼ cup cornstarch
Pinch of salt
3 large egg yolks
2 cups whole milk
2 tablespoons cold butter, cut into small bits
2 teaspoons vanilla extract

Topping
1 cup cold heavy cream
3 tablespoons granulated sugar

1. Preheat the oven to 350°F.

2. To make the crust: In a medium bowl, combine the pretzel crumbs, graham cracker crumbs, granulated sugar, and melted butter until they form an evenly moist, crumbly mixture. Press the mixture evenly onto the bottom and up the sides of a 9-inch pie plate. Bake until the crust is fragrant and firm, 8 to 10 minutes. Set aside to cool.

3. To make the filling: In a medium bowl, whisk together the brown sugar, cornstarch, and salt. Add the egg yolks and ½ cup of the milk and whisk thoroughly to combine.

4. In a large saucepan, bring the remaining 1½ cups milk to a boil over medium-high heat. Remove from the heat. Whisking constantly, very slowly pour the hot milk into the egg mixture. Keep whisking so that you don't scramble those eggs. Return the entire mixture to the pan. Cook over medium heat, stirring constantly, until the mixture comes to a boil and thickens, 3 to 5 minutes. Remove from the heat and whisk in the butter and vanilla until smooth.

5. Pour the filling into the cooled piecrust and smooth the surface with a small spatula. Cover the surface entirely with plastic wrap to prevent a skin from forming. Make sure the plastic wrap is right up against the filling.

6. Place the pie in the fridge until thoroughly cooled and set, at least 2 hours.

7. Just before serving, make the topping: In the bowl of an electric mixer fitted with the whisk attachment, or using a handheld mixer, whip the cream and granulated sugar at medium-high speed to form soft peaks. Spread the whipped cream over the pie and serve.

DECADENT DOUBLE-CHOCOLATE CREAM PIE

The only thing better than a chocolate cream pie is one in a wonderful chocolate cookie crumb crust. If a person has a craving for chocolate, I don't see the point of going halfway, y'all.

MAKES ONE 9-INCH PIE

Crust
1⅔ cups chocolate wafer crumbs (from about 30 wafers, such as Nabisco Famous Chocolate Wafers)
6 tablespoons (¾ stick) butter, melted
¼ cup sugar

Filling
⅓ cup sugar
2 tablespoons plus 1 teaspoon cornstarch
2 tablespoons unsweetened cocoa powder
½ teaspoon salt
1 large egg

2 large egg yolks
2 cups whole milk
7 ounces semisweet chocolate (61% cacao), finely chopped
3 tablespoons cold butter
2 teaspoons vanilla extract

Topping and Garnish
1 cup heavy cream
3 tablespoons sugar
1 teaspoon vanilla extract
Chocolate curls (see box, page 320)

1. Preheat the oven to 350°F.

2. To make the crust: In a medium bowl, combine the cookie crumbs, melted butter, and sugar until they form an evenly moist, crumbly mixture. Press the mixture evenly onto the bottom and up the sides of a 9-inch pie plate. Bake until the crust is fragrant and firm, 7 to 8 minutes. Set aside to cool.

3. To make the filling: In a medium bowl, whisk together the sugar, cornstarch, cocoa, and salt. Whisk in the whole egg, egg yolks, and ½ cup of the milk until thoroughly combined.

4. In a large, heavy-bottomed saucepan, bring the remaining 1½ cups milk to a boil over medium-high heat. Remove from the heat. Whisking constantly, very slowly pour the hot milk into the egg mixture. Keep whisking so that you don't scramble those eggs. Return the entire mixture to the pan. Cook over medium heat, stirring constantly, until the mixture comes to a boil and thickens, 3 to 5 minutes. Remove from the heat, add the chocolate, and let sit for a minute. Add the butter and vanilla and whisk until the chocolate is completely melted and smooth.

5. Pour the filling into the cooled piecrust and smooth the surface with a small spatula. Cover the surface entirely with plastic wrap to prevent a skin from forming. Make sure the plastic wrap is right up against the filling.

6. Place the pie in the fridge until thoroughly cooled and set, about 2 hours.

7. Just before serving, make the topping: In the bowl of an electric mixer fitted with the whisk attachment, or using a handheld mixer, whip the cream, sugar, and vanilla at medium-high speed to form medium peaks. Spread the whipped cream over the pie. Sprinkle all over with chocolate curls and serve.

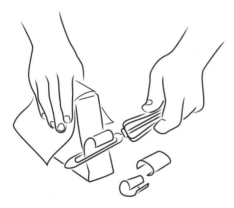

Create chocolate curls by running a vegetable peeler along a slightly softened block of chocolate as you would along a carrot or potato.

CURL UP

Chocolate curls are such a pretty and easy way to gussy up a pie or cake. To make yours, hold a block of chocolate with a paper towel (so your hand doesn't melt the chocolate) and use a vegetable peeler to scrape along the edge to create long, curly strips. Use a skewer to gently pick them up (the heat of your hand could melt them) and place them on the pie.

SWEET POTATO PRALINE CRUNCH PIE

■ ■

During the holidays, sweet potatoes, bourbon, cinnamon, ginger, brown sugar, butter, and pecans just seem to get together in the kitchen. This pie was a real hit at our family Thanksgiving and its smell while baking drove us all crazy.

MAKES ONE 9-INCH PIE

Pie

All-purpose flour, for dusting

Paula's Flaky Piecrust Dough (page 339), or one 9-inch unbaked prepared piecrust

1¾ cups mashed cooked sweet potato

1 cup packed light brown sugar

½ cup sour cream

4 tablespoons (½ stick) butter, melted

2 large eggs

2 tablespoons bourbon (optional)

1¾ teaspoons ground cinnamon

½ teaspoon ground ginger

½ teaspoon salt

Topping

1 cup pecan halves

2 tablespoons packed light brown sugar

¼ teaspoon ground cinnamon

1. To prepare the pie: Dust a work surface with a small handful of flour. Roll the dough into a 12-inch round about ¼ inch thick (skip this step if using a prepared crust). Use it to line a 9-inch pie pan and chill in the refrigerator for 30 minutes or up to overnight (cover lightly with plastic wrap if chilling for more than 2 hours).

2. When you are ready to bake the pie, preheat the oven to 375°F. Line the dough with parchment paper or foil and fill with dried beans or pie weights. Bake for 20 minutes. Remove the beans or pie weights and paper or foil.

3. While the piecrust is in the oven, whisk together the sweet potato, brown sugar, sour cream, melted butter, eggs, bourbon (if using), cinnamon, ginger, and salt. Pour the filling into the piecrust.

4. To make the topping: In a small bowl, stir together the pecans, brown sugar, and cinnamon. Sprinkle over the surface of the pie. Bake until the filling is set, 35 to 40 minutes. Let cool before slicing and serving up.

A STICKY SITUATION

If you'd rather avoid the flour and keep your work area neater, try rolling out your dough between 2 pieces of waxed or parchment paper. You'll have beautiful nonsticking crusts ready in no time!

BOURBON PECAN PIE

My pecan pie has just enough goop to hold together all those good, sweet, crunchy Georgia pecans. Whether you call them "pee-cans" or "pe-cahns," you'll adore this rich, slightly sticky pie.

MAKES ONE 9-INCH PIE

1 tablespoon all-purpose flour, plus extra for dusting

Paula's Flaky Piecrust Dough (page 339), or one 9-inch unbaked prepared piecrust

4 tablespoons (½ stick) butter

¾ cup packed light brown sugar

¾ cup cane syrup or corn syrup

3 large eggs, lightly beaten

½ teaspoon salt

2 tablespoons bourbon

1½ cups pecan halves

1. Dust a work surface with a small handful of flour. Roll the dough into a 12-inch round about ¼ inch thick (skip this step if using a prepared crust). Use it to line a 9-inch pie plate and chill in the refrigerator for 30 minutes or up to overnight (cover lightly with plastic wrap if chilling for more than 2 hours).

2. When you are ready to bake the pie, preheat the oven to 375°F. Line the dough with parchment paper or foil and fill with dried beans or pie weights. Bake for 20 minutes. Remove the beans or pie weights and paper or foil.

3. Reduce the oven temperature to 325°F.

4. While the piecrust is in the oven, in a small saucepan, melt the butter. Whisk in the 1 tablespoon flour. Whisk in the brown sugar and cane syrup. Bring to a simmer, then immediately remove from the heat and let cool for 10 minutes. Beat in the eggs, salt, and bourbon. Stir in the pecans.

5. Pour the filling into the piecrust. Bake until the filling is set but still jiggles slightly in the center, 45 to 50 minutes. Let cool completely on a wire rack before slicing and serving up.

IN SHAPE

Now, I know you're going to be excited to get down to making (and eating) this pie, but I'd like to stress how very important that 30 minutes in the fridge is for the pie dough. By getting the dough really cold before popping it into the oven, you'll help to ensure that the crust doesn't lose its shape and shrink up on you.

KENTUCKY WALNUT PIE

■ ■

The chocolate chip cookie of pies. I put these ingredients together when we had a whole bunch of walnuts on hand, and we all went nuts for it, if you'll pardon the pun.

MAKES ONE 9-INCH PIE

½ cup all-purpose flour, plus extra for dusting

Paula's Flaky Piecrust Dough (page 339), or one 9-inch unbaked prepared piecrust

1 cup sugar

Pinch of salt

8 tablespoons (1 stick) butter, melted

2 large eggs

2 tablespoons bourbon (optional)

2 teaspoons vanilla extract

1½ cups chopped walnuts

½ cup semisweet chocolate chips

1. Dust a work surface with a small handful of flour. Roll the dough into a 12-inch round about ¼ inch thick (skip this step if using a prepared crust). Use it to line a 9-inch pie plate and chill in the refrigerator for 30 minutes or up to overnight (cover lightly with plastic wrap if chilling for more than 2 hours).

2. When you are ready to bake the pie, preheat the oven to 350°F.

3. In a medium bowl, whisk together the sugar, the ½ cup flour, and the salt. In a small bowl, whisk together the melted butter, eggs, bourbon (if using), and vanilla. Using a rubber spatula, fold the butter mixture into the sugar mixture just until combined. Stir in the walnuts and chocolate chips. Spoon the filling into the unbaked piecrust. Bake until the filling is firm to the touch, 40 to 45 minutes. Let cool to room temperature before serving.

COLD STORAGE

The first order of business with nuts is to store them properly. And that means keeping them nice and cold. You see, all nuts contain oils that have a nasty habit of going rancid if they are left in the cupboard too long. So, I like to keep my nuts in the fridge or freezer. Wrap them up tightly and you can store them in the fridge for as long as 4 to 5 months. In the freezer they should keep for about 10 months.

LEMONY CHESS PIE

Chess pie is such an old-timey, homey dessert. You can make it any time of year with ingredients you have on hand: eggs, cornmeal, flour, butter, and sugar. I've heard theories that it was originally called chess pie because folks thought the pie contained a plain white cheese. And the filling *is* a bit like sweet ricotta, since it has a little texture from the cornmeal. I like mine nice and lemony. This is one of those pies I'll keep out on the counter nibbling at all day. You know, to even out the edges.

MAKES ONE 9-INCH PIE

1 tablespoon all-purpose flour, plus extra for dusting

Paula's Flaky Piecrust Dough (page 339), or one 9-inch unbaked prepared piecrust

1 cup sugar

1 tablespoon cornmeal

Pinch of salt

3 large eggs

Grated zest of 1 lemon

4 tablespoons (½ stick) butter, melted

⅓ cup fresh lemon juice (about 2 lemons)

1 teaspoon vanilla extract

1. Dust a work surface with a small handful of flour. Roll the dough into a 12-inch round about ¼ inch thick (skip this step if using a prepared crust). Use it to line a 9-inch pie plate and chill in the refrigerator for 30 minutes or up to overnight (cover lightly with plastic wrap if chilling for more than 2 hours).

2. When you are ready to bake the pie, preheat the oven to 375°F. Line the dough with parchment paper or foil and fill with dried beans or pie weights. Bake for 20 minutes. Remove the beans or pie weights and paper or foil.

3. While the piecrust is in the oven, whisk together the sugar, cornmeal, the 1 tablespoon flour, and the salt. Whisk in the eggs and lemon zest until thoroughly combined. Slowly whisk in the melted butter, lemon juice, and vanilla.

4. Pour the filling into the piecrust. Bake until the filling is set and jiggles like jelly, 30 to 35 minutes. Let this pie cool right through before serving.

THE BEST ZEST

My favorite tool for zesting citrus is my handy Microplane. But whatever tool you use to zest your citrus fruit, be sure not to press down too hard on the peel: you want to make sure you get only the thin colored layer on the outside, not the spongy white part underneath.

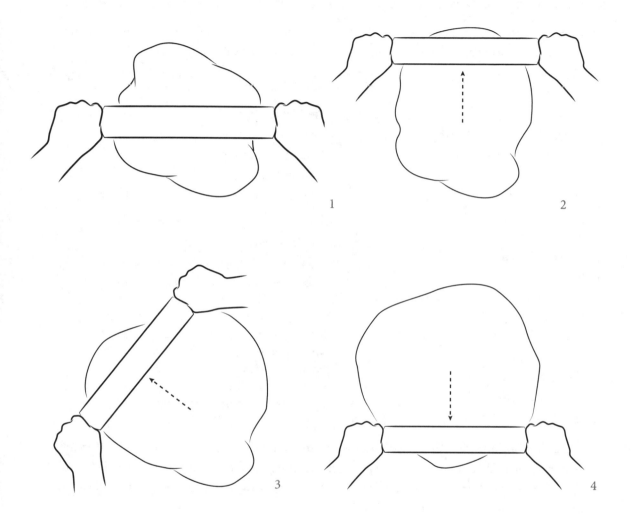

Roll the dough from the center out to the edges in all directions.

KEY LIME DIVINITY PIE

■ ■

When it comes to Key lime pie, the tarter the filling, the happier I am. Those little green limes sure pack a lot of puckery flavor. And that fluffy divinity topping just makes it out of this world!

MAKES ONE 9-INCH PIE

Pie

All-purpose flour, for dusting

Paula's Flaky Piecrust Dough
(page 339), or one 9-inch
unbaked prepared
piecrust

1¼ cups sugar

⅓ cup cornstarch

Pinch of salt

½ cup fresh Key lime or regular
lime juice (9 Key limes or
3 regular limes)

4 large egg yolks

4 tablespoons (½ stick) cold
butter, cut into
small bits

Meringue Topping

4 large egg whites

¼ teaspoon cream of tartar

Pinch of salt

1 teaspoon vanilla extract

KEY TO SUCCESS

The secret to the best Key lime pie is really no secret at all! All you have to do is make sure you use those tart Key limes. You can distinguish them from regular limes by their lighter color and smaller and rounder shape, as well as their thinner rind. If you can't find fresh Key limes, you can also buy their juice bottled. Regular limes will work, too, in a pinch. It just won't be quite as special.

1. Dust a work surface with a small handful of flour. Roll the dough into a 12-inch round about ¼ inch thick (skip this step if using a prepared crust). Use it to line a 9-inch pie plate and chill in the refrigerator for 30 minutes or up to overnight (cover lightly with plastic wrap if chilling for more than 2 hours).

2. When you are ready to bake the pie, preheat the oven to 375°F. Line the dough with parchment paper or foil and fill with dried beans or pie weights. Bake for 20 minutes. Remove the paper or foil and beans or pie weights, return to the oven, and bake until golden, 10 to 15 minutes longer.

3. Meanwhile, make the filling: In a large saucepan, whisk together the sugar, cornstarch, and salt. Slowly whisk in 1½ cups water, the lime juice, and egg yolks. Place the saucepan over medium heat and bring to a boil, stirring constantly. Let the mixture boil for 1 minute, then whisk in the butter. Pour the hot filling into the baked piecrust.

4. While the filling is still hot, make the meringue topping: Bring a medium saucepan of water to a bare simmer on the stove. In the bowl of an electric mixer fitted with the whisk attachment, or

using a handheld mixer, whisk together the egg whites, cream of tartar, salt, and vanilla at medium speed. Place the mixer bowl over the pan of simmering water. By hand, whisk the mixture constantly until it registers 140°F on an instant-read thermometer. Remove from the heat and return to the mixer. Whip at high speed until soft peaks form. Spread the meringue over the surface of the pie filling, being sure to spread the meringue to the edges of the crust to anchor it. Refrigerate the pie for at least 3 hours to set it before serving with a good old Southern smile.

DOWN-HOME GRITS PIE

■ ■

When I was working on *The Lady & Sons Just Desserts,* I took a look at my container of grits and said to myself, "Why not?" So I went ahead and started playing around with grits and came up with this very special pie. Just after I made it, I recall, a friend stopped in, so I served him up a slice. He couldn't guess what he was eating, but he just loved it, so I knew I had a hit on my hands.

SERVES 8

¼ cup quick-cooking grits (not instant grits)
⅛ teaspoon salt
8 tablespoons (1 stick) butter
¾ cup sugar
2 tablespoons all-purpose flour
3 large eggs, lightly beaten

¼ cup buttermilk
1 teaspoon vanilla extract
Paula's Flaky Piecrust Dough (page 339), or
    one 9-inch unbaked prepared piecrust
Sweetened whipped cream and strawberries,
    for garnish (optional)

1. Preheat the oven to 325°F.

2. In a small saucepan, bring ¾ cup water to a boil. Slowly whisk in the grits and salt. Cook for 20 minutes, whisking constantly. Add the butter and cook for an extra minute. Set aside to cool slightly.

3. In a small bowl, stir together the sugar, flour, eggs, buttermilk, and vanilla. Stir into the cooked grits. Pour the grits mixture into the unbaked piecrust and bake until set, 35 to 40 minutes. Serve warm or cold with whipped cream and strawberries piled on top, if desired.

EGGS, LIGHTLY BEATEN

By lightly beating the egg with a fork before adding it to the bowl, you ensure that the white and the yolk are evenly distributed with the rest of the ingredients. This is especially important when you're mixing by hand. It's just another little step that will help to make your baked goods the best they can possibly be.

ELVIS PIE

■ ■

The King loved his bananas and peanut butter, and I don't suppose he was opposed to cream cheese, either, so I make this fun, satisfying pie sprinkled with chopped peanuts in his honor.

MAKES ONE 9-INCH PIE

Filling

1 cup creamy peanut butter

1 package (8 ounces) cream cheese, at room temperature

⅓ cup sugar

1½ teaspoons vanilla extract

1 cup cold heavy cream

One 9-inch prepared graham cracker piecrust

2 large bananas, cut into ¼-inch-thick slices

Topping

1 cup cold heavy cream

¼ cup sugar

Chopped roasted peanuts, for garnish

1. To make the filling: In the bowl of an electric mixer fitted with the paddle attachment, or using a handheld mixer, cream together the peanut butter, cream cheese, sugar, and vanilla at medium speed. In a separate bowl, whip the cream until soft peaks form. You can do this by hand with a whisk or in the bowl of an electric mixer fitted with the whisk attachment. Using a rubber spatula, fold the cream into the peanut butter mixture until completely combined. Make sure you fold, not stir, as stirring will only deflate all the air you've just whipped into the cream. Scrape half the filling into the piecrust and smooth with a spatula. Layer the sliced bananas on top of the filling, then spread the remaining filling over the bananas. Cover with plastic wrap and refrigerate until set, at least 1 hour.

2. To make the topping: In the bowl of an electric mixer fitted with the whisk attachment, or using a handheld mixer, whip the cream and sugar together until soft peaks form. Spread over the surface of the pie. Sprinkle the chopped peanuts all over the top and serve to all your Elvis lovers out there.

WHIP IT UP

Homemade whipped cream is like a taste of heaven on just about anything. To make it easier and faster, be sure to chill your whisk, cream, and bowl in the fridge for about 15 minutes before you start whipping. Whip either by hand or with an electric mixer until the mixture thickens and forms soft peaks.

VANILLA BUTTERMILK PIE

Sometimes we forget the simple old-time foods like this sweet, homey pie. Put this one on your to-do list because it is a tangy, refreshing change of pace from richer pies, and if you've never had it, y'all, I know you'll just love it.

MAKES ONE 9-INCH PIE

¼ cup all-purpose flour, plus extra for dusting
Paula's Flaky Piecrust Dough (page 339), or one 9-inch unbaked prepared piecrust
1¼ cups sugar

⅛ teaspoon salt
4 large eggs, lightly beaten
1½ cups buttermilk
2 tablespoons (¼ stick) butter, melted
1 tablespoon vanilla extract

1. Dust a work surface with a small handful of flour. Roll the dough into a 12-inch round about ¼ inch thick (skip this step if using a prepared crust). Use it to line a 9-inch pie plate and chill in the refrigerator for 30 minutes or up to overnight (cover lightly with plastic wrap if chilling for more than 2 hours).

2. When you are ready to bake the pie, preheat the oven to 375°F. Line the dough with parchment paper or foil and fill with dried beans or pie weights. Bake for 20 minutes. Remove the beans or pie weights and paper or foil.

Blind bake the piecrust by covering it with parchment paper or foil. Fill with dried beans, pie weights, or uncooked rice, then bake to set the dough. Remove the paper or foil and the beans, weights, or rice. Bake again for a few minutes to brown, then add the filling.

3. Reduce the oven temperature to 350°F.

4. While the piecrust is in the oven, whisk together the sugar, the ¼ cup flour, and the salt. Add the eggs and whisk thoroughly to combine. Whisking constantly, slowly pour in the buttermilk, whisking out any lumps. Whisk in the melted butter and the vanilla.

5. Pour the filling into the piecrust. Bake until the filling is set and jiggles like jelly, about 40 minutes. Let the pie cool right through before serving.

ADD SOME ZEST

While I just adore this pie as is, if I've got lemons around, sometimes I grate zest into my custard to add a little zing. The lemon-vanilla flavor is just so delicate, and the little flecks of lemon-yellow in the custard look so pretty.

GREEN TOMATO PIE

■ ■

Tomatoes are a fruit, and green tomatoes are so tart and crunchy, they're just perfect cooked and sweetened like I do here. If you grow your own, or if you find green tomatoes at the market in late summer and early fall, do give this wonderful pie a try.

MAKES ONE 9-INCH PIE

All-purpose flour for dusting
2 batches Paula's Flaky Piecrust Dough (page 339), or two 9-inch unbaked prepared piecrusts
1¼ cups sugar, plus extra for sprinkling
2 tablespoons tapioca flour

1 teaspoon grated orange zest
½ teaspoon ground cinnamon
¼ teaspoon grated nutmeg
5 green tomatoes, or enough to fill the piecrust, thinly sliced
1 large egg white, lightly beaten

1. Dust a work surfce with a small handful of flour. Roll each disk of pie dough into a 12-inch round about ¼ inch thick (skip this step if using prepared crusts). Use one to line a 9-inch pie plate and chill in the refrigerator for 30 minutes or up to overnight (cover lightly with plastic wrap if chilling for more than 2 hours). Place the other on a baking sheet, cover with plastic wrap, and chill until you need it.

2. When you are ready to bake the pie, preheat the oven to 425°F.

3. In a large bowl, whisk together the 1¼ cups sugar, the tapioca flour, orange zest, cinnamon, and nutmeg. Lay the tomato slices in the unbaked piecrust until you fill the dish. (Overlapping will occur, but tomatoes will shrink in size when baked.) Sprinkle the sugar mixture over the tomatoes. Gently place the reserved round of dough over the pie, folding the extra dough under around the edges. Press the bottom and top crusts together by pinching (or pressing with the tines of a fork) to seal the edges. Using a knife, make several 2-inch slits in the top crust to allow steam to escape. Brush the crust with the egg white and sprinkle with sugar.

4. Place the pie in the oven and bake for 25 minutes. Reduce the oven temperature to 350°F and continue to bake until the crust is golden brown, about 20 minutes longer. Let cool on a wire rack before serving this little piece of Southern hospitality.

ANY WAY YOU SLICE IT

Unless you've got a very sharp slicing knife, I'd say go with a serrated knife to get a nice clean cut on your tomatoes before they go in the pie. While green tomatoes are generally easier to slice than ripe tomatoes, you still want to make sure you get as clean a cut as possible without bruising these little gems.

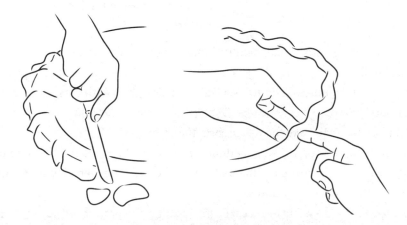

Trim the edges of the piecrust and crimp by pressing all around the top rim of the pie plate with the tines of a fork or the dull side of a knife. Alternatively, press the thumb and forefinger of one hand, held about 1 inch apart, along the inside rim of the crust while pushing into the space between these fingers along the outside rim with the forefinger of the other hand.

BLUEBERRY CRUMB PIE

■ ■

I adore the way that sweet-tart purple blueberry juices bubble up here and there through the crumb topping on this pie. Try it slightly warm with a scoop of ice cream for a real treat.

MAKES ONE 9-INCH PIE

All-purpose flour, for dusting
Paula's Flaky Piecrust Dough (page 339), or
    one 9-inch unbaked prepared piecrust

Crumb Topping
¾ cup all-purpose flour
¼ cup packed light brown sugar
¼ cup granulated sugar
½ teaspoon ground cinnamon
¼ teaspoon salt
4 tablespoons (½ stick)
    butter, melted

Filling
¾ cup granulated sugar
¼ cup cornstarch
¼ teaspoon salt
5 cups blueberries
Grated zest and juice of 1 lemon

MIDWINTER BLUEBERRY PIE
It's the middle of winter and fresh blueberries cost an arm and a leg. There's nothing to worry about, folks. Simply substitute frozen blueberries for the fresh ones.

1. Dust a work surface with a small handful of flour. Roll the dough into a 12-inch round about ¼ inch thick (skip this step if using a prepared crust). Use it to line a 9-inch pie plate and chill in the refrigerator for 30 minutes or up to overnight (cover lightly with plastic wrap if chilling for more than 2 hours).

2. When you are ready to bake the pie, preheat the oven to 375°F.

3. To make the crumb topping: In a medium bowl, whisk together the flour, both sugars, the cinnamon, and salt. Add the melted butter and stir until evenly moistened. Using your hands, roll the topping into balls the size of walnuts.

4. To make the filling: In a large saucepan, stir together the granulated sugar, cornstarch, and salt. Add the blueberries and toss to coat. Set the pan over medium-high heat and bring to a boil, stirring often. Remove from the heat and stir in the lemon juice and zest.

5. Spoon the blueberries and all the juices into the unbaked piecrust. Cover the surface with the crumb topping. Bake until the filling is bubbling and the topping is golden brown, 50 minutes to 1 hour. Let cool thoroughly before serving.

PEACHES AND CREAM PIE

I like my peach pie as juicy and full of fruit as can be, and I mellow out the filling with cream and stabilize it with a little tapioca, which gives it a real comforting feeling.

MAKES ONE 9-INCH PIE

All-purpose flour, for dusting
Paula's Flaky Piecrust Dough (page 339), or
    one 9-inch unbaked prepared piecrust
3 cups peeled (see box, page 422), pitted, and
    sliced peaches
½ cup sugar

3 tablespoons instant tapioca
Pinch of salt
1 cup heavy cream
2 large eggs
2 large egg yolks
2 teaspoons vanilla extract

1. Dust a work surface with a small handful of flour. Roll the dough into a 12-inch round about ¼ inch thick (skip this step if using a prepared crust). Use it to line a 9-inch pie plate and chill in the refrigerator for 30 minutes or up to overnight (cover lightly with plastic wrap if chilling for more than 2 hours).

2. When you are ready to bake the pie, preheat the oven to 400°F.

3. In a medium bowl, toss together the peaches, sugar, tapioca, and salt. In a small bowl, whisk together the cream, whole eggs, egg yolks, and vanilla. Place the peach mixture on the bottom of the piecrust. Pour the cream mixture evenly over the peaches, pushing down on the peaches to submerge them in the liquid.

4. Bake for 20 minutes, then reduce the oven temperature to 350°F. Bake until the center of the pie is set and the top is lightly browned, 25 to 30 minutes. Let this pie cool thoroughly before you serve it.

SHINING STAR

Instant tapioca is a starch thickener. It's the perfect choice for pies because it gives a glossy sheen to whatever it's tossed with. It also thickens quickly at a low temperature. Most important, though, it imparts no flavor to your pie, leaving the peaches and cream the real stars of this little beauty.

FRIED PEACH PIES

■ ■

My Grandmama Paul always made her fried pies with dried fruit that she'd simmer in syrup. The fruit plumps up beautifully and has an especially intense flavor. I will never forget how she would just roll her dough, cut it out, fill it, fold it, and crimp it with a fork in no time, sliding a pie into the oil with one hand while she started on the next one with her other.

MAKES 5 HAND PIES

1 cup dried peaches
2½ tablespoons sugar
1 tablespoon butter
½ teaspoon ground cinnamon
About 4 quarts vegetable oil, for deep-frying

All-purpose flour, for dusting
Paula's Flaky Piecrust Dough (page 339), or
    one 9-inch unbaked prepared piecrust
1 egg, lightly beaten, for brushing

1. In a small saucepan, combine the dried peaches and ½ cup water. Bring to a simmer over medium heat and cook until the fruit is softened, about 10 minutes. Let cool slightly, then stir in the sugar, butter, and cinnamon. Let cool completely.

2. In a deep pot, heat 3 inches of oil until it reaches 350°F on a deep-fry thermometer, about 15 to 20 minutes.

3. Sprinkle a small handful of flour over a work surface. Roll the pie dough into a 13-inch round. Using a 4½- to 5-inch round cookie cutter, cut out rounds of dough.

4. Divide the peach filling evenly among the dough rounds. Brush the edges of one half of each dough round with the egg. Fold the rounds over the filling to make half-moons. Crimp the edges of the dough with the tines of a fork to seal and decorate.

5. Working in batches of 2 at a time, add the pies to the hot oil and fry until golden and crisp, 2 to 3 minutes. Set on a paper towel–lined plate to drain. Serve while these little pies are still warm.

STUCK ON YOU

Oh, I just love these cute little pies! To make sure they fry up as neatly as possible, I give them a good brushing with the egg wash. You see, that's the glue that holds these little guys together. The egg wash, together with a firm crimping, should ensure that they don't bust open on you when you drop them into the oil.

PEACH BISCUIT COBBLER

A biscuit-topped cobbler is homey and satisfying like nothing else, and it works so well with real juicy fruit like ripe summer peaches. Bring this along to a picnic or potluck, or serve it at your next barbecue and celebrate summer.

MAKES 6 TO 8 SERVINGS

Peach Filling

3 pounds peaches, peeled (see box, page 422), pitted, and sliced ¼ inch thick
⅔ cup packed light brown sugar
¼ cup instant tapioca
1 teaspoon ground cinnamon
1 teaspoon fresh lemon juice
¼ teaspoon grated nutmeg
⅛ teaspoon salt

Biscuit Topping

1⅔ cups all-purpose flour, plus more for dusting
¼ cup granulated sugar
1½ tablespoons baking powder
⅛ teaspoon salt
6 tablespoons (¾ stick) cold butter, cut into small bits
⅔ cup heavy cream, plus extra for brushing
Coarse sugar, for sprinkling (optional)

1. Preheat the oven to 350°F. Grease a shallow 2½-quart baking dish with butter, oil, or cooking spray.

2. To prepare the peach filling: In a medium bowl, stir together all the ingredients. Pour the filling into the prepared dish.

3. To make the biscuit topping: In a food processor or large bowl, pulse or whisk together the flour, granulated sugar, baking powder, and salt. Pulse or cut in the butter just until the mixture resembles coarse meal. Slowly add the ⅔ cup cream, mixing until the dough just comes together. It will look scraggly and messy.

> ### A DIFFERENT KIND OF COBBLER
>
> Now, I usually go in for cobblers that have a cakelike consistency like my blueberry and blackberry cobblers. But sometimes I like to change things up and make a cobbler like this one. The biscuit topping is such a nice crunchy, toasty complement to the soft and silky peaches on the inside. I tell you, there just seems to be no end to the ways you can put biscuits to use!

4. Sprinkle a small handful of flour over a work surface. Place the dough on the surface and pat together. Pull off 2-inch pieces of dough and roll into balls. Flatten them with the palm of your hand and evenly arrange the dough rounds on top of the filling. Brush with cream and sprinkle with coarse sugar, if desired. Bake until the cobbler topping is golden and the filling is bubbling, about 1 hour. Serve warm.

BLUEBERRY COBBLER

■ ■

This one-bowl cobbler comes together in a minute and feeds a crowd. Keep a few cans of blueberry filling in your pantry and you can put it together at the drop of a hat. I just love how the lemon zest complements the sweet berries.

SERVES 8 TO 10

8 tablespoons (1 stick) butter
1 cup sugar
¾ cup self-rising flour
Grated zest of 1 lemon

Pinch of salt
¾ cup whole milk
2 cans (14 ounces each)
  blueberry pie filling

1. Preheat the oven to 350°F.

2. Put the butter in an 11 by 7-inch baking dish and place in the oven to melt. Tilt the pan and swirl the butter around to coat all sides.

3. In a medium bowl, whisk together the sugar, flour, lemon zest, and salt. Whisk in the milk slowly, to prevent clumping. Pour the batter evenly over the melted butter in the baking dish, but do not stir. Spoon the pie filling evenly over the batter. The batter will rise to the top during baking.

4. Bake until the cobbler is lightly browned and firm to the touch, 40 to 50 minutes. I like to serve this cobbler while it's still warm, but room temperature is perfectly fine, too.

CHERRY PICKING

This cobbler is just as nice with cherry pie filling in place of the blueberry pie filling. It all depends on what you're in the mood for.

BLACKBERRY COBBLER

Blackberries cook up to such a beautiful and dramatic deep black-purple, you could serve this at a fancy dinner party—or enjoy it on a picnic blanket.

SERVES 8 TO 10

4 cups blackberries

2 cups sugar

8 tablespoons (1 stick) butter

1½ cups all-purpose flour

2¼ teaspoons baking powder

¾ teaspoon salt

1½ cups whole milk

1. Preheat the oven to 350°F.

2. In a medium saucepan, combine the blackberries and 1 cup of the sugar and mix well. Bring to a boil over medium-high heat and simmer for 10 minutes. Remove from the heat.

3. Put the butter in a 13 by 9-inch baking dish and place in the oven to melt. Tilt the pan and swirl the butter around to coat all sides.

4. In a large bowl, whisk together the remaining 1 cup sugar, the flour, baking powder, and salt. Whisk in the milk slowly, to prevent clumping. Pour the batter evenly over the melted butter in the baking dish, but do not stir. Spoon the fruit on top, gently pouring in the syrup. The batter will rise to the top during baking.

5. Bake until the cobbler is lightly browned and firm to the touch, 30 to 40 minutes. I like to serve this cobbler while it's still warm, but room temperature is perfectly fine, too.

OR TRY FROZEN

If blackberries aren't around when you feel like making up this cobbler, go ahead and substitute frozen blackberries. You won't be disappointed!

PEAR CRISP

■ ■

When I see a bowl of juicy pears on the counter, I think about having me a snack, but I know that when Michael sees those pears, his mind turns immediately to one of his all-time favorites—a nice, homey pear crisp. With syrupy-sweet slices of pear underneath and plenty of that crunchy, buttery topping, it's a fine dessert. Just pull out some vanilla ice cream, and you got yourself a real treat.

SERVES 8 TO 10

Filling
5 large pears (about 2¾ pounds), peeled, halved, cored, and cut into ½-inch-thick slices
2 tablespoons sugar
¼ teaspoon ground cinnamon

Topping
⅔ cup sugar
⅔ cup all-purpose flour
¾ teaspoon ground cinnamon
¼ teaspoon salt
8 tablespoons (1 stick) cold butter, cut into small bits
½ cup sliced almonds

1. Preheat the oven to 375°F. Grease a 9-inch square baking dish with butter, oil, or cooking spray.

2. To prepare the filling: In a medium bowl, toss together the pears, sugar, and cinnamon. Place in the prepared baking dish.

3. To make the topping: In a medium bowl, whisk together the sugar, flour, cinnamon, and salt. Cut in the butter with a pastry blender, your hands, or two knives (see illustration, page 277) until the mixture resembles coarse meal. Add the almonds and stir to combine.

4. Scatter the topping over the surface of the pears. Bake until light golden brown and the pears have softened, 50 to 60 minutes. I like to serve a crisp just like my cobblers, while it's still warm, but room temperature is perfectly fine, too.

PEAR PICKING

There are so many tasty types of pears to choose from. Whichever type you choose for this lovely little crisp, make sure the pears are firm to the touch but give slightly under gentle pressure. Definitely steer clear of mushy and bruised pears. I love pears with cinnamon as I've flavored them in this crisp, but they're equally nice with ginger or nutmeg.

PAULA'S FLAKY PIECRUST DOUGH

I use chilled butter for flavor and chilled Crisco for texture in my pie dough, and just enough icy-cold water to bring the ingredients together without making things tough. Some pie doughs can get finicky on you, but this one always does me proud. You can easily double this if you need enough for a double-crust pie.

MAKES ENOUGH FOR ONE 9-INCH PIECRUST

1 cup all-purpose flour
¼ teaspoon salt
4 tablespoons (½ stick) cold butter,
   cut into small bits

¼ cup cold vegetable
   shortening
2 to 4 tablespoons ice-cold water

1. In a food processor, pulse together the flour and salt just until combined. Add the butter and shortening and pulse just until the mixture resembles coarse meal. Add the ice water, 1 tablespoon at a time, and pulse just until the dough comes together, taking care not to overwork the dough. The dough should be rough and not smooth.

2. Place the dough on a sheet of plastic wrap and press it into a flat disk. Wrap well and refrigerate for at least 2 hours before rolling out.

> **DO AHEAD**
> This pie dough will keep in the fridge for 3 days or so, and in the freezer for a good 3 months. Now, how convenient is that?

Chapter 14

CAKES, COOKIES, AND BARS

For many Southerners, cake is a way of life. And we don't need to wait for birthdays, weddings, or other special events to bake a big old layer cake, either—we woke up and the sun came out and that's all the occasion we need! We take cake so seriously here that if you go to a Southern town, you'll likely find one woman who specializes in making the best of each of the three big cakes: caramel, coconut, and chocolate layer.

Baking a great big cake can sure seem intimidating—but oftentimes it's as easy as stirrin' up a batch of brownies. Some of my recipes, like the Coconut Cake (page 363) I've been making for Jamie's birthday since he was small, begin with a mix, which, after all, is just your flour, leavening, and sugar all combined and ready for you. But even without this shortcut, I can pull together a recipe like Peachy Upside-Down Cake (page 359), one of my absolute favorites, in about the time it takes to preheat the oven.

Cake played a big part in my childhood, too. Back then, I attended church suppers and other buffets where all the best bakers in the community contributed their prized cakes. And while I do believe I did my share to help with a slice or two of the tall, fancy-looking layer cakes like Lady Baltimore Cake (page 381) or General Robert E. Lee Cake (page 386), I seem to recall that nothing made my eyes light up like the sight of a simple Texas Sheet Cake with Chocolate Fudge Frosting (page 380). Watching my grandbaby Jack get into that good fudgy frosting brings me right back.

Even to this day, I am a sucker for frosting. I frost my Nutty Fudge Brownies (page 346), and I spread my creamy Pecan Praline Cheesecake (page 357) with a fluffy sour cream topping. In my kitchen, dessert is absolutely the best place to add a little more—a special flourish on top, an extra layer to turn a cake into a real showstopper, a handful of chopped pecans or peanuts here, some chocolate chips there. Could there be anything more fun than fixin' the kind of dessert that makes everyone feel special—special occasion or not?

CHOCOLATE PECAN BARS

■ ■

You know I was born and raised in the pecan capital of the world, and I can assure you that there is no better place for a pecan than right here, stirred into these sweet, chocolate bar cookies. Pack a few of these in a lunch box and you will make someone very popular.

MAKES 24 SQUARES

Crust
2 cups all-purpose flour
2 sticks (8 ounces) butter, at room
    temperature
¾ cup confectioners' sugar
½ cup granulated sugar
Pinch of salt

Filling
1½ sticks (6 ounces) butter
½ cup light corn syrup
½ cup heavy cream
½ cup packed light brown sugar
¼ cup honey
1 teaspoon vanilla extract
3½ cups coarsely chopped pecans
1½ cups mini chocolate chips

1. Preheat the oven to 325°F. Lightly grease a 13 by 9-inch baking pan with butter, oil, or cooking spray.

2. To make the crust: In a food processor, combine all the ingredients. Pulse until a crumbly shortbread dough forms—it will be like wet sand. Press the dough into the prepared pan and bake until the crust is golden around the edges, about 20 minutes. (Leave the oven on.)

3. While the crust is baking, make the filling: In a large saucepan, melt the butter over low heat. Add the corn syrup, cream, brown sugar, and honey. Stir over low heat until well combined. Remove from the heat and stir in the vanilla.

4. Once the crust is finished baking, add the pecans and chocolate chips to the filling. Spread the filling mixture evenly over the crust. Return to the oven and bake until the filling is set and the mixture is bubbling around the edges, about 35 minutes. Let cool completely in the pan before cutting into 24 cute little squares.

> ## NUTS ABOUT NUTS
> If you just love your pecans and you don't want anything getting in front of that nutty flavor, go ahead and leave out the chocolate. You'll wind up with a more traditional pecan bar that is just as delicious as this tasty chocolate pecan bar.

NUTTY FUDGE BROWNIES

To me, a brownie ought to be frosted. Why hold back? I love mine with some nuts and enough salt in the batter to balance some of that sweetness.

MAKES 24 BROWNIES

Brownies

2 sticks (8 ounces) butter

8 ounces semisweet chocolate, chopped

4 ounces unsweetened chocolate, chopped

2 cups granulated sugar

4 large eggs, lightly beaten

1 tablespoon vanilla extract

1 cup all-purpose flour

1 teaspoon salt

1½ cups chopped pecans

Frosting

¾ cup granulated sugar

⅓ cup unsweetened cocoa powder, sifted

⅓ cup whole milk

3 tablespoons butter, at room temperature

1½ tablespoons light corn syrup

3¼ cups confectioners' sugar, sifted

1½ teaspoons vanilla extract

1. Preheat the oven to 350°F. Grease a 13 by 9-inch baking pan with butter, oil, or cooking spray.

2. To make the brownies: In a large saucepan, melt the butter and both chocolates over low heat, stirring constantly. Whisk in the granulated sugar. Then whisk in the eggs and vanilla.

3. In a medium bowl, whisk together the flour, salt, and pecans. Using a rubber spatula, fold the chocolate mixture into the flour mixture just until combined.

4. Pour the batter into the prepared baking pan and bake until firm and set, but not dry, 25 to 30 minutes. Let cool completely in the pan.

5. To make the frosting: In a large saucepan, whisk together the granulated sugar and cocoa powder. Whisk in the milk, butter, and corn syrup. Place the pan over medium-high heat and bring to a boil, whisking constantly. Take the pan off the heat and stir in the confectioners' sugar and vanilla. Spread the frosting over the surface of the cooled brownies, cut into 24 squares and enjoy!

KEEP IT SIMPLE

If you have a hankering for brownies but you don't feel like making your own frosting, feel free to substitute canned frosting for homemade. And choose whatever flavor you like! Or if you'd like, keep it real simple and leave the frosting out altogether.

BROWNIE PUDDING PUDDLES

This is a really cute little way to get a chocoholic his or her fix. I adore making desserts in mini muffin tins, so they're easy to serve and eat in one bite.

MAKES 24 BROWNIE BITES

Crust

¾ cup chocolate wafer crumbs (from about 15 wafers, such as Nabisco Famous Chocolate Wafers)

2 tablespoons sugar

2 tablespoons (¼ stick) butter, melted

Filling

6 tablespoons (¾ stick) butter

2 ounces unsweetened chocolate, finely chopped

¾ cup sugar

2 large eggs

⅓ cup all-purpose flour

1 teaspoon vanilla extract

½ cup semisweet chocolate chips

THE LIGHT TOUCH

Take care in removing the brownies from the pan. They can stick to the sides and be a little tricky to dislodge, so be real gentle with them as you are moving your spatula or paring knife around the edges to release them.

1. Preheat the oven to 350°F. Generously grease one 24-cup mini muffin tin or two 12-cup mini muffin tins with butter, oil, or cooking spray.

2. To make the crust: In a small bowl, combine all the ingredients until they form an evenly moist, crumbly mixture. Divide the mixture evenly among the muffin cups (about 1½ teaspoons per cup) and, using the back of a spoon or a shot glass, press the cookie crumb mixture firmly into each well. Bake until the crust is set and fragrant, 5 minutes. Remove from the oven and set aside to cool.

3. To make the filling: In a medium saucepan, melt the butter and chocolate over low heat, stirring constantly. In a medium bowl, whisk together the sugar and eggs until smooth and combined. Add the chocolate-butter mixture to the egg mixture and whisk to combine. Using a rubber spatula, gently fold in the flour just until combined. Fold in the vanilla and chocolate chips.

4. Spoon about 1 heaping tablespoon of the batter into each muffin cup. Bake until the brownies are set around the edges but nice and gooey in the center, 11 to 12 minutes. Let cool completely in the pan.

5. Using a small spatula or paring knife, carefully remove the brownies from the pan and enjoy them with a tall glass of cold milk.

CHOCOLATE CHIP–PEANUT COOKIES

■ ■

I always like to keep a container of salted roasted peanuts on hand for snacking, so it's no surprise that eventually they wound up in a batch of cookies I was making. Chocolate and peanuts are always a winning combination in my book! These cookies keep in an airtight container at room temperature for about 5 days. I like that this makes a big batch. That way, I've always got something sweet to put out when company comes round.

MAKES ABOUT 5 DOZEN COOKIES

2 sticks (8 ounces) butter,
   at room temperature
1⅔ cups packed light brown sugar
2 large eggs
1 teaspoon vanilla extract
2⅓ cups all-purpose flour

1 teaspoon baking powder
1 teaspoon baking soda
½ teaspoon salt
1 cup semisweet chocolate chips
1 cup chopped salted roasted peanuts

1. Preheat the oven to 375°F. Lightly grease several baking sheets with butter, oil, or cooking spray.

2. In the bowl of an electric mixer fitted with the paddle attachment, or using a handheld mixer, beat the butter at medium speed until creamy and smooth, 1 to 2 minutes. Add the sugar and beat the mixture until light and fluffy, about 5 minutes. Be sure to scrape down the sides of the bowl occasionally to incorporate all the sugar into the butter. Beat in the eggs, one at a time, beating well after each egg is added to thoroughly combine. Beat in the vanilla.

3. In a medium bowl, whisk together the flour, baking powder, baking soda, and salt. Add the flour mixture to the butter mixture, beating just until combined. Using a rubber spatula, fold in the chocolate chips and peanuts.

> ### DON'T GET STUCK
> Cookie batter tends to be a bit sticky, so I like to use two spoons to drop the batter onto the cookie sheets. First, I spray them with a little cooking spray so that the dough will slide off more easily. Then I scoop up my rounded spoonful in one spoon and use the other spoon to push it off and onto the baking sheet. Neat trick, don't you think? (Of course you can also use a mini ice cream scoop instead of spoons. Just be sure to coat it with cooking spray first.)

Portion out evenly sized cookie dough rounds by using a lightly greased mini ice cream scoop.

4. Drop the batter by rounded tablespoonfuls (a mini ice cream scoop is great for this) onto the prepared baking sheets and bake, one sheet at a time, until set around the edges and light golden brown, 9 to 10 minutes. Let cool on wire racks.

CRUNCHY OATMEAL-COCONUT-PECAN COOKIES

■ ■

Michael is my Cookie Monster. He just has to have his cookies, and he likes his cookies so crunchy, you gotta get out the Dustbuster after he eats one on the couch. I made up these loaded oatmeal cookies with him in mind, and they are crunchy enough that you'll have to put your conversation on hold while you enjoy one.

MAKES ABOUT 2½ DOZEN COOKIES

8 tablespoons (1 stick) butter,
   at room temperature
½ cup packed dark brown sugar
⅓ cup granulated sugar
1 large egg
1 teaspoon vanilla extract
¾ cup all-purpose flour

1 teaspoon ground cinnamon
½ teaspoon baking powder
½ teaspoon salt
¼ teaspoon baking soda
1½ cups old-fashioned rolled oats
¾ cup chopped pecans
½ cup shredded sweetened coconut

1. Preheat the oven to 350°F. Grease 2 baking sheets with butter, oil, or cooking spray.

2. In the bowl of an electric mixer fitted with the paddle attachment, or using a handheld mixer, beat the butter at medium speed until creamy and smooth, 1 to 2 minutes. Add both sugars and beat the mixture until light and fluffy, about 5 minutes. Be sure to scrape down the sides of the bowl occasionally to incorporate all the sugar into the butter. Add the egg and beat well, then beat in the vanilla.

3. In a medium bowl, whisk together the flour, cinnamon, baking powder, salt, and baking soda. Add the flour mixture to the butter mixture, beating just until combined. Using a rubber spatula, fold in the oats, pecans, and coconut.

4. Drop the batter by rounded tablespoonfuls (a mini ice cream scoop is great for this) onto the prepared baking sheets and bake, one sheet at a time, until set around the edges and light golden brown, 10 to 12 minutes. Let cool on the pans slightly, transfer to wire racks, and then watch these little beauties disappear.

ON A ROLL

You may see rolled oats labeled "old-fashioned" oats. If you can't find rolled or old-fashioned oats, you can substitute quick-cooking oats, but you won't get the same texture that the rolled oats will give you. Whatever you do, don't substitute instant oatmeal—that cooks up way too fast to be used in baking.

BENNE SEED WAFERS

■ ■

Benne seeds, also known as sesame seeds, are big in the South Carolina Low Country, and I just love to use them for these superthin wafers. These crispy, buttery wafers are just the thing with a cup of tea.

MAKES ABOUT 7 DOZEN WAFERS

¾ cup benne seeds (sesame seeds)

2 sticks (8 ounces) butter,
   at room temperature

1⅓ cups packed light brown sugar

1 large egg

1 cup all-purpose flour

½ teaspoon baking powder

¼ teaspoon salt

1 teaspoon vanilla extract

1. Preheat the oven to 350°F. Line several baking sheets with parchment paper.

2. Place the benne seeds on one of the prepared baking sheets and toast in the oven until lightly browned and fragrant, 3 to 5 minutes. Place in a small bowl and set aside to cool completely.

3. Reduce the oven temperature to 300°F.

4. In the bowl of an electric mixer fitted with the paddle attachment, or using a handheld mixer, beat the butter and sugar at medium speed until light and fluffy, about 5 minutes. Be sure to scrape down the sides of the bowl occasionally to incorporate all the sugar into the butter. Add the egg and beat well.

5. In a small bowl, whisk together the flour, baking powder, and salt. Add the flour mixture to the butter mixture, beating just until combined. Using a rubber spatula, stir in the vanilla and cooled benne seeds.

6. Drop rounded ½ teaspoonfuls onto the prepared baking sheets. Make sure they are at least 1 inch apart, as the wafers will spread during baking. Bake, one sheet at a time, until golden brown but not burned at the edges, 14 to 15 minutes. Let the wafers cool completely on the baking sheets before removing them from the parchment paper.

SLEEP ON IT

For the crispest wafers, make the dough a day ahead and refrigerate right up until you're ready to bake.

FLORIDA LEMON BARS

■ ■

Florida citrus comes to us so fresh and sweet here in Savannah, it just brightens even the gloomi-est midwinter days. I use a ton of citrus here—orange zest in the crust, and lemon juice and zest in the filling—to give my buttery lemon bars a genuine jolt of juicy, tangy flavor. They'll wake up a tea party faster than anything.

MAKES 24 SQUARES

Crust

3 cups all-purpose flour
½ cup granulated sugar
½ cup confectioners' sugar
1 teaspoon finely grated orange zest
¼ teaspoon salt
3 sticks (12 ounces) cold butter,
   cut into tablespoons

Filling

6 large eggs, lightly beaten
1½ cups granulated sugar
1 tablespoon finely grated lemon zest
½ cup fresh lemon juice (3 to 4 lemons)
¼ cup all-purpose flour
Pinch of salt

Confectioners' sugar, for sprinkling

1. Preheat the oven to 325°F. Lightly grease a 13 by 9-inch baking pan with butter, oil, or cook-ing spray.

2. To make the crust: In a food processor, combine the flour, granulated sugar, confectioners' sugar, orange zest, and salt and pulse to combine. Add the butter and pulse until a crumbly short-bread dough forms (it will resemble wet sand). Press the dough onto the bottom of the prepared pan. Bake until the crust is golden around the edges, about 45 minutes.

3. While the crust is baking, make the filling: In a large bowl, whisk together all the ingredients.

4. When the crust is ready, take it out of the oven and increase the oven temperature to 350°F. Carefully pour the filling onto the crust and return the pan to the oven. Bake until the filling is just set, about 20 minutes. Let cool thoroughly before cutting into 24 squares. Dust with confectioners' sugar to dress these pretty little bars up just before serving.

DIY SHAKER

Now, you can dust with confectioners' sugar by using a small metal strainer and shaking it over your dessert, but I always find that a bit of a mess. Instead, why don't you try this at home? Get yourself an empty spice container with a shaker top (with small holes), clean it out thoroughly, and fill it with sifted confectioners' sugar. Keep it in the cupboard so that it's always handy. Less mess, less cleanup!

TEA CAKES

In Savannah, people still take tea like the British, and these buttery, tender little cookies are a must-have on the tea table. Personally, I just love to enjoy my tea cakes with a tall glass of icy-cold lemonade.

MAKES 6 TO 8 DOZEN TEA CAKES

4 cups all-purpose flour,
    plus extra for dusting
1 teaspoon baking soda
2 teaspoons baking powder
2 cups sugar

2 large eggs
½ cup buttermilk
2 sticks (8 ounces) butter,
    at room temperature
1 teaspoon vanilla extract

1. In a large bowl, sift together the flour, baking soda, and baking powder. Stir in the remaining ingredients with a spoon. The dough will be soft and wet.

2. Sprinkle a large handful of flour over a work surface. Turn the dough out onto the surface and shape it into a disk. Wrap it in plastic and refrigerate for 1 hour.

3. Preheat the oven to 350°F. Lightly grease several baking sheets with butter, oil, or cooking spray.

4. Throw more flour onto the work surface and roll the dough out until about ¼ inch thick. Cut the dough with a cookie cutter into whatever shapes (about 2 inches) you like. Reroll the scraps (just once) and cut out more shapes. Bake, one sheet at a time, until pale golden, 10 to 12 minutes. No matter where I am in the world, these little cakes always bring me right on back to the South.

FOR A SPECIAL OCCASION

Tea cakes are an everyday affair here in the South. I like to have them on hand to enjoy with an afternoon cup of coffee or tea. But if I know I've got company coming round, I dress them up a bit by drizzling on a pretty frosting and shaking a few sprinkles on top.

GOOEY BUTTER CAKE

■ ■

My preference is for a moist cake. None of these dry egg white numbers for me. Heck, I sometimes think that cake batter tastes better than the cake, so I bake these gooey cakes so they're still real moist in the center. Now, I like to make it easy on everyone whenever I can, so this recipe, based on a box of cake mix and filled with the best sweet vanilla-scented cream cheese you ever put in your mouth, has been a standby in my kitchen forever.

SERVES 15 TO 20

Cake
1 box (18¼ ounces) yellow cake mix
1 large egg
8 tablespoons (1 stick) butter, melted

Filling
1 package (8 ounces) cream cheese,
    at room temperature
2 large eggs
1 teaspoon vanilla extract
8 tablespoons (1 stick) butter, melted
1 box (16 ounces) confectioners' sugar

VARIATIONS ON A THEME

There are just so many ways to change this cake up. Try these ideas on for size:

- For the holidays, add a 15-ounce can of unsweetened pumpkin puree to the filling along with ground cinnamon and nutmeg.
- Add a 20-ounce can of drained crushed pineapple to the filling for a tropical flavor.
- Use a lemon cake mix instead of yellow cake mix and add lemon juice and zest to the filling.
- Use a chocolate cake mix instead of yellow cake mix and sprinkle with chocolate chips and nuts on top.
- Use a spiced carrot cake mix instead of yellow cake mix and add chopped nuts and shredded carrots to the filling.
- Use mandarin oranges, bananas, blueberries, or strawberries in the filling and coordinate your extract flavorings.
- Use a chocolate cake mix instead of yellow cake mix and add ¾ to 1 cup peanut butter and nuts to the filling.

1. Preheat the oven to 350°F. Grease a 13 by 9-inch baking pan with butter, oil, or cooking spray.

2. To make the cake: Place the cake mix, egg, and melted butter in a large bowl and mix well, using a large spoon, until well combined. Scrape the batter into the prepared pan and smooth out.

3. To make the filling: In the bowl of an electric mixer fitted with the paddle attachment, or using a handheld mixer, beat the cream cheese at medium speed until smooth. Add the eggs and vanilla and beat well. Add the melted butter and beat until combined. Slowly add the confectioners' sugar, ¼ cup at a time, and beat well after each addition. Using a spatula, spread the filling over the cake mixture and bake for 40 to 50 minutes. You want the center to be a little gooey, so be careful not to overbake. Stick a toothpick into the center and you should see a few wet crumbs stick to it.

GEORGIA POUND CAKE

■ ■

There's nothing better to have on hand or in your freezer than a big buttery pound cake. I'll tell you why: Y'all can just take it so many different ways. You can fry it up in the skillet with butter for breakfast. Or turn it into strawberry shortcake or peach shortcake with a little whipped cream and a sprig of mint. I also like to make a pound cake into a trifle. This pound cake is not just rich and moist and delicious, it's also the key to turning out so many other desserts like you just pulled a rabbit out of a hat. Folks will think you're a magician.

SERVES 16 TO 20

3 cups all-purpose flour, plus extra for dusting	6 large eggs
	½ teaspoon baking powder
2 sticks (8 ounces) butter, at room temperature	½ teaspoon salt
	1 cup heavy cream
3 cups sugar	2 teaspoons vanilla extract

1. Grease a 10-inch Bundt pan with butter, oil, or cooking spray. Flour generously and shake out any excess.

2. In the bowl of an electric mixer fitted with the paddle attachment, or using a handheld mixer, beat the butter and sugar at medium speed until light and fluffy, about 5 minutes. Be sure to scrape

down the sides of the bowl occasionally to incorporate all the sugar into the butter. Add the eggs, one at a time, beating well after each egg is added to thoroughly combine.

3. In a medium bowl, sift together the 3 cups flour, the baking powder, and salt. Beat one-fourth of the flour mixture into the egg mixture. Beat in ⅓ cup of the cream. Continue adding the flour mixture and the cream in this fashion, alternating them and ending with the flour mixture. Mix just until incorporated and scrape the sides of the bowl down occasionally. Using a rubber spatula, stir in the vanilla.

4. Pour the batter into the prepared pan. Place in a cold oven, set the oven temperature at 325°F, and bake, without opening the oven door, until a toothpick inserted into the center comes out dry, 1 hour and 15 minutes. Bake for an extra 15 minutes if you think it needs it. Let the cake cool in the pan for 15 minutes, then invert it onto a cake plate. For a real treat, serve yourself a slice while it's still warm.

EXTRACT FLAVOR

While I absolutely love this traditional pound cake just the way it is, if I'm feeling zesty, I switch out the vanilla extract for lemon extract. Or I go nuts and switch out the vanilla for a teaspoon of almond extract.

PECAN PRALINE CHEESECAKE

■ ■

If you ask me, cheesecake deserves a creative crust and an exciting topping. I suppose you could say I'm not a purist in this department because I always enjoy playing around with new combinations. Here I believe I have hit upon a cheesecake trifecta: a crispy pecan-gingersnap crust; a smooth brown sugar and cream cheese filling with bits of crunchy pecan praline right in it; and a tangy sour cream and praline topping. Life is rich.

SERVES 10 TO 12

Praline
1¼ cups chopped pecans
8 tablespoons (1 stick) butter
1 cup packed light brown sugar
¼ teaspoon baking soda
1 teaspoon vanilla extract

Crust
1¼ cups finely crushed gingersnaps
   (about 24 cookies)
½ cup chopped pecans
3 tablespoons packed light brown sugar
6 tablespoons (¾ stick) butter, melted

Filling
3 packages (8 ounces each) cream cheese
¾ cup granulated sugar
½ cup packed light brown sugar
¼ teaspoon salt
3 large eggs, lightly beaten
¾ cup heavy cream
1 teaspoon vanilla extract
1 cup chopped praline (see Praline)

Topping
¾ cup heavy cream
½ cup sour cream
2 tablespoons granulated sugar
½ cup chopped praline (see Praline)

1. To make the praline: Preheat the oven to 325°F. Spread the pecans on a rimmed baking sheet and toast for 10 minutes. Grease another rimmed baking sheet with butter, oil, or cooking spray. In a large saucepan, melt the butter over medium heat. Stir in the brown sugar and 1 tablespoon water. Increase the heat to medium-high and cook at a rapid boil for 7 minutes. Add the baking soda and warm pecans and swirl the pan to incorporate them (do not stir). Take care while you're swirling the pan, as the mixture will spatter a bit. When the bubbling has subsided, swirl in the vanilla. Pour the mixture out onto the prepared baking sheet and use a small buttered spatula (preferably offset) to spread the mixture in as thin a layer as possible. Let cool before chopping.

2. Preheat the oven to 350°F. To make the crust: In a medium bowl, combine all the ingredients until they form an evenly moist, crumbly mixture. Press the mixture evenly onto the bottom and just slightly up the sides of a 9-inch springform pan. Bake until the crust is fragrant and firm, 9 to 10 minutes. Set aside to cool. (Leave the oven on but reduce the temperature to 325°F.)

3. To make the filling: In the bowl of an electric mixer fitted with the paddle attachment, or using a handheld mixer, beat the cream cheese at low speed until smooth and creamy, 3 to 5 minutes. Gradually add both sugars and the salt and continue beating until very smooth and no lumps remain, about 10 minutes. Be sure to scrape down the sides of the bowl occasionally to incorporate all the sugar into the butter.

4. In a small bowl, whisk together the eggs, cream, and vanilla. With the mixer going, gradually stream the egg mixture into the cream cheese mixture, beating well and scraping down the sides of the bowl until smooth and creamy, 2 to 3 minutes longer. Using a rubber spatula, fold in the 1 cup praline. Pour the filling into the crust and smooth the top.

5. Bake until the edges of the cheesecake are set but the center still jiggles, 40 to 45 minutes. Let the cheesecake cool completely at room temperature before covering with plastic wrap and refrigerating for at least 8 hours or overnight.

6. When you're ready to serve the cheesecake, make the topping: In the bowl of an electric mixer fitted with the whisk attachment, or using a handheld mixer, whip the heavy cream, sour cream, and granulated sugar at medium-high speed until medium peaks form. Using a rubber spatula, fold in the ½ cup praline. Spread over the surface of the cheesecake. Get yourself a hot, dry knife (heat under hot running water, then wipe dry with a towel) and cut out wedges to serve up.

PLENTY OF PRALINE

This recipe for praline will actually make more than the 1½ cups praline you'll need for the cheesecake and topping. This is a very good thing! The remaining praline is great to eat on its own, chopped into bits sprinkled on a sundae, or folded into cookie batter. The praline will keep in an airtight container in the pantry for up to a month.

PEACHY UPSIDE-DOWN CAKE

I cannot play favorites when it comes to cakes, but let's just say anything upside-down is up there in my top ten. First of all, upside-down cakes are so pretty when you turn them out, with the fruit slices nestled right into the buttery cake, and you know they're always so moist, with chewy, browned edges that I absolutely adore.

SERVES 6 TO 8

Cake

8 tablespoons (1 stick) butter, at room temperature

¾ cup granulated sugar

2 large eggs

1½ teaspoons vanilla extract

1½ cups all-purpose flour

2 teaspoons baking powder

¼ teaspoon salt

1 can (15 ounces) peach halves in heavy syrup

6 to 8 dried cherries (depending on the number of peach halves)

Glaze

4 tablespoons (½ stick) butter

¾ cup packed light brown sugar

2 teaspoons fresh lemon juice

HEAT UP

Because you make the glaze for this lovely cake over the stovetop burner, be sure to use a metal pan. Also, if the cake sits in the pan too long after coming out of the oven (which will cause it to stick to the bottom), just pop it back on the stovetop to reheat the glaze for a minute. This will loosen it back up so that you'll be able to unmold it cleanly.

1. Preheat the oven to 350°F.

2. To make the cake: In the bowl of an electric mixer fitted with the paddle attachment, or using a handheld mixer, beat the butter and granulated sugar at medium speed until light and fluffy, about 5 minutes. Be sure to scrape down the sides of the bowl occasionally to incorporate all the sugar into the butter. Add the eggs, one at a time, beating well after each egg is added to thoroughly combine. Beat in the vanilla.

3. In a medium bowl, whisk together the flour, baking powder, and salt. Reserving ¼ cup of the syrup, drain the peaches. Stir ½ cup water into the reserved peach syrup.

4. Beat one-third of the flour mixture into the butter mixture. Beat in half of the peach liquid. Continue alternately adding the two mixtures, ending with the flour mixture.

5. To make the glaze: Melt the butter in a 9-inch square metal baking pan on the stovetop over medium-low heat. Add the brown sugar and lemon juice and stir until the sugar has melted; remove from the heat. Arrange the cherries in the pan and cover each with a peach half. Pour the batter over the peaches and bake until a toothpick inserted into the center of the cake comes out clean, about 40 minutes.

6. Let cool on a wire rack for 5 minutes. No longer, now, or this cake will stick! Run a knife along the edges of the pan and invert the cake onto a platter. I like to serve this cake warm, but it's just as delicious at room temperature.

BLACKBERRY JELLY ROLL

Jelly rolls made with homemade preserves such as this one are such an old-fashioned Southern dessert—the kind of thing a farm family would enjoy after a long, hard day outdoors. I like to up the ante with a fluffy meringue frosting, which makes this pretty little dessert special enough for any occasion.

SERVES 6 TO 8

Jelly
2 bags (10 ounces each) frozen
    blackberries
1 cup granulated sugar
3 tablespoons cornstarch

Cake
6 large eggs, at room temperature
1½ teaspoons vanilla extract
½ cup granulated sugar
½ cup cake flour, sifted
½ cup cornstarch, sifted
1¼ teaspoons baking powder
¼ teaspoon salt

Frosting
1¼ cups granulated sugar
¼ teaspoon cream of tartar
2 large egg whites
1 tablespoon light corn syrup
1 teaspoon vanilla extract

Confectioners' sugar, for sprinkling

DIFFERENT BERRIES MAKE THE (JELLY) ROLL CALL
Blackberries are the traditional fruit for jelly rolls, but you can make this with any berry that strikes your fancy. Raspberries, strawberries, mixed berries—it's all good for the roll!

1. To make the jelly: In a medium saucepan, combine the blackberries and granulated sugar. Bring to a simmer over medium heat, and cook for 5 minutes. Meanwhile, place the cornstarch in a small bowl. Spoon out ½ cup of the blackberry juices and whisk into the cornstarch to make a slurry. Return the cornstarch slurry to the pan and bring to a boil. Cook until the mixture has jelled and thickened, 1 to 2 minutes. Let cool before using. Y'all can make this jelly 2 days in advance and keep it in the fridge.

2. Preheat the oven to 400°F. Grease a 17 by 11-inch jelly-roll pan with butter, oil, or cooking spray and line with parchment paper.

3. To make the cake: In the bowl of an electric mixer fitted with the whisk attachment, or using a handheld mixer, beat the eggs and vanilla at high speed until pale yellow and fluffy, 2 to 3 minutes. With the mixer going, slowly add the granulated sugar and beat at high speed for an extra 3 minutes.

4. In a small bowl, whisk together the flour, cornstarch, baking powder, and salt. Using a rubber spatula, fold the flour mixture into the egg mixture just until all the flour is moistened.

5. Using a small offset spatula, spread the batter in the prepared pan. Bake until the cake is dry, firm to the touch, and light golden brown, 8 to 10 minutes. Spread a clean dishtowel on a work surface and sprinkle with confectioners' sugar. Flip the cake onto the towel so the pan is on top; lift off the pan and peel off the parchment paper. Starting on a short side, roll up the cake and dishtowel into a cylinder while it is still warm (the dishtowel will be rolled up with the cake, which keeps the cake from sticking to itself). Leave the cake, seam side down, on the work surface to cool completely.

6. When the cake is cool, gently unroll it and spread evenly with blackberry jelly, leaving a ¾-inch border. Reroll the cake, then use the dishtowel on the outside to secure the cake in a log shape. Secure with tape to help the cake maintain its shape. Refrigerate for 1 hour before serving.

7. To make the frosting: Bring a medium saucepan of water to a bare simmer on the stove. In the bowl of an electric mixer fitted with the whisk attachment, or using a handheld mixer, beat all the ingredients together with ¼ cup water at medium speed, just until combined. Place the mixer bowl over the pan of simmering water and, by hand, whisk until the sugar dissolves and the mixture is hot, about 3 minutes. Set the bowl back on the mixer and beat at high speed for 3 minutes. Beat until stiff peaks form, 5 to 7 minutes.

8. Remove the dishtowel from the roll. Spread the frosting over the top and sides of the cake, taking care not to let the filling show through the sides. Dust with confectioners' sugar before serving.

To prevent cracking when rolling a jelly roll, turn the cake out onto a clean dish towel that has been lightly sprinkled with confectioners' sugar. Roll up the cake in the dish towel and let cool. When cooled, unroll, fill, and roll again.

COCONUT CAKE

■ ■

This is one of the trinity of traditional, big fluffy Southern layer cakes, and it is Jamie's birthday cake every year.

SERVES 12 TO 16

Cake
1 box (18¼ ounces) yellow cake mix
Whole milk, as called for by cake mix
1 cup sour cream
1½ cups sugar
12 ounces canned or frozen
   shredded coconut

Frosting
2 large egg whites
1½ cups sugar
2 teaspoons light corn syrup, or ¼ teaspoon
   cream of tartar
Pinch of salt
1 teaspoon vanilla extract
About ½ cup shredded sweetened coconut

1. Preheat the oven to 350°F. Grease three 9-inch round cake pans with butter, oil, or cooking spray. To make the cake: Follow the directions on the cake mix box, substituting milk for water. Divide the batter among the cake pans. Bake for 20 minutes. Remove from the oven and let cool in the pans for 5 minutes on a wire rack, then remove the cakes from the pans to cool completely.

2. In a medium bowl, stir together the sour cream, sugar, and coconut. Spread between the slightly warm cake layers, piercing each layer with a toothpick (see box below) as you stack them (see box, page 370), but don't pierce the top of the top layer. Store the cake in a container in the refrigerator for 2 to 3 days to allow the flavors to soak through.

3. On the day you are ready to serve the cake, make the frosting: In the top of a double boiler, combine the egg whites, sugar, corn syrup or cream of tartar, and salt. Do not place over the heat; instead, beat for 1 minute using a handheld electric mixer. Then place over simmering water and cook, beating constantly, until the frosting forms stiff peaks. This should take about 7 minutes. Remove from the heat. Add the vanilla and beat until it reaches spreading consistency, about 2 minutes. Frost the top and sides of the cake and sprinkle all over with shredded coconut. Besides tasting great, y'all, this cake is just so pretty.

PIERCE THROUGH

You want this cake to soak in as much coconut moisture and flavor as possible. By piercing the cake with a toothpick where the sour cream-coconut mixture will be, you open up the window to let all that lovely flavor flow in.

RED VELVET CAKE
WITH CREAM CHEESE–BOURBON FROSTING

■ ■

There is so much to love in a red velvet cake. First, since it is an oil-based cake, it has a moist, even consistency. It is a sweet cake, no doubt, but a little unsweetened cocoa and buttermilk go a long way to balancing that sweetness—not to mention the tangy cream cheese frosting. My cousin Johnnie, who owns Gabriel's Restaurant & Bakery in Marietta, Georgia, makes the best red velvet cakes, and I learned everything I know about them from her. I'm not certain she'd approve of the splash of bourbon in this frosting, but this recipe is quite traditional otherwise.

SERVES 8 TO 10

Cake

2 cups canola oil

2¼ cups granulated sugar

3 large eggs

6 tablespoons (3 ounces) red food coloring,
   or dissolve 1 teaspoon gel food coloring in
   6 tablespoons water

2 teaspoons vanilla extract

3½ cups cake flour

¼ cup unsweetened cocoa powder (not Dutch
   process), sifted

1½ teaspoons salt

1¼ cups buttermilk

2 teaspoons baking soda

2½ teaspoons distilled white vinegar

Frosting

12 ounces cream cheese, at room temperature

1½ sticks (6 ounces) butter, at room
   temperature

4 cups confectioners' sugar, sifted

4 teaspoons bourbon

1. Preheat the oven to 350°F. Grease three 9-inch round cake pans with butter, oil, or cooking spray. Cut out three 9-inch rounds of parchment paper and line the bottoms of the pans.

> **MELT FOR YOU**
> Here's a neat trick I sometimes like to use when greasing my cake pans. Place a teaspoon or so of butter in the pan. Place the pan in the preheating oven for a few minutes, until the butter melts. Remove the pan from the oven and, using a pastry brush, brush the interior bottom and sides of the pan with the melted butter. This is an easy and absolutely mess-free way to grease your pans.

2. To make the cake: In the bowl of an electric mixer fitted with the paddle attachment, or using a handheld mixer, combine the oil and granulated sugar and beat at medium speed until well blended. Add the eggs, one at a time, beating well after each egg is added to thoroughly combine. Turn the mixer to low speed and very slowly add the red food coloring. Be careful! It may splash, so wear an apron, y'all! Beat in the vanilla.

3. In a large bowl, whisk together the flour, cocoa powder, and salt. Beat one-third of the flour mixture into the egg mixture. Beat in half the buttermilk. Continue adding the mixtures alternately, ending with the flour mixture. Scrape down the bowl and beat just long enough to combine. Place the baking soda in a small dish, and stir in the vinegar. With the mixer running, add the vinegar mixture to the cake batter and mix for 10 seconds.

4. Divide the batter among the prepared pans and bake until a toothpick inserted into the center of each cake comes out clean, 40 to 45 minutes. Let the cakes cool in the pans or on wire racks for 20 minutes. Then invert the cakes onto the racks, peel off the parchment paper, and let them cool completely before frosting.

5. While the cake layers are cooling, make the frosting: In the bowl of an electric mixer fitted with the paddle attachment, or using a handheld mixer, combine the cream cheese and butter and beat at medium speed until light and fluffy, about 2 minutes. With the mixer at low speed, beat in the confectioners' sugar, ½ cup at a time. Add the bourbon once all the sugar has been mixed in. If you find the frosting is too soft, just chill it for 10 minutes in the fridge before using.

6. To assemble the cake, place 1 cake layer on a serving plate, with the flat bottom side facing down. (See box, page 370.) Spread about 1 cup of frosting over the surface of the cake. Top with another cake layer, inverted, so the bottom of the cake is facing up. Spread about 1 cup of frosting over this cake layer. Place the remaining cake layer, also inverted, on top. Spread the remaining frosting over the top and sides of the cake.

Frost cakes quickly and neatly using an offset spatula.

AMBROSIA CARROT CAKE
WITH FLUFFY COCONUT FROSTING

■ ■

Real, old-fashioned ambrosia is based on the divine combination of coconut and orange, and one day I figured out that those flavors would be so good with a regular old Southern layered carrot cake. I'm glad I went right into the kitchen and gave it a try before anyone could convince me not to.

SERVES 10 TO 12

Cake

2½ cups all-purpose flour

3 teaspoons ground cinnamon

2 teaspoons baking powder

2 teaspoons baking soda

2 teaspoons salt

1 cup finely chopped walnuts

2 cups granulated sugar

1 cup vegetable oil

6 large eggs

2 cups finely grated carrots (3 to 4 large carrots)

1 cup shredded sweetened coconut

Frosting

3 packages (8 ounces each) cream cheese, at room temperature

3 sticks (12 ounces) butter, at room temperature

5½ cups confectioners' sugar, sifted

1 tablespoon vanilla extract

Pinch of salt

1 can (11 ounces) mandarin orange segments in light syrup, drained

3 cups flaked sweetened coconut

1. Preheat the oven to 325°F. Grease three 9-inch round cake pans with butter, oil, or cooking spray. Cut out three 9-inch rounds of parchment paper and line the bottoms of the pans.

2. To prepare the cake: In a large bowl, whisk together the flour, cinnamon, baking powder, baking soda, salt, and walnuts. In a medium bowl, whisk together the granulated sugar, oil, and eggs. Using a rubber spatula, fold the carrots and coconut into the egg mixture. Fold the carrot mixture into the flour mixture just until combined.

3. Divide the batter evenly among the prepared pans and bake until a toothpick inserted into the center of each cake comes out clean and the cakes are firm to the touch and light golden brown, about 25 minutes. Let the cakes cool in the pans on wire racks for 10 minutes. Then invert the cakes onto the racks, peel off the parchment paper, and let them cool completely before frosting.

4. While the cake layers are cooling, make the frosting: In the bowl of an electric mixer fitted with the paddle attachment, or using a handheld mixer, beat the cream cheese and butter at medium speed until smooth and creamy, scraping the sides of the bowl often. Once the mixture is smooth, add the confectioners' sugar and beat until smooth. Beat in the vanilla and salt.

5. To assemble the cake, place one cake layer on a serving plate with the flat bottom side facing down. Spread 1 cup of frosting over the surface of the cake. Place half the mandarin oranges over the frosting. Top with another cake layer, inverted, so the bottom of the cake is facing up. Spread 1 cup of frosting over the cake layer and repeat with the remaining mandarin oranges. Place the remaining cake layer, also inverted, on top. Add 1 cup of the coconut to the remaining frosting and, using a rubber spatula, fold in to combine. Spread the remaining frosting over the top and sides of the cake. Sprinkle the remaining 2 cups coconut over the top and sides of the frosted cake, pressing gently to make sure the coconut stays put.

GRATE EXPECTATIONS

Grating carrots by hand can take a while, so try expediting the process in a food processor. You'll have a pile of grated carrots in as little time as it takes to say, "One, two, three!"

MISSISSIPPI MUD CAKE

This is a perfect cake to bring along to a potluck or bake sale, since you can carry and slice it right in the baking pan. Melting marshmallows on top of the just-baked cake is so fun that even when my grandbaby Jack isn't around, I find myself shouting "Yay!" as those marshmallows melt into a beautiful glaze.

SERVES 8 TO 10

Cake
1½ cups all-purpose flour
1½ cups sugar
¾ cup unsweetened cocoa powder, sifted
1½ teaspoons baking powder
1 teaspoon salt
1 cup whole milk
8 tablespoons (1 stick) butter, melted
2 large eggs

1 teaspoon vanilla extract
3 cups mini marshmallows

Glaze and Topping
1 cup pecan halves
¼ cup heavy cream
¼ cup light corn syrup
½ cup chopped semisweet chocolate
½ cup shredded sweetened coconut

1. Preheat the oven to 350°F. Grease a 13 by 9-inch baking pan with butter, oil, or cooking spray.

2. To prepare the cake: In a large bowl, whisk together the flour, sugar, cocoa powder, baking powder, and salt. In a medium bowl, whisk together the milk, melted butter, eggs, and vanilla. Using a rubber spatula, fold the milk mixture into the flour mixture just until combined. Pour the batter into the prepared pan. Bake until a toothpick inserted into the center of the cake comes out clean and the cake is firm to the touch, 30 to 40 minutes.

TAKING THE TEMPERATURE
Ovens really do have a tendency to fluctuate 5 to 10 degrees hot or cold and that can be a big problem when you're baking. I recommend investing in an oven thermometer that hangs from the rack in the oven. That way, you'll never have to guess what the temperature really is.

3. Take the cake out of the oven and scatter the marshmallows evenly over the top. Return the cake to the oven for 5 minutes to melt the marshmallows.

4. To make the glaze: Reduce the oven temperature to 325°F. Spread the pecans on a baking sheet and bake until fragrant, about 10 minutes. When cool enough to handle, coarsely chop the pecans.

5. In a medium saucepan, combine the cream, corn syrup, and chocolate. Stir over medium-low heat until the chocolate is melted. Pour the chocolate mixture over the top of the cake. Top with the pecans and coconut. Let cool completely before serving a slice of pure decadence.

NEW JAPANESE FRUITCAKE

■ ■

This is one for the history books, and as far as I can tell, it's been a Southern tradition for over a hundred years despite the fact that it has nothing to do with Japan. The basic formula looks something like this: a plain cake, a layer of spices, and a filling that includes coconut. I like versions with pineapple and cherries, like this one, though I use dried tart cherries in place of maraschino because I find they have more flavor. It leaves regular fruitcake in the dust.

SERVES 10 TO 12

Cake

2 sticks (8 ounces) butter,
   at room temperature
2 cups sugar
4 large eggs
3 cups all-purpose flour
1 tablespoon baking powder
1 teaspoon salt
1¼ cups whole milk
2 teaspoons vanilla extract

Spice Layer

2 teaspoons ground cinnamon
¼ teaspoon ground cloves
¼ teaspoon ground allspice
⅓ cup finely chopped crystallized ginger

Filling

1 cup sugar
2 tablespoons cornstarch
1 can (20 ounces) crushed pineapple, drained
1 cup shredded sweetened coconut
Pinch of salt
⅔ cup dried tart cherries

Frosting

½ teaspoon cream of tartar
2½ cups sugar
4 large egg whites
2 tablespoons light corn syrup
2 teaspoons vanilla extract

1. Preheat the oven to 350°F. Grease three 9-inch round cake pans with butter, oil, or cooking spray. Cut out three 9-inch rounds of parchment paper and line the bottoms of the pans.

2. To prepare the cake: In the bowl of an electric mixer fitted with the paddle attachment, or using a handheld mixer, beat the butter at medium speed until creamy and smooth, 1 to 2 minutes. Add the sugar and beat the mixture until light and fluffy, about 5 minutes. Be sure to scrape down the sides of the bowl occasionally to incorporate all the sugar into the butter. Add the eggs, one at a time, beating well after each egg is added to thoroughly combine.

3. In a medium bowl, whisk together the flour, baking powder, and salt. In a small bowl, whisk together the milk and vanilla. Beat one-third of the flour mixture into the egg mixture. Beat in

To determine soft peaks or firm peaks for whipped cream or whipped egg whites, turn the whisk upside down. If peaks are just starting to stand but quickly fall back on themselves, they are soft peaks. If peaks hold and ridges are more defined, with only the tips falling back on themselves, they are firm peaks.

half the milk mixture. Continue beating in the two mixtures, alternating them and ending with the flour mixture. Mix just until incorporated and scrape the sides of the bowl down occasionally.

4. Measure out one-third of the batter and place in a bowl. Stir in the cinnamon, cloves, allspice, and crystallized ginger. Spoon this spice-layer batter into one of the prepared pans and smooth the top. Divide the remaining batter between the two remaining pans and smooth the tops. Bake until a toothpick inserted into the center of each cake comes out clean, 23 to 25 minutes. Let the cakes cool in the pans for 10 minutes on wire racks. Then invert the cakes onto the racks, peel off the parchment paper, and let them cool completely before filling and frosting.

5. While the cake layers are baking, make the filling: In a large saucepan, whisk together the sugar and cornstarch. Whisk in 1 cup water. Add the pineapple, coconut, and salt. Bring to a boil over medium heat. Cook, stirring constantly, until the mixture thickens and jells, about 5 minutes. Stir in the dried cherries and let the mixture cool.

6. Once the cake layers and filling are cool, stack the cake layers, one on top of the other with the spice layer of cake in the middle, spreading each layer evenly with filling as you stack. (See the box for a guide to stacking.) Set aside while making the frosting.

7. To make the frosting: Bring a medium saucepan of water to a bare simmer on the stove. In the bowl of an electric mixer fitted with the whisk attachment, or using a handheld mixer, beat together all ingredients with ½ cup water just until combined. Place the bowl over the pan of simmering water and whisk by hand until the sugar dissolves and the mixture is hot, about 3 minutes. Set the bowl back on the mixer and beat at high speed for 3 minutes. Beat until stiff peaks form, 5 to 7 minutes more.

8. Spread the frosting over the top and sides of the cake, taking care not to let the filling show through the sides.

STACK IT UP

Here's a handy guide for stacking three layers of a cake so that they are as stable and even as possible. Place the bottom layer on the serving platter with the flat bottom side down for stability. Top with another cake layer, inverted, so the bottom of the cake is facing up. If it's a little unstable because the cake top domed a bit, you can slice off the mound to create a level base or just fill in with frosting or filling. Place the remaining cake layer, also inverted (i.e., bottom side up), on top. Push down on the layers gently with the palm of your hand just to make sure they are level. If they are not, use a serrated knife to shave the uneven parts to even them out.

OLD-TIME SPONGE CAKE

■ ■

I seem to recall that my mama made her cakes this way and called them hot milk cakes. It's the sort of recipe you can put together in the afternoon and surprise everyone with a few hours later. Feel free to use this simple cake recipe as a starting point for your own creations by slicing it and filling it with any fruit or frosting you like, or icing or glazing it.

SERVES 8

2 large eggs

1 large egg white

1¼ cups granulated sugar

6 tablespoons whole milk

1¼ cups all-purpose flour

1¼ teaspoons baking powder

½ teaspoon salt

2 teaspoons vanilla extract

2 tablespoons (¼ stick) butter, melted

Confectioners' sugar, for dusting

1. Preheat the oven to 350°F. Grease a 9-inch round cake pan with butter, oil, or cooking spray. Line the bottom of the pan with a round of parchment paper.

2. In the bowl of an electric mixer fitted with the whisk attachment, or using a handheld mixer, beat the whole eggs and egg white at high speed until frothy. With the mixer running, gradually stream in the granulated sugar and beat at high speed until the mixture has thickened and lightened to a pretty lemon yellow color.

A YELLOW RIBBON

Be sure to beat your eggs and granulated sugar for at least 5 minutes or so, so that they reach what's called the ribbon stage. That's when the mixture is thick enough that when you raise the beater, the batter falls back on itself in a ribbonlike swirl. If the ribbon trail sits on the surface for a few seconds before soaking back into the batter, you'll know you've whipped to the right consistency.

3. In a small saucepan, warm the milk to 200°F over medium heat.

4. In a small bowl, whisk together the flour, baking powder, and salt and, using a rubber spatula, fold into the egg mixture. Working quickly and gently, fold in the milk, vanilla, and melted butter until completely combined.

5. Gently spoon the batter into the prepared pan and bake until golden brown and firm to the touch, 30 to 35 minutes. Let the cake cool in the pan for 10 minutes on a rack. Then invert it onto a wire rack and peel off the parchment paper. Invert the cake again so the flat bottom is down and let it cool completely. Before serving, dust the cake with confectioners' sugar.

To dust a cake with confectioners' sugar or cocoa powder, place a few tablespoons of sugar or cocoa into a fine mesh strainer and tap lightly on the outside of the strainer as you move around the cake.

TENNESSEE WHISKEY BUNDT CAKE

■ ■

I just love a beautiful Bundt cake, with its ridges dripping with glaze. This one is a boozy, buttery bad boy that'll make you want to sass your mama!

SERVES 12

Cake
½ cup raisins
⅓ cup whiskey
2½ sticks (10 ounces) butter,
    at room temperature
1¾ cups packed light brown sugar
Grated zest of 1 lemon
5 large eggs
3¼ cups all-purpose flour
1 tablespoon baking powder

1 teaspoon salt
1 cup whole milk

Glaze
½ cup granulated sugar
2 tablespoons whiskey
Juice of ½ lemon

1. To make the cake: In a small bowl, stir together the raisins and whiskey. Let sit for at least 1 hour or overnight.

2. Preheat the oven to 325°F. Grease a 12-cup Bundt pan with butter, oil, or cooking spray.

3. In the bowl of an electric mixer fitted with the paddle attachment, or using a handheld mixer, beat the butter at medium speed until creamy and smooth, 1 to 2 minutes. Add the brown sugar and lemon zest and beat the mixture until light and fluffy, about 5 minutes. Be sure to scrape down the sides of the bowl occasionally to incorporate all the sugar into the butter. Add the eggs, one at a time, beating well after each egg is added to thoroughly combine.

4. In a medium bowl, whisk together the flour, baking powder, and salt. Beat one-third of the flour mixture into the egg mixture. Beat in half the milk. Continue adding the flour mixture and milk alternately, ending with the flour mixture. Mix just until incorporated, scraping the sides of the bowl down occasionally. Using a rubber spatula, fold in the raisins and whiskey.

5. Spoon the batter into the prepared pan, smoothing the top. Bake until a toothpick inserted into the center of the cake comes out clean, 1 hour to 1 hour and 5 minutes. Let the cake cool in the pan for 10 minutes on a wire rack before unmolding and letting the cake cool on the rack completely.

6. Once the cake is cool, make the glaze: In a small saucepan, whisk together the granulated sugar, whiskey, and lemon juice. Stir constantly over low heat until the sugar is dissolved.

7. Set the cake on the wire rack over a baking sheet or a piece of waxed paper. Brush the glaze evenly all over the cake. This one packs a punch!

SEE WHAT DEVELOPS

Be sure your raisins get a good soak in that whiskey! That process is called maceration, and what it does is soften up your raisins and gives them time to soak in the deliciously boozy flavor.

CINNAMON-GLAZED SOUR CREAM APPLE BUNDT CAKE

■ ■

There's just something about apples, cinnamon, and sour cream that is so satisfying, especially in the fall when you want your house to smell like sweet spices.

SERVES 10 TO 12

Cake

2 sticks (8 ounces) butter, at room
    temperature
1¾ cups granulated sugar
4 large eggs
2½ cups all-purpose flour
2 teaspoons baking powder
1 teaspoon baking soda
1 teaspoon salt
1 cup sour cream

2½ teaspoons vanilla extract
¼ teaspoon almond extract
2 medium Granny Smith apples, peeled,
    cored, and finely chopped

Glaze

1 cup confectioners' sugar, sifted
1 teaspoon ground cinnamon
2 to 3 tablespoons whole milk

1. Preheat the oven to 325°F. Grease a 12-cup Bundt pan with butter, oil, or cooking spray. Flour the pan generously, shaking out the excess.

2. To make the cake: In the bowl of an electric mixer fitted with the paddle attachment, or using a handheld mixer, beat the butter at medium speed until creamy and smooth, 1 to 2 minutes. Add the granulated sugar and beat the mixture until light and fluffy, about 5 minutes. Be sure to scrape down the sides of the bowl occasionally to incorporate all the sugar into the butter. Add the eggs, one at a time, beating well after each egg is added to thoroughly combine.

3. In a medium bowl, whisk together the flour, baking powder, baking soda, and salt. In a small bowl, whisk together the sour cream, vanilla, and almond extract. Beat one-third of the flour mixture into the egg mixture. Beat in half the sour cream mixture. Continue adding the mixtures alternately, ending with the flour mixture. Mix just until incorporated, scraping the sides of the bowl down occasionally. Using a rubber spatula, fold in the apples.

4. Spoon the batter into the prepared pan, smoothing the top. Bake until a toothpick inserted into the center of the cake comes out clean, 1 hour to 1 hour and 5 minutes. Let the cake cool in the pan for 10 minutes on a wire rack before inverting and letting the cake cool on the rack completely.

5. Once the cake is cool, make the glaze: In a small bowl, whisk together the confectioners' sugar and cinnamon. Whisk in the milk, 1 tablespoon at a time, until the glaze is thick but pourable. Set the cake on the wire rack over a baking sheet or a piece of waxed paper. Spoon the glaze evenly over the cake.

> **GRATE IDEA**
>
> Make quick work of bringing cold butter to room temperature by grating it on the coarse side of a cheese grater. Or slice it thinly and place it in a bowl set over another bowl that is filled with a little warm water. Just be sure not to melt the butter in the process!

FROSTED BUTTERMILK FIG CAKE

Right after I met Michael I noticed this huge fig tree in his yard, and when I asked him about it, he said, to my surprise, "Oh, we don't use 'em—the birds just eat 'em. So if you would like to come over and get you some figs, you're welcome to 'em anytime." Well, I went and dragged up a tall ladder and climbed up to get those figs. And his children were in the house, and some of their friends were over, and one of their friends said, "There's some old lady in one of y'all's trees. You know who she is?" Well, love conquers all, as they say, and we just laughed about that one. Then I made Michael the first fig preserves he ever had and he just loved it (see Fig Jam, page 421). I fold them into a cake whenever I get the itch.

SERVES 6 TO 8

Cake

3 cups cake flour

2 teaspoons baking powder

¾ teaspoon grated nutmeg

¾ teaspoon salt

1 cup chopped pecans

2 sticks (8 ounces) butter, melted

1 cup granulated sugar

1 cup packed dark brown sugar

3 large eggs, lightly beaten

1 cup Fig Jam (page 421) or fig preserves, chopped

½ cup boiling water

1½ teaspoons baking soda

Frosting

4 sticks (1 pound) butter, at room temperature

10 cups confectioners' sugar, sifted

⅔ to ¾ cup buttermilk

2 teaspoons vanilla extract

⅛ teaspoon salt

1. Preheat the oven to 325°F. Grease three 8-inch round cake pans with butter, oil, or cooking spray. Line the bottoms with rounds of parchment paper.

2. To make the cake: In a large bowl, whisk together the flour, baking powder, nutmeg, salt, and pecans. In a medium bowl, whisk together the butter, both sugars, and the eggs. Fold the fig preserves into the egg mixture. In a small bowl, whisk together the boiling water and baking soda, then whisk this into the egg mixture. Using a rubber spatula, fold the egg mixture into the flour mixture until combined.

3. Divide the batter evenly among the prepared pans. Bake until a toothpick inserted into the center of each cake comes out clean and the cakes are firm to the touch and golden brown, 25 to 30 minutes. Let the cakes cool in the pans for 10 minutes on wire racks. Invert the cakes onto the racks, peel off the parchment paper, and let them cool completely before frosting.

4. While the cake layers are cooling, make the frosting: In the bowl of an electric mixer fitted with the paddle attachment, or using a handheld mixer, beat the butter at medium speed until smooth and creamy, scraping the sides of the bowl often. Once the mixture is smooth, add the confectioners' sugar, 1 cup at a time, to incorporate and beat until smooth. Beat in ⅔ cup buttermilk, the vanilla, and salt. Add extra buttermilk if needed, 1 tablespoon at a time, until the frosting is thick but spreadable.

5. To assemble the cake, place 1 cake layer on a serving plate, with the flat bottom side facing down. Spread a generous cup of frosting over the surface of the cake. Top with another cake layer, inverted, so the bottom of the cake is facing up. Spread 1 cup of frosting over this cake layer. Place the remaining cake layer, also inverted, on top. Spread the remaining frosting over the top and sides of the cake. For a decorative touch, create pretty swirls in the frosting by sliding your spatula around in little S shapes.

PECAN SPICE LAYER CAKE
WITH CARAMEL FROSTING

■ ■

I've always been a quick cook, so I never make burnt sugar caramel to flavor my caramel frosting. Instead, I have found that using brown and confectioners' sugars gives you a quick, easy frosting with the deep, dark caramel flavor. It's a natural partner for the pecans and spice in this cake, which is one of the most handsome cakes you could hope for.

SERVES 10 TO 12

Cake

1¼ cups chopped pecans

1½ sticks (6 ounces) butter, at room
   temperature

¾ cup granulated sugar

¾ cup packed light brown sugar

3 large eggs

2½ cups cake flour, sifted

2 teaspoons ground cinnamon

2 teaspoons baking powder

¾ teaspoon baking soda

¾ teaspoon salt

1¼ cups buttermilk

1 teaspoon vanilla extract

Frosting

3 sticks (12 ounces) butter, at room
   temperature

1 cup packed light brown sugar

1 cup packed dark brown sugar

½ cup whole milk

4¼ cups confectioners' sugar, sifted

2 teaspoons vanilla extract

1. Preheat the oven to 325°F. Grease three 8-inch round cake pans with butter, oil, or cooking spray. Cut out three 8-inch rounds of parchment paper and line the bottoms of the pans.

2. To make the cake: Place the pecans on a baking sheet and bake until fragrant, about 10 minutes. Leave the oven on but increase the temperature to 350°F.

3. Meanwhile, in the bowl of an electric mixer fitted with the paddle attachment, or using a handheld mixer, beat the butter at medium speed until creamy and smooth, 1 to 2 minutes. Add both sugars and beat the mixture until light and fluffy, about 5 minutes. Be sure to scrape down the sides of the bowl occasionally to incorporate all the sugar into the butter. Add the eggs, one at a time, beating well after each egg is added to thoroughly combine.

4. In a medium bowl, whisk together the flour, cinnamon, baking powder, baking soda, and salt. In a small bowl, whisk together the buttermilk and vanilla. Beat one-third of the flour mixture

into the egg mixture. Beat in half the buttermilk mixture. Continue beating in the mixtures, alternating them and ending with the flour mixture. Mix just until incorporated, scraping the sides of the bowl down occasionally. Using a rubber spatula, fold in the pecans.

5. Divide the batter among the prepared pans, smoothing the tops. Bake until a toothpick inserted into the center of each cake comes out clean, 23 to 25 minutes. Let the cakes cool in the pans on wire racks for 10 minutes. Then invert the cakes out of the pans onto the racks, peel off the parchment paper, and let them cool completely before frosting.

6. While the cake layers are cooling, make the frosting: In a medium saucepan, melt the butter over medium heat. Stir in both brown sugars. Slowly whisk in the milk. Place the mixture in the bowl of an electric mixer fitted with the paddle attachment or use a handheld mixer. Add the confectioners' sugar, ½ cup at a time, and beat at medium-low speed until smooth. Beat in the vanilla.

7. To assemble the cake, place one cake layer on a pretty serving plate, with the flat bottom side facing down. Spread just less than 1 cup of frosting over the surface of the cake. Top with another cake layer, inverted, so the bottom of the cake is facing up. Spread just less than 1 cup of frosting over this cake layer. Place the remaining cake layer, also inverted, on top. Spread the remaining frosting over the top and sides of the cake.

FLOUR AND FOLD

Here's a neat little trick I like to use when I'm adding nuts or chopped dried fruit to my batter. Toss them in some flour before folding them in. This will help them to suspend better in the batter, evenly distributing them throughout your cake and preventing them from dropping to the bottom.

To frost the cake, first let the cake cool completely. Brush away any stray crumbs on the outside of the cake. Seal the cake by applying a very thin coating of frosting, touching the unfrosted cake as little as possible to avoid lifting crumbs into the frosting. Let it sit for about 15 minutes. Spoon a generous amount of frosting on top of the cake and push it around with an offset spatula.

TEXAS SHEET CAKE WITH CHOCOLATE FUDGE FROSTING

■ ■

Whatever you do with this recipe, try your best to bring the leftovers back home with you in the pan. There is no better snack than a leftover piece of Texas sheet cake. The frosting is so fudgy and chewy, and the cake is so moist and flavorful.

SERVES 8 TO 10

Cake
1 cup boiling water

⅓ cup unsweetened cocoa powder, sifted

2 sticks (8 ounces) butter, melted

2 large eggs, lightly beaten

½ cup buttermilk

1 teaspoon vanilla extract

2 cups all-purpose flour

1 cup packed light brown sugar

1 cup granulated sugar

1 teaspoon baking soda

¾ teaspoon salt

½ teaspoon baking powder

Frosting
1 cup granulated sugar

½ cup unsweetened cocoa powder, sifted

> **LIVING LARGE**
>
> Don't try to substitute another size egg for the large eggs called for in baking recipes. It makes a big difference because large eggs are required to fall within a specific weight range that works for standard baking recipes. Eggs that are larger or smaller can throw off your recipe's proportions and give you an unexpected result.

½ cup whole milk

4 tablespoons (½ stick) butter, cut into small bits

2 tablespoons light corn syrup

4 cups confectioners' sugar, sifted

2 teaspoons vanilla extract

1. Preheat the oven to 350°F. Grease a 13 by 9-inch baking pan with butter, oil, or cooking spray.

2. To make the cake: In a medium bowl, whisk together the boiling water and cocoa powder. Stir in the melted butter. Whisk in the eggs, buttermilk, and vanilla. In another medium bowl, whisk together the flour, both sugars, the baking soda, salt, and baking powder. Fold the flour mixture into the chocolate mixture until combined. Pour the batter into the prepared pan. Bake until a toothpick inserted into the center of the cake comes out clean, 30 to 35 minutes.

3. While the cake is baking, prepare the frosting: In a large saucepan, whisk together the granu-

lated sugar and cocoa powder. Whisk in the milk, then stir in the butter and corn syrup. Place the pan over medium-high heat and bring to a boil, whisking constantly. Off the heat, stir in the confectioners' sugar and vanilla.

4. Spread the frosting over the surface of the cake just as soon as it comes out of the oven. Let the cake cool on a rack, then serve it up.

LADY BALTIMORE CAKE

■ ■

Well, I leave it to the history buffs to debate whether or not this fine layer cake originated in Charleston at the Lady Baltimore Tearoom. But I have never met a Southerner who isn't fond of this combination of white cake, dried fruit in the filling, and fluffy white frosting.

SERVES 10 TO 12

Cake
2 sticks (8 ounces) butter, at room
    temperature
1½ cups sugar
3 cups cake flour, sifted
1 tablespoon baking powder
1 teaspoon salt
1 cup whole milk, at room temperature
1 tablespoon vanilla extract
6 large egg whites
¼ teaspoon cream of tartar

Filling
¾ cup chopped pecans
¾ cup chopped dried figs
3 tablespoons ruby or tawny port

Frosting
½ teaspoon cream of tartar
2½ cups sugar
4 large egg whites
2 tablespoons light corn syrup
2 teaspoons vanilla extract

1. Preheat the oven to 325°F. Grease three 9-inch round cake pans with butter, oil, or cooking spray. Cut out three 9-inch rounds of parchment paper and line the bottoms of the pans.

2. To prepare the cake: In the bowl of an electric mixer fitted with the paddle attachment, or using a handheld mixer, beat the butter at medium speed until creamy and smooth, 1 to 2 minutes. Add 1 cup of the sugar and beat the mixture until light and fluffy, about 5 minutes. Be sure to scrape down the sides of the bowl occasionally to incorporate all the sugar into the butter.

3. In a medium bowl, whisk together the flour, baking powder, and salt. In a small bowl, whisk together the milk and vanilla. Beat one-third of the flour mixture into the butter mixture. Beat in half the milk mixture. Continue beating in the mixtures, alternating them and ending with the flour mixture. Mix just until incorporated, scraping the sides of the bowl down occasionally.

4. In another mixer bowl, using the whisk attachment, beat the egg whites and cream of tartar at medium-high speed until frothy. With the mixer running, slowly stream in the remaining ½ cup sugar and beat at medium-high speed until stiff peaks form and appear glossy but not dry. Using a rubber spatula, gently fold the egg whites into the cake batter.

5. Divide the batter among the prepared pans, smoothing the tops. Bake until a toothpick inserted into the center of each cake comes out clean, 25 to 30 minutes. (Leave the oven on for the pecans; see step 6.) Let the cakes cool in the pans on wire racks for 10 minutes. Invert the cakes onto the racks, peel off the parchment paper, and then let cool completely before frosting.

6. While the cake layers are cooling, prepare the filling: Spread the pecans on a baking sheet and bake until fragrant, about 10 minutes.

7. In a medium bowl, stir together the figs, pecans, and port. Set aside.

8. Once the cake layers are cool, make the frosting: Bring a medium saucepan of water to barely a simmer. In the bowl of an electric mixer fitted with the whisk attachment, or using a handheld mixer, beat together all the ingredients with ½ cup water at medium speed just until combined. Place the bowl over the pan of simmering water and whisk by hand until the sugar dissolves and the mixture is hot, about 3 minutes. Set the bowl back on the mixer and beat at high speed for 3 minutes. Beat until stiff peaks form, 5 to 7 minutes more. Measure out 3 cups of the frosting and fold into the filling until thoroughly combined. Set the remaining frosting aside.

9. To assemble the cake, place 1 cake layer on a serving plate, with the flat bottom side facing down. Spread half of the filling over the surface of the cake. Top with another cake layer, inverted, so the bottom of the cake is facing up. Spread the remaining filling over this cake layer. Place the remaining cake layer, also inverted, on top. Spread the frosting over the top and sides of the cake.

FINEST FLOUR

Cake flour has a lower protein content than all-purpose flour and a soft texture that results in the lightest, fluffiest cakes. If you're having trouble finding it, you can use this substitution: for every 1 cup cake flour, use ¾ cup sifted bleached all-purpose flour mixed with 2 tablespoons cornstarch.

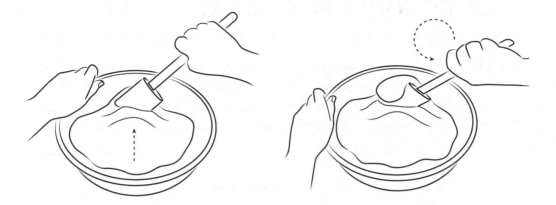

Always fold in whipped egg whites or whipped cream by hand, preferably with a rubber spatula, to avoid deflating the air in the whipped ingredient. Add a third of the egg whites or cream to the bowl and place the spatula in the center of the batter. Sweep the spatula up toward the side of the bowl to scoop batter from the bottom of the bowl, then fold over. Give the bowl a turn and repeat this motion. Add the remaining egg whites or cream in two batches, and mix only until incorporated.

OOEY GOOEY BUTTER LAYER CAKE

■■■■■■■■■■■■■■■■■■■■■■■■■■■■■■■■■■■■■

Now, y'all, the folks over at *Cooking with Paula Deen* magazine like to take a good idea and make it even better! We took my legendary gooey butter cakes and turned them into a sheet pan cake, adding a sweet cream cheese frosting. All these buttery, moist cake layers with the gooey orange filling all covered with frosting—now that's a real statement of pleasure, if you ask me.

SERVES 12 TO 16

Cake
3 sticks (12 ounces) butter,
   at room temperature
2¼ cups granulated sugar
5 large eggs
1 teaspoon vanilla extract
3½ cups all-purpose flour
1 tablespoon baking powder
½ teaspoon baking soda
¼ teaspoon salt
1¼ cups buttermilk
1 cup sour cream

Butter Filling
8 tablespoons (1 stick) butter
¾ cup granulated sugar
⅓ cup orange juice
3 large eggs
1 package (8 ounces) cream cheese, cubed, at
   room temperature

Frosting
1 package (8 ounces) cream cheese, at room
   temperature
8 tablespoons (1 stick) butter, at room
   temperature
1 tablespoon vanilla extract
6 cups confectioners' sugar

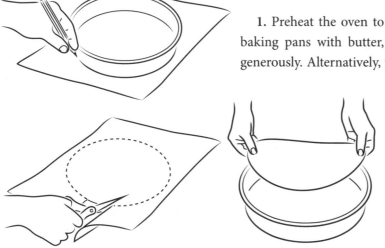

1. Preheat the oven to 350°F. Grease three 9-inch round baking pans with butter, oil, or cooking spray, then flour generously. Alternatively, you can cut out wax or parchment paper circles to line the bottoms of your cake pans.

2. To make the cake: In the bowl of an electric mixer fitted

Trace the base of the cake pan on parchment paper (waxed paper works, too). Cut out along the tracing and place inside the pan.

with the paddle attachment, or using a handheld mixer, beat the butter and sugar together at medium speed until light and fluffy, about 5 minutes. Be sure to scrape down the sides of the bowl occasionally to incorporate all the sugar into the butter. Add the eggs, one at a time, beating well after each egg is added to thoroughly combine. Beat in the vanilla.

3. In a medium bowl, combine the flour, baking powder, baking soda, and salt. Beat one-third of the flour mixture into the egg mixture. Beat in half of the buttermilk. Continuing beating in the flour mixture and buttermilk, alternating them and ending with the flour mixture. Mix just until incorporated, scraping the sides of the bowl down occasionally. Using a rubber spatula, stir in the sour cream.

4. Divide the batter among the prepared pans and smooth the tops. Bake until a toothpick inserted into the center of each cake comes out clean, 24 to 30 minutes. Let the cakes cool in the pans on wire racks for 10 minutes. Invert the cakes onto the racks, peel off the parchment paper, and let them cool completely before frosting.

5. While the cake layers are baking, make the butter filling: In the top of a double boiler or a bowl fitted snugly over a pan of simmering water, melt the butter. Remove from the heat and whisk in the granulated sugar, orange juice, and eggs until the mixture is smooth. Return the double boiler to the heat, and cook, whisking constantly, until the mixture is very thick (see box), 15 to 20 minutes. Whisk in the cream cheese. Remove the double boiler top or the bowl from the pan and let cool for 30 minutes.

6. Spoon the mixture into a bowl, cover with plastic wrap right up against the surface of the filling to prevent a skin from forming, and chill for at least 4 hours.

> ### WHISK AWAY
> When you're whisking your gooey butter filling and waitin' on that filling to get all nice and thick, just keep in mind that before it gets thick, it'll thin out at first. Don't worry about that. This happens because the mixture is heatin' up. But as moisture starts to evaporate, this filling will thicken up. Just remember to keep stirring and watch out for air bubbles—you don't want to beat air into your filling.

7. To assemble the cake, place 1 cake layer on a serving plate, with the flat bottom side facing down. Spread half of the butter filling over the surface of the cake. Top with another cake layer, inverted, so the bottom of the cake is facing up. Spread with the remaining butter filling. Place the remaining cake layer, also inverted, on top. Cover and freeze for at least 1 hour.

8. While the cake is in the freezer, make the frosting: In the bowl of an electric mixer fitted with the paddle attachment, or using a handheld mixer, beat the cream cheese, butter, and vanilla together at medium speed until light and fluffy, about 2 minutes. At low speed, beat in the confectioners' sugar, ½ cup at a time. If the frosting is too soft, chill it for 10 minutes before using.

9. Remove the cake from the freezer and spread the frosting over the top and sides of the cake. Refrigerate the cake, covered, until your guests arrive.

GENERAL ROBERT E. LEE CAKE

■ ■

I just love this old-fashioned cake invented to honor General Lee. It's a big, tall layer cake full of bright lemon and orange flavors and frosted with a citrus buttercream that is just so mouthwateringly delicious.

SERVES 10 TO 12

Lemon Curd Filling
2 large eggs
4 large egg yolks
1⅓ cups sugar
⅔ cup fresh lemon juice (2 to 3 large lemons)
Grated zest of 2 lemons
Grated zest of 2 oranges
1½ sticks (6 ounces) cold butter,
    cut into small bits

Cake
2 sticks (8 ounces) butter,
    at room temperature
2 cups sugar
Grated zest of 1 lemon
Grated zest of 1 orange
4 large eggs

3 cups cake flour, sifted
2½ teaspoons baking powder
1 teaspoon baking soda
1 teaspoon salt
1 cup buttermilk, at room temperature
1 tablespoon vanilla extract

Buttercream Frosting
4 sticks (1 pound) butter, cut into small bits,
    at room temperature
3 tablespoons fresh lemon juice
2 tablespoons fresh orange juice, strained
4 large egg whites
1 cup sugar
⅛ teaspoon cream of tartar
Pinch of salt

1. To make the lemon curd filling: In a heavy-bottomed saucepan, whisk together the whole eggs, egg yolks, sugar, lemon juice, lemon zest, and orange zest. Place the pan over medium heat and stir constantly until the mixture thickens enough to coat the back of a spoon, 10 to 15 minutes. Off the heat, whisk in the cold butter. Strain through a fine-mesh sieve into a bowl. Cover the surface directly with plastic wrap. Make sure that the plastic wrap is right up against the lemon curd filling so that it doesn't form a skin. Refrigerate until thoroughly chilled, at least 2 hours.

2. When you're ready to make the cake, preheat the oven to 350°F. Grease three 9-inch round cake pans with butter, oil, or cooking spray. Cut out three 9-inch rounds of parchment paper and line the bottoms of the pans.

3. In the bowl of an electric mixer fitted with the paddle attachment, or using a handheld mixer, beat the butter at medium speed until creamy and smooth, 1 to 2 minutes. Add the sugar, lemon zest, and orange zest and beat until light and fluffy, about 5 minutes. Be sure to scrape down the sides of the bowl occasionally to incorporate all the sugar into the butter. Add the eggs, one at a time, beating well after each egg is added to thoroughly combine.

4. In a medium bowl, whisk together the flour, baking powder, baking soda, and salt. In a small bowl, whisk together the buttermilk and vanilla. Beat one-third of the flour mixture into the egg mixture. Beat in half the buttermilk mixture. Continue beating in the mixtures, alternating them and ending with the flour mixture. Mix just until incorporated, scraping the sides of the bowl down occasionally.

5. Divide the batter among the prepared pans, smoothing the tops. Bake until a toothpick inserted into the center of each cake comes out clean, 23 to 25 minutes. Let the cakes cool in the pans on wire racks for 10 minutes. Invert the cakes onto the racks, peel off the parchment paper, and let them cool completely before frosting.

6. While the cake layers are cooling, make the buttercream frosting: In the bowl of an electric mixer fitted with the paddle attachment, or using a handheld mixer, beat the butter at medium speed until soft and creamy, 2 to 3 minutes. Beat in the lemon juice and orange juice until combined, about 1 minute. Place in a small bowl and set aside.

7. Bring a medium saucepan of water to barely a simmer. In the bowl of an electric mixer fitted with the whisk attachment, or using a handheld mixer, whisk together the egg whites, sugar, cream of tartar, and salt at medium speed. Set the bowl over the pan of simmering water and whisk by hand constantly until the mixture registers 140°F on a candy thermometer, about 10 minutes. Set the bowl back on the mixer and beat at high speed until the mixture has cooled and soft peaks form, 5 to 10 minutes. Add the creamed butter, ¼ cup at a time, beating well after each addition until smooth.

8. Once the cake layers are cool, assemble the cake: Place 1 cake layer on a serving plate, with the flat bottom side facing down. Spread half of the lemon curd filling over the surface of the cake. Top with another cake layer, inverted, so the bottom of the cake is facing up. Spread the remaining filling over this cake layer. Place the remaining cake layer, also inverted, on top. Spread the buttercream frosting over the top and sides of the cake. Then go on ahead and invite the ladies over for some tea and cake!

DO AHEAD
Save yourself some steps on the day you are making this lovely cake by making the lemon curd ahead of time. It can be made up to 2 days in advance and kept in the fridge. Make sure you cover it well with plastic wrap right up against the curd, so that it doesn't form a skin.

STACK CAKE

Cross a stack of pancakes and a wonderful layer cake and you have a sense of what stack cake is all about. Now, this cake is a real labor of love, since you will end up baking 6 layers in two batches, but when it's all stacked up and coated in glaze, people will fight over it. The thin layers make the ratio of icing to cake so fabulous, and it's a real looker, to boot.

SERVES 10 TO 12

Cake

2½ sticks (10 ounces) butter, at room temperature

2½ cups granulated sugar

5 large eggs

2½ cups cake flour

2 cups all-purpose flour

2½ teaspoons baking powder

2 teaspoons baking soda

2 teaspoons salt

2 cups whole milk

1 tablespoon vanilla extract

Glaze

4 cups granulated sugar

¾ cup packed light brown sugar

½ cup unsweetened cocoa powder, sifted

8 tablespoons (1 stick) butter, cut into small bits

1 can (12 ounces) evaporated milk

¾ cup whole milk

1 tablespoon vanilla extract

Pinch of salt

1. Preheat the oven to 400°F. Grease three 9-inch round cake pans with butter, oil, or cooking spray. Cut out three 9-inch rounds of parchment paper and line the bottom of the pans.

2. To make the cake: In the bowl of an electric mixer fitted with the paddle attachment, or using a handheld mixer, beat the butter at medium speed until creamy and smooth, 1 to 2 minutes. Add the granulated sugar and beat the mixture until light and fluffy, about 5 minutes. Be sure to scrape down the sides of the bowl occasionally to incorporate all the sugar into the butter. Add the eggs, one at a time, beating well after each egg is added to thoroughly combine.

3. In a medium bowl, sift together both flours, the baking powder, baking soda, and salt. In a small bowl, whisk together the milk and vanilla. Beat one-third of the flour mixture into the egg mixture. Beat in half the milk mixture. Continue adding the mixtures, alternating them and ending with the flour mixture. Mix just until incorporated, scraping the sides of the bowl down occasionally.

4. Spread a scant 1 cup batter in each prepared pan. Bake until light golden brown and firm to the touch, 9 to 10 minutes. While they're still warm, invert the cakes out of the pans onto wire

racks. Peel off the parchment paper. Regrease and reline the pans with new parchment paper rounds. Spread another scant 1 cup batter in each pan and bake again.

5. While the cakes are baking, make the glaze: In a large, heavy-bottomed saucepan, whisk together both sugars and the cocoa powder. Add the butter and both milks, place the pan over medium-high heat, and bring to a boil. Boil for 5 minutes, stirring constantly. Reduce the heat to a simmer and cook, stirring often, until slightly thickened, 5 to 10 minutes. Whisk in the vanilla and salt.

6. While the cake layers are still warm, assemble the cake. Place a cake layer on a large serving plate with the flat bottom side facing down. Pour ¼ cup of glaze over the cake layer, using a small spatula to spread the glaze to the edges. Repeat with the second batch of cakes as it comes out of the oven. Once all the cake layers have been assembled and glazed, glaze the top and sides of the cake with the remaining glaze. You will be able to see each cake layer right through this beautiful glaze.

IN THE THICK

If you find the glaze to be a little thin, just give it a little time to cool down so that it thickens up and really coats your layers when you pour it on.

Chapter 15

PUDDINGS AND FROZEN TREATS

To me, pudding is the epitome of a Southern dessert: simple, sweet, comforting, and everyday delicious. A bowl of pudding just makes things right. I remember when I was a kid, my brother and I would come home many a day and our mama would have the most incredible casserole dish of warm banana pudding waitin' on us for an after-school treat. Oh, my gosh, my brother and I would stand up and eat almost the whole dish!

Later, when I was older and doing my Bag Lady lunches, I made Fridays pudding days, and you know I just could not make enough of those—everyone wanted some. It is a comfort food and a great way to use up what you've already got in the kitchen. I think many puddings come from the Depression era, when women were in their kitchens without much of anything, trying to come up with something sweet to serve. And since a Southerner always has stale biscuits or bread lying around, they found a way to take that and give their family a wonderful dessert made with leftover products and few ingredients.

When I'm trying my hardest to rustle up something special from just about nothing, I always think of making a Creamy Rice Pudding (page 395), Cream Cheese–Chocolate Chip Bread Pudding (page 400), or even a Classic Trifle (page 401). I always keep milk and cream in the fridge, condensed milk in the pantry along with custard mix, and a plain ol' pound cake in the freezer. And, of course, my girls out in the chicken coop provide us eggs! With these basic ingredients on hand, the desserts in this chapter are real quick favorite treats around our house.

Another easy and delightful treat that we turn to a lot in our house is ice cream. Ice creams are about as easy as freezing a simple custard or pudding now that we have a countertop ice cream maker, and I am thankful for electricity every time. Where I grew up, at my grandmama's place in River Bend, Georgia, we would sit out there on the porch taking turns churning that ice cream crank. It was such a production, but of course we had plenty of incentive. If you haven't made yourself a batch of Real, Homemade Vanilla Ice Cream (page 403) on a summer night, you better fix that.

For a while there, Michael and I got into a bit of a nightly ice cream habit, mixing up little batches of ice cream flavored with whatever I could think of. Sweet Potato Ice Cream (page 406) was probably our most surprising success. Then we tried to lighten things up a bit, so I made up some real beautiful sherbets, using frozen fruit and jam like I do for my Quick Raspberry Sherbet recipe (page 407). Whatever you've got on hand can go into the ice cream maker. When it's watermelon season down here, we have so many we just have to keep at 'em, and one evening I discovered that Watermelon Ice (page 408) is just about the most refreshing thing a person can serve on a hot, humid night. Just goes to show you that sometimes the most indulgent pleasures can be some of the simplest and easiest ones to whip up.

CREAMY RICE PUDDING

■ ■

I just love a real creamy rice pudding studded with plump, juicy raisins—it is such a comforting treat. I like to serve this warm on a cold winter's night, topped with whipped cream and freshly grated nutmeg—it's like eggnog in a bowl. It's also tasty chilled the next day.

SERVES 6

4 cups whole milk
1 cup long-grain white rice
½ cup sugar
1 cinnamon stick
Pinch of salt
½ cup raisins

½ cup heavy cream
2 large egg yolks
1 teaspoon vanilla extract
Whipped cream and grated nutmeg,
    for serving

1. In a medium saucepan, combine 1 cup water, the milk, rice, sugar, cinnamon stick, and salt. Bring to a boil over medium-high heat. Reduce to a simmer and cook, uncovered, until the rice is tender and the milk has been absorbed, 40 to 45 minutes. In the last 5 minutes of cooking, stir in the raisins.

2. In a small bowl, whisk together the cream, egg yolks, and vanilla. Remove the saucepan from the heat and whisk the cream mixture into the rice. Serve with whipped cream and freshly grated nutmeg.

NICE PUDDING

While rice pudding can be found in the cooking lore of just about every culture, this recipe makes up a traditional American-style rice pudding. If you feel like changing up the flavors a bit, try adding some ground allspice or cloves. Or grate some lemon or orange zest into the mix. For even more flavor, the raisins can be plumped in sherry or orange juice before you stir them in.

OLD-FASHIONED BAKED CHOCOLATE PUDDING

■ ■

Don't even think of baking yourself a chocolate pudding unless you're planning to serve it with a dollop of freshly whipped cream. It just goes so perfectly with the silky chocolate pudding. Some things are just meant to be, y'all.

SERVES 6

½ cup sugar
¼ cup unsweetened cocoa powder, sifted
1½ cups whole milk
½ cup heavy cream
Pinch of salt

4 large egg yolks
4 ounces semisweet chocolate, finely chopped
Lightly sweetened whipped cream, for serving

1. Preheat the oven to 300°F. Have handy a large pot of boiling water. Place six 6- or 8-ounce custard cups in a large roasting pan.

2. In a large, heavy-bottomed saucepan, whisk together the sugar and cocoa powder. Whisk in the milk, cream, and salt. Bring to a simmer over medium-high heat.

3. Meanwhile, lightly whisk the egg yolks in a medium bowl. Whisking constantly, gradually pour the hot milk mixture into the egg yolks. Pour the mixture back into the saucepan and cook over medium-low heat, stirring constantly with a heatproof spatula, until the custard thickens slightly, 2 to 3 minutes. Be sure to scrape the bottom and sides of the pan and don't let the custard come to a boil.

A water bath provides moisture in the oven and protects delicate dishes such as puddings and custards from strong direct heat. To create a water bath, place a pan large enough to hold the custard cups on an oven rack. Fill with enough hot water to reach halfway up the height of the cups.

4. Place the chopped chocolate in a medium bowl. Remove the custard mixture from the heat and strain through a fine-mesh sieve set over the bowl of chocolate; whisk until the chocolate is melted and smooth.

5. Pour the custard into the custard cups. Pour enough boiling water into the roasting pan to come halfway up the sides of the custard cups. Bake until the custard is just set and jiggles like jelly, about 25 minutes (if using 8-ounce custard cups, check on the custard after 20 minutes). Let

cool to room temperature before covering the surface of each pudding entirely with plastic wrap and refrigerating until cold. Serve topped with a big dollop of whipped cream. (To make whipped cream, add 2 tablespoons sugar to 2 cups cold heavy cream and, using a whisk or a handheld electric mixer, whip until soft peaks form.)

> **AVOID A SPILL**
>
> It can be tricky moving your roasting pan full of boiling water and custard cups from the counter to the oven rack. For that reason, I recommend pouring the water into the roasting pan while it's sitting on the pulled-out oven rack. That way, all you have to do is gently push the rack in and close the oven door.

NOT YO MAMA'S BANANA PUDDING

I like to use Chessmen cookies because they're hearty and buttery and crunchy all at once—and they're a time-saver. But I *do* go to the trouble of making homemade whipped cream (instead of using whipped topping) because it's worth the time. No matter where I am, someone will shout out "Not Yo Mama's Banana Pudding." Make it and find out why it's so famous.

SERVES 12

2 bags (7¼ ounces each) Pepperidge Farm
    Chessmen cookies
6 to 8 bananas, cut into ¼-inch-thick slices
2 cups cold heavy cream
2 tablespoons sugar
2 cups whole milk

1 package (5 ounces) instant French vanilla
    pudding
1 can (14 ounces) sweetened condensed milk
1 package (8 ounces) cream cheese, at room
    temperature

1. Line the bottom of a 13 by 9-inch baking dish with 1 bag of cookies and layer the bananas on top.

2. In a chilled bowl, using a whisk or a handheld electric mixer (or in a chilled bowl of a stand mixer fitted with a whisk attachment) at medium-high speed, whip the cream and the sugar until stiff peaks form.

3. In a medium bowl, combine the whole milk and pudding mix and blend well using a hand-held electric mixer. In another medium bowl, beat the condensed milk and cream cheese together until smooth. Using a rubber spatula, fold the whipped cream into the cream cheese mixture. Add the cream cheese mixture to the pudding mixture and stir until well blended. Pour the mixture over the cookies and bananas and top with the remaining bag of cookies. Cover with plastic wrap and refrigerate for 3 hours.

NOT A COOKIE CUTTER

Sometimes I switch out the Chessmen cookies for chocolate cookies and add some chocolate shavings on top. The combination is pure decadence.

CLASSIC BANANA PUDDING

This is a nostalgic traditional banana pudding that folks go crazy for every time, and rightly so—there's just nothing more comforting and delicious. Set it out at a covered-dish buffet next to someone's fancy little fruit tart, and you'll see what I mean.

SERVES 8 TO 12

Filling
¾ cup granulated sugar
½ cup packed light brown sugar
½ cup cornstarch
¼ teaspoon salt
6 large egg yolks
4 cups whole milk
8 tablespoons (1 stick) cold butter,
   cut into small bits

4 teaspoons vanilla extract
About 50 vanilla wafers (or half an
   11-ounce box)
3 large or 4 medium bananas, cut into
   ¼-inch-thick slices

Topping
2 cups heavy cream
3 tablespoons granulated sugar

1. To make the filling: In a medium bowl, whisk together both sugars, the cornstarch, and salt. Whisk in the egg yolks and ½ cup of the milk until thoroughly combined.

2. In a large, heavy-bottomed saucepan, bring the remaining 3½ cups milk to a boil over medium-

high heat. Whisking constantly, gradually pour the hot milk into the egg mixture. Pour the mixture back into the saucepan and cook over medium heat, stirring constantly with a heatproof spatula, until a few bubbles rise to the surface and the mixture thickens, about 5 minutes. Remove from the heat and whisk in the butter and vanilla.

3. Spread half the custard into a 13 by 9-inch baking dish and smooth the top. Top the custard with the vanilla wafers in a single layer. Place all of the sliced bananas on top of the wafers. Spread the remaining custard over the surface. Cover the surface entirely with plastic wrap to prevent a skin from forming. Refrigerate until thoroughly cooled and set, at least 4 hours.

4. When ready to serve, prepare the topping: In the bowl of an electric mixer fitted with the whisk attachment, or using a handheld mixer, beat the cream and granulated sugar at medium-high speed to medium peaks. Spread the whipped cream over the surface of the custard and serve. Your mama will be so proud!

AN EGG-CELLENT IDEA

There are two ways I like to separate the egg yolk from the egg white.* Either way, the first thing you want to do is set up a couple of bowls on your counter, one for the yolks and one for the whites. If you're being extra careful, set up a bowl for each white and a separate bowl for the yolks. That way, if you make a mistake on one egg, you don't ruin all the work you've done on the previous ones.

The first way to separate an egg is to crack it on the edge of a surface and gently pry the egg open with your thumbs, leaving the shell intact on the underside of the egg. Gently transfer the yolk back and forth between the shell halves, letting the egg white drip into a bowl as you do so. When you've isolated as much of the egg white as you can, drop the yolk into another bowl.

Alternatively, crack an egg on the edge of a surface and, with your hand hovering over a bowl, let the entire egg plop into the palm of your hand. Hold the yolk in your palm and let the white drip out of your hand and into the bowl. When it has dripped out entirely, pop the yolk into another bowl. A little messier, I suppose, but probably a little easier.

By the way, don't just throw out all the egg whites you are not using in this recipe. Place them in an airtight plastic bag, label the number of whites, and store them in the freezer. They will keep for up to 3 months.

*It's important, for recipes like these, to separate whites and yolks properly. If your egg yolks get into the whites, it doesn't allow you to whip your whites properly.

CREAM CHEESE–CHOCOLATE CHIP BREAD PUDDING

■ ■

Bread pudding is such an old-fashioned way to revive every last bit of bread you have lying around. One of my favorite ways to have bread pudding is full of cream cheese and chocolate chips. It's out-of-this-world delicious!

SERVES 8

1 package (8 ounces) cream cheese, at room temperature

¾ cup plus ½ cup granulated sugar

1 teaspoon vanilla extract

Salt

5 large eggs

2 cups half-and-half

1 cup whole milk

6 cups cubed day-old egg bread

1¼ cups semisweet chocolate chips

½ cup packed light brown sugar

1. Preheat the oven to 325°F. Grease a 13 by 9-inch baking dish with butter, oil, or cooking spray.

2. In the bowl of an electric mixer fitted with the paddle attachment, or using a handheld mixer, beat the cream cheese at low speed until smooth and creamy, 2 to 3 minutes. Add the ¾ cup granulated sugar, the vanilla, and a pinch of salt and continue beating, occasionally scraping down the sides of the bowl to incorporate the sugar into the cream cheese, until very smooth and no lumps remain, about 5 minutes.

3. In a large bowl, whisk together the eggs and the ½ cup granulated sugar. Whisk in the half-and-half, milk, and ¼ teaspoon salt. Add the bread cubes and, using a rubber spatula, fold gently to moisten all the bread. Fold in the chocolate chips. Pour the egg-bread mixture into the prepared baking dish. Drop the cream cheese mixture by rounded spoonfuls evenly over the surface of the pudding. Sprinkle the brown sugar over the top. Bake until the top is light golden brown and a knife inserted into the center comes out clean, 45 to 50 minutes. Dig in while it's still warm.

EGG BREADS

There are all types of egg-based breads out there that will work for this recipe. Some options are challah, brioche, panettone, or any Easter breads.

CLASSIC TRIFLE

■■■

I keep the ingredients for trifle on hand whenever we're going to be entertaining a lot, because it is one of the easiest make-ahead desserts you can think of, and it is just drop-dead gorgeous, to boot. Besides, all that leftover cake and pudding and fruit make one of the most indulgent breakfasts you ever ate when no one was looking.

SERVES 6 TO 8

Custard
2½ cups whole milk
¾ cup sugar
2 large eggs
2 large egg yolks
Pinch of salt
2 teaspoons vanilla extract

Trifle Assembly
One 9-inch yellow cake, cut into ¾-inch cubes
¼ cup cream sherry
3 cups sliced strawberries
¾ cup strawberry jam
1 cup heavy cream
¼ cup sugar

1. To make the custard: In a large, heavy-bottomed saucepan, combine the milk and 6 tablespoons of the sugar. Bring to a simmer over medium heat. Meanwhile, in a medium bowl, whisk together the remaining 6 tablespoons sugar, the whole eggs, egg yolks, and salt. Whisking constantly, gradually pour the hot milk into the egg mixture. Pour the mixture back into the saucepan and cook over medium-low heat, stirring constantly with a heatproof spatula, until the custard is thick enough to coat the back of a spoon, 3 to 5 minutes. Be sure to scrape the bottom and sides of the pan and don't let it come to a boil. Remove from the heat and whisk in the vanilla. Strain through a fine-mesh sieve into a bowl. Cover with plastic wrap right up against the custard to prevent a skin from forming, and refrigerate. Chill the custard thoroughly before using.

2. To assemble the trifle: Using half the cake, place a layer of cake cubes in the bottom of a trifle bowl or 3-quart serving dish. Brush with some of the cream sherry. Place half the strawberry slices over the cake. Using a small spatula, spread half the jam over the strawberries. Pour half the custard over the jam. Repeat the layering. Cover with plastic wrap and refrigerate for at least 4 hours or up to overnight.

3. Just before serving, in the bowl of an electric mixer fitted with the whisk attachment, or using a handheld mixer, beat the cream with the sugar at medium-high speed until soft peaks form. Spread over the surface. Serve just as soon as you can.

> ### BEAUTY IN A BOWL
>
> A trifle bowl is a tall cylindrical glass bowl that allows you to layer the trifle ingredients and see them from the outside. Your layers, custard, and fruit will look so pretty, it'll be a real stunner of a dessert that your whole table will just love.

COCONUT FLAN

■ ■

You know I love Coco Lopez, the sweetened cream of coconut, because it makes this rich, smooth, eggy dessert so delicious and luxurious. This flan is a perfect way to show off that coconut flavor, which is just a little bit of the exotic, and the familiar, creamy goodness of the best custard you ever ate.

SERVES 10 TO 12

Caramel
1¼ cups sugar
Pinch of cream of tartar

Custard
1 can (14 ounces) sweetened condensed milk
1 can (14 ounces) coconut milk
1 can (15 ounces) Coco Lopez
1 cup heavy cream
5 large eggs
2 large egg yolks

> **AGAINST THE GRAIN**
>
> It's important that y'all don't stir your caramel once it has come to a boil. Stirring will only cause the sugars to recrystallize, resulting in an undesirable grainy texture. The cream of tartar will also help give the caramel a nice smooth texture.

1. To make the caramel: First be sure to have on hand a 9-inch round cake pan. In a small, heavy-bottomed saucepan, combine ¼ cup water, the sugar, and the cream of tartar. Bring to a boil over medium-high heat. Reduce the heat to a simmer and cook, without stirring, until the syrup begins to darken, 10 to 15 minutes. Swirl the pan until the syrup is dark amber in color. Immediately pour the caramel into the cake pan, moving the pan to allow the caramel to evenly cover the bottom of the pan. Set aside.

2. Preheat the oven to 325°F. In a large bowl, whisk together the condensed milk, coconut milk, Coco Lopez, and cream until combined. In a small bowl, whisk together the whole eggs and egg yolks. Whisk the eggs into the milk mixture.

3. Pour the custard into the caramel-coated cake pan. Place the cake pan inside a large roasting pan. Pour enough boiling water into the roasting pan to come halfway up the sides of the cake pan. Bake until the custard is just set, jiggles like jelly, and a knife inserted into the center comes out clean, 1 hour and 15 minutes to 1½ hours.

4. Let the flan cool to room temperature before covering the surface entirely with plastic wrap to prevent a skin from forming. Refrigerate overnight.

5. Just before serving, run a thin spatula around the sides of the flan to loosen it. Place a large serving plate over the cake pan and invert. If the flan does not readily release from the pan, place it right side up and place on the stove over low heat to loosen the caramel, then invert again. Cut into thin wedges and serve on pretty little cake plates.

REAL, HOMEMADE VANILLA ICE CREAM

Thank goodness for those countertop ice cream machines—they make ice cream making a cinch! When I make my own ice cream, I usually start with this recipe. You can throw in sweetened, sliced strawberries or peaches right before serving if you like, or use as a topping, and be sure to have on hand plenty of good ol' chocolate fudge sauce. But sometimes, a simple bowl of just plain vanilla ice cream is really all you need in the world.

MAKES ABOUT 2 CUPS

1½ cups whole milk

¾ cup sugar

⅛ teaspoon salt

6 large egg yolks

1½ cups cold heavy cream

1 tablespoon vanilla extract

1. Have ready a 2-quart bowl placed inside a larger bowl that is filled with ice and water.

2. In a medium, heavy-bottomed saucepan, combine the milk, sugar, and salt. Bring to a simmer over medium heat.

3. Meanwhile, in a medium bowl, gently whisk the egg yolks. Whisking constantly, gradually whisk about 1 cup of the hot milk mixture into the egg yolks. Pour the mixture back into the saucepan and cook over low heat, stirring constantly with a heatproof spatula, until the custard is thick enough to coat the back of a spoon, 3 to 5 minutes. Be sure to scrape the bottom and sides of the pan, and don't let it come to a boil. Remove from the heat and strain through a fine-mesh sieve into the bowl sitting in the ice bath. Stir in the cold cream and vanilla. Continue stirring over ice until cooled to room temperature.

4. Cover the surface entirely with plastic wrap right up against the custard to prevent a skin from forming. Refrigerate the custard for at least 2 hours or overnight, then freeze in an ice cream maker according to the manufacturer's instructions. Serve soft and custardy right away, or place the ice cream in a freezer container with a tight-fitting lid and freeze until firm, at least 4 hours.

BOILING OVER

Be sure to watch heating milk (or cream) very, very carefully! It has a tendency to boil over in a lickety-split minute. As soon as it comes to a simmer, whisk it off that heat.

PEACH ICE CREAM

▪ ▪

When peach season hits in Georgia, you better be ready, because ripe, juicy peaches are just every-where, and they're too good to pass up. I love to get my fill of this gorgeous fruit and just adore makin' ice cream with it.

MAKES ABOUT 4 CUPS

1½ pounds peaches, peeled (see box, page
    422), pitted, and finely chopped
⅓ cup plus ¾ cup sugar
1 teaspoon almond extract
Few drops of fresh lemon juice

2 cups heavy cream
1 cup whole milk
¼ teaspoon salt
6 large egg yolks

1. In a small saucepan, combine the peaches and the ⅓ cup sugar. Bring to a simmer over medium-low heat and cook until the sugar dissolves and the peaches just begin to release their juices, 2 to 3 minutes. Stir in the almond extract and lemon juice. Mash the peach mixture with a potato masher. Let cool to room temperature, then cover with plastic wrap and chill for at least 2 hours or overnight.

2. Have ready a 2-quart bowl placed inside a larger bowl that is filled with ice and water.

> ## PEACH PUREE
>
> If you don't have a potato masher, or if you want your peach mixture smoother, you can place the just-simmered peaches in the blender and puree until they are chunky-smooth.

3. In a medium, heavy-bottomed saucepan, combine the cream, milk, ½ cup of the sugar, and the salt. Bring to a simmer over medium heat.

4. Meanwhile, in a large bowl, whisk together the egg yolks and remaining ¼ cup sugar. Whisking constantly, gradually whisk about 1 cup of the hot cream mixture into the egg yolks. Pour the mixture back into the saucepan and cook over low heat, stirring constantly with a heatproof spatula, until the custard is thick enough to coat the back of a spoon, 3 to 5 minutes. Be sure to scrape the bottom and sides of the pan, and don't let it come to a boil. Remove from the heat and strain through a fine-mesh sieve into the bowl sitting in the ice bath. Continue stirring over ice until cooled to room temperature.

5. Cover the surface entirely with plastic wrap right up against the custard to prevent a skin from forming. Refrigerate the custard for at least 2 hours or overnight, then freeze in an ice cream maker according to the manufacturer's instructions. Pour in the chilled peach mixture for the last 10 minutes of freezing. Serve soft and custardy right away, or place the ice cream in a freezer container with a tight-fitting lid and freeze until firm, at least 4 hours. I tell you, this is just about the only ice cream I make when Georgia peaches are in season.

BUTTERMILK ICE CREAM

I just adore tangy buttermilk, and it makes the most refreshing ice cream, y'all. It's just perfect on its own or—oh, my goodness—right on top of a slice of warm apple pie.

MAKES ABOUT 4 CUPS

2 cups heavy cream
1¼ cups sugar
¼ teaspoon salt

6 large egg yolks
1½ cups buttermilk

1. Have ready a 2-quart bowl placed inside a larger bowl that is filled with ice and water.

2. In a medium, heavy-bottomed saucepan, combine the cream, 1 cup of the sugar, and the salt. Bring to a simmer over medium heat.

3. Meanwhile, in a large bowl, whisk together the egg yolks and the remaining ¼ cup sugar. Whisking constantly, gradually whisk about 1 cup of the hot cream mixture into the egg yolks. Pour the mixture back into the saucepan and cook over medium-low heat, stirring constantly with a heat-proof spatula, until the custard is thick enough to coat the back of a spoon, 3 to 5 minutes. Be sure to scrape the bottom and sides of the pan, and don't let it come to a boil. Remove from the heat and strain through a fine-mesh sieve into the bowl sitting in the ice bath. Stir in the buttermilk and continue stirring until cooled to room temperature.

4. Cover the surface entirely with plastic wrap right up against the custard to prevent a skin from forming. Refrigerate the custard for at least 2 hours or overnight, then freeze in an ice cream maker according to the manufacturer's instructions. Serve soft and custardy right away, or place the ice cream in a freezer container with a tight-fitting lid and freeze until firm, at least 4 hours. Just wait until y'all see how the buttermilk in this custard gives this ice cream the most beautiful velvety texture.

To test for the doneness of custard, dip a wooden spoon into the custard and run a finger along the back of the spoon. If the custard leaves an even film along the spoon and there is a distinct path where you ran your finger, the custard is done.

STRAIN AWAY

I like to strain my cooked custards as an extra bit of insurance that I don't end up with cooked eggy bits. You never know when you might miss a spot on the bottom or sides of the pan that cooked just a little too fiercely. I always use a fine-mesh strainer so that the egg can't sneak through.

SWEET POTATO ICE CREAM

■ ■

Try this one around the holidays—your guests will eat it up in no time! And it makes the best topping you've ever had on a piece of spiced gingerbread.

MAKES ABOUT 4 CUPS

1 cup cooked, pureed, and chilled sweet
   potato (1 large)
¾ cup packed dark brown sugar
½ teaspoon ground ginger
¼ teaspoon grated nutmeg
Pinch of salt

1½ cups heavy cream
1½ cups whole milk
4 large egg yolks
¼ cup granulated sugar
2 teaspoons vanilla extract

1. In a medium bowl, whisk together the sweet potato, brown sugar, ginger, nutmeg, and salt.

2. In a large, heavy-bottomed saucepan, combine the cream and milk. Bring to a simmer over medium heat.

3. Meanwhile, in a medium bowl, whisk together the egg yolks and granulated sugar. Whisking constantly, gradually add the hot milk mixture to the egg yolks. Pour the mixture back into the saucepan and cook over medium-low heat, stirring constantly, until the custard is thick enough to coat the back of a spoon, 3 to 5 minutes. Be sure to scrape the bottom and sides of the pan, and don't let it come to a boil. Remove from the heat, whisk in the vanilla, and strain through a fine-mesh sieve into a bowl. Whisk in the sweet potato mixture.

4. Cover the surface entirely with plastic wrap right up against the custard to prevent a skin from forming. Refrigerate the custard for at least 2 hours or overnight, then freeze in an ice cream maker according to the manufacturer's instructions. Serve soft and custardy right away, or place the ice cream in a freezer container with a tight-fitting lid and freeze until firm, at least 4 hours.

SWEET SUBSTITUTION

Feel free to simplify this recipe by substituting canned sweet potato for fresh. Just be sure that you don't use canned candied sweets. That will result in just a bit too much sweetness in this ice cream.

QUICK RASPBERRY SHERBET

■ ■

This is a quick-fix recipe that needs nothing more than frozen fruit and a jar of jam, and wouldn't you know, it tastes just like a berry patch. If you prefer another kind of berry, go ahead and use it.

MAKES ABOUT 3 CUPS

1 jar (12 ounces) seedless raspberry jam
1 bag (10 ounces) frozen unsweetened
   raspberries

1 cup whole milk
½ cup superfine sugar
Juice of 1 lemon

1. In a food processor, combine all the ingredients and process until smooth. Using a rubber spatula to give the mixture a gentle push, strain the mixture through a fine-mesh sieve into a bowl to remove the raspberry seeds.

2. Refrigerate the mixture for at least 2 hours or overnight, then freeze in an ice cream maker according to the manufacturer's instructions. Place in a freezer container with a tight-fitting lid and freeze until firm, at least 4 hours.

FINE TUNE

Because this sherbet base isn't cooked, superfine sugar is best to ensure that the end product is nice and smooth. It's simply granulated sugar that has been pulverized more finely, and because of that, it will dissolve more quickly. If you can't find superfine sugar, substitute granulated sugar and just give it a few pulses in the food processor on its own before you add the other ingredients.

WATERMELON ICE

■ ■

Juicy and refreshing, watermelon was the original Gatorade down South! Watermelon got a lot of hardworking people through their summer days out in the sun. You don't need to add much to make a beautiful ice that's just perfectly sweet and delicious—and you don't need an ice cream maker for this one, either.

MAKES ABOUT 4 CUPS

⅔ cup sugar

6 cups seedless watermelon chunks

1 tablespoon fresh lemon juice

Fresh mint sprigs, for garnish

1. In a small saucepan, bring ⅓ cup water and the sugar to a simmer over medium heat. Cook until the sugar completely dissolves. Pour the syrup into a medium bowl and refrigerate until cold.

2. In a blender, puree the cold sugar syrup, watermelon, and lemon juice until smooth.

3. Pour the mixture into a wide, shallow pan and freeze for 1 hour. Scrape the mixture with a fork (be sure to give the whole mixture a good scrape, now) and freeze for another hour. Scrape again and freeze for 1 more hour. Scrape into cups and serve. I like to decorate these beautiful watermelon cups with pretty little sprigs of mint.

> ### QUICK FREEZE
> The wider and shallower the pan that you use to freeze this watermelon ice, the better. That will help speed up the freezing time. Also, be sure to place the pan level in your freezer. That way, you won't have uneven freezing due to deeper areas in the pan.

Chapter 16

CANDIES, PRESERVES, AND BEVERAGES

I love how so many people are reviving the old-fashioned cooking that my grandmama used to do, and the candy and preserves recipes in this chapter are a perfect example. Down South, kitchen gardens grew so fast that cooks always had to scramble to keep up, and preserving was the best solution to not wastin' an ounce of that beautiful produce. A hot, sticky day or two of canning, and then you could put your feet up and sip a glass of Southern wine (sweet iced tea, that is) knowing your beautiful garden-fresh produce wouldn't ruin, and you'd have all your jams, jellies, and pickles to see you through the year.

I've been preserving since I was a little girl, and have fond memories of the preserving I did in my grandmama's kitchen. I love to revisit them by putting up just a small batch of Strawberry Jam (page 424) or Blackberry Jelly (page 423) whenever I can manage it. In smaller quantities, jelly making is not the big production we all tend to imagine.

For old-fashioned, home-style recipes, nothing beats making your own candies. When I was a child, and even when the boys were in school, to bring in homemade divinity or fudge for a bake sale, or to give homemade candies to the teacher at the end of the year, was such a point of pride. My mama's Divinity (page 414) always sold out at our school fund-raising events, and I'd walk with my head held high that whole week.

Whether it's eating a piece of homemade peanut brittle or spreading a hot biscuit with Fig Jam (page 421) from your own backyard, it will just bring you right back to an earlier era, when things were simpler and slower, and that's something we all seem to crave in these fast-moving times. When you're making your own Popcorn Balls (page 415) or peeling peaches for jam, you're also giving your mind a minute to slow down and enjoy the beautiful things that you can make with your own hands. That's why I love cooking, y'all, and I want to share with everyone the great feeling that comes from making beautiful, delicious things yourself.

THE ULTIMATE EASY
CHOCOLATE-PEANUT FUDGE

■ ■

Salted peanuts, sweetened condensed milk, and chocolate are hard to beat. You won't be able to stop yourself from poppin' pieces of this delicious fudge into your mouth!

MAKES 64 (1-INCH) PIECES

2 cups semisweet chocolate chips

1 can (14 ounces) sweetened condensed milk

2 tablespoons (¼ stick) butter, at room temperature

1 cup salted cocktail peanuts

1 teaspoon vanilla extract

Pinch of salt

1. Grease an 8-inch square baking dish with butter, oil, or cooking spray. Line with waxed paper, leaving the edges of the waxed paper to hang over all around the edges of the dish.

2. In a medium, heavy-bottomed saucepan, melt the chocolate chips with the milk over medium-low heat. Stir in the butter until completely melted. Stir in the peanuts, vanilla, and salt. Using a rubber spatula, spread the mixture on the bottom of the prepared dish, smoothing the top. Cover loosely with plastic wrap and refrigerate until firm, at least 4 hours. Using a hot, dry knife, cut into cute little 1-inch squares.

SMOOTH OPERATOR

The secret to perfectly smooth-edged squares of fudge is in the hot knife you use to cut it. Make sure you warm that knife up real good in hot water and wipe it fully dry before you slice into the fudge. First, score the top of the fudge lightly as soon as it is set enough to do so (about an hour or so into the chilling time): lightly slide the tip of a sharp knife over the surface of the fudge to mark where you will cut it when it is fully set. Then when it's set, you have guidelines for cutting the fudge all the way through, with the hot, dry knife.

DIVINITY

■ ■

My mama was the queen of divinity. I can still see that beautiful redheaded woman standin' up there at her counter with those two tablespoons, twirling the most incredible, perfect mounds of divinity you ever put in your mouth. My grandmama and my aunt Trina would try to make it and it would turn out to be a disaster. They finally just threw up their hands and said, "Okay, Corrie, we have given up. You are the divinity queen and we'll eat divinity only when you make it." Mama made hers just like this, with pecans. Now that you have the recipe, you can just go ahead and be a divinity queen yourself.

SERVES 8 TO 10

4 cups sugar

1 cup light corn syrup

3 large egg whites

1 teaspoon vanilla extract

2 to 2½ cups chopped pecans

1. Line a couple of wire racks with waxed paper.

2. In a medium, heavy-bottomed saucepan, stir together ¾ cup water, the sugar, and corn syrup. Place over medium heat and give it a good stir *only* when the sugar has just dissolved; do not stir after this point. Cook the sugar syrup until it reaches 250°F (hard-ball stage) on a candy thermometer.

3. While the syrup is cooking, in the bowl of an electric mixer fitted with the whisk attachment, or using a handheld mixer, beat the egg whites at medium-high speed until stiff peaks form. Once the sugar syrup has reached 250°F, with the mixer at high speed, carefully pour the hot syrup in a slow, steady stream into the stiffly beaten egg whites, beating constantly. Add the vanilla and continue to beat until the mixture holds its shape, about 5 minutes. Using a rubber spatula, stir in the pecans.

4. Using two tablespoons, drop the divinity mixture onto the waxed paper–lined rack, using one spoon to push the candy off the other. This may take a little practice because the technique is to twirl the pushing spoon, making the candy look like the top of a soft-serve ice cream. If the mixture becomes too stiff, add a few drops of very hot water. Y'all are going to need to work fast when making this candy! When you've used up all the mixture, let the candies cool completely. You can store them in an airtight container for up to 2 weeks.

MAMA'S WAY
If you feel like trying something new, dried cherries make a nice substitute for some or all of the pecans.

POPCORN BALLS

My grandmama used to make popcorn balls all the time. I especially love these around holiday time, but they are a wonderful, simple treat whenever you get the urge for them.

MAKES 14 BALLS

2 cups sugar

½ cup unsulfured molasses (not blackstrap)

1 teaspoon distilled white vinegar

½ teaspoon salt

1 teaspoon vanilla extract

18 cups popped corn

1. In a medium, heavy-bottomed saucepan, combine 1⅓ cups water, the sugar, molasses, vinegar, and salt. Bring to a boil over high heat. Cook the sugar mixture, without stirring, until it reaches 255°F (hard-ball stage) on a candy thermometer. Swirl in the vanilla.

2. Place the popped corn in a large bowl and pour the sugar mixture over, tossing gently to coat. When the mixture is cool enough to handle, with lightly greased hands, press the popcorn into 3-inch balls. Let cool completely on waxed paper before digging in.

CANDIED BACON

Sometimes I like to add ½ cup candied bacon, cut up real fine. To make candied bacon, lay 3 slices of nice, thick-cut bacon on a foil-lined baking sheet and sprinkle a teaspoon of light brown sugar on each slice. Bake at 325°F for 30 minutes, then check to see if the bacon is browned and crispy. If not, cook for another 10 minutes or so and check again. Once done, place the bacon on a paper towel–lined plate and let it cool—it'll "crisp" up even more. Then chop it up fine and add to your popcorn when mixing all the ingredients together.

CRUNCHY PRALINES

■ ■

I started making pralines when I was a young housewife—and I mean young. They're really easy to make so long as you take care not to overcook them, and there's nothing better. I remember making a big old can of pralines to take to Atlanta to my daddy when he was in the intensive care unit up there. Earl Hiers was a beautiful man, forty years old, and he'd just had a stroke, but he couldn't stop eatin' my pralines. Bless him!

MAKES ABOUT 2 DOZEN PRALINES

½ cup heavy cream
1 cup packed light brown sugar
1 cup granulated sugar
1½ cups coarsely chopped pecans

4 tablespoons (½ stick) butter, at room
   temperature
1 teaspoon vanilla extract
Pinch of salt

1. Grease a baking sheet and two tablespoons with butter, oil, or cooking spray.

2. In a medium, heavy-bottomed saucepan, stir together the cream and both sugars. Bring to a boil over high heat. Let the mixture cook, without stirring, until fragrant and starting to caramelize, about 5 minutes. Add the pecans and butter and swirl the pan to combine. Remove the pan from the heat and let cool for 10 minutes. Add the vanilla and salt, and using as few strokes as possible, stir vigorously to cool and thicken the sugar mixture.

3. Using the prepared spoons, drop by rounded tablespoonfuls onto the prepared baking sheet, If the mixture firms up, stir in a few drops of very hot water to loosen it. Let the candy cool before serving. Store any leftovers (if there are any!) in an airtight container.

A SOUTHERN SWEETIE

Praline may have started out in Europe as a candy made with almonds. But we here in the South have made it our own by cooking it up with our very favorite nut: pecans.

SPICY CANDIED PECANS

Whether you're drinking bourbon or lemonade, a spicy, salty-sweet candied pecan is just the thing on the side. Well, maybe more than one.

MAKES ABOUT 5 CUPS

1 cup sugar

1 large egg white

1 pound pecan halves

1 teaspoon salt

1 teaspoon ground cinnamon

⅛ teaspoon cayenne pepper

Pinch of ground cloves

1. Preheat the oven to 300°F. Line a rimmed baking sheet with parchment paper.

2. In a large bowl, whisk together the sugar and egg white. Add the pecans and toss to combine. In a small bowl, stir together the salt, cinnamon, cayenne pepper, and cloves. Sprinkle the spice mixture over the nuts and toss well.

3. Spread the nuts in a single layer on the prepared baking sheet. Bake, tossing occasionally, until the nuts are fragrant and almost dry to the touch, about 30 minutes. Put these out in pretty bowls when company comes round.

A HOMEMADE GIFT

During the holiday season, I love packaging up these beautiful pecans in cute little Mason jars. I pretty them up with ribbons and bows and bring them round to all my friends. I reckon homemade gifts mean so much more than the store-bought kind.

NUTTY BRITTLE

▪ ▪

Down around Savannah, peanut brittle is big business. Folks just love that sweet, salty, buttery crunch. I like to make my brittle with mixed nuts, which makes it look pretty and taste pretty darn addictive, so don't say I didn't warn y'all. It makes a great gift, too, if you're looking to get it out of the house before you eat the whole thing.

MAKES ABOUT 1½ POUNDS OF BRITTLE

2 cups sugar

½ cup light corn syrup

2 cups salted mixed nuts

4 tablespoons (½ stick) butter,
  at room temperature

1 tablespoon baking soda

2 teaspoons vanilla extract

¼ teaspoon salt

1. Grease a rimmed baking sheet with butter, oil, or cooking spray.

2. In a medium, heavy-bottomed saucepan, combine ½ cup water, the sugar, and corn syrup. Bring to a boil over high heat. Cook the sugar mixture, without stirring, until it registers 260°F (hard-ball stage) on a candy thermometer. Stir in the nuts and butter and continue cooking until the mixture reaches 300°F (hard-crack stage). Stir in the baking soda, vanilla, and salt until completely incorporated.

3. Pour the mixture onto the prepared baking sheet and, using an offset spatula, spread it as thinly as possible. Let the candy cool before breaking it into pieces and serving. Store any leftovers in an airtight container.

SUGAR STAGES

Back before candy thermometers were readily available, candy makers used to test the stage of their cooked sugar using a bowl of cold water. That's how we got the terms "hard-ball stage" and "hard-crack stage." So, for instance, if you dropped some of your cooking sugar at around 260°F into a bowl of cold water, it would form a hard ball. At that point, you've made nougat. At around 300°F, that same sugar placed in water would form brittle threads, just exactly what you need for nutty brittle. And that's some Candy Making 101, folks.

BUCKEYES

■ ■

Jamie adores these peanut butter and chocolate balls, and I always used to make them for the boys to give to their teachers as gifts. I remember how proud Jamie was that his mama could make a fine homemade candy.

MAKES ABOUT 48 (1-INCH) BALLS

3 cups confectioners' sugar
1 cup creamy peanut butter
4 tablespoons (½ stick) butter, at room
   temperature

1 teaspoon vanilla extract
3 cups semisweet chocolate chips

1. Line a baking sheet with parchment paper.

2. In the bowl of an electric mixer fitted with the paddle attachment, or using a handheld mixer, beat together the sugar, peanut butter, butter, and vanilla at medium speed. The dough should end up slightly crumbly. Roll the dough into 1-inch balls. Place the balls on the prepared baking sheet and stick a toothpick into each ball. Place in the freezer and chill for 1 hour.

3. In the top of a double boiler, or in a bowl snugly on top of a pan with a few inches of simmering water, melt the chocolate chips, stirring until smooth. Holding a ball by the toothpick and placing a fork under the ball to stabilize it, dip it into the hot chocolate, leaving a small hole of the peanut butter dough showing at the top of the ball as the "buckeye." Let the excess chocolate drip back into the pot. Return the buckeye to the baking sheet. Repeat with the remaining balls.

4. Cover loosely with plastic wrap and refrigerate for at least 2 hours or overnight. Remove the toothpicks before serving.

HOT AND COLD

The secret to getting a nice coating of chocolate on the buckeyes is to make sure the chocolate is very hot and the buckeyes are very cold. I like to bring my buckeyes out of the freezer in batches to make sure they don't heat up while I'm working.

CANNING BASICS

■ ■

Canning sauces, jams, and relishes is fun, economical, and easy. To ensure their freshness, all you need to know are some simple basics. First off, make sure your jars, lids, and screw bands are completely clean. Then sterilize them in a large pot of rapidly boiling water for a good 10 minutes, making sure that they are fully submerged in the water. After they have thoroughly dried on paper towels, fill them with whatever you are looking to preserve, leaving ½ inch of headroom. Wipe the rims clean and screw the lids on tightly. Place the sealed jars in a large pot of water on a rack of a folded-up kitchen towel, making sure they are fully submerged. Bring to a boil, covered, and continue boiling for 5 to 10 minutes. You should hear a small pop when the vacuum is fully sealed. Let them cool on a kitchen towel–lined counter for 24 hours and test that the lid is fully sealed by pressing on the center. If the lid is concave, it is fully sealed.

FIG JAM

■ ■

To me, there's nothin' better than pulling a whole soft preserved fig out of that syrup. For some reason, no one else in the family seems to agree, which is just fine by me—I don't need help working my way through a batch of Fig Jam on my own. Try it in my Frosted Buttermilk Fig Cake (page 375) if you like, or spread it over toasted pound cake for dessert, and you're in for a treat.

MAKES 6 HALF-PINTS

4 pounds fresh, ripe figs, stemmed
3 cups sugar

Finely grated zest of 1 lemon
¼ cup fresh lemon juice

1. In a large, wide, heavy-bottomed nonaluminum saucepan, toss the figs with the sugar. Add the lemon zest and lemon juice and bring to a boil over medium-high heat, stirring until the sugar is dissolved. Reduce the heat to a simmer and cook, stirring occasionally, until the fruit is glassy and the jam runs off a spoon in thick, heavy drops, 20 to 25 minutes. The mixture should register around 220°F on a candy thermometer. Skim off any foam that rises to the surface of the jam.

2. Spoon into hot, sterilized half-pint jars (leaving ½ inch of room at the top) and process for 10 minutes. (See Canning Basics, opposite.)

PAN PRIMER

Nonreactive pans are key in jam making. Pans that are made from aluminum or cast iron or copper can impart a metallic flavor to your jams because these materials react with the acids in the fruit. So stick with nonreactive materials like stainless steel or enamel. That way, nothing will get in the way of the fresh fruit flavor of your jams.

PEACH JAM

■ ■

When you are at a farm stand or market in the middle of peach season and you see a crate of soft, juicy peaches buzzing with bees, you've hit peach jam pay dirt: those ripe, sweet fruits are usually a real bargain, since they're too soft to eat out of hand, but they're just perfect for a jam so full of summertime goodness, it'll knock your socks off every time you open a new jar.

MAKES 6 HALF-PINTS

4 pounds ripe peaches, peeled (see box), pitted, and cut into ½-inch wedges
3½ cups sugar

Finely grated zest of 1 lemon
3 tablespoons fresh lemon juice

1. In a large, wide, heavy-bottomed nonaluminum saucepan, toss the peaches with the sugar and let stand off the heat, stirring occasionally, until the sugar is mostly dissolved, about 1 hour. Mash lightly with a potato masher.

2. Add the lemon zest and lemon juice to the peaches and bring to a boil over medium-high heat, stirring until the sugar is fully dissolved. Reduce the heat to a simmer and cook, stirring occasionally, until the fruit is glassy and the jam runs off a spoon in thick, heavy drops, 20 to 25 minutes. The mixture should register around 220°F on a candy thermometer. Skim off any foam that rises to the surface of the jam.

3. Spoon into hot, sterilized half-pint jars (leaving ½ inch of room at the top) and process for 10 minutes. (See Canning Basics, page 420.)

PEACH A-PEEL

Peaches, just like tomatoes, can be easily peeled using a pot of boiling water and a bowl of ice water. Clean the peaches well and, using a small knife, score a shallow X at the blossom end of each peach. Then dunk the peaches in the boiling water for about 40 seconds or so, depending on how ripe they are. Using a slotted spoon, lift the peaches out and place them directly in the ice water. Let them cool for a few seconds and peel away!

BLACKBERRY JELLY

∎∎∎∎∎∎∎∎∎∎∎∎∎∎∎∎∎∎∎∎∎∎∎∎∎∎∎∎∎∎∎∎∎∎∎∎

Eating blackberry jelly on toast brings me back to my grandmama's kitchen like nothing else. This is a beautiful jelly, and you can make more to give away as gifts if you do like my grandmama did and get someone else to pick a few flats of blackberries.

MAKES 6 HALF-PINTS

4 pounds blackberries (about 3 quarts)   4 cups sugar
1 package (1¾ ounces) powdered pectin

1. Wash the berries and mash them with a potato masher or the back of a wide spoon. Place them in cheesecloth and bundle up tightly, creating a knot on top of the bundle. Place in a colander set over a large bowl and, with your hands, squeeze the bundle to get the juices out. You want to extract about 3 cups of juice.

2. In a medium, wide, heavy-bottomed nonaluminum saucepan, stir together the blackberry juice, pectin, and sugar. Bring to a boil and cook for 1 minute. Skim off any foam that rises to the surface of the jelly.

3. Ladle into hot, sterilized half-pint jars (leaving ½ inch of room at the top) and process for 10 minutes. (See Canning Basics, page 420.)

PECTIN POWDER

Powdered pectin is readily available and is a great aid in jam and jelly making. A little added pectin helps to set your jelly just right. It's naturally occurring in fruit, but more so when the fruit is unripe. So when you're cooking up ripe fruit, it helps to give it this little natural boost to set properly.

STRAWBERRY JAM

■ ■

I make strawberry jam for my family because it tastes a thousand times more wonderful than what you'd buy in the store; it's full of lush strawberry flavor. And I have never met a soul who could turn away a good strawberry jam on a hot buttered biscuit.

MAKES 4 HALF-PINTS

3 pounds strawberries, hulled and halved

3 cups sugar

Finely grated zest of 1 lemon

⅓ cup fresh lemon juice

1. In a large, wide, heavy-bottomed nonaluminum saucepan, toss the strawberries with the sugar and let stand off the heat, stirring occasionally, until the sugar is mostly dissolved, about 1 hour. Mash lightly with a potato masher.

2. Add the lemon zest and juice to the strawberries and bring to a boil over medium-high heat, stirring until the sugar is fully dissolved. Reduce the heat to a simmer and cook, stirring occasionally, until the fruit is glassy and the jam runs off a spoon in thick, heavy drops, 20 to 25 minutes. The mixture should register around 220°F on a candy thermometer. Skim off any foam that rises to the surface of the jam.

3. Spoon into hot, sterilized half-pint jars (leaving ½ inch of room at the top) and process for 10 minutes. (See Canning Basics, page 420.)

SPREAD THE LOVE

You want to give your jams plenty of room to spread out in the pan so that they reduce as quickly as possible. So I always recommend using a wide-bottomed saucepan for making jam. Your jams will thicken up quicker, retaining the fresh, just-picked fruit flavor that you want.

Hull a strawberry by inserting a small knife just to the side of the core on the stem end. Angling the knife toward the core, carve a small circle and pop out the core with the tip of the knife.

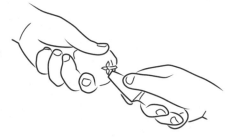

SOUTHERN-STYLE SWEET ICED TEA

■ ■

Here in the South, we like our iced tea cold and sweet. We like to brew ours fresh every day and serve it over plenty of ice. Not a summer's day goes by that I don't reach for a tall glass of this reviving, refreshing drink.

MAKES 8 CUPS

6 to 7 black tea bags, such as Luzianne or Lipton

4 cups boiling water
1 cup sugar

1. Place the tea bags in a large heatproof bowl or pot and pour in the freshly boiled water. Let steep for 5 minutes. Fill a large pitcher with 4 cups room-temperature water. Strain the hot tea into the pitcher and stir to combine.

2. In a small, heavy-bottomed saucepan, combine ½ cup cold water with the sugar. Simmer until the sugar completely dissolves, about 5 minutes. Pour the sugar syrup into the tea to taste. Refrigerate the tea until nice and cold. Serve over plenty of ice.

A HINT OF MINT

Y'all try adding some fresh mint to your iced tea next time. Just muddle a few leaves at the bottom of your glass using a wooden muddler or a knife handle, and pour the iced tea over it—it's out-of-this-world delicious.

Muddle mint to release its flavor by gently pressing down, never grinding, with a wooden muddler or the handle of a dinner knife.

LEMONADE

When I want lemonade, I go into the kitchen and start squeezin' me some lemons. It's a little bit of work for a whole lot of satisfaction. Sometimes it gets so hot down South, there ain't nothin' that'll refresh you better. Poured into a tall glass and garnished with a sprig of mint, I'm tellin' ya, it's as welcome as a cool breeze.

MAKES ABOUT 16 CUPS

2 cups sugar
2 cups fresh lemon juice
(about 8 large lemons)

Get the most juice possible out of a lemon by gently rolling the whole lemon under your palm along the countertop. This will break down some of the lemon membranes and make the juice flow more easily.

1. In a medium, heavy-bottomed saucepan, combine 2 cups water and the sugar. Cook over medium heat until the sugar fully dissolves. Remove from the heat and let cool to room temperature. Chill the syrup for at least 1 hour.

2. Before serving, fill a pitcher with 14 cups cold water. Stir in the lemon juice and chilled sugar syrup. Serve in tall glasses filled with ice.

LEMONADE WITH SPIRIT

Here in the South we love our lemonade and we love our iced tea. When we can't decide which to sip on, we just mix ourselves up an Arnold Palmer, a drink that is equal parts of each. If a cooling cocktail is what you're after, add a splash of vodka to the mix, or even a splash of bourbon for a Lynchburg Lemonade.

SPARKLING BERRY PUNCH

Mix up a pitcher of this beautiful and festive libation whenever you feel like celebratin'—it goes over just as well at a Mother's Day brunch as at a kid's birthday party (if you make the sparkling cider variation below).

SERVES 12 TO 16

2 bottles (750ml) cold champagne
4 cups cold lemonade
1 cup cold cranberry juice

2 pints fresh mixed berries, such as blueberries, raspberries, blackberries, and sliced strawberries

In a large pitcher, combine the champagne, lemonade, and cranberry juice. Stir in the berries and serve. Be sure to have lots of ice on hand!

Create an ice mold by placing sliced fruit in a ring mold, then filling with water. Freeze until set and float in a punch bowl.

VIRGIN VARIATION
To make an alcohol-free version of this cocktail, substitute sparkling cider for the champagne.

CHEATER'S BLACKBERRY WINE

Real blackberry wine was something I remember folks putting up along with their preserves, but of course it took months and months to be ready. I'd been missing the wonderful flavor, so I came up with this shortcut to get to the good stuff right away and wanted to share it with y'all. I don't know anyone who makes his own fruit wines anymore, but this one you can stir together just a day ahead.

MAKES ABOUT 1 QUART

1 cup fresh or frozen blackberries
⅓ cup sugar

1 bottle (750ml) white wine
1 lemon

1. In a small, heavy-bottomed nonaluminum saucepan, simmer the blackberries and sugar over medium heat until syrupy, about 5 minutes. Let the mixture cool completely. Pour the wine into a large bowl and stir in the blackberry syrup. Place in an airtight container and refrigerate overnight.

2. Using a vegetable peeler, peel ½-inch-wide strips of zest from the lemon (reserve the lemon in the fridge for another use). Pour the blackberry wine into chilled glasses. Before serving, twist a strip of zest over each glass and drop it in. Now, aren't you the cocktail maestro!

GLASS GARNISHES

Before twisting the zest, go on ahead and rub the rim of the serving glasses with the zest to give the drinks a lemony flavor when sipped. Or coat the rims with a little confectioners' sugar for a sweeter sip.

Chapter 17

SAUCES, DRESSINGS, AND RELISHES

JEZEBEL SAUCE

Serve over cream cheese with crackers. Or use as a glaze or condiment for meat or poultry. It can also perk up a turkey sandwich like nobody's business.

MAKES 2½ CUPS

1 cup pineapple preserves
1 cup apple jelly
½ cup prepared horseradish

2 tablespoons mustard powder
1 teaspoon black pepper

In a medium bowl, combine all the ingredients and stir well. The sauce will keep in an airtight container for several weeks in the fridge.

ONION RELISH

For your next weenie roast! This relish is tangy and sweet with a bit of crunch.

MAKES 2 CUPS

3 cups chopped yellow onion
2 tablespoons balsamic vinegar
2 tablespoons sugar
1 tablespoon tomato paste

1 tablespoon olive oil
½ teaspoon Worcestershire sauce
Salt and black pepper

In a medium saucepan, stir together 1½ cups water, the onion, vinegar, sugar, tomato paste, oil, and Worcestershire sauce. Bring to a boil over medium-high heat. Reduce the heat to a simmer and cook, stirring occasionally, until there is just enough liquid to cover the bottom of the pan, about 20 minutes. Season to taste with salt and black pepper. Store in an airtight container in the refrigerator for up to 3 weeks.

CHOWCHOW

■ ■

Similar to another great relish: piccalilli. Try it on hot dogs or hamburgers for a real treat.

MAKES 6 HALF-PINTS

4 cups coarsely chopped green tomato

4 cups coarsely chopped green cabbage

2 cups coarsely chopped yellow onion

2 cups coarsely chopped red bell pepper

2 tablespoons seeded and finely chopped jalapeño pepper, or more if more heat is desired

¼ cup salt

1½ cups apple cider vinegar

1½ cups distilled white vinegar

1 cup sugar

2 tablespoons pickling spice, tied in cheesecloth

1 tablespoon mustard seeds

1 tablespoon celery seeds

2 teaspoons ground turmeric

1. In a large nonaluminum bowl (like glass or stainless steel), combine the tomato, cabbage, onion, bell pepper, and jalapeño. Toss with the salt, cover, and let stand in a cool spot for 12 hours. Place in a colander to drain, rinse with water, and drain again.

2. In a large nonaluminum saucepan, combine the drained vegetables with 1½ cups water, both vinegars, the sugar, pickling spice, mustard seeds, celery seeds, and turmeric. Bring to a boil over medium-high heat. Reduce the heat to a lively simmer and cook for 30 minutes. Discard the cheesecloth-wrapped pickling spice.

3. Spoon into hot, sterilized half-pint jars (leaving ½ inch of room at the top) and process for 10 minutes. (See Canning Basics, page 420.)

SOUTH CAROLINA MUSTARD SAUCE

■ ■

So zesty but with a sweet edge. Use as a marinade or finishing sauce. Or put some in a squirt bottle on the table. I feel a pig pickin' coming on.

MAKES ABOUT 1 CUP

½ cup yellow mustard

⅓ cup packed light brown sugar

¼ cup apple cider vinegar

1 teaspoon Worcestershire sauce

1 teaspoon onion powder

¼ teaspoon cayenne pepper

¼ teaspoon salt

In a medium bowl, combine all the ingredients and stir well. Store in the refrigerator for up to 1 month.

GREEN TOMATO CHUTNEY

■ ■

Here in the South, we just can't get enough of those green tomatoes. We fry 'em, and that's what made 'em famous, but we also make this tasty chutney. It'll make you lick your fingers.

MAKES 6 HALF-PINTS

1 pound green tomatoes, coarsely chopped

1 pound Granny Smith apples, peeled, cored, and coarsely chopped

1 yellow onion, finely chopped

1 orange, unpeeled, thinly sliced and seeded

1 small clove garlic, finely chopped

¼ cup golden raisins

¼ cup dried cranberries

2 teaspoons mustard seeds

½ teaspoon black pepper

1½ teaspoons ground ginger

¼ teaspoon ground allspice

1 cup apple cider vinegar

1⅔ cups packed light brown sugar

1. In a large, heavy-bottomed saucepan, combine all the ingredients. Bring to a boil over medium-high heat, stirring frequently. Reduce the heat to a simmer and cook, stirring occasionally, until thickened, 30 to 45 minutes.

2. Spoon into hot, sterilized half-pint jars (leaving ½ inch of room at the top) and process for 10 minutes. (See Canning Basics, page 420.)

PEPPER JELLY

■ ■

If you don't like your jelly too spicy, substitute some bell pepper for the jalapeño. On the other hand, if you like even more heat, try adding some of the jalapeño seeds to the mix.

MAKES 5 HALF-PINTS

1 cup chopped green bell pepper

½ cup seeded and chopped jalapeño pepper

5 cups sugar

1½ cups apple cider vinegar

3 ounces liquid pectin or 1 packet Certo

4 drops green food coloring

1. In a food processor, puree the bell pepper and jalapeño pepper with ¼ cup water.

2. In a medium saucepan, combine the pepper mixture, sugar, and vinegar. Bring to a boil over medium-high heat, and boil vigorously for 5 minutes, stirring frequently (and watch out for it bubbling over).

3. Add the pectin and boil, stirring, for 1 minute longer. Remove from the heat, skim the foam if necessary, and stir in the food coloring.

4. Spoon into hot, sterilized half-pint jars (leaving ¼ inch of room at the top) and process for 5 minutes. (See Canning Basics, page 420.)

BOILED DRESSING

■ ■

Great on any kind of vegetable salad—cabbage, potato, green bean, beet—anything, including meat and poultry salads. It was created when vegetable oils were nearly impossible to come by in the South. Take that, mayonnaise!

MAKES 1 CUP

2 tablespoons all-purpose flour

1 tablespoon sugar

1 teaspoon mustard powder

1 teaspoon salt

½ cup apple cider vinegar

2 large egg yolks

¼ cup heavy cream

1. In a medium saucepan or in the top of a double boiler, whisk together the flour, sugar, mustard powder, and salt.

2. In a small bowl, whisk together ½ cup water, the vinegar, egg yolks, and 2 tablespoons of the cream. Whisk the vinegar mixture into the flour mixture. Cook over low heat, stirring constantly, until thickened, about 10 minutes. Remove from the heat and whisk in the remaining 2 tablespoons cream. Refrigerate until cool. Store in the refrigerator for up to a week.

PAULA DEEN'S HOUSE SEASONING

■ ■

Y'all, this is a wonderful all-around seasoning to have on hand. It's out of this world on anything from fish to poultry to meat. And the garlic powder makes it so much more interesting than just salt and pepper alone. I'm never without it.

MAKES 1½ CUPS

1 cup salt

¼ cup freshly ground black pepper

¼ cup garlic powder

Combine all the ingredients in a bowl. Store in an airtight container for up to 6 months.

HOMEMADE CHRISTMAS GIFTS

You know, sometimes you really don't realize what an impression a homemade gift makes on somebody. Jamie told me one day, "Mama, do you remember when at Christmastime, you'd go out and buy those little glass jars and you'd fill 'em with all your homemade candy and put a ribbon on 'em and that would be my gift to my teachers? I would be so proud. I remember my chest puffing out when the teacher would say, 'Jamie, thank you so much. That was the most wonderful candy I've ever eaten.' Mama," he said, "you will never, never know how proud those homemade candies made me feel."

When you don't have much money, a simple gift of food delivered in a brown paper bag that you have sponge-painted with a Christmas tree or holly leaf can send such a personal message of sharing and caring. I've chosen a few recipes that even children can do—they can certainly be taught to measure out the ingredients for the Fruited Rice Curry Mix (page 448) or the Lemon-Dill Rice Mix (page 449) or the Russian Spiced Tea Mix (page 447). Any of these would make such wonderful teacher gifts, and would provide welcome relief from the traditional coffee mug! For your salad-loving friends, give the Greek Salad Dressing (page 450) in a small carafe, and those with a sweet tooth will appreciate the Peppermint Bark (page 445) or the Pretzel-Peanut Bark (page 444). A small tin of Cheese Straws (page 22) is always welcome for an afternoon nibble. As for the Icebox Fruitcake (page 439), well, I think fruitcake gets a bad rap. My grand-mama always made a fruitcake for the holidays, placing a small open container of brandy in the center of the cake. The cake would absorb the brandy flavor as it aged. By the time you ate the last slice, it would knock your socks off! Now, that's a gift worth getting!

Happy gift giving!

ICEBOX FRUITCAKE

What are the holidays without fruitcake? I don't make traditional fruitcake like my grandmother made. Instead I make this unbelievably easy stir-together fruitcake and put it into mini loaf pans for gift giving. This recipe appeared in *The Lady & Sons Just Desserts*, but I wanted you to have it again in case you missed it!

MAKES 10 MINI LOAVES

1 can (14 ounces) sweetened condensed milk

1 bag (16 ounces) miniature marshmallows

1 box (16 ounces) graham crackers, crushed to crumbs

4 cups chopped pecans

1 can (3.5 ounces) flaked coconut (1⅓ cups)

2 packages (8 ounces each) chopped dates

1 jar (16 ounces) maraschino cherries, well drained and halved

½ cup bourbon

1. Spray 10 mini loaf pans with vegetable oil cooking spray.

2. In a 2-quart saucepan, heat the milk and marshmallows together over low heat. Stir constantly (condensed milk scorches easily!) until the marshmallows are melted. Remove the mixture from the heat. Combine the cracker crumbs, pecans, coconut, dates, and cherries in a large bowl. Add the bourbon to the milk mixture and pour over the crumb mixture. Mix well with your hands. Scoop the mixture into the prepared pans and press down firmly to mold into shape. Refrigerate for 2 days or longer before serving.

CHOCOLATE CHEWY COOKIES

■ ■

These cookies are best eaten within 24 hours, which is usually not a problem.

MAKES 18 BIG COOKIES

2 cups confectioners' sugar, sifted

2 tablespoons cocoa powder, sifted

¼ teaspoon salt

⅓ cup all-purpose flour, sifted

3 egg whites

1 cup chopped pecans, toasted

1. Preheat the oven to 350°F. Line two baking sheets with parchment paper.

2. Stir together the sugar, cocoa, salt, and flour. Add the egg whites one at a time. Beat well, then stir in the pecans. The batter will be very thin.

3. Drop by tablespoonfuls onto the prepared baking sheets. Bake for 12 to 15 minutes, until the cookies have begun to brown on the bottom and appear set. Allow to sit for about 2 minutes undisturbed, then remove the cookies to wire racks to cool completely. Store in cookie tins, or package in Chinese food take-out cartons lined with waxed paper.

CHOCOLATE CHIP–COFFEE COOKIES

■ ■

These are just downright delicious, ya'll. You'll need to make two batches—one to get eaten up while you're cooking and the other to save for the party. Put them in resealable plastic freezer bags and freeze them. Take them out that morning and they'll taste like you just baked them.

MAKES ABOUT 24 COOKIES

½ cup (1 stick) butter, softened

1 cup light brown sugar

¼ cup granulated sugar

1 egg

2 teaspoons vanilla extract

1¾ cups all-purpose flour

½ teaspoon baking soda

½ teaspoon baking powder

½ teaspoon salt

1½ teaspoons instant coffee, powdered or freeze-dried

1 bag (6 ounces) chocolate chips (1 cup)

½ cup chopped pecans, lightly toasted

1. Preheat the oven to 375°F. Line a cookie sheet with parchment paper.

2. In a large mixing bowl, using an electric mixer, cream the butter and sugars until light and fluffy. Beat in the egg and vanilla. Sift together the flour, baking soda, baking powder, and salt. Add the flour mixture to the butter mixture and, using a spatula, stir together until they are completely blended. Stir in the instant coffee, chocolate chips, and pecans.

3. Drop by tablespoonfuls, 1 inch apart, onto the prepared cookie sheet. Bake in batches for 11 minutes, until crisp on the bottom. (Reuse parchment paper for each batch.)

4. Remove the cookie sheet from the oven and allow the cookies to cool undisturbed for about 3 minutes, then transfer to a wire cooling rack to cool completely before storing in airtight tins or freezer bags. Store in cookie tins, or package in Chinese food take-out cartons lined with waxed paper.

GEORGIA COOKIE CANDY

■ ■

What better way to top off any party than with peanut butter and chocolate?

MAKES 36 TO 40 PIECES

1 cup (2 sticks) butter or margarine, softened
1 cup crunchy peanut butter
3 cups confectioners' sugar, sifted

1½ cups graham cracker crumbs
1½ cups semisweet chocolate chips

1. Line a 13 by 9 by 2-inch pan with foil.

2. Combine the butter, peanut butter, sugar, and graham cracker crumbs in a food processor. Process until the mixture forms a ball. Press into the foil-lined pan using your hands or a spatula.

3. Melt the chocolate chips in a double boiler over simmering water or in a microwave-safe glass dish in the microwave for 1 minute on high (100%). Stir. If the chocolate has not completely melted, microwave for 10 seconds more, then stir. Spread evenly over the cookie layer with a spatula. Chill for several hours.

4. When ready to serve, allow the candy to come to room temperature before cutting into pieces. Store in an airtight container in the refrigerator. Store in cookie tins, or package in Chinese food take-out cartons lined with waxed paper.

OVEN CARAMEL CORN

■ ■

This is positively addictive. Put about 2 cups in a clear plastic bag and tie with a beautiful Christmas bow.

MAKES 7 TO 8 QUARTS

7 to 8 quarts of popped popcorn

2 cups unsalted peanuts, shelled pumpkin seeds, and/or sunflower seeds

1 cup light brown sugar

1 cup (2 sticks) butter or margarine

1 teaspoon salt

½ cup light corn syrup

1 teaspoon maple-flavored pancake syrup

1 teaspoon vanilla extract

1 teaspoon baking soda

1. Preheat the oven to 250°F. Spray rimmed cookie sheets or jelly-roll pans with vegetable oil cooking spray.

2. In a very large bowl, combine the popcorn and your choice of nuts and/or seeds. In a medium saucepan, combine the sugar, butter, salt, syrups, and vanilla. Bring to a boil over medium-high heat and continue boiling for 5 minutes. Stirring constantly. Remove from the heat and add the baking soda. The mixture will bubble up. Stir vigorously until the mixture is smooth.

3. Pour the hot syrup over the popcorn mix. Stir until the popcorn is coated. This is messy; take your time and use a long-handled spoon.

4. Spread the coated popcorn in the prepared pans. Bake for 1 hour, stirring several times. The mixture will be very sticky.

5. Remove the popcorn from the oven and allow to cool for 15 minutes. Break big hunks apart while the mixture is cooling. When cooled, the sugars will have candy-coated the popcorn. Store in large, airtight plastic containers.

PRETZELS DIPPED IN WHITE CHOCOLATE

■ ■

MAKES ABOUT 24 PRETZELS

8 white chocolate baking squares
   (1 ounce each)

1 bag (10 ounces) pretzel rods
Pink sprinkles

1. In a glass dish in the microwave, melt the chocolate on high (100%) for 60 seconds. Remove, stir, and microwave for 10 seconds more until the chocolate has melted. Continue heating in 10-second bursts until all the chocolate is melted.

2. Allow the chocolate to cool slightly to thicken. Dip the bottom half of each pretzel rod in the melted chocolate.

3. Twist the rod so that the chocolate forms a "tail" at the end. Over a paper plate, sprinkle the warm chocolate with pink sprinkles. Place on waxed paper to harden. Store in cookie tins, or package in Chinese food take-out cartons lined with waxed paper.

PRETZEL-PEANUT BARK

■ ■

This is terribly yummy.

MAKES ABOUT 8 CUPS

18 white chocolate baking squares
   (1 ounce each)
2 cups dry salted peanuts

3 cups skinny pretzel sticks, broken into small
   pieces but not crushed, then measured

1. Line a rimmed cookie sheet with parchment or waxed paper.

2. In a double boiler over simmering water, melt the chocolate until smooth, or melt in the microwave in a 2-quart glass dish. Microwave on high (100%) for 1 minute, stir, and microwave on high for 10 seconds more. If necessary, microwave on high for an additional 10 seconds, and

stir until the chocolate is melted and smooth. Stir in the peanuts and pretzel pieces. Stir well with a flexible spatula.

3. Spoon onto the prepared cookie sheet, spreading the mixture out so that the ingredients are relatively evenly distributed.

4. Allow the chocolate to cool for several hours or refrigerate for 45 minutes or until firm. Break the bark into irregular pieces, like peanut brittle. Store in cookie tins, or package in Chinese food take-out cartons lined with waxed paper.

PEPPERMINT BARK

■ ■

The weekend when I was walking the red carpet for the screening of *Elizabethtown* (the movie I appeared in with Orlando Bloom and Kirsten Dunst), I had time to teach actress Judy Greer how to make this simple but delicious candy. Package it in Chinese food take-out cartons for individual gifts.

MAKES ABOUT 6 CUPS

Peppermint candy canes
18 white chocolate baking squares
   (1 ounce each)

Peppermint extract (optional)

1. Line a rimmed cookie sheet with parchment or waxed paper. In a heavy-duty plastic bag, place the candy canes and hammer into ¼-inch chunks or smaller. You should have about 1 cup.

2. Melt the chocolate in a double boiler over simmering water until smooth, or melt in the microwave in a 2-quart glass dish. Microwave on high (100%) for 1 minute, stir, and microwave on high for 10 seconds more. If necessary, microwave on high for an additional 10 seconds, and stir until the chocolate is melted and smooth.

3. Combine the candy cane chunks with the melted chocolate. Add 1 drop of peppermint extract, if desired. Pour the mixture onto the prepared cookie sheet and place in the refrigerator for 45 minutes or until firm. Remove from the cookie sheet and break the bark into irregular pieces, like peanut brittle. Store in cookie tins, or package in Chinese food take-out cartons lined with waxed paper.

RUSSIAN SPICED TEA MIX

■ ■

This is fun for really young children. They can measure and mix the ingredients, and could even be invited to "tea" by the recipient!

MAKES 5 CUPS, ABOUT 60 SERVINGS

1 jar (3 ounces) Lipton Sweetened
   Iced Tea Mix
1 container (21.1 ounces) Tang

1 tablespoon ground cinnamon
1 tablespoon freshly grated nutmeg
1 tablespoon ground allspice

1. In a medium bowl, combine the tea mix, Tang, cinnamon, nutmeg, and allspice. Mix well with a metal spoon.

2. Store in small plastic containers or glass jars with tight-fitting lids. Attach the recipe.

RECIPE

Use 2 heaping teaspoons in 6 ounces of hot water for hot tea or 2 heaping teaspoons in 6 ounces of cold water for a refreshing summer beverage over ice.

FRUITED RICE CURRY MIX

■ ■

This goes well with roast pork or chicken.

MAKES 3 CUPS, ABOUT 6 SERVINGS

1¼ cups raw white rice
¼ cup chopped dried mixed fruit
¼ cup slivered almonds
2 tablespoons golden raisins

2 teaspoons curry powder
2 beef bouillon cubes, crushed, or
   2 teaspoons granulated bouillon
½ teaspoon salt

1. In a small bowl, combine the rice, mixed fruit, almonds, raisins, curry powder, bouillon, and salt. Mix well with your fingers.

2. In a sandwich-size resealable plastic bag, place the mixture and attach the recipe.

> ### RECIPE
> Combine the contents of this package with 2½ cups water and 2 tablespoons butter in a 2-quart saucepan. Bring to a boil, cover, reduce the heat to low, and simmer for 20 minutes.

LEMON-DILL RICE MIX

■ ■

This is particularly good with seafood, although I also like it with baked chicken.

MAKES 3 CUPS, ABOUT 6 SERVINGS

1¼ cups raw white rice

2 chicken bouillon cubes, crushed, or
   2 teaspoons granulated bouillon

1½ teaspoons dried grated lemon zest

1 teaspoon dried dill weed

½ teaspoon dried minced onion

½ teaspoon salt

1. In a small bowl, combine the rice, bouillon, zest, dill weed, minced onion, and salt. Mix well with your fingers.

2. In a sandwich-size resealable plastic bag, place the mixture and attach the recipe.

RECIPE

Bring 2½ cups water and 1 tablespoon butter to a boil in a 2-quart saucepan. Add the contents of this package. Reduce the heat to low, cover, and simmer for 20 minutes.

GREEK SALAD DRESSING

■ ■

By all means include the recipe; your friends are going to want to keep this on hand at all times in the fridge. After you shake the dressing, pour it into an attractive bottle (or bottles) with a stopper.

MAKES A LITTLE MORE THAN 1 CUP

½ cup olive oil

¼ cup canola oil

⅓ cup fresh lemon juice (about 3 lemons)

1 teaspoon salt

1 clove garlic, minced

¾ teaspoon dried oregano

¼ teaspoon sugar

1. In a pint jar with a tight-fitting lid, combine both oils, the lemon juice, garlic, salt, oregano, and sugar.

2. Seal and shake well. Store in the refrigerator. When ready to use, allow the dressing to come to room temperature and shake well.

ORANGE-GINGER BUTTER

■ ■

This is terrific with cake or muffins and is also delicious smeared on broiled fish.

MAKES ABOUT ¾ CUP

½ cup (1 stick) butter, softened
3 tablespoons orange marmalade

¼ teaspoon grated fresh ginger (the kind in
   the jar is fine)

1. In a small bowl, combine the butter, orange marmalade, and ginger. Pack into a small crock or baby food jar with a decorative lid. Or roll in waxed paper into a log and twist the ends.

2. Chill thoroughly. Wrap in colorful paper.

CINNAMON-HONEY BUTTER

■ ■

I serve this the morning after Christmas on homemade waffles.

MAKES ABOUT ½ CUP

½ cup (1 stick) butter, softened
2 tablespoons honey

½ teaspoon ground cinnamon

1. In a small bowl, combine the butter, honey, and cinnamon. Pack into a small crock or baby food jar with a decorative lid. Or roll in waxed paper into a log and twist the ends.
2. Chill thoroughly. Wrap in colorful paper.

HERB BUTTER

■ ■

Delicious on homemade bread. Killer slathered over grilled steak or chicken.

MAKES ABOUT ½ CUP

½ cup (1 stick) butter, softened
1 clove garlic, minced
1 teaspoon dried parsley flakes

½ teaspoon dried basil
½ teaspoon dried thyme

1. In a small bowl, combine the butter, garlic, parsley, basil, and thyme. Pack into a small crock or baby food jar with a decorative lid. Or roll in waxed paper into a log and twist the ends.
2. Chill thoroughly. Wrap in colorful paper.

Acknowledgments

— — — —

This book has been a real labor of love, and it would not have come together so beautifully without all the amazing people who helped make it happen.

My deepest thanks go out to my manager, Barry Weiner, who goes beyond his role and looks after me like his own child. Huge heartfelt thanks to my literary agent, Janis Donnaud, who continues to be the best literary agent I could have ever asked for.

Big thanks go out to Jonathan Karp, as well as to all those at Simon & Schuster who have made this book a reality. Thanks to my meticulous editors, Priscilla Painton and Michael Szczerban, who are as dedicated as they are thorough. Huge thanks to Sybil Pincus, senior production editor; Kate Slate, the copy editor; Nancy Singer, director of interior design, for the beautiful interior of the book; Jackie Seow, executive art director, for a stunning jacket; Richard Rhorer, associate publisher; Brian Ulicky, publicity manager; Nina Pajak, marketing manager; Irene Kheradi, executive managing editor; and Gina DiMascia, managing editorial assistant. Thanks to photographer Ben Fink and his team, who made every dish look mouthwateringly delicious. Thanks to illustrator Jason Snyder for his clear drawings.

Many thanks to my coauthor, Melissa Clark, who helped shape this book into a comprehensive compendium of Southern food, and to her intrepid team: Sarah Huck, Olga Massov, Jaimee Young, Zoe Singer, Rebecca Klus, and Nancy Duran.

I don't know where I'd be without Nancy Assuncao, my tireless and enthusiastic publicist, who possesses unparalleled dedication. Thanks to Phyllis Hoffman and her amazing staff, who publish my beautiful magazine, *Cooking with Paula Deen*. Thanks to all my friends at the Food Network, and to Gordon Elliot, the executive producer of my show *Paula's Best Dishes*. Thanks to my hairstylist, Jamie Cribbs, and makeup artist, Courtney Fix, who always make me look and feel pretty. A mountain of thanks to my Deen Team, who can be counted on day and night, rain or shine, and who keep my schedule in impeccable order: Brandon Branch, Theresa Feuger, Holis Johnson, and Sarah Meighen.

Huge thanks to my ever-reliable staff at The Lady & Sons, particularly Dora Charles, Rance Jackson, Dustin Walls, and Scott Hopke. Also, big thanks to everyone at Uncle Bubba's Oyster House.

And to my amazing family: my darling husband, Michael; my two boys, Jamie and Bobby; my beautiful daughter-in-law, Brooke; and to all my grandsons, Jack, Matthew, and Henry; the Groover kids, Anthony and Michelle; and Michelle's husband, Daniel Reed. Thanks to my baby brother, Bubba; my niece, Corrie, and her husband, Brian Rooks. Also huge thanks to Michael's brothers, Father Hank and Nick; and his cousins, aunts, and uncles; and my darlin' aunt Peggy Ort. Y'all are my most precious gift—thank you for being there.

And last but not least, a big-thank you to all my fans: I hope y'all find this book to be your own Southern cooking bible.

Index

*Recipe photo appears in photo insert.

Fruitcake
  Icebox, 439
  New Japanese, 369–70
frying. *see also* fried
  best oils for, 190
  deep-fry thermometer for, 159, 195
  reusing oil from, 308
fudge
  Brownies, Nutty, 346
  Chocolate, Frosting, 380–81
  Chocolate-Peanut, Ultimate Easy,* 413
  cutting smooth-edged squares of, 413

G
Game Hens, Molasses, 179
garlic
  Butter, 216
  peeling cloves, 9
  powder, in Paula Deen's House Seasoning, 435
  sautéing, 266
gelatin
  7-Layer Molded Salad, 62–63
  unmolding, 63
General Robert E. Lee Cake, 386–87
Georgia Pound Cake, 355–56
German Potato Salad with Bacon, Hot,* 56
gifts
  packing food items for, 417
  recipes as, 437–51
gingersnap crumb crust, 357–58
glazes
  Chocolate, 368, 388–89
  Cinnamon, 374–75
  egg, for baked goods, 304
  Lemon, 359–60
  Whiskey, 372–73
Gooey Butter Cake, 354–55
  Ooey, Layer, 384–85
Gooey Gorilla Bread, 305
gravy
  Chocolate,* 276
  Cream, Cajun Chicken-Fried Livers with, 181
  Cream, Chicken-Fried Steak with,* 127
  Fried Beef Tenderloin with Grits and, 132–33
  getting to right consistency, 181
  Quails in, 180
  Redeye, Ham Steaks with, 141
  Sawmill, 276
  Tomato, Fried Pork Chops with, 142
  whisking smooth, 276

green beans
  with Bacon and Tomato, Southern-Style, 262
  removing stem ends of, 262
Green Goddess Dip, Buttermilk, 28
greens
  Best Braised Southern, 240
  prepping, 240, 241
  Turnips and, 242
  Very Veggie Braised, 241
greens, salad
  dressing, 45
  Fried Chicken Salad,* 44–45
  washing and drying, 57
  Wilted Salad with Hot Bacon Dressing, 57
green tomato(es)
  Chowchow, 432
  Chutney, 433
  Fried, 254
  Pie, 330–31
  slicing, 331
griddle cakes
  Buttermilk Pancakes,* 299
  Cornmeal Blueberry Pancakes, 300
  Hoecakes, The Lady & Sons, 297
  Lace Hoecakes, 298
  Okra Lace Cakes, 298
Grillades and Grits, 149–50
grill baskets, 224
grilled, 207–27. *see also* BBQ/barbecue
  Burgers, Butter, 219
  Chicken, Beer Can, 211
  Chicken, Quick BBQ, 213
  Filet Mignon, Perfect Char-Grilled, 217
  Flank Steak with a Kick, Cajun, 218
  Pork Loin, BBQ,* 227
  Pork Ribs, BBQ, 143
  Rib Eyes, Mustard-Glazed, 215
  Rib Eye with Garlic Butter, 216
  Ribs, Memphis Dry-Rub,* 225
  Salmon, Maple-Glazed,* 221
  Scallops, Red Pepper, 220
  Shrimp Kebabs, 214
  Steak Fajitas, Smoky, 226–27
  Tuna Burgers, Bobby's, 223
  Tuna Steaks, Benne Seed, 222
  Veggie Basket, 224
Grilling Sauce, Daddy's Tangy, 212
grilling with charcoal
  direct heat in, 217
  indirect heat in, 225